A Happier Eden

ALSO BY HEATHER DUBROW

Captive Victors: Shakespeare's Narrative Poems and Sonnets

Genre

The Historical Renaissance: New Essays
on Tudor and Stuart Literature and Culture (co-editor)

A Happier Eden

The Politics of Marriage in the Stuart Epithalamium

Heather Dubrow

Cornell University Press

Ithaca and London

The publisher gratefully acknowledges a grant
from the Hyder E. Rollins Fund of Harvard University
that aided in bringing this book to publication.

First published 1990 by Cornell University Press.

International Standard Book Number 0–8014–2296–5
Library of Congress Catalog Card Number 89–71200
Printed in the United States of America
*Librarians: Library of Congress cataloging information
appears on the last page of the book.*

⊗ The paper used in this publication meets the minimum requirements
of the American National Standard for Permanence
of Paper for Printed Library Materials Z39.48—1984.

To my Carleton colleagues

thus these two
Imparadised in one another's arms,
The happier Eden, shall enjoy their fill
Of bliss on bliss.

John Milton, *Paradise Lost,*
IV. 505–508

Contents

Preface

Pyramidal patterns attract students of literary history as well as students of dramatic form: the theory that plays involve a structure of rising action, climax, and falling action finds its analogue in the supposition that genres develop, reach an apogee that is typically signaled by a major work, and then decline. This assumption is problematical in its premises: it is prone to oversimplify historical patterns and to neglect the ways our own processes of interpretation and valuation may intervene in those patterns. More to the point here, the pyramidal model is problematical in its results. It has led many critics to misread the epithalamium tradition: they have presumed it exemplifies that model, with Edmund Spenser's "Epithalamion" the culmination of the genre and the seventeenth-century wedding poem its decline. Hence we have too often ignored or dismissed texts composed after Spenser's two poems in the genre.

This book maps the largely unexplored terrain of the Stuart epithalamium, focusing particularly on the attitudes to marriage which so deeply affect that institution and the genre commemorating it. *A Happier Eden* is concerned with both cultural tensions and formal decisions—and above all with connections between the two. Why, for instance, do Stuart poets favor one subgenre, the so-called lyric epithalamium, over the many alternatives? In investigating such questions we will find that many generic norms which may at first appear merely arbitrary, such as a predilection for dialogic structures, in fact express (or in some instances repress) responses to gender, sexuality, and marriage. Even when poets decide to adopt a generic norm precisely because they wish to root their poem in convention and tradition, their decision may reflect other drives as well: literary imitation functions as a metaphor for other types of conservatism. And the workings of marriage in Stuart England influence not only which generic norms poets in that period select and emphasize but also how those norms are interpreted by their readers.

This is not to say, however, that generic formulas are merely a by-product of cultural attitudes. The epithalamium also demonstrates the ways a genre may itself inform such attitudes, as Thomas M. Greene briefly but suggestively notes in his important article "Spenser and the Epithalamic Convention" (CL, 9 [1957]), thus anticipating the contemporary emphasis on the interactive dynamics of a culture. Nor am I implying that formal decisions are mere codes or ciphers for the ideologies of Stuart England. Literary genres, like many contemporary children, may have several sets of parents and stepparents: to read them solely as the progeny of cultural forces is to misread them. Hence we will examine other explanations for generic conventions and strategies, including the poet's sheer delight in virtuosity.

The issues I am exploring in this book are, then, broad ones, ranging from the construction of gender to the construction of generic norms. And in one sense the examples I adduce are wide-ranging, too: though I am concerned specifically with the lyric and narrative poetry celebrating weddings, I have also traced some parallels between that tradition and the masque, as well as other types of drama and poetry. Yet in another sense my scope is narrow: this book addresses itself specifically to the Stuart wedding poem. Hence it necessarily focuses exclusively on lyrics composed by men; Katherine Philips experimented with the epithalamium later in the seventeenth century, and several modern women poets have composed wedding poetry, but in Stuart England the genre remained the preserve of male authors. This fact is germane to the tradition in many ways; for instance, as we will see, the men who wrote these poems, like those who composed the conduct books on marriage, are concerned at once to celebrate and to circumscribe the power of the women they evoke. The compass of A Happier Eden is delimited in another regard as well: though the book refers at several points to wedding poems written in other cultures, it does not aim to provide a comparatist survey of the epithalamium or even a historical survey of the genre within England.

One reason for defining my subject in this way is that the need for a comparatist history of the genre has already been admirably filled by Virginia Tufte in *The Poetry of Marriage* (Los Angeles, 1970). Moreover, concentrating specifically on the English epithalamium allows one to examine the connections between generic decisions and social pressures that were especially intense in Renaissance England, such as tensions about what actually constituted a valid wedding ceremony. But why focus on the Stuart period rather than encompass Tudor epithalamia as well? In important respects the Stuart wedding poem is the product of a distinct and distinctive cultural milieu; the role of marriage in the court, for example, distinguishes this period from the Tudor era. Elizabeth had discouraged marriages among her courtiers and her clergymen, whereas James actively encouraged and on occasion even financed weddings; many of them, such as the union of Princess Elizabeth and the Elector Palatine, were major social occasions at the court. And commemorating such events became a principal and well-traveled route to patronage; epithalamia written for the weddings of patrons or their children were the exception in sixteenth-century England but the norm in the seventeenth century. Moreover, commonplace comparisons between marriage on the one hand and church and state on the other acquired more force in Stuart culture. Since a stable marriage metaphorically represented the stability of those two other institutions, the acceleration of the events that threatened both church and state and eventually resulted in the Civil War deepened the significance of wedlock.

Another reason for focusing on the Stuart epithalamium is polemical. The two principal Tudor wedding poems, Spenser's "Epithalamion" and "Prothalamion," have been exhaustively scrutinized, but seventeenth-century instances of the genre have been neglected. This book aims to redress that balance; it maintains that the Stuart epithalamium deserves sustained attention in its own right. The later tradition represents not a decline in its genre but rather a redevelopment and redeployment of generic potentialities. And it is not a footnote to the sixteenth-century epithalamium but rather an important new chapter in the history of its own literary type and of the relationship between such types and cultural pressures.

My emphasis on the Stuart epithalamium does not, however, imply radical and consistent discontinuities between this form and its counterparts in other periods and countries. The epithalamium is deeply conventional in more than one sense of that word. The distinctions between the wedding poems of different periods often blur; Rothko is better suited than Mondrian to paint the development of the form. Nonetheless, in important respects the Stuart epithalamium represents a distinguishable tradition. These poems approach sexuality, for example, very differently from many of their counterparts on the Continent. And we will also see how a familiar generic convention may acquire, in response to new circumstances, new resonances for poets and their readers. Writing in a genre whose very conservatism made it appealing, Stuart poets often react to cultural tensions subtly, by emphasizing or reinterpreting an existing convention. Thus a dialogue between the outside and the inside, in many senses of those words, structures wedding poems in other eras, but a deeper and different significance accrues to its terms when women are perceived as spending too much time away from their homes rather than staying safely within. Similarly, the lyric epithalamium characteristically relies on commands, yet that speech act takes on new resonances when performed within the seventeenth-century patronage system. Several Stuart poets follow Spenser's lead in comparing the bride to Queen Elizabeth; but that comparison functions very differently in seventeenth-century poems than it does in Spenser's "Epithalamion," contributing to a pattern of nostalgia and an urge to recover and revivify the apparently lost past. The presence of so many similarities with earlier wedding poems makes dissimilarities like these all the more striking.

As even this brief introduction suggests, *A Happier Eden* is deeply indebted to feminism and, in particular, to the new historicism. Yet its genealogy, like that of the epithalamium itself, is complex. If it participates in new historicist projects, it has other aims as well, and it does not share certain assumptions central to that movement. Moreover, it uses critical approaches that one often does not associate with new historicism, notably linguistic and formalist analyses and detailed scrutiny of lyric poetry. I attempt to justify this eclecticism implicitly throughout the book and address it explicitly in the Conclusion.

My introductory chapter charts the two coordinates against which Stuart poets plot their lyrics: generic traditions and cultural responses to marriage. It focuses on the anxieties at the core of those responses and on the source of many anxieties, the uneasy coexistence of conflicting assumptions about wedlock. Chapter 2 explores the relationships between generic strategies and cultural pressures. That interaction, it argues, assumes a range of forms: the pressures are sometimes, for example, simply inscribed in the text, sometimes suppressed or displaced in the interests of an idealized fantasy about marriage, and sometimes resolved. Chapter 3 reexamines generic strategies in a different context, the literary milieux that shape them. It investigates the familial relationships between the epithalamium and other genres, including ones that at first seem quite dissimilar, such as epic; and it relates the wedding poem to the patronage system, deploying the tools of pragmatics to do so and questioning some of the conventional wisdom about patronage. The next two chapters trace the significantly different ways three principal poets of the period, John Donne, Ben Jonson, and Robert Herrick, respond to this complex generic inheritance. I have singled out these three writers for particular attention because of their significance in the development of seventeenth-century literature in general and the epithalamium tradition in particular. Situating this study within the controversies that characterize contemporary Renaissance studies, the Conclusion interrogates some ideologies and methodologies that currently dominate that field.

The discussion of the epithalamium in Julius Caesar Scaliger's *Poetices libri septem* has not previously been available in English, although Scaliger's Latin is unusually problematical; my appendix is a translation of this important chapter by Jackson Bryce.

I wrote *A Happier Eden* under virtually Edenic scholarly conditions: living in Harvard University's Adams House and working at the Bunting Institute. I am grateful to the staff of Adams House for their assistance and to the Master and Co-Master, Robert and Jana Kiely, for their hospitality. The stimulating and supportive atmosphere at the Bunting facilitated my work in many ways, and I am pleased to have the opportunity to acknowledge my debt to the staff and to my colleagues there. I am grateful as well for a Senior Fellowship granted by the National Endowment for the Humanities and for many types of support, financial and less tangible, provided by Carleton College. I was fortunate enough to work once again with Bernhard Kendler, my editor at Cornell University Press, and with his efficient associates. Librarians at Carleton College and at Harvard's Houghton Library have been helpful throughout this project. Many colleagues have read sections of the manuscript and answered queries about it; though I cannot list everyone, I thank in particular Ilona Bell, Mary Thomas Crane, Margaret Morganroth Gullette, Richard Helgerson, John Hildebidle, Carol Ann Johnston, Constance Jordan, Arthur Marotti, Katherine Maus, Margaret Mikesell, Frank Morral, Joseph Porter, Anne Lake Prescott, Richard Strier, and Robert Watson. I am indebted as well to Virginia Tufte, who kindly made available to me invaluable notes and other materials from her own book on the epithalamium. With his customary generosity Gwynne Blakemore Evans agreed to read the entire manuscript, and with his customary erudition he improved it in many ways; his contributions exemplify the connections between traditional and contemporary critical modes advocated in Chapter 6.

Sections of this book appeared in earlier form in *Studies in English Literature* (1976), *The Eagle and the Dove: Reassessing John Donne,* ed. Claude Summers and Ted-Larry Pebworth (Columbia: Univ. of Missouri Press, 1986), and *The Historical Renaissance: New Essays on Tudor and Stuart Literature and Culture,* ed. Heather Dubrow and Richard Strier (Chicago: Univ. of Chicago Press, 1988), © 1988, the University of Chicago; I am grateful for permission to make use of my work. I quote Henry Goodyer by permission of the British Library.

Heather Dubrow

Northfield, Minnesota

CHAPTER I

Introduction

Enuie. Hymen, thou canst not chase vs so away,
For, looke how long as thou mak'st marriages,
So long will we produce incumbrances.
                    Samuel Daniel, *Hymens Trivmph*

I

The lovers in *A Midsummer Night's Dream* must pass through their forests and confront their hobgoblins, internal and external, before they can wed. Similarly, the brides and grooms in Stuart epithalamia confront not only scenes of pastoral tranquillity but also forests of the night; the generic conventions of these poems are shaped and reshaped by tensions about marriage and the process of celebrating it. These pressures assume different forms; in some cases they erupt, uncontrolled and unmediated, into the poem, though more frequently lyrics in the genre deploy a whole range of strategies for explicating and quieting concerns about the wedding. Stuart epithalamia are indeed primarily joyful, but their joy is often hard-won and qualified: the attempt variously to repress, reinterpret, and resolve the dangers and fears associated with marriage is central to the praxis of these lyrics.

Though recent Renaissance critics have tended to focus on the fault lines in the culture of the period rather than on the optimism that concerned Jacob Burckhardt and the generation of scholars he influenced so deeply, on the whole these changing emphases have not yet

I

affected our interpretations of the epithalamium.[1] Most readers are
programmed to associate wedding poetry with unmitigated happiness and serenity and hence are prone to overlook the tensions and
ambivalences in the Stuart wedding poem, as well as those in earlier
instances of the genre. One consequence of that neglect is misreading
particular lyrics. Surprised and puzzled by the dark and bitter tone
of John Donne's "Epithalamion made at Lincolnes Inne" and Richard
Crashaw's "Epithalamium," scholars have labeled those poems parodies or anti-epithalamia;[2] in fact, many Stuart epithalamia in some
measure share the apparently discordant notes we encounter in these
two works, and so their relationship to their tradition is far more
complex than we admit. The disturbed and disturbing wedding poems of Donne and Crashaw are twins of the more conventional
works in the genre—fraternal rather than identical, but twins nonetheless. Similarly, the ironic vision of Sir John Suckling's "A Ballade.
Upon a Wedding" finds its counterparts even in straightforward versions of its genre.

Another consequence of neglecting the anxieties that characterize
Stuart wedding poems in particular and their genre in general is a
distortion of the history of that tradition. Some readers have claimed
that the epithalamium declined in the seventeenth century because its
serene vision of marriage proved incompatible with the conditions of
Stuart weddings.[3] But in important ways those conditions were at
once the progenitors and the progeny of seventeenth-century wed-

[1] One of the best studies of this and related trends in contemporary Renaissance
studies is Jean E. Howard's survey of the new historicism, "The New Historicism in
Renaissance Studies," *ELR,* 16 (1986), 13–43.

[2] See, e.g., David Novarr, "Donne's 'Epithalamion made at Lincoln's Inn': Context
and Date," *RES,* 7 (1956), 250–263, and Virginia Tufte, *The Poetry of Marriage: The
Epithalamium in Europe and Its Development in England,* Univ. of Southern California
Studies in Comparative Literature, 2 (Los Angeles: Tinnon-Brown, 1970), chap. 3.
The pessimistic strains in the genre have been analyzed, though from a different perspective, in Celeste Marguerite Schenck's *Mourning and Panegyric: The Poetics of Pastoral Ceremony* (University Park: Pennsylvania State Univ. Press, 1988); she sensitively
traces the connections between epithalamic and elegiac modes in a range of poems
and discusses the anti-epithalamium in chap. 4. A few recent critics have analyzed the
somber elements in Spenser's "Epithalamion" (see, e.g., Douglas Anderson, " 'Vnto
My Selfe Alone': Spenser's Plenary Epithalamion," *Spenser Studies,* 5, ed. Patrick
Cullen and Thomas P. Roche, Jr. [New York: AMS, 1985]).

[3] See Paul W. Miller's influential article "The Decline of the English Epithalamion," *TSLL,* 12 (1970), 405–416. This viewpoint has been widely accepted, but a

ding poems, and this book argues that the epithalamium flourished in Stuart England precisely because many of its generic norms lent themselves variously to expressing or suppressing the problems associated with wedlock.

But if neglecting tensions in the genre, and in Stuart poems in particular, is dangerous, studying them involves its own perils. The principal one is exaggerating those tensions. In reaction to the New Critical tendency to see literary works as aesthetically unified and emotionally balanced, Renaissance critics have recently been moving in the opposite direction, focusing intensely on dissonances and contradictions. To return to our earlier example, we are now unlikely to overlook the dark forests in *A Midsummer Night's Dream;* indeed, we are more at home with the blood-red colors of Liviu Ciulei's 1985 production of that play at the Guthrie Theater than with Mendelssohn's pastels. These correctives are sound and sanative. Yet in the current critical climate it is particularly important to remind ourselves that though the authors of Stuart epithalamia emphasize the tensions associated with marriage, they celebrate the pleasures and the achievements of that institution as well. For all their doubts and ambivalences, these poems are in many respects joyous responses to happy occasions; that joy may sometimes be tarnished by the attempt to resolve the doubts that threaten it, but it is joy nonetheless. In drawing attention to anxieties that were largely ignored by an earlier generation of critics, in other words, we need to right a delicate balance, not seesaw between ignoring the tensions in texts and ignoring everything but tensions. In a sense, indeed, as critics of the epithalamium tradition we confront the very challenge that its authors and readers faced: on the one hand frankly acknowledging the threats that imperil both marriage and the poems that celebrate marriage while on the other hand continuing to recognize more optimistic elements in both the institution and its poetry.

The second danger inherent in my emphasis on tensions can be suggested only briefly here, but it will recur throughout this book. References to "cultural anxieties" are common in many critical cir-

---

few critics have interpreted the tradition differently; see Thomas M. Greene, "Spenser and the Epithalamic Convention," *CL,* 9 (1957), 218; Ruth Leah Michelson, "The English Epithalamium from Spenser to Marvell: A Marriage of Literary and Social Forms," undergraduate History and Literature thesis, Harvard University (1986), pp. 2–3.

cles and even obligatory in some, but such phrases need to be deployed with care. Despite the contemporary distrust of universalist
assumptions, scholars have never adequately examined the ways perceptions and manifestations of anxiety vary from culture to culture.[4]
In addition, the members of a culture may of course react to the
same pressure in different ways; for instance, if some Renaissance
readers were disturbed by inconsistencies in the conduct books on
marriage, others may not have noticed, say, the contradictions between how the authors of two such volumes, William Whately and
Henry Smith, talk about even as controversial an issue as physical
abuse.[5] Consciously or unconsciously one may read selectively, seeing only what one expects or wants to see.

Moreover, the tensions in question can vary significantly from decade to decade and region to region. Fears that the bride or groom
would die young haunted wedding celebrations, but those fears must
have been particularly intense in the instance of Princess Elizabeth,
since her brother, the beloved Prince Henry, had himself died shortly
before her marriage. Similarly, the lavish wedding of Elizabeth and
the Elector Palatine is likely to have intensified both interest in the
potentialities of marriage and concern about the financial and other
excesses often associated with it—but primarily for those in geographical and psychological proximity to the court. Marilyn L.
Williamson's important study, *The Patriarchy of Shakespeare's Comedies,* has aptly demonstrated that patriarchy is not an unchanging institution but rather a series of attitudes that shift significantly from
decade to decade,[6] and the same is true of many of the other intellectual, social, and psychological systems with which this book is
concerned.

---

[4]For a thought-provoking analysis of this issue, see William J. Bouwsma, "Anxiety
and the Formation of Early Modern Culture," in Barbara C. Malament, ed., *After the
Reformation: Essays in Honor of J. H. Hexter* (Philadelphia: Univ. of Pennsylvania Press,
1980); his assertions about the decline of anxiety in early modern Europe are, however, unpersuasive.

[5]The customary opposition to wife-beating is exemplified in Henry Smith, *A
Preparatiue to Mariage* (London, 1591), pp. 54–58. William Whately, a troubling and
no doubt troubled misogynist, does accept this abuse, though he emphasizes that it
should be used only rarely and as a last resort (*A Bride-bvsh* [London, 1619], pp.
169–173).

[6]Marilyn L. Williamson, *The Patriarchy of Shakespeare's Comedies* (Detroit: Wayne
State University Press, 1986).

II

The problems associated with weddings are not, of course, unique to Stuart England: marriages are emotionally charged occasions for many other cultures as well. For one thing, they represent a threshold between two different states, two different stages of life, and thresholds are perilous, as Victor Turner and other anthropologists have demonstrated.[7] In one German ballad, "Graf Friedrich," for instance, the bride is injured on the bridegroom's sword during the journey home, bleeds heavily, and ultimately dies.[8] The phallic significance of the injury is obvious; less obvious but no less significant for our purposes is the fact that the injury occurs during a journey, a transitional period that mimes the transition represented by the wedding itself. Folk rituals also testify to the dangers associated with literal and metaphoric thresholds. Such customs include the well-known rite of lifting the bride as she enters the house, and in his *Poetices libri septem*, Julius Cæsar Scaliger notes that grooms anoint the doors of their houses.[9] Yorkshire couples were advised to be particularly cautious at bridges.[10] Ben Jonson, whose classical scholarship is funded in part by his antiquarian enthusiasms, explains such practices in the notes he attaches to "The Masque of Hymen": the bride is carried so that she will not come into contact with the magical drugs that witches bury at thresholds.[11]

[7]Victor W. Turner, *The Ritual Process: Structure and Anti-Structure* (Chicago: Aldine, 1969), esp. pp. 95–96. Also compare John R. Gillis, *For Better, for Worse: British Marriages, 1600 to the Present* (New York: Oxford Univ. Press, 1985), p. 57.

[8]See the summary of versions of this ballad in Francis James Child, *The English and Scottish Popular Ballads*, 5 vols. (Boston and London: Houghton, Mifflin and Henry Stevens, 1882–1898), I, 142–143. This summary, however, neglects some salient differences among the versions; for instance, in one variant he shoots her in the foot and then stabs himself, and in another the reason for her death is not given.

[9]See the translation of and commentary on Scaliger in the Appendix of this book.

[10]On these and other rituals connected with thresholds, see Gillis, pp. 64–66, 71, 75; George Elliott Howard, *A History of Matrimonial Institutions*, 3 vols. (1904; rpt. New York: Humanities Press, 1964), I, 172.

[11]The Jonson passage is discussed in Tufte, *The Poetry of Marriage*, pp. 211–212. Twentieth-century popular culture, too, testifies to the dangers associated with the transitional process of getting married. The harpies and Spenser's Archimago are not the only guests rude enough—or in other instances prescient enough—to interrupt a wedding; that situation recurs even in such movies as *The Graduate* and *Spaceballs*, the latter boasting two interrupted marriages. Of course, the situation in which evil forces disrupt the event differs from the beneficent disruption at the end of *The Graduate,* but the fact remains that the recurrence of the situation, whether its effects be good or ill, yet again reminds us of the danger of thresholds.

However they responded to the threat posed by thresholds, the writers and readers of Stuart epithalamia also confronted the complications attending marriage in their own culture. The nature of the occasion celebrated in these poems, the wedding itself, was controversial and ambiguous. To what extent, if at all, was it a spiritual event? Marriage was not a sacrament in England after the Reformation; yet, as several commentators have observed, the recurrence of such phrases as "holy matrimony" throughout the service in the Book of Common Prayer suggests a reluctance to consider the occasion as wholly secular.[12] One response was to view the church ceremony as a "solemnization" of a marriage that had already occurred.

These ambivalences surface as well in a debate about what actually constituted a wedding. The authors of conduct books on marriage, a genre we will examine in more detail, differ radically and saliently on this question, with Robert Cleaver and John Dod, for instance, asserting that proper marriages in all ages included "an apparent and open contract, and . . . publicke marriage, the true and vnfained confirmation thereof," whereas William Gouge, who wrote the popular tract *Of Domesticall Dvties,* assures us that a contract is desirable but not strictly necessary.[13] And William Perkins, perhaps responding to the widespread fear of secret marriages, insists that three actions constitute a proper and lawful wedding: the parents must bring the bride to the bridegroom, the minister must perform the ceremony, and the couple must consummate the marriage.[14] Even those

---

[12]See Horton Davies, *Worship and Theology in England,* 5 vols. (Princeton: Princeton Univ. Press, 1961–1975), I, 33, 63; Chilton Latham Powell, *English Domestic Relations 1487–1653* (1917; rpt. New York: Russell and Russell, 1972), pp. 37–44. Davies maintains that the Anglican tradition emphasized the holiness of marriage even though it was not a sacrament, whereas Puritans were determined to regard it as wholly civil; I am arguing for more division even within the Puritan tradition.

[13]Robert Cleaver and John Dod, *A Godly Forme of Hovshold Government* (London, 1621), sig. G7; William Gouge, *Of Domesticall Dvties* (London, 1622), p. 198. After the initial citation to these and other conduct books, page references will appear in the text. Though I am following common practice in attributing the tract to Cleaver and Dod, the authorship of *A Godly Forme of Hovshold Government* is in dispute; see A. W. Pollard et al., *A Short-Title Catalogue of Books Printed in England, Scotland, and Ireland,* 2d ed., 2 vols. (London: Bibliographical Society, 1976–1986), I, 242. Here and elsewhere in the chapter I refer to Elizabethan conduct books as well as Stuart ones. A sharp distinction between the two would be artificial: some Elizabethan books went through several editions, including ones published in the seventeenth century, and in any event we do not find major differences between the Protestant marriage manuals of the two periods.

[14]William Perkins, *Christian Oeconomie* (London, 1609), p. 84.

who assented to the importance of prenuptial contracts disagreed about their nature, debating whether witnesses were necessary, whether the de futuro contract, in contrast to the de praesenti one, had any validity, and so on.[15] In one of his sermons, Donne sharply attacks nonbinding contracts, associating their legal looseness with sexual looseness: "no half-mariage, no lending away of the minde, in conditionall precontracts before, no lending away of the body in unchaste wantonnesse before."[16] Some of these concerns were to be resolved during the Commonwealth when a statute unequivocally established marriage as civil. In the meantime, however, Stuart epithalamia responded to both the question about the sacredness of weddings and the debate about whether they should be open and public.

Many other procedures connected with weddings also proved controversial. For instance, as we have just observed, the arguments about contracts are related to another source of tension, a preoccupation with secret marriages that surfaces not only in many tracts but also in so much dramatic literature during the English Renaissance, most notably The Duchess of Malfi.[17] The Tudor and Stuart stages testify as well to tensions about whether parents should determine the choice of partners, and the extraordinary popularity that Francis Quarles's Argalus and Parthenia enjoyed despite its indifferent style may be traced in part to its focus on that issue.

These disagreements about the nature and proper procedures for weddings reflect and were no doubt intensified by more fundamental disagreements about the nature of marriage.[18] The conventional

[15]See, e.g., Gouge, pp. 198–203.

[16]All citations from Donne's sermons are to The Sermons of John Donne, ed. George R. Potter and Evelyn M. Simpson, 10 vols. (Berkeley: Univ. of California Press, 1953–1962). This passage appears in III, 248; future volume and page references will be incorporated into the text.

[17]On the fear of secret marriages see esp. Constance Jordan, Renaissance Feminism: Literary Defenses of Women in Early Modern Europe (Ithaca: Cornell Univ. Press, 1990). I am grateful to the author for making her work available to me prior to publication and for a number of useful suggestions about this book.

[18]In addition to the work of social historians summarized in this chapter, in the past two decades numerous studies of marriage and the role of women have been written by literary critics. This body of work is too vast to be enumerated in full here, but a few studies with particular relevance to the issues raised by the conduct books include Linda Woodbridge, Women and the English Renaissance: Literature and the Nature of Womankind, 1540–1620 (Urbana: Univ. of Illinois Press, 1984), and " 'What Says the Married Woman': Marriage Theory and Feminism in the English Renaissance," Mosaic, 13 (1980), 1–22 (published under the name Linda T. Fitz); Ruth Kelso,

wisdom offers two conflicting theories about marriage in late Elizabethan and Stuart England, the one emphasizing the types of freedom and openness that arguably distinguished Protestant and
Catholic concepts of marriage and the other instead drawing our attention to authoritarian repression.[19] Ronald Mushat Frye, Charles
and Katherine George, William and Malleville Haller, and L. L.
Schücking are among the scholars who developed the theory of "the
Puritan art of love."[20] According to this interpretation, the Reformation sparked and Puritanism nurtured a distinctive type of marriage.
Rooted in Thomistic misogyny, Catholic doctrine emphasized the
value of celibacy and regarded marriage as at best a necessary evil
that could ensure procreation. Protestantism, in contrast, privileged
marriage over celibacy and defined the aims of that institution as
companionate, not merely procreative or financial. In Puritan marriages, so the theory runs, sexuality was respected, even celebrated.
Though the husband's superiority remained unchallenged, his relationship to his wife was becoming more egalitarian. The household
itself assumed a new importance because of the significance of family
worship, and the wife's role in the spiritual education of her children
further enhanced her status.

Lawrence Stone and his students have developed a very different
paradigm for marriage in Stuart England.[21] The period between

---

Doctrine for the Lady of the Renaissance (Urbana: Univ. of Illinois Press, 1956); Mary
Beth Rose, *The Expense of Spirit: Love and Sexuality in English Renaissance Drama* (Ith-
aca: Cornell Univ. Press, 1988); Mary Beth Rose, "Moral Conceptions of Sexual
Love in Elizabethan Comedy," *Renaissance Drama*, 15 (1984), 1–29.

[19] A third type of approach, population studies, has produced invaluable information about marriage patterns but has not generated a cohesive theory about attitudes
to marriage. See, e.g., Peter Laslett, *The World We Have Lost: Further Explored*, 3d ed.
(London: Methuen, 1983).

[20] Ronald Mushat Frye, "The Teachings of Classical Puritanism on Conjugal Love,"
Studies in the Renaissance, 2 (1955), 148–159; Charles H. and Katherine George, *The
Protestant Mind of the English Reformation, 1570–1640* (Princeton: Princeton Univ. Press,
1961), chap. 7; William and Malleville Haller, "The Puritan Art of Love," *HLQ*, 5
(1942), 235–272; Levin L. Schücking, *The Puritan Family: A Social Study from the Literary Sources*, trans. Brian Battershaw (London: Routledge and Kegan Paul, 1969).

[21] Lawrence Stone, *The Family, Sex and Marriage in England, 1500–1800* (New York:
Harper and Row, 1977). Also see, e.g., two studies by Miriam Slater, *Family Life in
the Seventeenth Century: The Verneys of Claydon House* (London: Routledge and Kegan
Paul, 1984); and "The Weightiest Business: Marriage in an Upper-Gentry Family in
Seventeenth-century England," *Past and Present*, 72 (1976), 25–54.

about 1580 and 1640, Stone maintains, was the era of what he terms the Restricted Patriarchal Nuclear Family. Though he acknowledges the presence of conflicting and contradictory currents, what he primarily finds in these decades is an intensification of patriarchal authority in the relationship of husband to wife and of father to child. Whereas our first theory discovers significant evidence of companionate marriage in Stuart England, Stone instead locates the rise of that type of wedlock in the eighteenth century.

The controversies surrounding each of these models have intensified. Opponents of the theory of "the Puritan art of love" have debated whether that form of Protestantism did in fact encourage equality and companionship, variously arguing that the so-called Puritan ideals of marriage may be found in Catholic and Anglican tracts or that Puritanism generated more suppression than freedom within marriage.[22] Stone's work has also proved far more controversial than the literary critics citing it sometimes acknowledge. In particular, many social historians have taken issue with his methodology, especially his reliance on French sources, and with his mode of analyzing the primary texts that purportedly demonstrate the paucity of emotion within the Restricted Patriarchal Nuclear Family.[23]

What evidence should we adduce in adjudicating between these rival theories? Sermons, family letters and diaries, tracts in the misogynist debate about women, and literary works can all illuminate the nature of marriage in Stuart England, though these texts are not without their own interpretive problems, especially those center-

[22]See, e.g., Kathleen M. Davies, " 'The sacred condition of equality'—How Original Were Puritan Doctrines of Marriage?" *Social History*, 5 (1977), 563–580; Margo Todd, "Humanists, Puritans and the Spiritualized Household," *Church History*, 49 (1980), 18–34. Another version of the Davies essay appears under the title "Continuity and Change in Literary Advice on Marriage" in *Marriage and Society: Studies in the Social History of Marriage*, ed. R. B. Outhwaite (New York: St. Martin's, 1981). John Halkett maintains that the marital attitudes generally labeled Puritan appear in Milton but not in most of the Puritan divines (*Milton and the Idea of Matrimony: A Study of the Divorce Tracts and "Paradise Lost"* [New Haven: Yale Univ. Press, 1970]). Ralph A. Houlbrooke argues that during the period 1450–1700 the family did not in fact undergo fundamental changes (*The English Family, 1450–1700* [London: Longman, 1984]).

[23]Though Alan Macfarlane's own historiography has proved very controversial, the objections against Stone that he and other historians have raised are trenchantly summarized in his review essay on *The Family, Sex and Marriage in England, 1500–1800* (*History and Theory*, 18 [1979], 103–126). For other critiques of Stone, see, e.g., Houlbrooke, pp. 14–15; Keith Thomas, "The Changing Family," *TLS*, 21 October 1977, pp. 1226–1227.

ing on the ways social and literary conventions may influence discourse.[24] The conduct books on marriage, however, represent the most valuable single resource for weighing the two rival theories of marriage and, indeed, for considering many other issues about that institution as well.

Manuals specifically on marriage were virtually unknown in medieval England, but they enjoyed a tremendous popularity in the sixteenth and seventeenth centuries, a vogue that may itself attest to a preoccupation with and concerns about the subject of wedlock.[25] A couple of these volumes were translations of Continental treatises, notably Heinrich Bullinger's *The Christen State of Matrimonye*. Most of their authors, however, were Englishmen and, in the case of the later treatises, Puritans. Some conduct books had only one edition, others proved far more popular; Gouge's *Of Domesticall Dvties* went through three editions, and Cleaver and Dod's *A Godly Forme of Hovshold Government* boasted nine. Tracts in this tradition typically discuss not only the relationship between husband and wife but also that between father and child and master and servant: they are, in other words, guides to running a household. That slant testifies to the extent to which marriage was regarded as public and communal, functioning not merely as the link between two people but also as one relationship within a larger social unit. And their preoccupation with "household government" in the sense of ordering, controlling, and ruling anticipates the intensely though covertly political discourse of the Stuart epithalamium.

Though this intriguing group of books can indeed guide us in digging love's mine, the procedure, like the investigation in "Love's Alchemy" itself, is demanding. How representative are the attitudes expressed in these tracts? Many of their authors, after all, were divines with Puritan sympathies. We may wonder whether their views differed from those of other ministers—and, even more to the point,

---

[24]See esp. Woodbridge's ultimately unpersuasive but thought-provoking argument that the formal controversy about women was primarily an exercise (*Women in the English Renaissance*, esp. Part I). We can more persuasively assert that at least some of the expressions of affection in family letters were formulaic, though when the rest of the letter is intimate and loving in tone we have good reason to assume that in the instance in hand the author invested formulaic phrases with real emotion.

[25]Compare D. E. Underdown, "The Taming of the Scold: The Enforcement of Patriarchal Authority in Early Modern England," in *Order and Disorder in Early Modern Europe*, ed. Anthony Fletcher and John Stevenson (Cambridge: Cambridge Univ. Press, 1985), p. 136.

whether any clergyman is not likely to have biased and partial views on marriage. (John Gregory Dunne's flawed but fascinating novel *True Confessions* directs our attention to one type of bias: as the principal priest in the book observes, "But one thing you learn about being a pastor, Tommy, and that's that no one ever rings your doorbell, even if it works, unlike mine, to tell you the whole family's working and John's on the wagon and the little ones are getting nothing but the highest marks in parochial school.")[26] Moreover, are the authors of these treatises representative even of their own profession? It is likely that a certain type of clergyman would be attracted to the writing of conduct books on marriage, whether because he had unusually strong opinions to express or unusually strong prejudices to release. Then, too, the authors of such treatises evidently had an urge to publish that itself distinguishes them from many other ministers and may gesture towards other distinguishing qualities as well.[27]

Nor, as Margaret J. M. Ezell and Steven Ozment have reminded us, can one assume that theoretical treatises consistently reflect or influence actual behavior.[28] Take the issue of wife-beating, one of the clearest and most disturbing instances of the assertion of power within marriage. With the exception of Whately, among the most misogynist men in the group, the authors of the conduct books on marriage condemn the practice, and "An Homilie of the State of Matrimonie," one of a group of sermons regularly read in Elizabethan churches, unequivocally seconds the injunctions against such abuse.[29] Yet the space devoted to the subject (for instance, it occupies

[26]John Gregory Dunne, *True Confessions* (New York: E. P. Dutton, 1977), p. 21.

[27]Such questions are further complicated by the possibility that these popular conduct books sometimes shaped the attitudes of other clergymen: they may form an approach to marriage rather than or in addition to being formed by it. I am grateful to Margaret Mikesell for pointing out this possibility, as well as for drawing my attention to the significance of Vives's tracts and providing other useful bibliographical references.

[28]See Ezell, *The Patriarch's Wife: Literary Evidence and the History of the Family* (Chapel Hill: Univ. of North Carolina Press, 1987), esp. pp. 161–163; Ozment, *When Fathers Ruled: Family Life in Reformation Europe* (Cambridge: Harvard Univ. Press, 1983), pp. 55, 70. Ezell's book, which I read after I had completed work on this chapter, provides a valuable corrective to the tendency to emphasize patriarchy at the expense of noting the challenges to it; at times, however, she overstates her case, neglecting the ambiguities in the documents she is quoting.

[29]*Certaine Sermons or Homilies Appointed to be Read in Churches in the Time of Queen Elizabeth I (1547–1571)*, ed. Mary Ellen Rickey and Thomas B. Stroup (Gainesville, Fla.: Scholars' Facsimiles and Reprints, 1968), pp. 245–247.

more than a page of the ten-page homily on marriage) hints that on this issue the authors of sermons and marriage manuals were not always preaching to the converted. And to what extent were readers actually influenced by the pronouncements on marriage they encountered? The Short-Title Catalogue can demonstrate that many of the conduct books sold well; but the number of editions does not indicate how thoroughly or how impartially they were read. When we apply the questions that reader-response critics have taught us to the texts of social history, we may come to wonder if some readers at least perused these treatises selectively, searching out the passages that supported their preconceptions.

But these problems are not insuperable. My caveats represent not a counsel of despair but rather a reason for interpreting the marriage manuals carefully. Certain of the issues I have cited can be resolved by redefining the significance of the conduct books; for instance, the very fact the authors of the conduct books considered it appropriate and politic to present the arguments they did, whether or not readers practiced what was preached at them, is revealing. And other potential problems can be forestalled by refining the relevant methodologies; thus one can address the dilemma of representativeness by playing the conduct books against the many other texts that concern marriage, such as sermons and family letters.

Indeed, the question of representativeness is ultimately not a barrier but rather an invitation to understand the central characteristic of marriage in Stuart England: the coexistence of conflicting and competing theories and practices. The marriage manuals, as I will demonstrate, manifest a striking degree of inconsistency from treatise to treatise and within the same treatise. If so much divergency and so many contradictions and ambivalences appear in even a relatively homogeneous group of authors, one may anticipate greater inconsistency in the culture at large.[30]

Recognizing that inconsistency allows us to resolve the conflicts between the principal constructions of marriage that I identified earlier, the Puritan art of love and the Restricted Patriarchal Nuclear

[30]In *The Expense of Spirit*, Mary Beth Rose also notes the range of interpretations of wedlock in the period; however, her book, unlike mine, emphasizes the movement towards the Protestant idealization of marriage (see esp. pp. 4–5 and chap. 1). I regret that this important study appeared after I had completed work on my manuscript. For a thought-provoking discussion of competing discourses on other subjects, see Clark Hulse, Andrew D. Weiner, and Richard Strier, "Spenser: Myth, Politics, Poetry," *SP*, 85 (1988), 378–411.

Family. Many of the apparent contradictions between these theories stem from the assumption that Renaissance attitudes to marriage attained a consistency and a clarity that are hardly evident in our own culture's meditations on the subject. In fact, neither the Catholic nor the Protestant position was monolithic. Medievalists such as Theresa Coletti and Lee Patterson have recently demonstrated that Catholic attitudes to sexuality, marriage, and women varied widely and shifted considerably in the course of the Middle Ages.[31] Certainly a significant gap separates Erasmian from Thomistic discussions of marriage,[32] though the Counter-Reformation may have suppressed some of that variety, as one historian has recently argued.[33] And we shall find far more variety within the Puritan tradition, with several interwoven strands of thought comprising its texture.

This heterogeneity does not preclude all generalizations, of course: some strands predominate in the patterns, and others are only faintly visible. Thus Catholic pronouncements continue to privilege celibacy, though marriage is not of course totally condemned; we do not encounter in the Protestant tradition a distrust of marriage quite as deep as that emerging from the conduct books by the Spanish humanist Juan Luis Vives or an attraction to virginity quite as ecstatic as that expressed by the Catholic writer Leo Lessius.[34] Nonetheless, variety and change are among the most salient characteristics of both Tudor and Stuart thinking on marriage; we need to talk in terms of Protestant discourses of marriage, not the Protestant discourse, of Puritan arts of love rather than a unified and monolithic art.[35]

[31]See the paper Theresa Coletti presented at the 1987 English Institute, "Wyves and Gossipis, Vergynes and Maides: Christian Myth and Female Sexuality in Medieval Drama"; Lee Patterson, " 'For the Wyves love of Bath': Feminine Rhetoric and Poetic Resolution in the *Roman de la Rose* and the *Canterbury Tales*," *Speculum*, 58 (1983), 656–695.

[32]On Erasmus's attitudes to marriage and their relationship to his antimonasticism, see Emile V. Telle, *Erasme de Rotterdam et le Septième Sacrement* (Geneva: Droz, 1954).

[33]See Todd, "Humanists, Puritans, and the Spiritualized Household."

[34]A sample of the Catholic praise of virginity may be found in Leo Lessius, *The Treasvre of Vowed Chastity* (St. Omer, France: English College Press, 1621).

[35]Most scholars have either totally ignored this variety or alluded to it only in passing. For brief but apt references to the disagreements among Protestant divines, see S. D. Amussen, "Gender, Family and the Social Order, 1560–1725," in Fletcher and Stevenson, esp. p. 201; George, p. 265; Rose, pp. 18–19, 28. In disagreeing with Stone, Keith Wrightson suggests that companionate and patriarchal marriage coexisted, a position close to my own (*English Society, 1580–1680* [London: Hutchinson, 1982], esp. pp. 90–104). Margaret Lael Mikesell comments acutely on divergent attitudes to marriage in Renaissance England, though her analyses, unlike mine, focus on

Even the distinction separating the work of Vives from that of the authors of Protestant conduct books is often one of degree, not of kind.[36] It is, after all, easier to rewrite prayer books than to reshape attitudes.

In short, we should embrace rather than resolve the contradictions among the theories of marriage put forth by contemporary historians. These contradictions reflect not the inadequacies of our historiography but the complexities of marriage in Renaissance England: conflicting theories of the nature of that institution coexist in contemporary scholarship precisely because they coexisted in that era. Indeed, not the least source of the anxiety in question is the lack of a stable vision. Nor does Renaissance England witness a steady and consistent change from a more patriarchal to a more egalitarian construction of marriage (hence this chapter does not emphasize chronological distinctions among the texts or between sixteenth- and seventeenth-century practices and attitudes). In both Tudor and Stuart England, attitudes towards marriage are characterized above all by contradictions, ambivalences, and flux.

Despite the significant inconsistencies that characterize them in other respects, on certain issues the Protestant marriage manuals are uniform and predictable, which may explain why most twentieth-century scholars have emphasized similarities among them at the expense of observing their divergences and dissonances. The manuals' reliance on the Bible explains some of these similarities, of course.

---

the distinctions between the Protestant and Catholic positions. See her articles "The Formative Power of Marriage in Stuart Tragedy," *Modern Language Studies*, 12 (1982), 36–44; "Catholic and Protestant Widows in *The Duchess of Malfi*," *Renaissance and Reformation*, 19 (1983), 265–279. For an important and exhaustive treatment of an issue closely connected to controversies about matrimony, the disagreements in Renaissance interpretations of Genesis, and related issues concerning sexuality and marriage, see James Grantham Turner, *One Flesh: Paradisal Marriage and Sexual Relations in the Age of Milton* (Oxford: Clarendon Press, 1987). Also, cf. Margaret Loftus Ranald, *Shakespeare and His Social Context: Essays on Osmotic Knowledge and Literary Interpretation* (New York: AMS, 1987), esp. pp. 4–6, on the survival of Roman canon law in Protestant England. I regret that this study appeared after I had completed my manuscript.

[36]For a different interpretation of the relationship of Vives to the Protestant tradition, see the paper that Margaret Mikesell presented at the 1987 Center for Medieval and Early Renaissance Studies conference at the State University of New York at Binghamton, "Vives' *Instruction* Replicated." Mikesell trenchantly argues that in the Protestant tracts a preoccupation with obedience replaces the Catholic focus on chastity.

Moreover, their authors are not above parroting, and at times even plagiarizing, sections from earlier treatises. Perhaps, too, the authors of these tracts so determinedly echo one another on certain issues as a defense against uncertainties and disagreements on other topics.[37] In particular, they sedulously repeat particular doctrinal commonplaces. Confounding longevity and worth as determinedly as the presidents of certain distinguished American universities, they remind us that marriage was made in heaven and instituted in Eden. They unite in declaring that the purposes of the institution are providing companionship and solace, preventing sin (especially fornication), and encouraging procreation. In defending the institution against its detractors, they cite similar biblical evidence, such as Christ's miracle in Cana. The conventional comparison of wedlock to the church and the commonwealth also recurs regularly. These analogues with state and church demonstrate one reason why problems in the institution of marriage could appear so threatening; as Perkins, the author of *Christian Oeconomie,* puts it, "the corruption or declination of this first gouernment, must of necessitie giue way to the ruinating of the rest" (sig. ¶ 3ᵛ).

The marriage manuals also second one another in their assertions of the wife's inferiority and her obligation to obey her husband. Thomas Pritchard, for instance, warns unruly wives (and perhaps in so doing reassures their husbands) that God views disobedience towards a husband as seriously as disobedience towards himself,[38] and Daniel Rogers, who enumerates marital duties at some length, lists subjection as the primary one the wife must fulfill, devoting an entire chapter to this obligation.[39] Such assertions appear, predictably, elsewhere in the cultural discourse on wedlock, most notably in the marriage ceremony in the Book of Common Prayer; in the service itself, the wife promises "to obey him and serve him,"[40] and the sermon to be used if the minister does not wish to write his own crams in repeated references to her subjection and submission. As we will see, the intensity and frequency of such pronouncements may well

[37]I am indebted to Margaret Mikesell for this observation.
[38]Thomas Pritchard, *The Schoole of Honest and Vertuous Lyfe* (London, 1579), p. 77.
[39]Daniel Rogers, *Matrimoniall Honovr* (London, 1642), chap. 13.
[40]All citations from the Book of Common Prayer are to John E. Booty, ed., *The Book of Common Prayer 1559: The Elizabethan Prayer Book* (Charlottesville: Univ. Press of Virginia, 1976).

have been reactive, a defensive response to types of power achieved by women in the culture.[41]

Despite their unanimity on such points, the authors of marriage manuals and of other treatises on wedlock contradict one another—and often themselves—on many issues that are especially germane to marriage and its celebration. In particular, the conventional wisdom would have us believe that the value of marriage was firmly established in Stuart England: in contrast to and reaction against the Catholic distrust of sexuality and privileging of celibacy, the Reformers and their followers celebrated the married state. One can amass some evidence for that position; for instance, in his treatise on choosing a wife, Alexander Niccholes poses the rhetorical question, "Where is the man this day liuing whose Virginity may be compared with *Abrahams* Mariage, in whom all the Nations of the earth were blessed."[42] But unqualified tributes to marriage at the expense of celibacy are not the norm: instead, both the Protestant conduct books and other Elizabethan and Jacobean discussions of wedlock testify to a continuing and uneasy debate on the relative virtues of those two states.[43]

The earlier pronouncements on marriage in which these texts are grounded are themselves sufficiently ambiguous and ambivalent to spark further dissension. Certainly the Pauline pronouncements on marriage in 1 Corinthians 7 lend themselves to divergent interpretations.[44] The apostle's famous declaration that it is better to marry than burn, like many of his other statements, seems to reduce marriage to a necessary evil. Yet by elevating it to the status of a "gift" only a few verses earlier ("For I would that all men were even as I myself. But every man hath his proper gift of God, one after this

[41]Several critics have suggested that other types of patriarchal assertions may be reactive. See esp. Louis Adrian Montrose, " 'Shaping Fantasies': Figurations of Gender and Power in Elizabethan Culture," *Representations,* 1 (1983), 61–94.

[42]Alexander Niccholes, *A Discourse, Of Marriage and Wiving* (London, 1615), p. 6.

[43]For a different perspective on this issue, see C. L. Barber and Richard P. Wheeler, *The Whole Journey: Shakespeare's Power of Development* (Berkeley: Univ. of California Press, 1986), esp. pp. 31–34, 46, 295, 333; their argument about transmutations of the cult of the Virgin Mary indirectly supports my contention about Protestant ambivalence on the subject of marriage vs. celibacy.

[44]On the problems of interpreting these Pauline passages, see *The Anchor Bible: I Corinthians,* by William F. Orr and James Arthur Walther (New York: Doubleday, 1976), esp. pp. 205–225; *The Anchor Bible: Ephesians,* by Markus Barth, 2 vols. (New York: Doubleday, 1974), II, 651–753. Other useful observations may be found in Jordan, *Renaissance Feminism.*

manner, and another after that" [1 Cor. 7.7])[45] he imbues it with a kind of dignity that provided a basis for the Reformers' attack on the Catholic cults of virginity and celibacy.

Both Luther and Calvin emphatically defended marriage, and both Reformers themselves had wives.[46] Yet their writings on wedlock are not without ambivalence. Luther is torn between his drive to reject the Catholic privileging of virginity and his distrust of the alternative state, which, he maintains in "A Sermon on the Estate of Marriage," can degenerate into "a filthy sow's sty" if one does not control lust.[47] In fact, even while praising marriage he complains that Paul himself fails to express enough respect for celibacy, presenting this ambivalent sentiment in strikingly ambivalent and guarded language: "If it were not St. Paul, I should truly be vexed that he gives such miserly praise and small honor to the noble state of celibacy."[48] Luther in part resolves—or possibly merely rationalizes—these apparent contradictions by developing Paul's own observation on the cares associated with marriage: while marriage is instituted by God and helps to prevent sin, it brings with it a host of daily problems. "If one cannot have the happy days of celibacy, then one must accept the evil days of marriage, for it is better to suffer evil days without sin in marriage than happy days without marriage in sin and unchastity"[49]—an endorsement of wedlock, but hardly an enthusiastic one. Calvin firmly opposes priestly celibacy and defends marriage for those who cannot be continent; yet in his reminder that celibacy is a special gift that can promote piety and in his warning that we should beware of lust within marriage we encounter reservations that anticipate those in the conduct books, sermons, and other texts on wedlock.[50] The tensions in Luther's and Calvin's own

[45]All citations from the Bible are to the King James version.

[46]For a useful analysis of the Reformers' defense of marriage, see Steven Ozment, *The Age of Reform, 1250–1550: An Intellectual and Religious History of Late Medieval and Reformation Europe* (New Haven: Yale Univ. Press, 1980), chap. 12.

[47]Martin Luther, *The Christian in Society I*, trans. and ed. James Atkinson (Philadelphia: Fortress Press, 1966), p. 11, in *Luther's Works*, ed. Helmut T. Lehmann and Jaroslav Pelikan, 55 vols. (St. Louis and Philadelphia: Concordia Publishing House and Fortress Press, 1955–). For Luther's other pronouncements on marriage see esp. *Commentaries on 1 Corinthians 7, 1 Corinthians 15, Lectures on Timothy*, ed. Hilton C. Oswald (St. Louis: Concordia Publishing House, 1973), in Lehmann and Pelikan.

[48]*Commentaries on 1 Corinthians*, p. 47.

[49]*Commentaries on 1 Corinthians*, p. 12.

[50]Calvin, *Institutes of the Christian Religion*, trans. John Allen, rev. ed., 2 vols. (Philadelphia: Presbyterian Board of Christian Education, n.d.), I, 437–441.

attitudes anticipate as well the reluctance of many German priests to marry even when urged to do so by the Reformers.[51]

In light of this background, it is not surprising that even the marriage ceremony in the Book of Common Prayer declares that wedlock was established for those lacking "the gift of continency."[52] Nor is it surprising that the authors of conduct books disagree among and with themselves when they weigh the relative merits of marriage and celibacy. Their ambivalence is reminiscent of the conflicts in the Petrarchan discourse on a related subject, the lady's chastity.[53] To be sure, all of these manuals are committed to establishing marriage as a holy alternative to celibacy: it is, they repeatedly affirm, a remedy for sin, not its source. But at this point they part company, arranging themselves along a spectrum from seeing marriage as an unhappy state, a necessary evil for those unfortunate enough to lack the gift of celibacy, to viewing it as a joyous alternative to celibacy.[54] Bullinger, whose treatment is often close to that of Paul, writes, "it is aquyct [sic] state of lyuying for a man not to touch or lye wyth a womman . . . if God haue graunted hym & geven him the gift that he may well and without burnyng lyue chast & unmaried. But yf a man or woman may not so do God hath geuen them the medicyne of mariage."[55] Celibacy is a gift, marriage a mere medicine. In telling contrast, Cleaver and Dod inform us that both states involve gifts (sig. H7^v). Such contradictions are further complicated by the contradictions we sometimes encounter within the work of a single author.

Bullinger's tract is far earlier than Cleaver and Dod's (the Coverdale version was first published in 1541 in Antwerp), and it represents a Continental tradition. Yet neither fact explains away his attraction to celibacy: the unease he expresses persists in the Puritan treatises of the seventeenth century.[56] As late as 1642, when Rogers balances the merits of the married and single states in his treatise

---

[51]See Ozment, *The Age of Reform*, pp. 394–395.

[52]Booty, p. 290.

[53]I am grateful to Ilona Bell for drawing this parallel with Petrarchism to my attention.

[54]Compare George, p. 266.

[55]Heinrich Bullinger, *The Christen State of Matrimonye*, trans. Myles Coverdale (London?, 1541), sig. Dii^v.

[56]Compare J. C. H. Aveling, who briefly observes that a number of Protestant tracts declare that celibacy is preferable to marriage ("Catholic Households in Yorkshire, 1580–1603," *Northern History*, 16 [1980], 100).

Matrimoniall Honovr, his own discourse is unbalanced, uncertain: he repeatedly implies the very preference for celibacy that he seems loath to admit directly. He condemns the Catholic emphasis on virginity and asserts that marriage is an honorable state, but most of his animosity is reserved for the hypocrisy with which the ideal of celibacy is espoused, not the ideal itself. In talking about determining to which state God has called one, he emphasizes the disadvantages of celibacy far less than those of marriage:

> thou maist gather the will of God by the signe, and so thou art to yeeld thy selfe to a single life; wherein although there cannot but fall out some petty discommodities (in some kinde) yet they ought to be digested meekely, for the avoyding of worse, and the attaining of the benefit of a single estate. . . . Then secondly, if not withstanding this triall, thou shalt finde, that God hath alotted marriage to thee, know, its a lawfull condition of life, be resolved it is so, be not snared with feare, melancholy, or any distemper. (p. 50)

These hints about the fears, melancholies, and distempers attending marriage are enforced at the conclusion of the treatise, where Rogers praises marital chastity in telling terms: "Thy marriage shall not prejudice nor stain this virginity" (p. 386). He is apparently deploying "virginity" metaphorically to represent "purity," but the usage is still revealing: even though he unqualifiedly condemns the Catholic respect for celibacy elsewhere in his tract, the highest praise he can bestow on marriage involves the term in question.[57]

Yet the Catholic positions on marriage and virginity are criticized even more harshly than are talkative women in the marriage manuals. Nor are these attacks confined to that particular genre; Nicholas Gibbens's commentary on the Bible, for example, lambasts Catholicism in the course of defending marriage.[58] How does the lingering attraction to celibacy that I am attributing to so many Renaissance writers relate to their antipapist diatribes? Given the intensity and frequency of antipapist attacks in Reformation literature, it would be foolish to read these passages solely as a blind for an interest in the

[57]After completing this chapter I discovered that Roberta Hamilton also notes that in several instances the term "virginity" is used to praise marriage; but the only implication she draws is that this usage reflects an urge to defend marriage and marital sex (*The Liberation of Women: A Study of Patriarchy and Capitalism* [London: George Allen and Unwin, 1978], pp. 56, 60).

[58]Nicholas Gibbens, *Qvestions and Dispvtations Concerning the Holy Scriptvre* (London, 1602), esp. pp. 84–85.

position being attacked, but I would suggest that at least some of their virulence may be attributed to the authors' uneasy and ambivalent attraction to the very ideal their Catholic opponents were espousing.

Acknowledging the presence of that attraction in the conduct books suggests that other manifestations of it are less idiosyncratic than they might otherwise have appeared. The contradictions in Edmund Spenser's comparisons between celibacy and wedlock are sometimes traced simply to the political exigencies of flattering his monarch; but the conduct books indicate instead that the ambivalent comparisons of those two states which we find in Book III of *The Faerie Queene* reflect a deeper, recurrent pattern in the culture and in Spenser himself.

Similar ambivalences appear in many seventeenth-century texts. The critical debate about the meanings of chastity in *Comus* is complicated, though not resolved, when one acknowledges that a Protestant writer might well have been attracted to chastity in the sense of virginity as well as that of continence within marriage. Donne's sermons repeatedly contradict themselves on the relative worth of marriage and celibacy; the conduct books on marriage encourage us to trace these contradictions not only to his divided religious heritage but also to tensions experienced even by his contemporaries who had not been raised Catholics. Thus in a sermon on riches he informs us that "the chastity of virginity, is the proper, and principal chastity" (III, 68). Similarly, in another sermon he defends the Protestant position from putative Catholic attacks in terms that indeed elide the distinction between the positions normally associated with each of those churches: "If they charge us that wee prefer Mariage before Continency, they charge us unjustly, for we do not so: Let them contain that can, and blesse God for that heavenly gift of Continency, and let them that cannot, mary, and serve God, and blesse him for affording them that Physick for that infirmity" (III, 131). Like Bullinger, he elevates continency into a "heavenly gift" while reducing marriage to a "Physick." Elsewhere, however, his defense of the institution is less equivocal. In particular, when preaching at the marriage of Lady Mary, daughter of the earl of Bridgewater, he emphasizes that vestal virgins "were preferred before all that liv'd unmaryed, but not before maryed persons" (VIII, 101), implying that the same ranking pertains to their counterparts in his own society. He proceeds to stress that we should not praise virginity in any terms that discredit marriage and to celebrate wedlock himself with intense though not unqualified enthusiasm.

Not only literary texts but also political semiotics should be reinterpreted in light of the ambivalences about virginity in Protestant England. Thus Elizabeth's cult as the Virgin Queen emerges as a policy even more astute than scholars have recognized: confronted with subjects who found the closely related ideals of virginity and celibacy somewhat appealing but did not wish to be associated with the Catholic position on the subject, she provided them with a safe way to express their values. The genre of pastoral romance flourished at the beginning of the seventeenth century in part at least because in the absence of the Virgin Queen the culture welcomed another mode of expressing the attraction of virginity.

Even when the authors of marriage manuals and other texts on wedlock are not explicitly comparing marriage and celibacy, they may express considerable ambivalence about the institution they are analyzing and advocating. Within a decade of publishing *A Bride-bvsh* (1617), Whately wrote *A Care-cloth* (1624); its ostensible purpose is to advise caution in marrying, but in many passages his view of marriage is dark enough wholly to discourage potential brides and grooms. Whately's tone is unusually negative, but his sentiments are not unique. For instance, Henry Smith entitles his tract *A Preparatiue to Mariage,* but his conclusion seems intended instead to prepare us to avoid it. He introduces his final remarks by emphasizing that they represent his summative wisdom. What is "most needfull to beare away" (p. 86), he announces, is the peril of marriage, not its potential benefits. Quoting 1 Corinthians 7.32 on how marriage tends to distract one from spiritual concerns, he wishes to "warne him to liue in marriage as in a temptation, which is like to make him worse then he was" (p. 87). Such language is reminiscent of the contemporaneous misogynist debate on women (for example, Joseph Swetnam, one of its most vitriolic participants, warns, "In the beginning a womans loue seemeth delightfull, but endeth with destruction"[59] and proceeds with pathological intensity to describe that destruction).

While not denying that marriage may carry with it some problems, certain writers sing its praises in terms very different from the somber warnings issued by Smith and Whately. Several texts laud

[59]Joseph Swetnam, *The Araignment of Lewde, Idle, Froward, and Vnconstant Women* (London, 1615), p. 36.

the institution by punning on "merry-age." And as early as 1560, Thomas Becon expresses commonplaces about the relationship of marriage to civilization in intense, hyperbolic prose: "Out of it as oute of a moste riche and golden floud all other orders and degrees of life issue and flow forth: yea as a moste fruteful mother bringeth it forth such as may worthely lyve . . . without whom . . . whole Realmes, whole kingdomes, whole Common weales fal to ruine."[60] These treatises on wedlock sometimes include enthusiastic and sympathetic defenses not only of marriage but of women; for instance, the authors of marriage manuals, like the polemicist who attempt to counter misogynist attacks such as Swetnam's,[61] often assert that the faults attributed to women should really be blamed on men. When read in the context of more pessimistic evaluations of marriage, passages such as Becon's lend qualified support to theories distinguishing medieval and Renaissance attitudes towards wedlock—and unqualified support to assertions about the range of responses to marriage in Tudor and Stuart England.

Another controversy that recurs in the conduct books and other treatments of marriage involves the moral limitations inherent in woman and the degree of subordination appropriate to her, issues that, as James Grantham Turner has acutely demonstrated, proved controversial in other types of theological discourse as well.[62] The marriage manuals contain both virulent misogyny and equally intense critiques of misogyny; they stress woman's spiritual equality and her inequality in other respects. And they move back and forth between emphasizing the husband's dominion and bestowing some measure of both power and authority on the wife as well.[63] We cannot be sure whether that bestowal represents the growing respect for her suggested by the doctrine of the Puritan art of love or, alternatively, a minor concession designed to make patriarchal power more palatable; the answer no doubt varies from tract to tract, as well as

[60]The Worckes of T. Becon, 3 vols. (London, 1564), I.sig. QQqiiiiv. The title pages of Volumes 1 and 2 are dated 1560.

[61]See, e.g., C[hrisopher] N[ewstead], An Apology for Women (London, 1620), p. 3 ("Eue then tempted Adam, but now Adam tempts Eue").

[62]See esp. chap. 3. The tension between equality and subjection is also trenchantly discussed in Amussen, pp. 201–203.

[63]In "The Formative Power of Marriage in Stuart Tragedy," Mikesell uncovers a somewhat similar series of contradictions in the genre she explores: the heroines, she argues, deviate from societal norms in their actions, but dramatic convention assigns them a subsidiary role that conforms to more traditional expectations about women.

from marriage to marriage. In any event, however, the marriage manuals repeatedly acknowledge the wife's power within the family. Several authors emphasize that she too is a governor of the family—but a subsidiary one. They wish, in other words, at once to grant and to delimit power, to give with one hand and take away with the other. That wish emerges in the titles assigned to define the wife's status, which vary subtly but significantly in their degree of egalitarianism; she is, we are variously told, "an vnder-officer," "the associate" to "the prince and chiece [*sic*] ruler," the "fellow-helper" for the "chiefe gouernour" or a "ioynt Gouernour."[64] To name something is often to attempt to control it, and so we may perhaps sense some anxiety about the woman's dual status as governed and governor not only in the range of these appellations but also in these writers' preoccupation with bestowing an apt title on that role.

Similar ambivalences about the status and value of a wife appear in other types of discourse as well. Two of Thomas Gataker's marriage sermons, published under the title *A Good Wife Gods Gift,* do indeed celebrate the joys of happy wedlock. But he does not hesitate to devote considerable space to the misogynist critique of wives, acknowledging that "many a one neuer knew what *miserie* meant, till he came to know what *a wife* was."[65] Family letters vary as much as the conduct books in the degree of power and responsibility they assign to the wife and the amount of subordination ascribed to her, suggesting that Renaissance families differed as much as their modern counterparts in their approaches to these questions. Furthermore, as the letters among other documents remind us, the wife's role within a given family need not remain essentially constant: it could vary not only from one family unit to the next but also from one period to another in the history of a given family. The illness of the husband or his absence from home during an era when communications systems were slow and irregular obviously could lead to the temporary reassignment of responsibilities, as the correspondence of Lady Katherine Paston testifies;[66] the firm divisions between the roles of husband and wife that we find in some of the literature on marriage may well represent a nervous antidote to the

---

[64]See respectively Smith, p. 52; Perkins, p. 173; Cleaver, sig. B2; Gouge, sig. ¶4.
[65]Thomas Gataker, *A Good Wife Gods Gift* (London, 1623), p. 49.
[66]*The Correspondence of Lady Katherine Paston, 1603–1627,* ed. Ruth Hughey (Norwich: Norfolk Record Society, 1941), p. 33.

shifts in power that occurred in practice. Moreover, as Margaret J. M. Ezell reminds us, the death of her husband could transfer to the wife responsibilities we would normally classify as patriarchal.[67]

Other ambiguities and ambivalences about the status of women recur in the intriguing biography that Lucy Hutchinson wrote of her husband, the Parliamentarian colonel John Hutchinson. Though this work slightly postdates the other texts we are examining, its commentary illuminates theirs in several ways. In particular, these memoirs enable us to view marriage from the perspective of the wife—but a wife who, for all her independence and pride, has internalized many patriarchal attitudes towards marriage. Thus, using the third person for herself as she does throughout, she declares that "he soon made her more equal to him than he found her,"[68] a statement that acknowledges her own achievements but in so doing establishes her husband as both their yardstick and their source. This surely goes beyond the demands of modesty and tact, as does the adjoining description of herself as "a very faithful mirror, reflecting truly, though but dimly, his own glories upon him" (p. 53).

The marriage manuals grant the wife a type of power that no doubt troubled their authors and many of their readers as much as questions about her compliance and subordination. In 1 Corinthians 7.3–5 Paul establishes the concept generally known as "due benevolence" or "the marriage debt":

> Let the husband render unto the wife due benevolence: and likewise also the wife unto the husband.
>
> The wife hath not power of her own body, but the husband: and likewise also the husband hath not power of his own body, but the wife.
>
> Defraud ye not one the other, except *it be* with consent for a time, that ye may give yourselves to fasting and prayer; and come together again, that Satan tempt you not for your incontinency.

Though the glosses in the Geneva Bible suggest a range of meanings for the concept of due benevolence, its primary one is not in question: both husband and wife have the right to demand sexual relations, and the partner may not refuse. It is no wonder that the Wife

---

[67]See Ezell, esp. p. 161.

[68]Lucy Hutchinson, *Memoirs of the Life of Colonel Hutchinson*, ed. Julius Hutchinson and C. H. Firth, rev. ed. (London: George Routledge and Sons, 1906), p. 53. Subsequent page references will appear in the text.

of Bath seizes on this theory with such enthusiasm; it is, as James Grantham Turner observes, "astonishingly egalitarian."[69] That egalitarianism involves a recognition of female sexual desire—a recognition that in some readers might even breed fears about being unable to pay the debt, or performance anxieties. But the implications of the marriage debt extend beyond the bedroom; the recurrence of the word "power" in the Pauline text, as well as in glosses on it in the marriage tracts, gestures towards a metaphoric equation connecting sexual rights and other types of rights, as well as other types of power.

Though the primary implications of due benevolence would be likely to threaten male readers accustomed to patriarchal authority, the concept invites other types of interpretation as well. It potentially both excites and assuages anxieties, a pattern that recurs repeatedly in the texts, literary and extraliterary, concerning marriage. For one thing, the fears of overindulgence in marital sex that so many scholars have charted[70] in some instances no doubt interfered with collecting the debt or even experiencing the desire to do so. Moreover, the rhetoric of the Pauline passages in question and the commentaries on them in the marriage manuals circumscribe and control the very passion ostensibly being unleashed. The language of debt and obligation makes sexuality seem less an anarchic and uncontrollable force and more a mercantile commodity subject to measurement and control. Similarly, the allusion to duty in "due benevolence" achieves the very transformation that is so often performed by the genre of the epithalamium itself: sexuality is constructed not as a self-indulgent, uncontrollable pleasure but rather as a socially sanctioned and even mandated responsibility. Ozment offers a different but not incompatible explanation of how due benevolence, like procreation, makes passion respectable: it "placed sex safely under God's commandments to be fruitful and multiply and avoid illicit fornication."[71] Hence if the concept invites fears of sexually aggressive Argantes, it also holds out the promise of a race of Britomarts who channel their sexuality to socially acceptable ends.

---

[69]Turner, p. 27. His subsequent discussion of due benevolence (pp. 221–226) is different from but compatible with my own; for instance, he draws attention to how the concept intensified fears of polluted sexuality.

[70]See, e.g., Stephen Greenblatt, *Renaissance Self-Fashioning from More to Shakespeare* (Chicago: Univ. of Chicago Press, 1980), esp. pp. 241–252.

[71]Ozment, *When Fathers Ruled*, p. 11.

The multiple interpretations to which due benevolence lends itself
help explain why the authors of the marriage manuals respond to it
so differently. Some devote little attention to the concept in question,
probably because they find it deeply problematical and perhaps fear
their readers will do so as well. Despite—or because of—the misogynist anxieties latent in *A Bride-bvsh* and overt in *A Care-cloth,*
Whately emphasizes that due benevolence and chastity are the two
principal duties of marriage. Gouge's popular tract discusses the concept at some length, both stressing the notion of obligation implied
in the language of debt and warning readers of the danger that either
husband or wife may use the privileges of due benevolence to enforce
excessive sexual demands.

But how did such passages actually affect the readers of the conduct books on marriage? The concept of due benevolence must have
influenced some people little or not at all: I have suggested that
countervailing emphases on the dangers of sexuality, especially female sexuality, may have made many hesitate to collect the debt (it is
hard to think of a more potent anaphrodisiac that the concept of
duty, as George Orwell's *1984* memorably demonstrates through the
character of Winston Smith's wife Katharine). Yet Gouge's warnings
about excessive demands do indicate either a climate in which at least
some women did not hesitate to express their sexual desires—or
male anxieties, whether justified or not, about such a climate. Indeed, those anxieties may well have generated an intensified conservatism: the assertions of patriarchy that we encounter in the tracts
were surely at least in part reactive, responses not only to the assertions of independence that many feminist scholars have traced in late
Elizabethan and Jacobean culture[72] but also to the degree of autonomy that the authors of these tracts were themselves ascribing to
women.

But just as we must note that due benevolence both intensifies and
subdues anxieties, so we should not conclude our survey of potentially explosive tensions in the discourses of marriage without drawing attention as well to one of the authors' strategies for defusing the
mines they plant. The very act of writing a manual or delivering a
sermon on marriage gestures towards the principal strategy: the act

---

[72]See, e.g., Underdown, "The Taming of the Scold"; Woodbridge, *Women and the
English Renaissance,* pp. 265–267. Natalie Zemon Davis has written a seminal study of
female rebelliousness in France (*Society and Culture in Early Modern France* [Stanford:
Stanford Univ. Press, 1975], chap. 5).

implies that wedlock is an institution that can indeed be regulated, controlled, and ordered by someone who assumes the authority to do so. And the rhetoric of the marriage manuals in particular is in fact grounded in ordering in the sense both of giving commands and of establishing order—and grounded as well in the connection between those two activities. Witness some of their titles: *A Godly Forme of Hovshold Government: for the ordering of private families, according to the direction of Gods word*; *Of Domesticall Dvties*; *Christian Oeconomie: Or, A short svrvey of the right manner of erecting and ordering a familie, according to the Scriptures* (emphases added). Moreover, the authors of these books delight in the process of hierarchical enumeration: they list and rank the duties of the husband and wife, the functions of the contract, and so on. The activity of listing naturally occurs in many treatises, but the authors of these books do it with particular frequency and to particular ends: like the speech act of naming that in so many ways it resembles, it involves an assertion of control.

These discussions of marriage, then, warn us against exaggerating the pressure associated with marriage in Stuart England or neglecting contrary influences. But they also draw our attention to the many problems surrounding that institution. This era witnessed conflicting theories about the procedures appropriate for weddings (is a church ceremony necessary? is a *de futuro* contract binding?) and about the very nature of marriage itself. The Stuart epithalamium, like the conduct books, responds to such tensions by substituting its own narratives of marriage and in so doing ordering (in both senses) the disorderly.

III

The Stuart wedding poem is, of course, the product of generic potentialities as well as cultural pressures: its poets turn to the norms and conventions they inherited to interpret, control, and suppress the anxieties we have been surveying. Since the history of the genre has been so thoroughly mapped by Virginia Tufte in *The Poetry of Marriage,* as well as by other critics,[73] that inheritance can be briefly

[73]For summaries of the history and development of the genre, see Greene, "Spenser and the Epithalamic Convention"; Masoodul Hasan, "English Epithalamic Verse of the Earlier Seventeenth Century," *Indian Journal of English Studies,* 8 (1967), 10–24; Barbara Kiefer Lewalski, *"Paradise Lost" and the Rhetoric of Literary Forms*

summarized here. Even a short summary, however, indicates the range of possibilities that the genre offered Stuart poets. Like adherents of the Whig view of history, we may assume that it was natural, even virtually inevitable, that the primary model adopted by Spenser and seventeenth-century poets was Catullus 61 rather than, say, Catullus 62 or the epithalamium written by the neo-Latin poet Johannes Secundus. But the history of the genre reminds us how many other options were available and hence prepares us to recognize the significance of the choices that were made—and those that were not. In literary criticism as in sociolinguistics, what is not said can be as revealing as what is. And a survey of the genre clarifies the Stuart epithalamium in a second way: such a summary demonstrates that the vision of marriage in earlier instances of the genre is not without its tensions. Many Stuart wedding poems express their reservations and fears about wedlock with unusual intensity and in unusual ways, but precedents for these sentiments can be traced to earlier epithalamia, including lyrics that are sometimes read as uniformly celebratory.

Though little tangible evidence survives, the folk epithalamium apparently enjoyed a long history. Both poets and rhetoricians prove conscious of these antecedents; thus, focusing on the folk epithalamium throughout his chapter on the genre, George Puttenham asserts that it divided into three parts, a song when the couple went to bed, another one later in the evening, and a third the next day when they arose.[74] Influenced by the common assumption that the Bible is a compendium of all literary types, Renaissance writers were no doubt also aware that both the Song of Solomon and Psalm 45 are poems about weddings.

(Princeton: Princeton Univ. Press, 1985), pp. 190–195; James A. S. McPeek, *Catullus in Strange and Distant Britain*, Harvard Studies in Comparative Literature, 15 (Cambridge: Harvard Univ. Press, 1939), and "The Major Sources of Spenser's *Epithalamion*," *JEGP*, 35 (1936), 183–213; Camillo Morelli, "L'epitalamio nella tarda poesia latina," *Studi italiani di filologia classica*, 18 (1910), 319–432; Charles G. Osgood, "Epithalamion and Prothalamion: 'and theyr eccho ring,' " *MLN*, 76 (1961), 205–208; Tufte, *The Poetry of Marriage;* Cortlandt Van Winkle, ed., "Introduction," in Edmund Spenser, *Epithalamion* (New York: F. S. Crofts, 1926); Enid Welsford, *Spenser, Fowre Hymnes, Epithalamion: A Study of Edmund Spenser's Doctrine of Love* (Oxford: Basil Blackwell, 1967), pp. 64–70; Arthur Leslie Wheeler, *Catullus and the Traditions of Ancient Poetry* (Berkeley: Univ. of California Press, 1934), and "Tradition in the Epithalamium," *AJP*, 51 (1930), 205–223.
[74]George Puttenham, *The Arte of English Poesie*, ed. Gladys Doidge Willcock and Alice Walker (1936; rpt. Cambridge: Cambridge Univ. Press, 1970), chap. 26.

Greek literature includes several influential epithalamia, notably fragments by Sappho and Theocritus's eighteenth idyll, a poem that was to be both imitated and translated by English writers. The primary models adopted by Elizabethan and Stuart poets, however, derive from the Latin tradition, which has been classified in terms of two subgenres, the "lyric" and the "epic" types.[75] Exemplified by such narratives as Claudian 10 and Statius *Silvae* 1.2, the epic epithalamium recounts a mythological story connected with weddings; typically, Venus and Cupid discuss marriage, and the goddess of love deigns to attend the ceremony at hand. Elements of this type are also present in Catullus 64, an intricately structured celebration of the marriage of Peleus and Thetis. In the lyric epithalamium, in contrast, the poet describes the events of the wedding day in chronological order. Catullus 61, the best and most influential classical instance, demonstrates the principal characteristics of this type. Serving as both a master of ceremonies and a wedding guest, the speaker invokes Hymen, invites nymphs and other guests, lists Roman marriage customs such as sprinkling wine, praises the couple, alludes to perils that their marriage should avoid, and offers prayers for good fortune in general and heirs in particular. In referring to perils, Catullus 61 exemplifies the tensions that were to be echoed, often in a louder and harsher voice, in the Stuart epithalamia; for instance, in one relevant passage the speaker imitates the Fescennine taunts by urging the bridegroom to abandon former loves.

Yet the binary division of lyric and epic epithalamia, like so many other binary divisions, turns out to be problematical, in part because it does not readily admit Catullus 62, a dialogue between maidens and youths about marriage.[76] That poem begins on an allusion to the approach of evening, an opening Jonson and other English poets were to imitate. The participants then debate the advantages and perils of marriage, with the maidens defending the single life and their male counterparts arguing for the wedded state instead. Thus the girls declare that the bride becomes a faded flower after losing her virginity. In response the youths compare the virgin to an unwedded vine, fruitless and untended. They buttress their analysis

---

[75]For this system of classification, see esp. Van Winkle, pp. 10–21. On the characteristics of the epic epithalamium, see Gary M. McCown, "Milton and the Epic Epithalamium," *Milton Studies*, 5 (1973), 39–66.

[76]A sensitive and trenchant reading of this poem is offered by Steele Commager in "The Structure of Catullus 62," *Eranos*, 81 (1983), 21–33.

with a strikingly materialistic argument: young women must remember, they assert, that only one-third of their maidenhead is their
own, for the other two-thirds belong to their parents, who have bestowed their rights on the bridegroom. Predictably, the young men
have the last word, and the poem concludes on the traditional invocation of Hymen. The format of this dialogue was to influence English poets in both obvious and subterranean ways; its debate
structure, for example, undergoes a sea-change and surfaces in a very
different guise in the Stuart epithalamium.

During most of the Middle Ages the term "epithalamium" was
applied primarily to religious poems, such as works in praise of Mary,
that had little influence on the English wedding poem. The Continental Renaissance, however, witnessed a resurgence of interest in the
secular epithalamium. If the customary categorization into lyric and
epic types may tempt us to underestimate the significance of Catullus 62, it may also lead us to neglect the range of models Continental
poets offered their English counterparts. Thus, for example, the French
tradition includes poems that fit into those two categories, such as
Marc-Claude de Buttet's celebration of the marriage of Philibert of
Savoy and Marguerite of France, which, like Catullus 61, addresses
Hymen, recounts the events of the wedding day, and concludes on a
prayer for heirs. Pierre de Ronsard's "Epithalame de . . . Antoine de
Bourbon et de Jeanne, reine de Navarre," however, is not primarily
an account of the wedding day; instead, like so many other works in
the genre, it concentrates on praising the couple and offering good
wishes for their happiness. An epithalamium by Clément Marot, his
"Chant nuptial du mariage de madame Renée . . . avec le duc de
Ferrare," exemplifies yet another option for the genre: though this
lyric includes a few allusions to the events of the wedding day, by
and large it focuses on the night instead. As these poems suggest,
scholars might profitably qualify the lyric-epic division by enumerating several subgenres that fit neither category, such as lists of good
wishes and poems addressing the wedding night itself.

Despite his emphasis on the wedding night and the explicitness of
some of his other poetry, Marot is tactfully vague in most of his
allusions to the consummation of the marriage. The neo-Latin poets
Gioviano Pontano and Johannes Secundus, in contrast, write far
more erotic evocations of the night (indeed, the epithalamium that
Pontano composed for the wedding of Giovanni Brancati can best be
described as an explicit sex manual for the bridegroom), and Giovanni Battista Marino's wedding poem "Il Letto" focuses on the

events in the marriage bed, as its name would suggest. Leonard Forster has asserted that the epithalamium tradition functioned as a
safety valve for Petrarchism as it allowed writers to express sensuality that could not be so freely included in the sonnet tradition;[77] this
claim accords well to poems like these, though not to the many
other Continental lyrics that refer to sex far more tacitly and tactfully. In the treatment of the sexual aspects of marriage, as in so
many other areas, English poets inherited a wide range of models
from which to choose.

Among the earliest members of the native tradition are John Lyd-
gate's "On Gloucester's Approaching Marriage" and William Dunbar's "The Thrissil and the Rois." Epithalamia also appear in a few
Tudor translations, such as Bartholomew Young's anglicized version
of Gil Polo's continuation of Montemayor's *Diana* and Henry Wotton's rendition of a work by Jacques Yver, *A Courtlie Controversie of
Cupids Cautels.* Sir John Davies also wrote a wedding poem, apparently for the union of Elizabeth Vere and the earl of Derby.[78]

On a casual perusal—the type of reading critics typically give it—
the epithalamium in the Third Eclogues of Sir Philip Sidney's *Arcadia*
appears bland and predictable. In fact, however, it repays closer analysis. For this lyric both reflects and responds to several of the concerns that electrify so much of the *Arcadia.* Thus it is exemplary,
demonstrating a pattern that we will encounter throughout this
book: the poem works, with considerable though not complete success, to control the pressures and dangers that, as it repeatedly reminds us, threaten marriage.

As many readers have observed, the Third Eclogues are closely related to Sidney's prose narrative and, in particular, to Book III: they
implicitly comment both on the behavior of the royal and noble
characters and on the ethical and psychological problems raised by
that behavior.[79] Celebrating the marriage of Kala and Thyrsis,[80]

[77]Leonard Forster, *The Icy Fire: Five Studies in European Petrarchism* (Cambridge:
Cambridge Univ. Press, 1969), chap. 3.

[78]For the text of this obscure lyric and the evidence that it was intended for the
wedding in question, see Robert Krueger, "Sir John Davies: *Orchestra* Complete, *Epigrams,* Unpublished Poems (Concluded)," *RES,* 13 (1962), 113–118.

[79]On these connections see Walter R. Davis, *A Map of Arcadia: Sidney's Romance in
Its Tradition,* in Walter R. Davis and Richard A. Lanham, *Sidney's Arcadia* (New Ha-
ven: Yale Univ. Press, 1965), p. 106; John A. Galm, *Sidney's Arcadian Poems,* Salzburg
Studies in English Literature: Elizabethan Studies (Salzburg: Institut für Englische
Sprache und Literatur, 1973), pp. 176–177.

[80]Thyrsis is named Lalus in the Old Arcadia.

these eclogues appear in the *Old Arcadia* immediately after Pyrocles and Philoclea consummate their passion, as though Sidney wishes and needs to temper his ecstatic evocation of extramarital passion with an instance of sanctioned desire. But the lyrics in question manifest broader and deeper connections with earlier sections of the romance: they too investigate gender, sexuality, and marriage, and they too are equivocal and troubled in their explorations of those issues.

Thus three of the four other eclogues in the group directly involve forces that might threaten the vision of domestic happiness in the epithalamium,[81] as well as the happiness of Pyrocles and Philoclea. One is a fabliau-like narrative about a wife tricking her husband. In a sonnet delivered by Pas, a husband is instructed how to make his wife chaste; this sonnet concludes on the ambiguously inconclusive couplet, "This done, thou hast no more, but leave the rest / To vertue, fortune, time and woman's brest" (13–14).[82] The instabilities of Sidney's responses to women and sexuality emerge in the conflict between the closural certainty of the couplet and the uncertainties involved in the curiously juxtaposed items on which the couplet ends. Though one reader glosses this passage as an assertion that "fidelity is largely a matter of luck,"[83] it in fact resists any neat summary: is "vertue" a stable anchor for behavior or as unreliable a force as "fortune"? does relying on "woman's brest" imply depending on the strength of a Pamela or the lasciviousness of a Gynecia? Here, as in so many of Sir Thomas Wyatt's poems, cynical assertions represent not a neatly conclusive answer but rather a dominant voice in a cacophony of conflicting ones. Similarly, the final poem in this group of eclogues exemplifies Renaissance debates about marriage, with Histor explaining his reluctance to take a wife and Geron arguing the opposite case. The latter seems to win, but the advice on which his speech culminates is telling:

> Marrie therefore; for marriage will destroy
> Those passions which to youthfull head doo clime,
> Mothers and Nurses of all vaine annoy.
>
> (115–117)

[81] Another eclogue, not directly connected with marriage, was inserted in the Third Eclogues in the 1593 edition. See *The Poems of Sir Philip Sidney*, ed. William A. Ringler, Jr. (Oxford: Clarendon Press, 1962), pp. 496–497.

[82] All citations from Sidney's poetry are to Ringler, *The Poems of Sir Philip Sidney*.

[83] Galm, p. 179.

In other words, in the very process of defending women and advocating marriage, Geron genders unruly passions as female ("Mothers and Nurses"), thus transferring them to the Other. And in so doing he clouds maternity, a role normally celebrated in defenses of marriage, with negative connotations. If Philip Sparrow renounces the implications of his name, he simply deflects them onto his mate.

The epithalamium in the Third Eclogues addresses itself to the very tensions expressed by the other lyrics in what we might call Sidney's Marriage Group. Each stanza focuses on a particular wish for the couple's happiness. Here, as in Catullus 61 and many of the lyrics we will examine in Chapter 2, such hopes and wishes are frequently constructed as the banishing of a threat ("But thou foule *Cupid,* syre to lawlesse lust, / Be thou farre hence with thy empoyson'd darte" [55–56]), a formulation that recalls those threats while attempting to dismiss them.

One such danger is especially revealing. "Yet let not sluttery, / The sinke of filth, be counted huswifery" (78–79), Sidney writes, and in his final stanza he refers again to "loathsome sluttishnes" (97). Yet allusions to housekeeping are not common in either classical or Renaissance wedding lyrics, and they seem all the more out of place in a pastoral epithalamium. Et in Arcadia ego, we assume, refers to death, not dustballs. One explanation for this curious reference is that "sluttery" functions synecdochally, representing not only the untidiness of a given house but also all the kinds of poetic and social disorder that the marriage attempts to control. Another explanation lies in the word's semantic sluttishness. As the *Oxford English Dictionary* informs us, though its primary meaning in the sixteenth century was indeed dirtiness, it could refer as well to sexual licentiousness.[84] The preoccupation with such licentiousness that occurs in the episodes and lyrics immediately surrounding this one is manifest in Sidney's choice of words. As I will argue shortly, its recurrence later in the poem is also telling.

On the whole the final stanza effects a conclusive resolution to the potential tensions and threats that the lyric has concerned. Dismissed through prayers and pleas earlier in the poem, here they are again exorcised through several prosodic and linguistic strategies:

> The earth is deckt with flowers, the heav'ns displaid,
> Muses graunt guiftes, Nymphes long and joyned life,

[84]*OED,* s.v. "slut," "sluttery."

Pan store of babes, vertue their thoughts well staid,
Cupid's lust gone, and gone is bitter strife,
Happy man, happy wife.
No pride shall them oppresse,
Nor yet shall yeeld to loathsome sluttishnes,
And jealousie is slaine:
For *Himen* will their coupled joyes maintaine.

                                              (91–99)

The optatives that characterized earlier sections of the poem stabilize
here into the reassurance of declaratives: "Let mother earth now
decke her selfe in flowers" (1) is transformed into "The earth is
deckt with flowers," and the refrain "O *Himen* long their coupled
joyes maintaine" (9, 18, 27, and so on) becomes "For *Himen* will
their coupled joyes maintaine." Thus the lyric enacts the movement
from anticipation to assurance that so often occurs in the genre. Similarly, it is telling that many of those declaratives rely not on verbs of
action but on verbs of being, or, to put it another way, verbs relax
into participial adjectives, with "decke" (1) becoming "is deckt" and
so on. Stasis and calm replace activity, anticipating the closure of the
poem itself. The final stanza achieves and advocates stability in yet
another way. The Second Maker who composed it is experimenting
with the "collector" device, or correlative verse: with one telling exception, to which we will turn shortly, the final stanza includes one
item from each of the previous stanzas, with each reference appearing
in the order in which it originally occurred in the poem.[85] Thus separate and disparate elements come together in harmony, a rhetorical
version of the social and marital values the lyric is celebrating. Prosodically, as in so many other ways, this epithalamium attempts to
reassert order and resolve uncertainties.

   Yet the final stanza hints, faintly but suggestively, at a threat to
such attempts. Though the collector device otherwise involves incorporating one item from each of the previous stanzas, in fact Sidney
includes two from the ninth stanza, "pride" and "sluttishnes." Literary critics need to remind themselves how often technical pressures
like the need for a rhyme may determine aesthetic decisions, but one
cannot explain away this particular oddity in that fashion. The au-

---

[85]Jon S. Lawry also notes the presence of this device but analyzes it differently,
comparing it to the curtain call at a play (*Sidney's Two "Arcadias": Pattern and Proceed-
ing* [Ithaca: Cornell Univ. Press, 1972], p. 112).

thor of the *Arcadia* could easily have crafted another rhyme for "oppresse" (96)—"happiness' and "bless" spring to mind immediately. Rather, he violates the neatness of his correlative verse by referring to "sluttishnes" a second time because he is preoccupied with the moral and social disorder that the word represents. Notice, too, the curious ambiguity, "Nor *yet* shall yeeld to loathsome sluttishnes" (italics added). Satan is clearly barred from this particular Eden, but we cannot forget that he lurks outside its walls.

In short, then, Sidney's lyric is more complex than it appears on first reading. Comparatively few Stuart epithalamia are located in the pastoral world; that setting exemplifies the many generic alternatives that seventeenth-century poets choose to ignore. But the poem we have just explored anticipates subsequent lyrics in a more important respect: both the tensions the author of the *Arcadia* addresses and the ways he addresses them foreshadow Stuart wedding poems.

The principal native source of those poems is, however, Spenser's "Epithalamion." Though writers in seventeenth-century England do not follow Spenser's innovative lead in casting the bridegroom as the speaker, in many other respects the echo of this lyric, as well as of the "Prothalamion," rings clearly and loudly in their work. For instance, a number of Stuart poets experiment with the type of shifting refrain that Spenser deploys. His comparisons of the bride and Queen Elizabeth also appear repeatedly in Stuart epithalamia, though these references come to assume a different function.

To understand a deeper and subtler parallel between Spenser's "Epithalamion" and Stuart works in its genre, we need to review its recent critical history. The commentary on the "Epithalamion," like that on the Herrick lyrics examined in Chapter 5, provides a convenient microcosm of changes in our discipline. Studies of this wedding poem published in the 1960s and early 1970s typically emphasized its serenity: representative titles tellingly read, "The Harmonious Universe of Love" and "Order and Joy in Spenser's 'Epithalamion.' "[86] Certainly Spenser's lyric provides evidence for such interpretations. The poem repeatedly advocates order: "Bynd vp the locks the which hang scatterd light" (62), "Set all your things in seemely good aray"

[86]A. R. Cirillo, "Spenser's *Epithalamion:* The Harmonious Universe of Love," *SEL,* 8 (1968), 19–34; W. Speed Hill, "Order and Joy in Spenser's 'Epithalamion,' " *Southern Humanities Review,* 6 (1972), 81–90.

(114), and so on.[87] And, of course, the epithalamium itself enacts the
values it advocates, with its extraordinary numerological patterning
establishing parallels between poetic, human, and natural rhythms.

Predictably enough, however, more recent criticism of this poem,
as of other Renaissance texts, has drawn attention to its anxieties.
Douglas Anderson stresses its silence and isolation.[88] Incompleteness,
poverty, and desperation are uncovered in Joseph Loewenstein's
thoughtful reading; the poem's presiding spirits, he argues, are Orpheus, the singer who loses his beloved, and Echo, who represents
not only man's control over nature but also his loss of control.[89]

The conflict between these two modes of reading the "Epithalamion," like that between the two rival paradigms for Stuart marriage, should be resolved by acknowledging that both are to some
degree right: in more senses than one, the poem contains both darkness and sunshine. Like Sidney, however, Spenser is concerned to de-
vise strategies that resolve or release the tensions that darken the
vision he evokes.[90] These tensions are often different from and less
intense than those in Stuart wedding poems, but Spenser's basic pattern of acknowledging and attempting to defuse threats anticipates
the seventeenth-century tradition.

The early stanzas of the poem incorporate mild and playful allusions to threats, such as,

> And let the ground whereas her foot shall tread,
> For feare the stones her tender foot should wrong
> Be strewed with fragrant flowers all along.
>
> (48–50)

The potential danger is subordinated, grammatically and psychologically. Lines like these do, however, anticipate references to graver
menaces.

Indeed, Spenser devotes the entire twentieth stanza of his lyric to
detailing and derailing dangers more threatening than stones—"Let

---

[87]The Variorum Spenser, ed. Edwin Greenlaw, Charles Grosvenor Osgood, Frederick Morgan Padelford, 11 vols. (Baltimore: Johns Hopkins Univ. Press, 1932–
1957). This edition is cited throughout my text.

[88]Anderson, " 'Vnto My Selfe Alone': Spenser's Plenary Epithalamion."

[89]Joseph Loewenstein, "Echo's Ring: Orpheus and Spenser's Career," ELR, 16
(1986), 287–302.

[90]Though his analysis of the threats involved in the poem differs significantly from
mine, Loewenstein also observes that assertions of order and stability represent a reactive defense against those threats (see "Echo's Ring," esp. 287–288).

not the shriech Oule, nor the Storke be heard" (345), and so on. Such pleas, like the comparable references in Sidney's lyric, invoke the anxieties about marriage in general and sexuality in particular that are never far from the surface of this poem. And Spenser, like Sidney, attempts to subdue these anxieties in the process of invoking them: the stanza aims to banish the dangers that may threaten the marriage. That aim is not wholly successful at this point in the lyric: the repeated allusions to the perils this marriage should avoid both reflect and create some measure of anxiety.

But Spenser's enumeration of the owls, storks, and other beasties of the night is in fact preceded by a more subtle and more successful attempt to control them. The lines in question are telling enough— and neglected enough—to invite lengthy quotation:

> Behold how goodly my faire loue doth ly
> In proud humility;
> Like vnto Maia, when as Ioue her tooke,
> In Tempe, lying on the flowry gras,
> Twixt sleepe and wake, after she weary was,
>
> . . . . .
>
> Now welcome night, thou night so long expected,
> That long daies labour doest at last defray,
> And all my cares, which cruell love collected,
> Hast sumd in one, and cancelled for aye:
> Spread thy broad wing ouer my loue and me,
> That no man may vs see,
> And in thy sable mantle vs enwrap,
> From feare of perrill and foule horror free.
> Let no false treason seeke vs to entrap,
> Nor any dread disquiet once annoy
> The safety of our ioy:
> But let the night be calme and quietsome,
> Without tempestuous storms or sad afray:
> Lyke as when Ioue with fayre Alcmena lay,
> When he begot the great Tirynthian groome.
>   (305–309, 315–329)

The initial emphasis on the pastoral in this graceful description of Maia—she is lying "on the flowry gras" after bathing in the brook—serves both to eroticize the poem's natural landscape and also, more to our purposes here, to make the erotic itself seem natural and hence unthreatening, as in the evocation of Adam and Eve's nuptial couch in *Paradise Lost*. Moreover, the description emphasizes Maia's sexual passivity; Jove "tooke" her when she was half-asleep. Thus female sexuality is drained of the threatening aggressiveness latent in the concept of due benevolence. This is no Argante, nor even a Britomart. Of course, for obvious reasons Spenser would hardly have wished to link his bride to a sexually demanding woman, but the degree of passivity here is striking. Yet the lines do not comment merely on female sexuality, as we may be tempted at first to believe; the allusion to sleep anticipates the ways the next stanza implicitly associates all sexuality neither with the male aggressiveness implied by "tooke" nor with the anarchic energy it often represents in the marriage manuals and other contemporary documents on wedlock, but rather with calm and stasis.

By alluding in the beginning of the next stanza to the cancellation of his cares, Spenser is rendering overt and thematic the poetic strategy in question: his poem itself both acknowledges and attempts with varying degrees of success to cancel "for aye" the cares associated with Cupid. The following lines illustrate one way he does so: "Spread thy broad wing ouer my loue and me, . . . And in thy sable mantle vs enwrap." Night—and by implication the sexual act connected with it—is reinterpreted to represent not the "perrill and foule horror" often associated with them in the conduct books and other texts on marriage but rather the antithesis and the antidote to those dangers. The Virgilian image of the brooding wing makes night seem maternal, an image that anticipates the emphasis on procreation later in the stanza. That emphasis transforms the sexual act from a potential threat to society and its participants into a social responsibility. The reference to a "calme and quietsome" night, which echoes the preoccupation with rest and fatigue that A. Bartlett Giamatti and others have found in Spenser's epic,[91] further helps to still any anxieties associated with the consummation of the marriage. The calm night clearly mirrors an inner calm, and yet the lines perhaps also allude to the sexual act itself, implying that it will be as serene as the night, as ceremonious as Spenser's refrain and alliteration. And the Spenserian doublings here ("calme and quietsome," "tempestuous storms or sad afray," and so on) enact verbally the kinds of balance and stability that the poem is advocating.

[91]See, e.g., A. Bartlett Giamatti, *The Earthly Paradise and the Renaissance Epic* (Princeton: Princeton Univ. Press, 1966), pp. 240–242.

The two mythological allusions towards the end of the stanza both reinforce and undermine the ways the previous lines have attempted to tame the potentially anarchic sexuality associated with the wedding. The stress in both instances is on procreation: providing for the future rather than satisfying one's own desires. Yet in *The Faerie Queene* Spenser refers to Alcmena in a different context: Jove made the night last as long as three nights to prolong her pleasure (III.xi.33). By invoking the myth in question, the author of the "Epithalamion" is invoking that aspect of it as well and hence covertly stressing the erotic even while overtly emphasizing the procreative. And how do we interpret yet another component of the myth: driven by her usual jealousy, Juno tormented Alcmena with a prolonged labor? It is likely that Spenser knew that part of the story: it figures prominently in *Metamorphoses* (IX.285–323), and Spenser, like Chaucer, could well claim Ovid as his "owne auctor." When the "Epithalamion" alludes to Alcmena, then, some measure of anxiety about childbirth and about the sins it supposedly punishes and commemorates seems to surface via the part of the myth that lies beneath the surface of the poem. Yet these tensions, like the others in the poem, are delimited; after these mythological references we again encounter a refrain, which, like the refrains that we will examine in more detail in Chapter 2, reestablishes an impression of the very "custom and ceremony" to which William Butler Yeats refers in his own mediations on marriage.

Even this brief examination of Spenser's "Epithalamion," then, reveals the presence of many of the anxieties witnessed in the conduct books, notably an impulse to control and purify sexuality. But again we need to guard against exaggerating the potency of such pressures: Spenser's lyric, like Sidney's and those of the seventeenth-century poets who were to follow them, is concerned less with expressing its author's fear of the beasts and goblins of the night than with confronting and caging those creatures.

Stuart poets inherited not only these native, Continental, and classical traditions but also a collection of theoretical precepts about wedding poetry. Many of these rules codify the practices I have been outlining, especially the emphasis on creating order and containing disorder. Puttenham, as we have seen, concentrates primarily on the folk epithalamium, but earlier rhetoricians detail the literary conventions of the genre at some length. Thus Menander Rhetor enumerates the topics that wedding poems should encompass, including a description of the bridal chamber, praise of the bride and bridegroom, and praise of Hymen. The epithalamium, he asserts, should emphasize the advantages of marriage: "You should go on to say that the ordering of the universe—air, stars, sea—took place because of Marriage. . . . You should develop this section by showing how it is due to Marriage that the sea is sailed, the land is farmed, philosophy and knowledge of heavenly things exist, as well as laws and civil governments. . . . Marriage subdues to his rite even the savage and horribly roaring lion."[92]

Classifying the epithalamium among poems of praise, the Renaissance rhetorician Julius Cæsar Scaliger analyzes it at length in his *Poetices libri septem*. His list of the topics appropriate to the epithalamium includes a description of the courtship, praises of the lineage, beauty, and other attributes of the couple; an enumeration of the favorable omens connected with their wedding; a section of joking; prophecies about the future, including the birth of offspring; and an exhortation to make love. Scaliger proceeds to enumerate wedding customs in some detail; his repeated emphasis on charms and rituals designed to protect the couple anticipates a similar dimension in the epithalamium tradition. The chapter then divides wedding poetry into several types, including drinking songs, the mythological wedding poetry that characterizes the epic epithalamium, and mixtures of narration and lyric, such as Catullus 64.

Both Scaliger and Menander urged poets to compose epithalamia, and a host of Stuart writers responded with alacrity. The union of Princess Elizabeth and the Elector Palatine alone inspired more wedding poems than had been written throughout the Elizabethan period. One explanation for the vogue the epithalamium enjoyed in seventeenth-century England is that Queen Elizabeth had discouraged weddings whereas her successor actively promoted them;[93] but this does not completely explain the popularity of the genre. Why, then, are Stuart poets so attracted to the epithalamium? And, given the range of subgenres, the wealth of competing norms and forms, why are these poets attracted to some types of epithalamia rather than others?

As Chapter 2 will argue, many—though by no means all—of the answers to those questions may be traced to the cultural pressures

[92]*Menander Rhetor*, ed. and trans. D. A. Russell and N. G. Wilson (Oxford: Clarendon Press, 1981), p. 139.
[93]See, e.g., Frye, 149–150.

explored earlier in this chapter. Stuart poets sift and deploy generic conventions in response to, as it were, the influence of anxiety. That process works in many ways; sometimes, for instance, generic norms serve to repress a problem, elsewhere they resolve it. Above all, however, these writers respond to the tensions we have traced by crafting a mythic vision of wedlock that variously denies and reconciles the problems in the institution and, indeed, other problems in the culture as well. Like other myths, theirs is less a rendition of the actual events surrounding weddings than a story that the culture wishes and needs to tell about itself, a story designed, as stories so often are, to guide its tellers and its listeners through their forests of the night.

CHAPTER 2

Choices and Constraints

Marriage . . . put an end to dispute and joined heaven
with earth in concord.

Menander Rhetor

I

Writing in a genre, like using any other form of language, involves a continuing series of choices. As sociolinguists have
shown us, such choices often include both a positive and a negative
component: one decides to deploy one linguistic form or register and
to avoid others. And if the initial choice closes some doors, it makes
others swing open, necessitating further decisions; casting one's discourse in Standard English does not preclude (and under some circumstances may even encourage) incorporating certain usages from
Black English Vernacular.[1] The epithalamium tradition encompasses
a broad selection of "dialects," and in selecting one, the authors of
Stuart epithalamia confront options that are complex in their consequences and revealing in their implications. The tensions associated
with marriage may, however, complicate and even subvert these decisions: generic choices, like other aspects of linguistic behavior, are
not invariably rational and consistent.

Such processes help us understand the vogue that the wedding
poem enjoyed in Stuart England. Though several critics have assumed that the genre of the epithalamium was uncongenial to Stuart

[1]On the sociolinguistic implications of Black English Vernacular, see, e.g., Peter
Trudgill, *Sociolinguistics: An Introduction to Language and Society,* rev. ed. (Harmondsworth: Penguin, 1983), pp. 59–77.

poets,[2] it was in fact singularly well suited to that era: some of its conventions embodied a view of marriage that proved especially attractive to the English at the beginning of the seventeenth century, whereas other conventions readily lent themselves to being reshaped by poets in the interest of such a view. This is not to say, however, that we can always distinguish Stuart wedding poems from other versions of the genre. Sometimes idiosyncratic problems, such as ambivalence about the religious implications of marriage or about the status of prenuptial contracts, do encourage idiosyncratic responses to generic conventions. But some of the cultural pressures that we traced in Chapter 1, such as anxieties about sexuality, are of course not unique to Stuart England, though they were present there in especially intense form. Hence it is not surprising that certain generic decisions that result from such tensions occur in earlier and later epithalamia as well as in Stuart versions. This is not a comparatist study, but it will be worth reminding ourselves from time to time that the distinctions between these seventeenth-century poems and their counterparts are often of degree, not of kind. Or, to put it another way, the problems and pressures traced in Chapter 1 frequently do not breed new generic norms; rather, they render familiar norms more attractive and more germane.

The relationship between those problems and those norms exemplifies an issue that confronts contemporary Renaissance studies: What models best explain the intersections between cultural and textual practices? In particular, one may assume that literature reflects its milieu or, alternatively, one may stress the interactions between the two. Many new historicists have abandoned the reflective paradigm in favor of the interactive. In one sense, both paradigms are present in and justified by the Stuart epithalamium; in another, that tradition elides the distinction between the two.

The Stuart wedding poem is indeed reflective in a very specific sense: its closural and anticlosural devices mime the nature of marriage, its refrains mirror the values associated with that institution, and so on. These mimetic patterns are not surprising, for sixteenth- and seventeenth-century England witnessed a vogue for two of the most extreme versions of reflective art: pattern poetry and numerology.[3] A culture that produces poems with the shape of George

[2]See, e.g., Paul W. Miller, "The Decline of the English Epithalamion," *TSLL*, 12 (1970), 405–416.

[3]I am grateful to Ronald Bush for useful comments on this issue.

Herbert's "Altar" or the extraordinary numerological resonances of Edmund Spenser's "Epithalamion" is likely to encourage and honor other versions of reflection as well.

In another sense, however, the epithalamium interacts with the conditions of marriage in Stuart England. Louis Adrian Montrose has written trenchantly of the "dynamic, unstable, and reciprocal relationship between the literary and the social."[4] Many Renaissance genres aptly demonstrate such a relationship. Thus the country-house poem serves as much to create a way of life as to describe it: this literary type provides a framework for, as it were, reading the house and hence helps create and define its significance. But no genre exemplifies the reciprocity of which Montrose writes better than the epithalamium. The Stuart wedding poem, like its predecessors, shapes its readers' perceptions and interpretations of marriage and thus in some important senses shapes the workings of the institution itself. For example, the epithalamium ascribes a range of interpretations to such wedding customs as crossing a threshold; some of these meanings are clearly present in the rituals even without the intervention of the poem, but in other instances the lyric defines meaning and thus affects the ways its audience will regard future weddings inside and outside literary texts.

Ultimately, of course, the apparent distinction between interaction and mere reflection blurs and even collapses. Mirrors become lamps. For in reflecting the characteristics of Renaissance marriage, as we will see, the genre shapes them as well. The literary choices and constraints involved in the Stuart epithalamium focus and clarify—for readers and for authors—the choices and constraints associated with marriage itself.

II

The Stuart epithalamium assumes a range of forms. The series of wedding poems written by the minor poet Henry Peacham for the marriage of Princess Elizabeth exemplifies this variety: in addition to one text that deploys the traditional epic format, they include a general celebratory poem, a lyric about dressing the bride, and an epi-

[4]Louis Adrian Montrose, "The Elizabethan Subject and the Spenserian Text," in *Literary Theory / Renaissance Texts,* ed. Patricia Parker and David Quint (Baltimore: Johns Hopkins Univ. Press, 1986), p. 305.

thalamium primarily modeled on Catullus 61.[5] A similar pattern occurs elsewhere in the tradition: the focus on the night in Continental epithalamia, for instance, finds its counterpart in a lyric by John Donne's friend Henry Goodyer and in a wedding poem included in Francis Beaumont and John Fletcher's *The Maid's Tragedy.* George Chapman follows many of his predecessors in writing a tribute to the god of marriage, aptly if predictably entitled "A Hymn to Hymen," and Ben Jonson composes a poem consisting of a list of good wishes when writing to the ill-fated and ill-mated earl of Somerset.[6]

Yet this variety does not preclude generalizations about the choices made by Stuart poets. First of all, these poets are, with only a handful of exceptions, consistent in the types of wedding poem they decide *not* to write. Though many of their epithalamia include pastoral elements and some, such as Sir John Suckling's "Upon my Lord Brohalls Wedding," assume the form of dialogues, few are pastoral dialogues like those composed by Jacques Grévin and Clément Marot in France. Poems addressed to the wedding night are common, but poems concentrating primarily and explicitly on sex are rare. Moreover, in England as on the Continent[7] the lyric epithalamium predominates. Its popularity in Stuart England is manifest not only when one counts the lyrics that fit this category rather than the epic type but also when one examines the works that do not conform to either model: many epithalamia that would be classified as neither lyric nor epic nonetheless isolate and privilege one element present in the former literary type. Thomas Dekker, Henry Chettle, and William Haughton, for instance, devote an entire poem, the epithalamium in Act 5, scene 2 of *Patient Grissil,* to the command to arise. Even the appeals to night and its embodiment in Hesperus on which many epithalamia focus isolate a single motif from the lyric epithalamium. One of the works by Peacham I mentioned above, the lyric on dressing the bride, might also be seen as a discrete section of a putative lyric epithalamium.

[5]See the "Nuptiall Hymns" in Henry Peacham, *The Period of Mourning* (London, 1613).

[6]See the conclusion of Chapman's "Masque of the Middle Temple and Lincoln's Inn" and Jonson's "To the most noble, and aboue his Titles, Robert Earle of Somerset."

[7]On the predominance of the lyric form in Continental vernacular epithalamia, see Virginia Tufte, *The Poetry of Marriage: The Epithalamium in Europe and Its Development in England,* Univ. of Southern California Studies in Comparative Literature, 2 (Los Angeles: Tinnon-Brown, 1970), p. 87.

Why are Stuart poets attracted to the lyric epithalamium? Even a preliminary reading of poems of the type warns us not to confine our explanations to the patterns in Stuart culture outlined in Chapter 1. Some of the characteristics that make this literary type so attractive are unrelated to cultural tensions about gender, sexuality, and marriage; others respond to those tensions but serve many other functions as well. Aesthetic choices are generally influenced but not determined by cultural constraints. For literary decisions, like psychological ones, are in fact typically overdetermined; and, again like psychological decisions, they develop from tangled and far-reaching roots.

Thus, for example, one reason the lyric type is popular is that it aptly communicates and generates excitement: the external audience of the poem, as well as the poet himself, can identify with the internal audience that is so joyously participating in the event. The lyric epithalamium is also appealing because its temporal structure represents a series of progressions from hope to fulfillment, from anticipation to satisfaction: we await the bride and she appears, we look forward to night and it comes, and so forth. Behind these instances lies the most central and most urgent version of the pattern: the movement towards sexual consummation. Several poems emphasize the anticipatory mode of their genre by referring overtly to it; thus, for instance, George Wither writes, "*Hymen* now will haue effected / What hath been so long expected" (sig. B4ᵛ),[8] and the epithalamium in Jonson's masque *Hymenaei* opens, "Glad *time* is at his point arriu'd / For which *loues* hopes were so long-liu'd."[9] (An Elizabethan epithalamium, the wedding song in the Third Eclogues of Sir Philip Sidney's *Arcadia*, enacts grammatically the point that Jonson and Wither establish more explicitly: as we observed earlier, Sidney shifts the optatives that characterize most of his poem to declaratives in the final stanza, so that statements like "Let mother earth now decke her selfe in flowers" [1] metamorphose into "The earth is deckt with flowers" [91].) One reason the progress from a desire to its realization pleases us is that such a model implies that even more uncertain events, such as the birth of heirs, will come to pass in an equally predictable fashion.

[8]All citations from Wither's epithalamia are to *Epithalamia* (London, 1613).

[9]Throughout this book Jonson's poems and masques are quoted from *Ben Jonson,* ed. C. H. Herford and Percy and Evelyn Simpson, 11 vols. (Oxford: Clarendon Press, 1925–1952).

In analyzing the popularity of the lyric epithalamium, I have thus far concentrated on factors largely unconnected to tensions in the Stuart milieu. Those tensions become more germane, however, if we consider the implications of literary imitation. When Stuart poets copy Catullus and Spenser, the act has political as well as aesthetic implications:[10] a respect for literary tradition can represent and recommend a respect for social tradition and stability as well. The poet who practices literary imitation is willing to subordinate or at least shape the imperatives of his individual talent in response to the demands of tradition; he is able, even eager, to accept his place within an order, to take his place on a long line. Hence it is no accident that certain poets who are preoccupied, even obsessed, with political or psychic turmoil loudly advertise their allegiance to their literary predecessors. Witness, among many other instances, Ben Jonson; as we will see, the social conservatism of his wedding poems is closely related to their literary conservatism.

The structure and plot of the lyric epithalamium also respond to the tensions attending marriage in Stuart England. For instance, the fictive weddings described in these poems emphasize the participation of the whole culture in the event: guests join the celebration, young girls scatter flowers, matrons undress the bride, and so on. In other words, in contrast to and in reaction against the fear of secret marriage we noted in Chapter 1, poems of this type present a vision of marriage as social, communal, and public. That vision is expressed as well through many of the generic norms I will explore shortly, such as the emphasis on the roles assigned to the participants in the festivities.

The parallel with sociolinguistic decisions reminds us that the decision to write a lyric epithalamium (or a poem that incorporates many of its elements) also involves a decision not to choose other versions of the genre. The debate structure of Catullus 62 aptly bodies forth its combative, conflictual mode. The maidens are contradicted by the youths, virginity is pitted against marriage, the withered flower is contrasted with the untended vine. Troubled by the disagreements and uncertainties attending on marriage in their era, Stuart poets idealize and mystify that institution in one crucial

[10]Many critics have traced the deep debts owed by authors of epithalamia. See, e.g., James A. S. McPeek's controversial study "The Major Sources of Spenser's *Epithalamion*," *JEGP*, 35 (1936), 183–213; Cortlandt Van Winkle, ed., "Introduction," in Edmund Spenser, *Epithalamion* (New York: F. S. Crofts, 1926), pp. 5–26.

respect: they choose to construct it as a source and a symbol of concord. Hence most of them reject Catullus 62 and in so doing downplay or conceal many of the tensions that, as the conduct books remind us, clouded marriage in Stuart England. This is not to say, however, that the discord present in Catullus 62 is wholly absent from Stuart wedding poetry. Rather, some types of disharmony are tamed or muzzled and then welcomed into the lyric in question. And other types appear indirectly and often, one suspects, unwittingly in the rhetoric of these lyrics—the uninvited guests who threaten to interrupt an otherwise harmonious wedding celebration.

Perhaps the single most revealing decision made by the authors of Stuart epithalamia, however, is their rejection of the erotic wedding tradition exemplified by poems by Pontano, Marino, and Johannes Secundus. This choice is all the more striking when one recalls that George Puttenham singles out Secundus for the highest praise in his highly influential *Arte of English Poesie*.[11] The neglect of Secundus and what he represents is no accident. The open eroticism of some Continental epithalamia, like the open conflict of Catullus 62, represents a kind of negative identity for the Stuart epithalamium, a road not taken: one can cite some telling exceptions, but by and large that unabashed and uncontrolled sexuality is not the value Stuart poems wish to advocate but rather the threat they attempt to control. Or, to put it another way, though one twentieth-century folklorist indexes "marriage" as a subdivision of "sex,"[12] the authors of Stuart epithalamia attempt to establish a very different lexicon.

But why do erotic marriage poems like Secundus's threaten Stuart poets? Weddings and the process of celebrating them poetically intensify anxieties about sexuality and gender. The act of composing an epithalamium mimes the process of staging a wedding in that in both cases the woman's body is opened up, made vulnerable in itself and a source of threatening vulnerability for others.[13] The bride is revealed to the gaze of others through the descriptive and epideictic passages

[11]George Puttenham, *The Arte of English Poesie*, ed. Gladys Doidge Willcock and Alice Walker (1936; rpt. Cambridge: Cambridge Univ. Press, 1970), p. 53.

[12]See Stith Thompson, *Motif-Index of Folk-Literature*, rev. ed., 6 vols. (Bloomington: Indiana Univ. Press, 1955–1958), VI, s.v. "marriage."

[13]On the open female body see the distinctions between classical and grotesque bodies explicated by Peter Stallybrass in "Patriarchal Territories: The Body Enclosed," in *Rewriting the Renaissance: The Discourses of Sexual Difference in Early Modern Europe*, ed. Margaret W. Ferguson, Maureen Quilligan, and Nancy J. Vickers (Chicago: Univ. of Chicago Press, 1986).

of the poem,[14] a rhetorical analogue to the loss of virginity that opens her to the sexual desires not only of her husband but also of other men. In response to these tensions, Stuart poets eschew the models offered by such poets as Secundus. And they adopt or develop a range of generic conventions and norms that serve in various senses to enclose the opened body of the bride.

The fundamental generic decisions that shape the Stuart epithalamium, then, testify to values behind that genre and the institution of marriage itself. Stuart poets typically envision marriage as public, a source and a symbol of an orderly and harmonious society;[15] their poems are concerned not only with the couple but also with the community, not only with sexual politics but also with politics in the more customary sense. One way these poems evoke harmony is by playing down the conflicts and tensions that threaten the wedding. In particular, sexuality is rechanneled and the bride's body reinterpreted; on the whole the tutelary deity of such lyrics is not one of the Lawrentian dark gods but rather the tame child Donne tellingly refers to as "Our little Cupid" ("Epithalamion at the Marriage of the Earl of Somerset," 87).[16] To be sure, one finds exceptions to all patterns. Nonetheless, when we examine the details of the Stuart epithalamium, such as the ways it describes the bride or its strategies for effecting closure, what we most frequently encounter is a vision of Edenic serenity and order—a paradisaical vision evoked by poets who dwell, and know they dwell, in a garden infested with snakes.

III

"Taxonomists love the molar teeth of mammals," Stephen Jay Gould observes in *Illuminations,* "for each group displays such a distinctive pattern that a single tooth identifies the animal. . . . A popular legend grants paleontologists such arcane anatomical wisdom

[14]For a related argument about the dangers of praise, see Nancy J. Vickers, " 'The blazon of sweet beauty's best': Shakespeare's *Lucrece,*" in *Shakespeare and the Question of Theory,* ed. Patricia Parker and Geoffrey Hartman (London: Methuen, 1985). The essay also appears in *The Female Body in Western Culture: Contemporary Perspectives,* ed. Susan Rubin Suleiman (Cambridge: Harvard Univ. Press, 1986).

[15]Compare Celeste Marguerite Schenck's emphasis on marriage as communal (*Mourning and Panegyric: The Poetics of Pastoral Ceremony* [University Park: Pennsylvania State Univ. Press, 1988], pp. 13–14) and her suggestion that the genre moves towards "conservative resolution and transcendence" (p. 14).

[16]Quotations from Donne are from *The Epithalamions, Anniversaries, and Epicedes,* ed. W. Milgate (Oxford: Clarendon Press, 1978).

that they can unerringly reconstruct the entire animal from a single
bone. . . . [Instead] we know that a rhino once surrounded a pi-
shaped tooth simply because this distinctive molar has never been
found in any other kind of animal but a rhino."[17] In one sense the
appearance of a command to awake would not reliably guide a tax-
onomist of genres. Allusions to waking up occur in genres besides
the epithalamium, notably the dream vision, as Geoffrey Chaucer's
splendidly imperious eagle reminds us. But in another sense that
command is as idiosyncratic as a rhinoceros's dental equipment: the
forms it assumes and the functions it serves clearly demarcate the
epithalamium from other genres. Even more to our purposes here,
the allusion to awakening functions with the extraordinary precision
attributed to paleontology by the popular legend to which Gould refers: this motif encompasses so many of the predilections of the wedding poem that one could reconstruct the skeleton of the genre
around it.

Those who have written on the genre tend to confine references to
this convention to the command that the bride awake. Yet that command should be inserted in a much broader context: the generic
norm in question is frequent in its appearances, protean in its forms.
And it appears in wedding poems from a range of countries and periods. Sometimes poets do present the motif in its most obvious version, the allusion to the bride's awakening; Thomas Carew's "An
Hymeneall Song on the Nuptials of the Lady Ann Wentworth, and
the Lord Louelace" devotes four of its twelve stanzas to the subject.
In other instances, however, elements of the natural world or characters other than the bride are the object of the command. Thus in
Theocritus's eighteenth idyll the maidens tell the bridegroom that he
should not be sleeping. Spenser's "Epithalamion" directs not only his
beloved but also the muses to arise; the second stanza of Sidney's
wedding poem opens "O heav'n awake" (10). (The example from
the Arcadia is all the more striking when one recalls that Sidney's
poem is a list of good wishes, not an exemplar of the lyric epithalamium; as we have observed, elements associated with the lyric epithalamium often surface in other subgenres.) In the epithalamium
Joachim Du Bellay composed for the wedding of the duke of Savoy
and Princess Marguerite, the three young women who present songs
within the framework of the epithalamium are commanded to get

[17]Rosamond Wolff Purcell and Stephen Jay Gould, *Illuminations: A Bestiary* (New
York: Norton, 1986), p. 85.

up. Many Stuart poets follow these examples. Wither, for instance, tells the nymphs he is inviting to the wedding to awaken, and Thomas Nabbes's "An Epithalamium on the hopefull happy Mariage of Master Bvrlacye, and Mistris Alice Bankes" opens, "Vp grey-ey'd morning" (1).[18] Suckling's "Upon my Lord Brohalls Wedding" opens, "In bed dull man? / When *Love* and *Hymens* Revels are begun."[19]

Epithalamia often include a closely related command: the injunction to rise up, to begin to perform one's duties. In Catullus 62 the verb "consurgo" appears when the youths exhort each other, as well as when the maidens tell their fellows to meet the youths: "Vesper adest, iuvenes, consurgite . . . cernitis, innuptae, iuvenes? consurgite contra" (1, 6) ("The evening is come, rise up, ye youths. . . . See ye, maidens, the youths? Rise up to meet them"). Very similar lines appear in Stuart epithalamia; Jonson, for instance, opens the wedding poem in *The Haddington Masque* with "Vp *youthes* and *virgins, vp.*"

The recurrence of the motif of awakening may be traced in part to the conversations literary genres conduct with one another. Such references acknowledge a link between the visionary wonder that characterizes certain epithalamia and the dream vision itself (William Dunbar's "The Thrissil and the Rois" and a minor Stuart epithalamium by Augustine Taylor in fact exemplify that medieval genre).[20] More to the point, allusions to awakening signal the distinction between the aubade and the epithalamium: awakening marks the abandonment of sexual pleasure in the first genre and the initial step towards its realization in the second. Or, to put it another way, the aubade assumes a conflict between the nighttime world of the erotic and the daytime world of the practical, whereas the epithalamium effects a reconciliation between the two.[21]

[18] All citations from Nabbes are to *The Springs Glorie* (London, 1638).

[19] *The Works of Sir John Suckling: The Non-Dramatic Works*, ed. Thomas Clayton (Oxford: Clarendon Press, 1971). I cite this edition throughout.

[20] See Taylor's *Epithalamium Vpon the All-Desired Nvptials of Frederike . . . and Elizabeth* (London, 1613). To the best of my knowledge this poem has not been discovered by previous students of the genre; its reliance on the dream vision demonstrates yet again the variety within the Stuart epithalamium tradition.

[21] For different interpretations of the relationship between the epithalamium and various types of dawn-song, see A. R. Cirillo, "Spenser's *Epithalamion:* The Harmonious Universe of Love," *SEL*, 8 (1968), 24; Leonard Forster, *The Icy Fire: Five Studies in European Petrarchism* (Cambridge: Cambridge Univ. Press, 1969), chap. 3; Enid Welsford, *Spenser, Fowre Hymnes, Epithalamion: A Study of Edmund Spenser's Doctrine of Love* (Oxford: Basil Blackwell, 1967), p. 72.

Another reason the motif of awakening recurs so often is that it helps establish the types of order and balance that epithalamia typically advocate and aim with varying degrees of success to embody.[22] The bride (and in some instances other participants in the wedding), the poem, and the day all, as it were, awaken at once, implying a pleasing harmony between the lyric itself and its subject matter, as well as between the natural world and its human inhabitants. This harmonious chord prepares us for the one struck at the end of many poems in the genre: just as they open at daybreak, so they close at nightfall. In his perceptive reading of Catullus 62, Steele Commager draws our attention to a similar type of harmony: by using the same verbs for the rising of Hesperus and the rising of the couple, the poet, he argues, "suggests that their own activity in the marriage ceremony is as natural, regular, and even inevitable . . . as the movement of nature herself."[23]

Though allusions to awakening in Stuart epithalamia and in other instances of the genre may look similar on the page, they sometimes function differently: for many Stuart poets and their readers, one suspects, the harmony effected within the epithalamium stood in sharp contrast to the dissonances associated with contemporary marriages or even, in the case of the notorious wedding of Frances Howard and Somerset, the particular wedding at hand. Hence the peace and order created by the structure of the poem contrasts with the postlapsarian dissonances in the world the poem mimes, one of many contrasts between happy and less happy Edens.

The convention of alluding to awakenings relates to Stuart civilization and its discontents in other ways. Once again that relationship reflects not a radical distinction between Stuart wedding poems and earlier versions of the genre but rather a reinterpretation or intensification of existing meanings in light of the heightened sexual anxieties to which the conduct books and other treatises on marriage so eloquently testify. In this genre as in the Song of Songs, the motif of waking up may well allude not only to getting up in the morning but also to sexual awakenings: in one sense the bride and bridegroom are being exhorted to go to bed through the very act of telling them to arise from their beds. A subterranean reference to the presumed

---

[22]On the role of order in the epithalamium tradition also see, e.g., Ruth Leah Michelson, "The English Epithalamium from Spenser to Marvell: A Marriage of Literary and Social Forms," undergraduate History and Literature thesis, Harvard University (1986), pp. 56–57; Schenck, p. 16; Tufte, *The Poetry of Marriage*, pp. 257–258.

[23]Steele Commager, "The Structure of Catullus 62," *Eranos*, 81 (1983), 23.

result of that sexual awakening, the awakening of one's generative faculties and the engendering of heirs, is probably present as well. Catullus's own vocabulary supports such interpretations: the verb he uses in the passage I quoted earlier, "consurgo," can be used for tumescence, as Ovid's *Amores* III.vii.75 testifies.[24]

But what is most significant for our purposes—and most reassuring for those of Stuart poets—is the way the convention connects sexual awakening and its control. That connection is especially telling in the case of the bride's awakening. Though the bride abandons the private world of sleep for a public world in which she potentially may threaten and be threatened, the poet carefully delimits those perils. The process of arising is disassociated from her own volition: it occurs in response to an injunction. Moreover, a male poet commands the sexuality of the bride, just as her husband may later do. Thus the writer delimits the fears potentially excited by the concept of due benevolence: if desire involves debts, a male clerk writes and reads the ledger and does so to his own ends. It is telling, too, that this form of control is exercised through the process of asserting authority and giving commands, the very pattern witnessed in the titles of Renaissance conduct books on marriage. In other words, through their allusions to awakening, Stuart epithalamia, like many of their predecessors, construct the woman's desires as the creature of masculine imperatives.

The implications of this control of desire emerge in the two ways poets develop the convention of the awakening bride. First, they sometimes hint that she is in a sense being born again or born anew; witness, for instance, the opening of Robert Herrick's "A Nuptiall Song, or Epithalamie, on Sir Clipseby Crew and his Lady":

> What's that we see from far? the spring of Day
> Bloom'd from the East, or faire Injewel'd May
>   Blowne out of April; or some New-
>   Star fill'd with glory to our view,
>
>   .   .   .   .   .
>
>   or rather the
>   Emergent *Venus* from the Sea?
>   (1–4, 9–10)[25]

[24] I am grateful to Mary Thomas Crane for drawing my attention to the usage in Ovid.

[25] Throughout my text I quote *The Poetical Works of Robert Herrick,* ed. L. C. Martin (Oxford: Clarendon Press, 1956).

Such lines suggest further ways poets in the genre respond to the sexual threats we explored in Chapter 1. If she is being born, she has no erotic past. Not only her sexuality but also her very self is created by this poet and this marriage. Poets also sometimes develop the convention of the awakening bride by indicating that she is reluctant to arise. This reluctance foreshadows the explicitly sexual hesitation expressed by brides in many Stuart wedding poems, as in their classical and Continental predecessors. Such responses testify to an attractive modesty and sexual restraint.

In emphasizing the process of awakening, the poet asserts his power over and against that of the bride in another, more subterranean sense. Not only she but the day and the poem itself awake—all called into being by the poet. He is, in other words, competitively drawing attention to his own generativity at the very point of commemorating an occasion that celebrates female fertility.[26] Because the process of patronage in the Stuart court was prone to compromise poets' sense of power and self-respect, as Chapter 3 will indicate, these assertions of generativity no doubt attracted seventeenth-century writers.

Yet to read allusions to awakening only as an instance of a patriarchal culture responding to female sexuality and fertility is to tell a partial story. For one thing, not only the bride but also her bridegroom and male guests are sometimes commanded to arise. Moreover, in dressing the bride the maidens who figure so prominently in many epithalamia are performing an action analogous to that of the male poet: they too are in a sense shaping or even creating the bride. She is, as we have already noted, the creature of the entire community, not only of its male leaders.

Furthermore, to read the awakening of the bride solely in terms of a monolithic imposition of patriarchal authority is to ignore the ambivalent tributes to the bride's own power and authority in many Stuart epithalamia. The compliments associated with the convention in question, though wholly conventional, typically serve to elevate and aggrandize her:

> Svch should this day be, so the Sun should hide
> His bashfull face, and let the conquering Bride

[26]For an instance of a defensive assertion of male generativity under different circumstances, see Constance Jordan, *Renaissance Feminism: Literary Defenses of Women in Early Modern Europe* (Ithaca: Cornell Univ. Press, 1990), "Introduction."

Without a Rivall shine.
>   (Thomas Carew, "On the Mariage of T. K.
>   and C. C. the morning stormie," 1–3)[27]

>   thy radiance wee'le supply
> With brighter beames shot from the Brides faire eye.
>   (Thomas Nabbes, "An Epithalamium on
>   the hopefull happy Mariage of Master
>   Bvrlacye, and Mistris Alice Bankes," 13–14)

Such passages remind us that the bride is seldom merely the passive and powerless object of authoritarian commands. As these comparisons between the rising bride and rising sun indicate, the very fact that the poem and the wedding day begin when she gets up is a tribute to her power.

How does such a tribute relate to the ways Stuart epithalamia attempt to control and even on occasion belittle the bride? On one level we should not be surprised to find that lyrics in this genre, like those in the Petrarchan tradition, juxtapose praise and condescension: admiration, even adulation, does not of course necessarily imply treatment of the object as an equal, and even if it did the history of gender relations in twentieth-century culture would hardly encourage one to anticipate logic and consistency in its counterpart in other cultures. More to the point, however, apparently conflicting responses are likely to generate each other: adulation of the bride could well seem threatening and hence produce a backlash of condescension (witness Petrarchism), whereas the attempt to assert control over her could variously be mystified or justified through extravagant praise.

The two passages quoted above offer further insights into the interplay between adulation and domination that so often characterizes the treatment of the bride in Stuart epithalamia. Carew's tribute to her power is in itself unmitigated and apparently reflects no sense of threat. Towards the end of the poem, however, he reshapes the conventional imagery of battle into a form that is not only more overtly erotic than in many other epithalamia but also more violent and even brutal:

> Then boldly to the fight of Love proceed,
> 'Tis mercy not to pitty though she bleed,

[27]All citations from Carew are to *The Poems of Thomas Carew*, ed. Rhodes Dunlap (Oxford: Clarendon Press, 1949).

Wee'le strew no nuts, but change that ancient forme,
For till to morrow wee'le prorogue this storme,
Which shall confound with its loude whistling noyse
Her pleasing shreekes, and fan thy panting joyes.
                                                    (31–36)

This rhetoric of acceptable and even admirable violence nervously attempts to counterbalance the power ascribed to the bride earlier by asserting the power of the bridegroom.

Nabbes's lines ("thy radiance wee'le supply / With brighter beames shot from the Brides faire eye") indubitably compliment the woman: her eyebeams not only rival but actually supplant the sun. Yet Nabbes immediately delimits that compliment—not the bride herself but rather a vague "we" that evidently includes the poet actually performs the action of unseating the sun. Later we will observe other respects in which the bride is demoted from subject to object, and it is telling in this instance that neither the bride nor her eyebeams is the grammatical subject of the sentence in question: both are reduced to prepositional phrases. In short, in each of these passages the command to awaken represents a paradoxical process that recurs on many levels in the genre, as in the Petrarchan love poetry that these lines so closely resemble: at once celebrating and circumscribing the authority of the bride. Like the treatises on marriage discussed in Chapter 1, these lyrics demonstrate that patriarchy in Stuart England is neither static nor monolithic: it involves instead a continuing series of actions and reactions, visions and revisions. Indeed, both passages exemplify the very shifts between granting and delimiting power that we encountered in Chapter 1 when examining the debates on the wife's status.

The command to awaken, then, aptly introduces the ways the other conventions and motifs of the genre function. The mere presence of that command does not distinguish the Stuart epithalamium from other versions of the genre; in the norms it deploys as in its social values the wedding poem of the period is deeply conservative. But nonetheless this motif, like many others, is variously deployed by Stuart poets and interpreted by Stuart audiences in response to their own cultural conditions and attitudes. The injunction to awaken further resembles the other generic norms we will explore in its genesis. It is the progeny both of pressures specific to Stuart England and of many other aesthetic decisions and predilections as well; and in demonstrating the pull between aggrandizing the bride and delimiting her power it reminds us yet again of the complexities and contradictions inherent in those cultural pressures.

In the lyric epithalamium, shortly after commanding the bride to awake, the poet performs two functions that are closely related: he in effect posts wedding invitations, variously urging Hymen, other deities, and human participants to join the celebration, and he encourages these guests to form the wedding procession.[28] Even poems that are not lyric epithalamia often include some version of or allusion to these conventions. The complexities of the command to awaken may prepare us for the resonances of these two apparently straightforward generic motifs. They dramatically enact what is at once the overt social blueprint of this genre and its covert core fantasy: the vision of a culture in which diverse and conflicting individuals and forces form a cohesive and harmonious whole, much as the couple will become one when the marriage is consummated.

Claude Lévi-Strauss's seminal but controversial *Elementary Structures of Kinship* helps us understand the attraction of that vision. In drawing on this study feminist scholars have generally focused most of their attention on its observations about woman as a medium for exchange. But Lévi-Strauss offers a related though often neglected insight about marriage that is more germane to Stuart weddings and to the poetry that celebrates them. The reason such exchanges are necessary, he maintains, is that they bind people together: exogamy, like feasts and other ceremonies, builds a cohesive group by integrating partial units.[29]

Whether or not one accepts Lévi-Strauss's contention that exchange is the fundamental purpose of all marriages (scholars who condemn universalist assumptions in other arenas sometimes prove curiously uncritical of those propounded by Lévi-Strauss), his point about binding groups together is particularly germane to Stuart marriages. For unification must have seemed especially attractive—and especially urgent—in the early seventeenth century. The fantasy of a unified social order attracted a culture marked by severe power

[28]For an argument about the procession that is related to though significantly different from my own, see Jordan's "Introduction"; she links the orderly movement of the procession to the woman's role in a system of exchange and attending fears about property and ownership.

[29]Claude Lévi-Strauss, *The Elementary Structures of Kinship*, trans. James Harle Bell, John Richard von Sturmer, and Rodney Needham, rev. ed. (Boston: Beacon Press, 1969), pp. 480–481.

struggles among socioeconomic groups and also, perhaps, by a separation between court and country that many historians consider a
crucial cause of the English Civil War.[30] Religious groups were splin-
tering as well, with the Puritans in particular dividing from the Anglican tradition. Moreover, as we saw in Chapter 1, the arranging of
a marriage risked creating or intensifying other divisions, such as
those between child and parent when they disagreed on the choice of
a spouse.

   Stuart epithalamia negotiate these problems and conflicts through
a vision of unity and unification—a vision that, like so much else in
the genre, is based both on order in the sense of harmony and on
orders in the sense of commands. The fundamental mode of these
poems involves lines, lists, and sequences: people and abstract enti-
ties such as Hymen come together in a linear pattern that unites all
of them while at the same time emphasizing their separate identities
and roles. Such patterns, like the social tensions that encourage
them, exist in other epithalamia and other cultures, but they appear
tailored to the lineaments of Jacobean England.

   These patterns typically involve several components. The invitation to guests and the description of the procession act out a fantasy
of unification: separate and potentially even antagonistic participants—gods and mortals, young and old, men and women—all join
together in celebrating the marriage. An echo of this pattern appears
even in Dunbar's "The Thrissil and the Rois," which is atypical of its
genre in most other respects: the parliament of nature that Dunbar
evokes is yet another bringing together of what was separate. In
much the same way, the literary imitation that characterizes the
genre involves a metaphoric procession, a line of writers that the individual poet willingly joins. And these poems culminate, of course,
in another version of union, the sexual consummation of the marriage. Several of the generic strategies that I discuss later in this
chapter, such as the predilection for lists and other accretive gram-

---

[30]The relationship of court and country and the distinctions between the gentry
associated with each milieu are among the most controversial issues in Renaissance
historiography. See, e.g., two studies by H. R. Trevor-Roper, "The General Crisis of
the Seventeenth Century," esp. pp. 72–78, in Trevor Aston, ed., *Crisis in Europe,
1560–1660: Essays from "Past and Present"* (London: Routledge and Kegan Paul, 1965);
and *The Gentry, 1540–1640*, The Economic History Review Supplements (London:
Cambridge Univ. Press, 1953). Also cf. the revisionist interpretation in Derek Hirst,
"Court, Country, and Politics before 1629," in *Faction and Parliament: Essays on Early
Stuart History*, ed. Kevin Sharpe (Oxford: Clarendon Press, 1978).

matical structures, in turn offer a rhetorical analogue to this predilection for unity.

Individual poets also design more idiosyncratic ways of embodying the vision I am describing. It is worth returning to a Tudor version because it provides such a skillfully wrought instance of that vision. In the wedding poem that appears within the Third Eclogues of the *Arcadia*, Sidney crafts a prosodic version of the myth of unification: he deploys a type of correlative verse sometimes known as "the collector," listing a number of items and then repeating and bringing them together in the final stanza. Many seventeenth-century poets work out other means of suggesting the type of unity and harmony Sidney's lyric embodies. For instance, Herrick's "Connubii Flores" consists of a series of choruses, variously comprised of young girls, priests, shepherds, and so on, each of which comments on the wedding; in the final stanza, however, they speak together in a single chorus, hence enacting the very unity that I am arguing is so central to the genre. Through references like these, the wedding becomes not only a source but also a symbol of a united society.

To some extent that unity involves a loss of individual identity;[31] in many epithalamia the bride and groom are not identified by name. But their individual identity is traded not for total aggregation in the group of celebrants but rather for a defined social role: the principal participants in the wedding become "the bride" and "the groom," much as the individual wedding guests are transformed into "the matrons" and so on.[32] Thus both the wedding procession and subsequent events in the celebration hint at another source of social harmony: not only do all members of the culture join the festivities, but they do so by willingly fulfilling the roles assigned to their stations. The boys strew nuts, the maidens gather flowers; this version of self-fashioning involves an identity assigned by and within the community. Indeed, in Jonson's poem on the Weston marriage even the church building joyously performs its allotted role: "thou more happy place, / Which to this use, wert built and consecrate" (129–130).

[31]Compare Schenck's description of the genre as "a literary rite of aggregation" (p. 13); my analysis attempts to distinguish unification from aggregation.

[32]On this loss of identity, compare Michelson, p. 9. Nelly Furman comments on the depersonalization in the pronouns used in the wedding ceremony ("The Politics of Language: Beyond the Gender Principle?" in *Making a Difference: Feminist Literary Criticism*, ed. Gayle Greene and Coppélia Kahn [London: Methuen, 1985], p. 66).

This emphasis on predetermined duties and responsibilities appears in the classical, Continental, and native wedding poems that preceded the Stuart tradition, but once again Stuart poets and their readers had good reason to find a traditional motif especially attractive. On the closely related issues of rank and of the rights and obligations associated with each station, as on the issue of marriage itself, late Elizabethan and Stuart England witnessed competing and conflicting discourses. The conservative defense of immutable social roles is exemplified by the sumptuary laws, as well as the epithalamium itself. But, like the professions of patriarchy examined in Chapter 1, that defense was all the more emphatic because it was under attack from several quarters. James I's lavish bestowal of titles and the continuing redistribution of the land that Henry VIII had impounded from the church intensified class mobility at the beginning of the seventeenth century.[33] The erosion of a clear-cut and apparently stable class system coincided chronologically with the perception, whether justified or not, that many members of the culture were refusing to perform the responsibilities assigned to them. Puritans targeted absentee ministers, and pamphlets recorded the fear that landlords were neglecting their tenants;[34] these lords neither dwelt nor built but rather ran away to London. Such situations were disturbing not only because of their practical consequences but also because of their semiotic implications. For they involve the erasure of distinctions: the middle-class man who joined the gentry and the country landlord who became a Londoner were in effect participating in a version of crossdressing.

But crossdressing in its more customary sense also helps explain the appeal of the conservative vision in the epithalamium. Recent studies have analyzed crossdressing within and outside the theater in relation to cultural anxieties about gender. Thus, for example, in distinguishing the male version of the phenomenon from that performed by women, Jean Howard has argued that the latter process

---

[33]See, e.g., Lawrence Stone, *The Crisis of the Aristocracy, 1558–1641*, rev. ed. (Oxford: Clarendon Press, 1979), esp. chap. 3 and pp. 36–39. Though many historians have questioned aspects of Stone's methodology and conclusions, few would disagree that the redistribution of land and the bestowal of titles significantly affected England's class system.

[34]On this problem and the contemporary response to it see William A. McClung, *The Country House in English Renaissance Poetry* (Berkeley: Univ. of California Press, 1977), pp. 28–35.

involved a threatening though limited subversiveness,[35] and Phyllis Rackin finds in the drama of the period a growing fear of androgyny and a growing distrust of marriage.[36] The epithalamium, in contrast, offers reassuringly stable gender roles in that both bride and groom perform the distinctive functions assigned to them.

If, as I am arguing, the epithalamium provided a reassuring antithesis to tensions about social roles in general and gender roles in particular, many members of Stuart culture attempted to construe marriage itself as such an antithesis. It is telling that the marriage tracts so carefully distinguish and list the marital responsibilities of husband and wife;[37] here as elsewhere enumeration reflects a desire to order and control. The poetry of marriage pursues the same endeavor by crafting a vision of an idealized society; the willing performance of roles on the wedding day implies and advocates a similar willingness throughout the year.

This preoccupation with filling one's proper social role emerges even, or especially, in Michael Drayton's pastoral epithalamium, where the characters ask a whole string of questions about who will assume certain responsibilities:

> By whom then shall our Bride be led
> To the Temple to be wed.
>
> . . . . .
>
> Whose lot will be the way to strow,
> On which to Church our Bride must goe?
>
> . . . . .
>
> By whom must *Tita* married be,
> 'Tis fit we all to that should see?
>
> . . . . .
>
> But comming backe when she is wed,
> Who breakes the Cake above her head.
>
> . . . . .

[35]Jean Howard, "Theatrical Crossdressing and the Political Stakes of Historicism," paper presented at The Renaissance, a conference at the State University of New York at Binghamton, October 1987.

[36]Phyllis Rackin, "Androgyny, Mimesis, and the Marriage of the Boy Heroine on the English Renaissance Stage," *PMLA*, 102 (1987), 29–41. Many other critics have also studied crossdressing. See, e.g., Linda Woodbridge, *Women and the English Renaissance: Literature and the Nature of Womankind, 1540–1620* (Urbana: Univ. of Illinois Press, 1984), chaps. 6 and 7.

[37]For example, in William Gouge's *Of Domesticall Dvties*, the "third treatise" concerns the duties of the wife and the "fourth treatise" lists those of the husband. Also see Smith, *A Preparatiue to Mariage*, pp. 43–88.

But when night comes, and she must goe
To bed, deare Nimphes what must we doe?
("The Eighth Nimphall," 147–148,
159–160, 171–172, 183–184, 207–208)[38]

The recurrence of these questions suggests a preoccupation with the fulfillment of roles and duties—but in each instance the reassuring answer ensues immediately and unequivocally. Notice, too, the recurrent choice of the verb "must" rather than "shall" or "may."

Shortly after describing the wedding procession, lyric epithalamia praise the bride or bride and groom; wedding poems of other types also typically include or even focus on such compliments. These tributes demonstrate a central distinction between Stuart epithalamia and many of their Continental and classical predecessors. Catullus 61 enumerates the virtues of both bride and groom. Julius Cæsar Scaliger advocates complimenting both members of the couple, and Continental writers typically follow that injunction; for instance, in the poem Remy Belleau wrote for the duke of Lorraine and Madame Claude, daughter of the king of France, the nymphs of the Meuse praise the groom and those of the Seine praise the bride. In lieu of Belleau's symmetrical equality, English poems usually focus on the bride, devoting less attention to the groom's virtues, or even none at all. Such generalizations admit of important exceptions: some classical and Continental poems, such as Theocritus's eighteenth idyll, do give most of their attention to the bride,[39] and some English lyrics, such as John Tatham's "An Epithalamium on the two happie Paire, Thomas B. Esquire, the younger, and his faire Bride," Suckling's satirical "A Ballade. Upon a Wedding," and many of the poems written for the wedding of Princess Elizabeth and the Elector Palatine, laud the groom. Nonetheless, by and large the privileging of the bride is marked enough to demand explanation.

To begin with, English poets are writing under the influence of Spenser's "Epithalamion," which for obvious reasons does not compliment the groom. But that response, like most traditional source studies, begs the question why a particular motif is copied while others are discarded. In what ways do Jacobean texts gloss—or self-consciously avoid glossing—James I's homosexual attraction to his

---

[38]I quote from The Works of Michael Drayton, ed. J. William Hebel, 5 vols. (Oxford: Basil Blackwell, 1931–1941). All citations are from this edition.

[39]Compare Tufte, The Poetry of Marriage, p. 17, on this issue in Theocritus.

favorites, especially Buckingham? That question deserves more sustained attention from critics than it has received; we might, for example, trace the continuing popularity of the epyllion tradition in
part to its propensity for evoking atypical sexual behavior while at
the same time safely situating it in a distant never-never land.[40] In
the instance of the epithalamium itself, it seems likely that the king's
homosexuality intensified his courtiers' nervousness about sexual
ambiguities, making some of them hesitant to praise a young man.
The primary reason for this emphasis on celebrating the bride, however, is that Stuart epithalamia assume the cultural work of resolving
a range of tensions about women; like marriage itself, these lyrics
control the very fires they fan. If the genre is the site of many cultural conflicts about women and sexuality, it is the source of solutions as well.

Whatever the reasons for their emphasis on the bride, a few Stuart
epithalamia celebrate her in one particularly revealing way. They assert that she resembles—or even reincarnates—Queen Elizabeth:

> To none I better may compare
> Your sweet selfe then one so rare:
> Like grac't you are from aboue,
> You succeed her in her loue,
>   As you enjoy her name:
>   Likewise possesse her fame.
> For that alone liues after death;
> So shall the name *Elizabeth.*
>   (Thomas Heywood, *A Marriage
>   Trivmphe,* sig. E1ᵛ)[41]

In the *Arcadia* Strephon and Klaius must mourn the loss of Astraea in
vain—but in the Stuart epithalamium she lands again on England's
green and pleasant shores.

The obvious source for such references is Spenser's joyous an-
nouncement that his own bride "seeme[s] lyke some mayden
Queene" (158). But identifying an echo of the "Epithalamion" is

---

[40]For a different but not incompatible commentary on the effects of James's homosexuality, see Mary Beth Rose, *The Expense of Spirit: Love and Sexuality in English
Renaissance Drama* (Ithaca: Cornell Univ. Press, 1988), pp. 60–61; Woodbridge, *Women
and the English Renaissance,* p. 144.

[41]All citations are to Thomas Heywood, *A Marriage Trivmphe* (London, 1613).

again more likely to spur than to satisfy our inquiries into the work of Spenser's successors: we still need to ask why poets adopted this particular aspect of the "Epithalamion" yet ignored others. One is hardly surprised that some of the poets who celebrate the marriage of James's daughter Elizabeth and the Elector Palatine do so: the correspondence of names no doubt made this mode of flattery hard to resist, as Heywood's graceless but determined rendering of such tributes might suggest. Such comparisons also arise, however, in epithalamia honoring other brides, again inviting further explanations of this generic predilection.

Poets, like scientists, admire elegant solutions. Comparisons with Elizabeth offer a convenient shorthand for representing several points about the bride. Since her own poets so often described the queen as the ideal Petrarchan mistress, allusions to her transfer that whole storehouse of compliments to the young woman about to wed. But if the tropes in question establish the bride as a desirable young maiden, they also present her as an imperial monarch. Once again, in other words, authors of Stuart epithalamia invest the bride with dignity and potency.

Above all, the lines that compare the bride to Elizabeth represent strategies for coping with the ambivalences about virginity charted in Chapter 1. Most obviously, the compliments in question quiet potential anxieties about the bride's fidelity after marriage (and also, perhaps, about her chastity before marriage) by comparing her to the ultimate symbol of sexual restraint, the Virgin Queen. These compliments can also assuage their authors' more generalized unease about the relative merits of celibacy and the married life. As I have indicated, the authors of some Elizabethan and Stuart conduct books find themselves attracted, however ambivalently and half-heartedly, to an ideal they associate with the worst abuses of papacy, such as sexual looseness in monasteries and nunneries; they must have been uncomfortable about the company they were keeping. One response is a version of reaction formation: they condemn Catholicism even more virulently than they might otherwise have done. It is probable that the poets who composed Stuart epithalamia shared this respect for celibacy; it was, as I have argued, widespread in their culture, and contemplating the sexual excesses and infidelities that the wedding could generate might well intensify or even activate it. Unlike the authors of the marriage manuals, however, the authors of epithalamia avoid identification with Catholicism by locating their attraction to celibacy in the safest of sites: their praise of the Protestant queen. Dramatic and prose romances provide Stuart culture with one outlet for the ambivalent interest in celibacy that some of its members experienced; the epithalamium offers another. The wedding poem renders that attraction safe in another way as well: if its authors deflect their latent respect for virginity onto the queen, they do so in the very process of celebrating the official norm of Protestant England, married love.

The paradox of comparing the bride to a queen renowned for her virginity suggests yet another function for these compliments: they permit male poets—and the patriarchal interests that they in several senses represent—at once to celebrate the destruction of the bride's virginity and displace that value onto Elizabeth. Renato Rosaldo has suggested that colonial cultures characteristically experience nostalgia for what they have willingly destroyed;[42] in the case of the epithalamium the myth of the Virgin Queen becomes the milieu for such a nostalgia. The parallel with colonialism demands several qualifications (for instance, I have already suggested that poets and many of their male readers may have been ambivalent about the loss of virginity, and we have seen that power relations in the epithalamium are far more complicated than the model of imperial domination may suggest). Nonetheless, the political analogue suggested by Rosaldo's work does draw our attention to the paradoxes involved in praising the bride for the very quality she will soon surrender.

Those paradoxes suggest that allusions to Elizabeth can be dysfunctional. The bride is, as it were, only a virgin queen for a day: the wedding culminates in her loss of maidenhood, the attribute emphasized and celebrated by adducing Queen Elizabeth. Acknowledging that loss puts pressure on the copula "is" in these compliments, drawing attention to the ways metaphor and simile at once bind and unbind their terms. The bride is like Elizabeth in that she is a virgin but unlike the queen in that she will not remain one for long. Hence if in certain respects the comparisons assuage concerns about virginity, in another sense they can intensify those anxieties. Genres, like biological organisms,[43] are not always ideally adapted: in this case a rhetorical flourish that works admirably in some regards fails in others.

---

[42]See Renato Rosaldo's unpublished paper "Imperialist Nostalgia: Longing for What We Have Destroyed." I am grateful to the author for making his work available to me prior to publication.

[43]In other respects, however, the parallel between genres and biological organisms is problematical. On that subject see my book *Genre* (London: Methuen, 1982), p. 117.

The epithalamium also demonstrates that the same literary convention may assume different functions in different cultures; comparing a bride to a dead queen differs significantly from Spenser's act of comparing her to a living one. For the poets who associate the bride with Queen Elizabeth look backwards, over their shoulders, to find their symbol of beauty and of chastity. In so doing they recall the many Stuart plays that also allude to Elizabeth's reign.[44] The impulse to compare the bride to her is nostalgic,[45] conservative, even reactionary, and as such it stems from the same generic values that encourage close imitation of one's literary fathers and repeated allusions to Roman wedding customs. Whether it be manifest in copying an older poet, replicating outdated rituals, or praising a dead queen, the conservatism we are observing is the outward and visible sign of one of the most subterranean fantasies that impels the Stuart epithalamium: returning to an ideal past. We will explore that fantasy in more detail when analyzing the family resemblances between the epithalamium and some versions of pastoral, but for now we can observe that the very genre that celebrates a return to Eden in effect celebrates a once and future queen.

Two tropes closely related to these comparisons between the bride and Queen Elizabeth appear towards the middle of the lyric epithalamium and in a range of positions in other versions of the genre: in Stuart epithalamia as in many earlier ones the bride is depicted as a prize to be won and an object to be positioned and adorned. The first group of allusions is more overt in its appearances and more predictable in its significances. Henry Goodyer, for example, writes,

> And you braue Pallatine,
> That art the Destenies greate Instrument,
> For this important business sent,
> Enter into possession of your Myne,
> Here you maye fittly fayne
> These sheetes to bee a Sea
> And you in it an Argosie,
> And shee an Iland, whose discouerie Spaine

[44]On those plays see Anne Barton, "Harking Back to Elizabeth: Ben Jonson and Caroline Nostalgia," *ELH,* 48 (1981), 706–731.

[45]Barbara Kiefer Lewalski observes the nostalgic elements in Milton's epithalamic passages (*"Paradise Lost" and the Rhetoric of Literary Forms* [Princeton: Princeton Univ. Press, 1985], p. 195).

(W^{ch} seldome vs'd to miss) hath sought in vaine.
("Epithalamion, of the
Princess Mariage," 56–64)[46]

Though this imagery is in part explained by the abortive attempt to arrange a marriage between Princess Elizabeth and the king of Spain,[47] it is clearly motivated by gender relations as well as international relations. Indeed, in representing Princess Elizabeth as the mine that waits to be exploited, the island that waits to be conquered, Goodyer suggests the connections between sexual and political imperialism. He suggests, too, the primacy of status systems based on gender over nationalistic determinations of status: the English princess becomes the prize and the willing conquest of her foreign husband. Palatine's role is more ambiguous. He is not entirely a free agent, having been drafted by the destinies. Yet he is evidently more a subject than an object in both the grammatical and the figurative sense: witness the sexually suggestive verb of action ("Enter) [59]) associated with him and his syntactical status as subject in all constructions save the relative one in line 58. It is suggestive, too, that while the male poet may perhaps assert a degree of power over the bride through his ability to turn her into a reincarnation of Elizabeth, here Palatine participates in the poet's own feigning.

The second and more subtle trope represents the bride as an object moved about by other people. Though epithalamia do sometimes depict her as confidently striding forth in the wedding procession, she is more typically carried, led, or positioned by others. This mode of description occurs a few times in the early sections of Spenser's "Epithalamion": "Bring her vp to th'high altar" (215), "bring home the bride againe" (242). Several of these references cluster at the moment before the marriage is consummated:

> Now bring the Bryde into the brydall boures.
> Now night is come, now soone her disaray,
> And in her bed her lay;
> Lay her in lillies and in violets,
> And silken courteins ouer her display.
>
> (299–303)

[46]All citations from Goodyer are to British Library Add. Ms. 25707.
[47]On this and other circumstances surrounding the wedding, see G. P. V. Akrigg, *Jacobean Pageant; or, The Court of King James I* (Cambridge: Harvard Univ. Press, 1962), p. 142; David Harris Willson, *King James VI and I,* The Bedford Historical Series (1956; rpt. London: Jonathan Cape, 1959), p. 282.

Seventeenth-century poets follow Spenser's lead. Jonson writes in the epithalamium in *Hymenaei*, "Place you our *Bride* to night" (495); if the pronoun expresses some affection and respect for her, it expresses as well the sense of control implied in the idea of placing. Christopher Brooke declares in "An Epithalamium; or a Nuptiall Song, applied to the Ceremonies of Marriage," "Forth honour'd Groome; behold, not farre behind / Your willing Bride; led by two strengthlesse Boyes" (18–19).[48] She is the object—the "willing" (18) object—not only of her husband's gaze but also of the attentions of other males. The promise Sir John Beaumont makes in "An Epithalamium to my Lord Marquesse of Buckingham, and to his faire and vertuous Lady" echoes the convention of leading and positioning the bride: "we shortly will adorne / Thee with a ioyfull Mothers name, when some sweet Childe is borne" (14–15).[49] These lines play down her own role in bearing the child and giving birth to it; rather, motherhood is something bestowed on her by others. Another intriguing instance of presenting the bride as an object that is moved about by others occurs in the wedding poem in Samuel Daniel's *Hymens Trivmph*:

> From the Temple to the Board
> From the Board vnto the Bed,
> We conduct your maidenhead.
> (III. iv. 1–3)[50]

The term "maidenhead" can refer to both the hymen and the state of virginity it represents.[51] Synecdochically identified with her maidenhood and her maidenhead, then, the bride is depersonalized, reduced to a signifier in the semiotics of female chastity. It is hardly surprising that she is led by others rather than moving of her own accord.

Spenser's repeated renderings of his bride's passivity immediately before the marriage is consummated suggest one obvious but crucial reason Stuart poets themselves so often describe the bride as a prize to be won or an object to be moved around. Such images negate the fears of sexual promiscuity or even sexual energy that the marriage

[48]Brooke is cited from *England's Helicon 1600, 1614*, ed. Hyder Edward Rollins, 2 vols. (Cambridge: Harvard Univ. Press, 1935).

[49]Sir John Beaumont, *Bosworth-field* (London, 1629). I cite this edition throughout my text.

[50]Samuel Daniel, *Hymens Trivmph* (London, 1615).

[51]*OED*, s.v. "maidenhead."

intensified. The limitation of the bride's physical movements may well displace an impulse to limit her verbal ones: the woman who is carried about and set in place by others is, I suggest, an analogue of the silent woman.[52] Her immobile limbs gesture towards her equally immobile tongue. A concern about the bride's silence and the subservience it implies is not unique to Stuart culture, if we can trust the information relayed in Giles Fletcher's *Of the Rus Commonwealth:* he reports, "Neither three days after [the ceremony] may she be heard to speak, save certain few words at the table in a set form with great manners and reverence to the bridegroom."[53] In any event, in suggesting that the bride is led willingly, without protest, Stuart poets both foreshadow and recommend a similar obedience after marriage.

Yet once again we find that though gender relations lie at the core of many allusions and conventions in the Stuart epithalamium, other explanations are germane as well. In emphasizing that the bride is led, poets imply that she belongs to the community leading her. Jonson asserts possession of the bride through his first person plural pronoun, and, similarly, John Tatham writes, "Bring thou *our* Bride to Church," "Who bids Good-night unto *our* Bride," and so on ("An Epithalamium on the happie Nuptials of his much respected friend Geo. F. Gent," 11, 21; italics added).[54] I have argued that one attraction of the lyric epithalamium is its rendering of marriage as public and communal; just as the marriage ceremony in the Book of Common Prayer stresses the festive and public manifestations of marriage through its allusion to Cana,[55] so the very structure of the lyric ver-

---

[52]Many recent critics have scrutinized the preoccupation with women's speech and silence in a number of Renaissance texts. See, e.g., Christine Brooke-Rose, "Woman as a Semiotic Object," in Suleiman, pp. 310–313; Jordan, "Introduction"; Woodbridge, *Women and the English Renaissance,* pp. 208–210. Jordan's discussion is especially germane to my argument because she links silence to the woman's status as an object. Ruth Kelso cites some Continental texts that also demonstrate this emphasis on silence (*Doctrine for the Lady of the Renaissance* [Urbana: Univ. of Illinois Press, 1956], pp. 100–101). Several conduct books discuss the subject; see, e.g., Robert Cleaver and John Dod, *A Godly Forme of Hovshold Government* (London, 1621), sig. F7; William Gouge, *Of Domesticall Dvties* (London, 1622), pp. 281–286.

[53]Giles Fletcher, *Of the Rus Commonwealth,* ed. Albert J. Schmidt (Ithaca: Cornell Univ. Press for the Folger Shakespeare Library, 1966), p. 138.

[54]This and subsequent citations are to John Tatham, *The Fancies Theater* (London, 1640).

[55]See *The Book of Common Prayer 1559: The Elizabethan Prayer Book,* ed. John E. Booty (Charlottesville: Univ. Press of Virginia, 1976), p. 290. Anne Lake Prescott drew the significance of this reference to my attention.

sion of the genre emphasizes public rituals and celebrations. The convention at hand serves that same end by transforming the bride into a possession not only of her husband but also of the entire community. Or, to put it another way, it is no accident that the guests adorn her: she is in a sense the creation of those celebrating her marriage as well as of the poet describing it.

But only in a sense. Children and property are moved about by others—but so too were the most honored members of Renaissance society. Elizabeth and James were carried in processions, as were icons of the saints whom Tudor monarchs displaced and attempted in some respects to replace. Another passage from Brooke's "An Epithalamium; or a Nuptiall Song, applied to the Ceremonies of Marriage" is as revealing as the first one we scrutinized, for here Brooke juxtaposes within a few lines the disempowerment and the enshrinement of the bride:

> The Board being spread, furnish't with various Plenties;
> The Brides faire Obiect in the Middle plac'd;
> While she drinkes Nectar, eates Ambrosiall dainties,
> And like a Goddesse is admir'd and grac'd.
>
> (32–35).[56]

The opening lines of this quotation could be lifted from a feminist textbook: however one interprets the ambiguities of line 33, the bride herself is constructed as an object, virtually part of the table setting. Yet immediately afterwards she is elevated to the status of an iconic goddess—a paradox very like the one we so often encounter in Petrarchan poetry. These patterns are further complicated by the possibility of a double entendre in the phrase "faire Obiect" (33).[56] Finding a bawdy joke in a poem—and a literary tradition—dedicated to controlling and purifying sexuality is not in fact surprising: in literature as in other forms of discourse, suppression often generates a counter-reaction. In short, these lines by Brooke again demonstrate that authors of Stuart epithalamia give with one hand and take away with the other: they honor the bride in the very process of disempowering her, idealize her in the very act of subjecting her to locker-room jokes. An extraordinary film about Chinese peasant culture, *Yellow Earth,* makes a similar point visually: its bride is carried to her

---

[56]I am grateful to G. B. Evans for this insight.

tragic wedding in an elaborate procession, her eyes covered.[57] Like other sacrificial victims, she is honored in the very process of being destroyed. The ambivalence about women that is manifest in so many areas of Stuart culture is nowhere better demonstrated than in the epithalamium.

We encounter a different type of ambivalence in the treatment of the religious component of the wedding. Marriage was no longer sacramental in Protestant England—but to what extent was it sacred? The authors of the conduct books on marriage disagree among themselves about the significance of the church ceremony, some arguing that it merely "solemnizes" a marriage that has already occurred, others maintaining that the marriage would not be valid without it. Stuart epithalamia are themselves engaged in negotiating such problems. By and large poets of the period devote far less attention to the rituals in the church than Spenser, for example, does in his "Epithalamion," though on this issue, as on so many others in Stuart wedding poetry, we find considerable variety. Some authors virtually ignore the religious events connected with the wedding. Thus Wither dismisses that ceremony in one line, "Now vnto the *Church* she hies her" (sig. C1ᵛ), and even that line emphasizes the bride herself, reducing the church to a prepositional phrase. Brooke, in contrast, labels one stanza "Going to Church." We even find divergences within the work of a single poet; as we will see, Donne handles the religious ceremony quite differently in his two principal wedding poems. The many poets who ignore or touch lightly on the ceremony decide that omission is the better part of valor: rather than confront the tense and controversial question of what the religious rites really signify, they treat them only in passing, if at all.

Stuart poets respond to contemporary controversies about the marriage ceremony in a more subtle way as well: they displace the sacred and numinous from the religious arena to other aspects of the wedding, much as Queen Elizabeth skillfully responded to the loss of saints' days by transforming herself into a type of secular saint. Thus Chapman casts his poem on the marriage of Princess Elizabeth and the Elector Palatine in the form its title indicates—"A Hymn to Hymen"; the pagan ceremonies he evokes are an analogue to and substitute for the Christian ones that were proving controversial.

---

[57]This film, produced in 1985, was directed by Chen Kaige.

And some poets imbue the events of the wedding day with the sacred.[58] Playing on the several senses of "mystery," Henry Goodyer writes,

> O most misterious night
> W^{ch} by the setting of a Sunne, & Moone,
> Art dearer [sic] then a daye at noone
> How art thou happie, by their sacred light?
>   . . . . .
> But though this night affords
> Light enough, manie Misteries to see.
>   ("Epithalamion, of the Princess
>   Mariage," 23–26, 34–35)

As this passage suggests, the consummation of the marriage can itself become a sacred act, a point to which we shall return. And in some instances yet another function of the hyperbolic praise of the bride is in effect to deify her, ascribing to her the numinousness absent from the religious ceremony itself. The implicit parallel with an icon in a procession contributes to this beatification. Another version of the process occurs in an intriguing stanza by Herrick that we examined from a different perspective earlier and will return to again in Chapter 5:

> Say, or doe we not descrie
> Some Goddesse, in a cloud of Tiffanie
> To move, or rather the
> Emergent *Venus* from the Sea?
> ("A Nuptiall Song, or Epithalamie, on
> Sir Clipseby Crew and his Lady," 7–10)

Ceremonious in diction and tone, many Stuart epithalamia themselves function as an analogue to and substitute for the controversial religious ceremonies associated with seventeenth-century weddings.[59]

---

[58]This response is not unique to seventeenth-century marriage poems; W. Speed Hill suggests that Spenser treats marriage sacramentally even though it was no longer a sacrament ("Order and Joy in Spenser's 'Epithalamion,' " *Southern Humanities Review*, 6 [1972], 84).

[59]In "The Function of Ritual in the Marriage Songs of Catullus, Spenser and Ronsard" (*Illinois Quarterly*, 35 [1972], 50–64), John Mulryan argues that epithalamia, like weddings themselves, are ritualistic.

Though they differ in their treatment of those ceremonies, Stuart wedding poems typically resemble each other—and other poems in their genre—in their emphasis on the moment of entering the house. Many lyric epithalamia play up this incident; and even poems assuming a different form may contrive to draw attention to it, most notably as Herrick does when he entitles one of his lyrics "The Entertainment: or, Porch-verse, at the Marriage of Mr. Hen. Northly, and the most witty Mrs. Lettice Yard."

The act of crossing a threshold is important in wedding poems in part simply because it was and is important in weddings: references to thresholds variously recall the folk customs described in Chapter 1 and religious traditions of holding part of the ceremony on the church porch, as well as the symbolic significance of transitions. Equally obvious and equally germane is the connection between entering the house and the sexual entrance that will shortly ensue (in *Hymenaei* Jonson fashions the double entendre "So, now you may admit him in" [501], and "Vpon the Marriage," a bawdy epigram on weddings in Richard Brathwaite's *A Strappado for the Diuell*, plays on the same idea).

In addition, though, in drawing attention to the act of entering the house Stuart epithalamia render overt and thematic a pattern that structures these poems on many subterranean levels the relationship of outside and inside.[60] So far I have emphasized the discords within the genre, but epithalamia also characteristically effect and celebrate the harmony of the natural and civilized worlds. Denizens of the two spheres, such as forest nymphs and matrons, march together in the procession, and the wedding itself represents the socialization of the potentially anarchic natural force of sexuality. When the wedding party enters the house or, in some instances, the church, the plot of the poem enacts this mediation of outside and inside, natural and civilized.[61]

But the metaphor in question has other resonances as well: it involves not only reconciliation but also rejection and repression. For one thing, we will shortly observe that the movement into the house

[60]Max A. Wickert notes a similar pattern in Spenser's "Epithalamion" but treats it differently, relating it to the movement of the procession and a pattern of concentric circles representing society, nature, and the supernatural ("Structure and Ceremony in Spenser's 'Epithalamion,' " *ELH*, 35 [1968], 135–157).

[61]For a different but not incompatible interpretation of the movement of the wedding party in Spenser's poetry, see Sandra R. Patterson, "Spenser's *Prothalamion* and the Catullan Epithalamic Tradition," *Comitatus*, 10 (1979–1980), 98.

symbolizes the shutting out of discordant forces that may threaten
the marriage. Spenser anticipates the pattern we find in seventeenth-
century wedding poems when he evokes the owl, the stork, the
night raven, vultures, and frogs to represent the forces that must be
kept at bay for the marriage to succeed: he chooses creatures who
literally dwell outside the house to suggest that they must remain
metaphorically outside it as well. Or, as Carew puts it, "Let Tempests struggle in the Ayre, but rest / Eternall calmes within thy
peacefull brest" ("On the Mariage of T. K. and C. C. the morning
stormie," 13–14).

Stuart epithalamia concern themselves with what is shut inside the
house as much as with what is shut out. In going within the house
the bride and groom are becoming stable, secure; Daniel Rogers's
conduct book, *Matrimoniall Honovr*, refers to married love as
"habited and settled" (p. 150). Allusions to thresholds imply the
source of this stability. When they enter the house, the bride and
groom are entering the society it represents: the architectural construction represents the cultural constructs they are accepting and
gracing.[62] In more senses than one they are leaving what is liminal
for what is—at least ostensibly—stable. Thus we return again to the
resonances of the phrase that recurs in the lyrics of Jonson and
Tatham, "our bride," and we are now in a position to understand
why Tatham also refers to "our Bridegroome" (16) in the same lyric:
marriage is a way of being welcomed in—and enclosed within—the
community and the family. It is telling that "casar," the Spanish verb
for "to marry," comes from the root "casa," or "house."

Another Spanish usage, terming a married man a "casado" and a
married woman a "casada," may prepare us to observe that epithalamia often allude to both bride and groom entering the house. But
such references acquire additional significance in the case of the
woman. Many epithalamia that precede the Stuart tradition emphasize the bride's entrance into the house; for instance, when he writes
"ac domum dominam voca" ("Call to her home the lady of the
house" [Catullus 61, 31]), Catullus deploys the homophonic wordplay to suggest that the connection between the house and its lady is
natural, even inevitable. But precedents do not wholly explain the

---

[62]Though he does not allude to houses, an observation by Leonard Forster in *The
Icy Fire* is germane here: he aptly observes that the epithalamium "affirms the
divinely ordered structure of society, into which the newly married couple enter"
(p. 89).

treatment of the motif in seventeenth-century wedding poetry: once again Stuart poets invoke and Stuart readers interpret an existing convention in light of local conditions.

Scholars have found in late sixteenth- and seventeenth-century England an intensified reaction against women spending time outside their homes; though that reaction was directed in part against women who spent too much time with their female friends, Linda Woodbridge has shown that it also involved concerns about middle-class women who were taking jobs or even women who were simply standing at windows.[63] The symbolic resonances of the open, the unenclosed, intensified these pragmatic concerns about women who spend too little time within their own houses. Marriage opens the virginal bride's body not only to her husband but also to his potential rivals;[64] and the open mouth and loose tongue of women could symbolize the openness of their sexual orifices and the looseness of their morals. In describing the bride entering her house epithalamia offer an implicit antidote to this poisonous distrust: they evoke a dream of woman as once again enclosed, controlled. In other words, their response to the many types of threat that Natalie Zemon Davis aptly terms "women on top"[65] is women indoors.

After describing the entrance into the house, epithalamia often allude to the marriage feast.[66] Many poems treat it positively; thus Thomas Heywood virtually implies that God himself has signed on as caterer:

> Because that as the Heauens gaue free assent,
> With th'Earth to fill these Bridals with content,

[63]See Woodbridge, *Women and the English Renaissance*, chap. 9 and pp. 174–176; Jordan, "Introduction." Also compare D. E. Underdown, "The Taming of the Scold: The Enforcement of Patriarchal Authority in Early Modern Europe," in *Order and Disorder in Early Modern England*, ed. Anthony Fletcher and John Stevenson (Cambridge: Cambridge Univ. Press, 1985); he finds an intensified concern about independent women in late Elizabethan and Jacobean literature, though he himself acknowledges the difficulty of measuring such attitudes reliably. The conduct books on marriage frequently warn women against spending too much time away from their homes (see, e.g., Cleaver and Dod, sig. F7).

[64]Compare the notion of virginity as an invisible armor in Nancy Huston, "The Matrix of War: Mothers and Heroes," in Suleiman, p. 129.

[65]The phrase is the title of the fifth chapter of Davis's *Society and Culture in Early Modern France: Eight Essays* (Stanford: Stanford Univ. Press, 1975).

[66]Schenck relates the feasts to Orphic rituals (pp. 62–63).

Euen so the Seas their bounties would afford
With seasonable Cates to Crowne their bord.
(*A Marriage Trivmphe*, sig. D3ᵛ)

In uncovering the tensions and dissonances in the genre, we must continue to remind ourselves of such joyous, celebratory passages. Other lyrics, however, refer to the feast more gravely:

Go to your banquet then, but use delight,
So as to rise still with an appetite.
(Herrick, "Connubii Flores," 18–19)

The feast, with gluttonous delaies,
Is eaten, and too long their meat they praise.
(Donne, "An Epithalamion, or
Mariage Song on the Lady Elizabeth,
and Count Palatine," 65–66)

One explanation for these admonitions is simply that wedding celebrations were in fact often extravagant. In an era in which a schoolmaster's annual salary was under £25,[67] the festivities surrounding the marriage of Princess Elizabeth and the Count Palatine cost £93,294.[68] Only a few months after this expensive event, King James also paid for the lavish wedding of Frances Howard and Somerset. As admonitions about sumptuous feasts in the conduct books on marriage indicate,[69] many of James's subjects imitated his extravagance in planning their own weddings. It is no accident that these expensive celebrations occurred during a period that witnessed the building of extensive and lavish homes: the same impulses that drove the gentry and aristocracy to erect the so-called prodigy houses led them to organize prodigious weddings.[70]

[67]See, e.g., John Carey, *John Donne: Life, Mind, and Art* (London: Faber and Faber, 1981), p. 15.
[68]William Sanderson, *A Compleat History of . . . Mary Queen of Scotland And . . . James the Sixth* (London, 1656), p. 405. On the cost of the wedding and the festivities surrounding it also see Akrigg, pp. 145–156; Willson, p. 286.
[69]See, e.g., Perkins, *Christian Oeconomie*, pp. 96–97.
[70]On the vogue for erecting new dwellings and the architecture of the prodigy houses, see G. R. Hibbard, "The Country House Poem of the Seventeenth Century," *Journal of the Warburg and Courtauld Institutes*, 19 (1956), 160–161; McClung, chap. 3; John Summerson, *Architecture in England, 1530 to 1830*, rev. ed. (Harmondsworth: Penguin, 1958), chaps. 4, 5.

But these cultural conditions are not the only valid explanations for the negative portrayals of the wedding feast. Many criticisms of that celebration focus on its untimeliness: it lasts too long, delaying the consummation of the marriage. In such allusions the latent tensions between the public, communal aspects of the wedding and its private, sexual conclusion surface, though that pattern is further complicated by the fact that these poems render even sexuality public by emphasizing the conception of heirs. More to the point, references to the delays occasioned by the feast participate in the concern about untimeliness that recurs throughout the genre: thus some poems complain that the bride sleeps too late or the day itself moves too slowly, and the refrain in Chapman's "Parcarum Epithalamion," like its model in Catullus 64, urges the Fates to speed up their work ("Haste you that guide the web, haste spindles haste").[71] One of Herrick's epithalamia is entitled "The Delaying Bride." Such allusions to time often reflect the sexual energy and anticipation that impel many epithalamia. Also, references to time relate to one of the most central patterns in the genre: the tension between orderly and controlled behavior and the anarchic forces that rival and threaten it. We have already encountered many instances of the former: the bride rises when the sun does, the celebrants perform the duties assigned to them, and so on. The feast that lasts too long symbolizes the disorder that threatens the wedding day—and threatens as well the harmonious marriage and the stable society that it prefigures and represents.[72]

Warnings about culinary overindulgence, I suggest, also encode anxieties about sexual overindulgence; they caution us not only against disorder in general but also against a particular form of it. Feasting is in this sense a symbol of sexuality, not an activity that may delay or prevent it. A few Stuart epithalamia imply this link between gustatory and sexual appetites. The wedding poem in Philip Massinger's *The Guardian* includes the lines, "freely taste / The Mar-

---

[71]George Chapman, *Andromeda Liberata* (London, 1614). All citations are from this edition. Many critics have discussed the significance of time in Spenser's "Epithalamion." See, e.g., A. Kent Hieatt, *Short Time's Endless Monument: The Symbolism of the Numbers in Edmund Spenser's "Epithalamion"* (New York: Columbia Univ. Press, 1960), and Harry Berger, "Spenser's *Prothalamion:* An Interpretation," *Essays in Criticism,* 15 (1965), 368–369.

[72]Many contemporary critics have been interested in feasting, often focusing on its relationship to order and disorder. See, e.g., Joseph Loewenstein, "The Jonsonian Corpulence; or, The Poet as Mouthpiece," *ELH,* 53 (1986), 491–518.

riage Banquet ne'er deny'd / To such as sit down chaste" (IV.ii.20–22),[73] and in his epithalamium on the marriage of Hierome Weston and Frances Stewart, Jonson observes, "There is a Feast behind, / To them of kind" (141–142). William Whately renders the connection explicit in *A Bride-bvsh*, one of his two treatises on marriage: "The belly and groyne, you know, are neare neighbours; hee that stuffes the one, prouokes the other; he that moderates the former, keepes the latter also in good temper" (pp. 10–11).

Allusions to feasting, however, testify not only to the prevalence of sexual anxieties but also to the potentialities the epithalamium offers for addressing those fears. Contemporary critical trends have too often encouraged us to see sexual anxieties merely as uncontrolled and unmediated intruders into texts. Passages like the ones I have quoted, however, demonstrate how skillfully a text can mediate tensions that might prove more destructive in other arenas: the process of describing the feast allows poets to issue warnings that are tacit and hence tactful, but clear nonetheless.

Another motif of the epithalamium also involves a type of warning: poems in the genre typically enumerate the dangers the marriage must avoid in order to survive, often presenting their list of these perils in the form of a prayer or command that they be absent. A familiar myth credits Hymen with rescuing the woman he loves from pirates.[74] The convention of cataloguing perils is in effect a lyric rendition of that myth: it involves protecting and rescuing the couple, their marriage, and even their whole community from the dangers that threaten them. Though students of the epithalamium generally devote little attention to this convention, it is central to these poems.

In many lyric epithalamia this convention appears after the description of the feast or at the very end of the poem. In these instances, a mirroring effect further structures the ceremonious patterns of these poems: at their beginning the poet calls forth the bride, the sun, and so forth, while at or near their conclusion he dismisses a different order of beings. Thus the balanced structure of the poem mimes the social and marital harmony that the author is both celebrating and advocating. But whatever position the motif in

---

[73]The citation is to *The Plays and Poems of Philip Massinger*, ed. Philip Edwards and Colin Gibson, 5 vols. (Oxford: Clarendon Press, 1976).

[74]See J. Lemprière and F. A. Wright, *Lemprière's Classical Dictionary* (New York: Dutton, 1951), s.v. "Hymen."

question assumes in a given poem, it remains related to the processes of awakening the participants and calling them together: the acts of gathering insiders and banishing outsiders represent yet another version of the inside-outside structures we noted earlier.

It is worth tracing instances of the convention of averting dangers in earlier wedding poems as well as in Stuart ones, in part to demonstrate its prevalence and in part to explore its protean variations. In the third of his Fescennine poems, Claudian declares "cessent litui saevumque procul / Martem felix taeda releget" ("Let trumpets of war cease and the propitious torch of marriage banish savage Mars afar" [3–4]).[75] Marot's "Chant nuptial du Roy d'Escoce & de Madame Magdelene" notes the importance of calming the winds, and in Dunbar's "The Thrissil and the Rois" Nature and Juno warn the wind to behave itself. The sixteenth-century English tradition offers many examples both of meteorological threats and of the metaphoric storms that lie behind these allusions to the weather. As we saw earlier, the epithalamium in the Third Eclogues of Sidney's *Arcadia* consists of a series of prayers for good fortune, many of which are linked to allusions to dangers that must be averted: "But thou foule *Cupid,* syre to lawlesse lust, / Be thou farre hence with thy empoyson'd darte" (55–56), and so on. Spenser includes some playful versions of this motif, such as the command that the sun not burn his bride's skin, and towards the end of the "Epithalamion" he devotes more than a stanza to banishing the evils that imperil the marriage.[76]

Stuart poets, like their predecessors, load their lyrics with examples of the dangers threatening the marriages they are celebrating. For instance, one of the epithalamia in Francis Quarles's *Argalvs and Parthenia* includes the prayer:

> From satiety, from strife,
> From Iealousie, domestick jars,
> From those blows, that leave no scars
> *Juno* protect your mariage life.
>
> (p. 106)[77]

[75]The quotation is from *Claudian,* trans. Maurice Platnauer, 2 vols. (Cambridge and London: Harvard Univ. Press and William Heinemann, 1956).
[76]On the threats in the "Prothalamion" and "Epithalamion," see, e.g., Eileen Jorge Allman, "*Epithalamion's* Bridegroom: Orpheus-Adam-Christ," *Renascence,* 32 (1980), 244–245; Welsford, p. 77.
[77]Francis Quarles, *Argalvs and Parthenia* (London, 1634?).

In the epithalamium in *The Two Noble Kinsmen,* as in so many other works, threats from denizens of the natural world clearly symbolize threats emanating from their human counterparts:

> The crow, the sland'rous cuckoo, nor
> The boding raven, nor [chough hoar],
> Nor chatt'ring pie,
> May on our bridehouse perch or sing,
> Or with them any discord bring,
> But from it fly.
>
> (I.i.19–24)[78]

Indeed, most Stuart epithalamia include some version of the motif at hand. Moreover, we find suggestive analogues to that motif both within the genre and in related works. When Beaumont refers to "holy fires" ("An Epithalamium to my Lord Marquesse of Buckingham, and to his faire and vertuous Lady," 25) or when Jonson describes sex as "fayre and gentle strife" (*Hymenaei,* "Epithalamion," 457), the adjectives in effect control and even banish the dangers suggested by the nouns. We will shortly examine an antithetical formula that recurs often in the genre, assuming the form "not x but y"; this syntactical structure also mirrors the motif of banishment and exclusion. Figures like Malvolio and Jacques, who depart from the stage rather than sour the comedic resolution, are the dramatic embodiments of the threats variously represented in the epithalamium tradition by owls, thunderstorms, and allegorical figures such as Jealousy.

The presence of this motif even in modern epithalamia, which in so many other ways depart from generic norms, testifies further to its significance. A. E. Housman, like a number of Renaissance poets, in effect employs a version of occupatio, referring to perils by saying they are not present:

> All is quiet, no alarms;
> Nothing fear of nightly harms.
> Safe you sleep on guarded ground,
> And in silent circle round

---

[78] *The Riverside Shakespeare,* ed. G. B. Evans et al., 2 vols. (Boston: Houghton Mifflin, 1974).

> The thoughts of friends keep watch and ward,
> Harnessed angels, hand on sword.
> ("Epithalamium," 39–44)[79]

In a sense this is reassuring; but ground must be guarded and angels harnessed only if danger lurks nearby. It is no accident that a few twentieth-century epithalamia, such as Gertrude Stein's "Prothalamium for Bobolink and His Louisa A Poem," Robert Graves's "At the Savoy Chapel," and John Masefield's "Prayer for the Royal Marriage," were written during or immediately after a war. War aptly exemplifies the threats represented in other ways in earlier epithalamia, much as the death of Prince Henry shortly before the marriage of his sister Elizabeth enacted the interplay between mourning and celebration that also characterizes the genre. For the writers of epithalamia, like so many other poets, life often imitates art.

Why, then, does this motif in all its varied forms recur so frequently throughout the history of the epithalamium? To begin with, the authors of these poems are translating into lyric form a preoccupation present in many of the rites and rituals connected with weddings. Classical epithalamia, most notably Catullus 61, remind us that Roman marriage customs included the Fescennine taunts; these bawdy or insulting comments functioned as apotropaic magic, the type of ritual aimed at averting danger.[80] As we have observed, folk traditions also included many procedures for warding off evil. Thus even in the twentieth century rural Egyptian brides sometimes wear a verse from the Koran sewn into a little packet of cloth; this object, the *hijab,* is intended to protect them from evil.[81] The word "hijab," which is used for other types of amulets as well, comes from a verb meaning to cover, veil, or seclude;[82] as its etymology indicates, the object protects someone by shutting her off from evil—the very pattern that epithalamia repeatedly enact and describe. In Western culture, the practices for crossing thresholds to which we referred earlier and a number of charms are designed to serve the same end.[83]

---

[79]The citation is to *High Wedlock Then Be Honoured: Wedding Poems from Nineteen Countries and Twenty-five Centuries,* ed. Virginia Tufte (New York: Viking, 1970).

[80]On this aspect of the Fescennine chants, see Tufte, *The Poetry of Marriage,* p. 23.

[81]I am indebted to Cynthia Nelson for this information.

[82]*A Dictionary of Modern Written Arabic,* by Hans Wehr and J. Milton Cowan, 3d ed. (Ithaca, N.Y.: Spoken Language Services, 1976).

[83]For example, see Gillis, pp. 70–73.

Such customs appear in an intriguing passage from the Sarum missal: in blessing the bedchamber the priest asks God to guard the couple against "all phantasies and illusions of devils."[84] As I argued in Chapter 1, attitudes associated with Catholicism, like Catholic priests themselves, survived in England long after the Reformation, disguised and hidden perhaps but present nonetheless, and we know that Spenser himself recalls and alludes to the Sarum rites.[85]

Rhetorical traditions and precepts as well as religious ones lie behind the motif of enumerating dangers. When the authors of epithalamia play the happiness they anticipate in the wedding against the dark forces that threaten the couple, they are defining by contrasts, a practice routinely advocated by classical rhetoricians.[86] Indeed, although the marriage ceremony in the Book of Common Prayer does not refer to devilish dangers in the way its Catholic predecessor did, one of its admonitions implicitly adduces them through a version of defining by contrasts: wedlock, we are warned, is not to be "taken in hand unadvisedly, lightly, or wantonly, to satisfy men's carnal lusts and appetites, like brute beasts that have no understanding, but reverently, discreetly, advisedly, soberly, and in the fear of God."[87] Often, too, in evoking the dangers that are to be averted the authors of epithalamia exemplify another respected rhetorical practice: they adduce what has been termed the "negative formula," in which one defines something by saying what it is not. Thus in "An Epithalamium vpon the happy marriage of our Soueraigne Lord King Charles, and our gracious Lady Queene Mary," Beaumont writes, "*Leander* here no dang'rous iourney takes"(7).

Yet though ritualistic and rhetorical practices may explain the convention of alluding to threats, they cannot wholly explain its force or its frequency. If the motif had not already existed, the authors of epithalamia would surely have invented it: these references to dangers that must be averted lie at the very core of the praxis of the genre. It is telling that many of the threats in question are externalized and

[84]See *The Sarum Missal in English*, ed. Vernon Staley, trans. Frederick E. Warren, 2 vols. (London: Alexander Moring, 1911), II, 160. I am grateful to Anne Lake Prescott for drawing my attention to this passage.

[85]On the influence of the Sarum Missal on the *Amoretti*, see Anne Lake Prescott, "The Thirsty Deer and the Lord of Life: Some Contexts for *Amoretti* 67–70," in *Spenser Studies*, 6 (New York: AMS Press, 1986).

[86]See, e.g., *Rhetorica ad Herennium*, trans. Harry Caplan (Cambridge and London: Harvard Univ. Press and William Heinemann, 1954), pp. 377–379.

[87]Booty, p. 290.

allegorized versions of forces that may be prevalent within the couple themselves or in their cultural milieu, such as jealousy and infidelity. Hence such allusions, like the references to excessive wedding feasts, provide a polite and politically safe way of writing monitory verse. Once again the genre attempts to control political pressures and cultural tensions rather than merely reflect them.

Though references to dangers that must be averted serve such a function throughout the epithalamium tradition, they play a particularly important role in poems written in and for the Jacobean court, which was notorious for its sexual laxness. The authors of epithalamia composed during that period faced the challenge of warning couples about real moral dangers without offending the patrons who might themselves exemplify those vices. The motif we are examining responds to that challenge. It is subtle enough to avoid insult: its recurrence throughout the genre veils its implications for the Stuart court, and references to an allegorized Jealousy or to a storm that may represent the disturbances occasioned by lust are less threatening than direct accusations. Nonetheless, admonitions about the passions that may damage the marriage—and the culture in which it takes place—clearly emerge. The few critics who have written on the epithalamium of this era typically stress that it celebrates the court's achievements, allowing its members to contemplate themselves with admiration.[88] True—and yet it is also true that allusions to potential danger draw attention to the court's signal failures, the marital strife and jealousy to which this motif so often alludes, in the process of warning the couple to avoid them. Although Stuart literature does of course often serve the interests of the powerful in the ways so many recent studies have documented, like certain theatrical characters it could prove a tricky servant indeed.

The motif in question fulfills psychological needs as well as political ones: it allows the poet to confront in a less threatening form fears that he and many of his readers no doubt shared. Sigmund Freud has observed that the word "no" allows us to say the unsayable, think the unthinkable. Similarly, the convention of referring to dangers that have been averted allows one to dismiss them in the very process of confessing them. The anxieties surrounding the marriage—will the bride remain chaste? will the couple be happy? will an early death interrupt the marriage?—are at once admitted and as-

[88]See, e.g., Margaret M. McGowan, " 'As Through a Looking-glass,' " in *John Donne: Essays in Celebration*, ed. A. J. Smith (London: Methuen, 1972).

suaged. Yet here, as in allusions to virginity, the epithalamium does not always function smoothly: sometimes the length of the list of dangers does suggest that the poet is dwelling on them obsessively. The forests of the night to which I referred at the beginning of this book have thick and tangled undergrowth; those who think they can stride through with confidence may find they are mistaken.

These allusions to perils that must be avoided participate in the complex semiotic systems that express gender and patronage relationships in the epithalamium. Some of the dangers that recur, such as thunderstorms, are not intrinsically so alarming as to justify these intense and detailed references: such apparent threats gesture towards other threats, towards metaphoric thunderstorms. In particular, many Stuart poets, like their predecessors, deflect onto the hobgoblins, climactic disturbances, and allegorical abstractions they are banishing anxieties and hostilities originally directed towards the bride. The positioning of the references in question is telling: they often occur in close conjunction to the evocation of the consummation of the marriage, the moment most associated with the dangers of female sexuality. Moreover, a sexually open and accessible body is often associated with the monstrous, as Peter Stallybrass and Allon White among others have demonstrated;[89] and the link between women and meteorological disturbances is a commonplace. And might not the same convention reflect and deflect concerns about patronage as well? Resentments of a patron do emerge in other texts as violence directed towards a safer target; witness Spenser's treatment of Lucifera, the demonic parody of Elizabeth.

Many generic norms and motifs involve controlling and rechanneling both tangible threats to the marriage and the anxieties that these and other threats provoke. Nowhere is this pattern clearer than in the treatment of sexuality at the end of these poems. Marriage itself of course serves in many cultures to channel sexuality into a form that promotes cultural norms rather than threatens them: children are produced and provided for, sex is regulated, and so on. Similarly, the authors of both Stuart and earlier epithalamia typically tame and civilize desire: they transform it from the anarchic lust that can threaten the couple and their culture to the love that produces harmony in this generation and generates heirs for the next.

[89]See Stallybrass and White, *The Politics and Poetics of Transgression* (London: Methuen, 1986), esp. pp. 21–25, 64–66.

These generalizations are sound, but like most of the others generated by the epithalamium, they immediately call for qualification: we have seen that works in the genre differ significantly among themselves in many respects, but the divergences in their treatment of sexuality are especially striking. These distinctions among the texts remind us yet again to modulate generalizations about cultural anxieties by remembering how differently members of the culture may respond to those tensions. In particular, when describing the bride's responses to consummating her marriage Stuart epithalamia vary widely. Thus at one end of the spectrum some poems, such as Tatham's "An Epithalamium on the happie Nuptials of his much respected friend Geo. F. Gent.," play up her fears and regrets. A far more extreme version of this position appears in Richard Crashaw's peculiar "Epithalamion," which repeatedly describes the wedding as a kind of death: "helpe me to mourne a matchlesse maydenhead / that now is dead" (11–12).[90] Some poets suggest that the bride's sorrow at her loss of virginity is brief or even hypocritical; Herrick enjoins the newly married woman:

> And beautious Bride we do confess y'are wise,
> In dealing forth these bashfull jealousies:
>   In Lov's name do so; and a price
>   Set on your selfe, by being nice.
>   ("A Nuptiall Song, or Epithalamie, on
>   Sir Clipseby Crew and his Lady," 51–54)

Other epithalamia locate themselves on the far end of the spectrum that acknowledges and celebrates female desire. The epithalamium in Thomas Campion's *Hayes Masque,* for example, emphasizes that the evening star heralds the bride's "wish't joyes" (p. 226).[91]

Many Stuart epithalamia associate the consummation of the marriage and the loss of virginity with ambivalence, though that ambivalence may be experienced by a range of people and assume a variety of forms. The most extreme and most intriguing versions of ambivalence, as I will argue in Chapter 5, inform Herrick's wedding poetry, but many analogues may be found elsewhere in the tradition as

[90] *The Poems English Latin and Greek of Richard Crashaw,* ed. L. C. Martin, 2d ed. (Oxford: Clarendon Press, 1957). All citations are to this text. I discuss the relationship of Crashaw's poem to the epithalamium tradition in Chapter 3.
[91] All citations from Campion are to *The Works of Thomas Campion,* ed. Walter R. Davis (London: Faber and Faber, 1969).

well. One of the choruses in Chapman's "Epithalamion Teratos," a
poem included in his continuation of "Hero and Leander," reads,
"Love paints his longings in sweet virgins eyes" (471, 479).[92] This
rendition of female desire contrives at once to acknowledge it and at
the same time to limit its threats. Chapman attributes to the sweet
virgins a passivity that may remind us of the rhetoric that renders
the bride as a movable object: the longings are in a sense those of
the male Cupid, transferred to women at his will, much as the bride
will presumably respond to her husband's passion at his behest.
Hence even while ostensibly declaring that young women feel desire,
Chapman contrives to suggest that they are the object of it, not the
subject experiencing it.

Both cultural pressures and literary traditions help explain the attitudes in question. Common sense should direct our initial response:
the references in question surely recall the responses of actual brides,
for the dangers of childbirth alone would probably make some of
them ambivalent about consummating their marriages. But allusions
to that ambivalence call for other, less obvious explanations as well.
Chapman's line seems to be motivated by a wishful fantasy: his
passive women, like the sleepy Maia in Spenser's "Epithalamion,"
are hardly likely to assert the claims to which the doctrine of due
benevolence entitles them. Some of the poets who stress the bride's
divided feelings or her regrets about the loss of virginity may be
projecting their own ambivalence about celibacy onto her. Literary
precedents encourage those projections: the internalized divisions attributed to the bride recall the debate about virginity that structures
Catullus 62. As I suggested earlier, Stuart epithalamia generally aim
to play down overt social conflict; in this instance, they transform
the open conflict between male and female speakers that structures
Catullus 62, variously locating such a debate within the bride or
within the rhetoric of the poem.

The best clues to the attitudes to sexuality in Stuart epithalamia,
however, are three images used in describing the consummation of
the marriage: the battle, the debt, and the rite. Presenting love or
sex as a battle is, of course, a literary cliché; Ovid, for instance, uses
it in the *Amores,* though the notion is so common that one could not

---

[92]Chapman is quoted here from *The Complete Works of Christopher Marlowe,* ed.
Fredson Bowers, 2 vols. (Cambridge: Cambridge Univ. Press, 1973).

and need not trace specific literary precedents.[93] But the trope in question aptly expresses Stuart concerns about sexuality to which the marriage manuals and other treatises on wedlock so eloquently testify. If the psychoanalytic theory that men perceive the female genitals as a wound is correct, meditations on the consummation of the marriage and guilt about the male responsibility for taking a woman's virginity might well generate fantasies of warfare. The extended renderings of this pattern in Gioviano Pontano's epithalamium for the wedding of Giovanni Brancati lend force to such speculations: he explicitly describes the man's genitals as a weapon. It is possible, too, that fears of the *vagina dentita* encourage poets to apply the imagery of the battlefield to weddings. One antiquarian study in fact records a custom of the bride wearing knives[94]; though that tradition could of course be interpreted in a range of ways, it is suggestive that she is constructed as the source, not the recipient, of violence. Thus the trope of the battlefield reverses potential anxieties about castration by representing the man as victor and the woman as helpless victim. In short, the epithalamium once again both expresses and suppresses anxieties.

Whatever its origins, the convention of referring to love as a battle assumes several functions specific to the epithalamium tradition. This generic norm contains an allusion to marriage by capture.[95] Many wedding rituals themselves allude to that type of dating service long after it had been abandoned; a folk custom that the young men plucked off the bride's garters, sometimes throwing her to the floor in the process, actually enacts a type of battle.[96] More to our purposes, this pattern of imagery is a microcosm of the way the genre as a whole so often operates: like the hijab, the packet of cloth worn by Egyptian brides, it acknowledges tensions and anxieties while at the same time attempting to contain and reduce them. The authors of Stuart epithalamia repeatedly stress that these skirmishes, unlike most others, are mild and unthreatening; through the trope of

[93]On this image in the Italian epithalamium tradition, see Tufte, *The Poetry of Marriage*, p. 109.

[94]John Brand and Sir Henry Ellis, *Observations on Popular Antiquities*, rev. ed., 3 vols. (London: Charles Knight, 1841–1842), II, 82–83.

[95]On marriage by capture see Howard, I, 156–179; Lévi-Strauss, pp. 19–20.

[96]On the custom concerning garters, see Brand and Ellis, II, 79–80. Also compare Gillis, pp. 59–60, on mock battles connected with Welsh weddings; here and elsewhere, however, one needs to inquire closely into whether the customs he cites are specific to a given region, period, or class.

the battle they incorporate a safe, subdued violence into the poem, much as the custom of plucking off the bride's garters incorporates a harmless attack into the wedding itself. These poets typically deploy oxymora (yet another rhetorical manifestation of the ambivalences we noted earlier) to suggest that the battle of love is relatively harmless; thus in "A Hymn to Hymen" Chapman refers to "the nuptial battle's joys" (76).[97] In such instances, the allusion to warfare recognizes the potential for conflicts between husband and wife and the violence implicit in the loss of virginity but does so in a form that is comparatively unthreatening, much as the convention of averting dangers admits those perils into the poem while praying and in many cases implying that they will not be admitted into the marriage.

The rhetoric of the battlefield serves several other functions. In the many poems that suggest the bride's hesitations about sex, the notion of the fight emphasizes her virginity and predicts her resistance to potential adulterous advances in the future. At the same time this imagery presents the husband's victory in a form that makes it more palatable to any readers, male or female, who experience doubts about it: epithalamia render the sexual battle playful and benign, rather like Damon the Mower's "harmless snake," and in many cases these epithalamia imply the woman's pleased assent to her husband's victory.

A second rhetorical pattern functions like the imagery of battle in that it too renders more benign the violence and loss that might be associated with the consummation of the marriage: several Stuart poets develop the concept of due benevolence by referring to the commonplace notion that the sexual union of the couple is the payment of a debt. We will scrutinize a particularly telling example when we turn to Donne's wedding poems, but instances occur elsewhere; a song in John Dowland's *Pilgrimes Solace,* for instance, alludes repeatedly to "Love's due debt."[98] Such references, like their analogues in the conduct books, socialize and civilize sexual desire. It becomes not an irresistible passion but an obligation; the bride and groom will make love, such rhetoric implies, because they should rather than because they want to. We may note in this context that one of the most influential Protestant conduct books on marriage,

[97]The citation is to *The Plays and Poems of George Chapman,* ed. Thomas Marc Parrott, 2 vols. (London and New York: George Routledge and E. P. Dutton, 1910–1914).
[98]John Dowland, *A Pilgrimes Solace* (London, 1612), Song XX.

Miles Coverdale's translation of Heinrich Bullinger, actually uses the term "worke" for the payment of the debt ("nether of them maye denye vnto the tother [sic] the due worke of matrimonye" [sig. Diii]). Read in relation to the financial rhetoric also associated with due benevolence, this usage hints at one way the marriage manuals civilize sex: they treat it as yet another form of work in the economy of the household.[99] Thus these books, like the epithalamia themselves, associate responsibility, not pleasure, with sexuality and construct it not as an individualistic and anarchic urge but rather as a socially mandated duty.

A third pattern of imagery is closely related. Several poets refer to sexual intercourse as the "rites of love"; we find the phrase, for example, in an epithalamium in *The Maid's Tragedy* (I.ii.212), and in "An Epithalamium" Thomas Randolph speaks of love's "misticke rites" (38).[100] In some contexts the phrase clearly refers to sex, but it can be ambiguous, as the debate about Desdemona's use of the same term demonstrates.[101] That ambiguity is, I suggest, the point. For one thing, by describing sex in terms that could be used for a religious ceremony poets yet again channel the sacredness of the event away from the problematical rituals in church and towards its seemingly secular components. Moreover, in so doing they enact linguistically the process that marriage itself performs: legitimizing the sexual drive. The play on "rites" in the sense of rituals and "rights" in the sense of legal commitments establishes sexuality as a component of social obligations and regulations rather than as an enemy to them. Thus in the wedding poem included in his continuation of *Hero and Leander,* Chapman declares, "Loves right claims more then banquets" (480); "claims" encourages us to read "right" in the sense of entitlement, but the other meanings are surely present as well.

Allusions to heirs, yet another link between the epithalamium and the Protestant marriage service, perform the same transformation. The significance of this convention throughout the history of the genre is manifest in its typical position at the culmination of the poem. Though Stuart poets differ in the amount of attention they

[99] A number of scholars have in fact linked attitudes to marriage to economic changes. For a useful summary of some of the issues, see Fitz, " 'What Says the Married Woman,' " 9–10.

[100] Thomas Randolph, *Poems* (Oxford, 1638).

[101] For a commentary on this controversy, see William Shakespeare, *Othello,* ed. M. R. Ridley, Arden Edition (London: Methuen, 1958), p. 36.

bestow on this motif, very few omit it completely. Their adoption of
it is hardly surprising, for the motif serves the same ends as the images we have been exploring: it reminds both the couple and the
readers that sexuality can serve society by producing a new generation rather than threaten it by creating turmoil in the current one.
This implication subtly emerges in the concluding lines of Nabbes's
"An Epithalamium on the hopefull happy Mariage of Master Bvrlacye, and Mistris Alice Bankes": "Whilst all mens zealous wishes are
to see / Those pleasures blest in a posteritie" (47–48). "Blest" may of
course simply mean "made happy," but the lines also imply that the
creation of a posterity renders sexual pleasure acceptable and even
holy. Allusions to heirs contribute as well to the preoccupation with
unification that we have noted; Beaumont, for instance, expresses a
wish for a "race of Sonnes" ("An Epithalamium vpon the happy
marriage of our Soueraigne Lord King Charles, and our gracious
Lady Queene Mary" (56). The orderly succession of generations
(and, in Beaumont's poem, of monarchs) is an analogue to another
linear pattern, the procession of wedding guests.

Yet here, as is so often the case in the Stuart epithalamium, tensions and threats lurk just beneath the surface of the poem, much as
they may lie near the threshold the couple must pass. It is not
wholly fortuitous that allusions to death often immediately follow
references to heirs. Child mortality was so high that a plague bill
that carefully specifies causes of death for adults merely notes "infant" as an apparent explanation for the demise of babies.[102] Jonson's
Somerset epithalamium is one of the few Stuart wedding poems to
allude specifically to the fear that the wished-for heirs might not survive infancy, but one suspects that in other cases such anxiety is not
absent but repressed.

Lyric epithalamia often conclude on requests or prayers for the
couple's happiness, and such statements also appear prominently in
other versions of the genre; some poems, indeed, are essentially lists
of wishes. This convention, the mirror image of the references to
dangers that must be averted, assumes several forms. For instance,

[102]See STC 4472.3, "A Generall Bill of All Those Which Have Been Buried . . . "
(Cambridge, England, 1638). Mortality rates in general and infant mortality in particular have, of course, been widely studied. See esp. the controversial but illuminating work by Peter Laslett, *The World We Have Lost: Further Explored*, 3d ed. (London:
Methuen, 1983), chap. 5; he points out that we sometimes overestimate the number
of early deaths.

heirs are sometimes mentioned here rather than in the discussion of consummating the marriage. Like their predecessors, many Stuart epithalamia express the hope that the bride and groom will enjoy long lives. Tropes concerning heat and cold also frequently appear at this point in the epithalamium. In one typical passage, Beaumont declares, "neuer must [Time's] freezing arme, their holy fires asswage" ("An Epithalamium to my Lord Marquesse of Buckingham, and to his faire and vertuous Lady," [25]); Jonson expresses the wish that "eu'ry birth encrease the heate of Loue" ("To the most noble, and aboue his Titles, Robert, Earle of Somerset" [20]); and Brooke prays that the couple avoid "cold affect" ("An Epithalamium; or a Nuptiall Song, applied to the Ceremonies of a Mariage" [96]). Although such lines could refer either to maintaining affection or to preserving physical desire and capability, in fact both meanings are germane; in particular, "affect" can be glossed both as "mood" and as "lust."[103] Certainly the Renaissance predilection for describing sexuality in terms of heat[104] does encourage us to find physiological as well as psychological concerns in such passages.

Often the good wishes that appear in epithalamia are vague and general. In particular, it is striking that they seldom include direct allusions to issues on which the conduct books focus: Stuart poets typically do not pray that the wife be obedient, that the couple enjoy a companionate relationship, or that they establish a devout household. Such absences support my contention that those issues were more controversial than scholars' analyses of Renaissance marriage have sometimes admitted; engaged in evoking a harmonious society by repressing or reinterpreting potential conflicts, Stuart poets do not wish to stir up discord by focusing on tense subjects.

In miming anthropologists who are prone to treat culture as monolithic, literary critics have often been tempted to elide the disagreements and fluctuations that characterize the culture—or, more precisely, the many cultures—of Elizabethan and Stuart England. But we could more profitably borrow an alternative anthropological paradigm that incorporates the distinctions within a society and in so doing proves especially useful for explaining the vagueness and

---

[103]*OED*, s.v. "affect."

[104]Though the incident of hermaphroditism interpreted by Stephen Greenblatt is more problematical than he acknowledges, his emphasis on the heat of generative "friction" is persuasive (*Shakespearean Negotiations: The Circulation of Social Energy in Renaissance England* [Berkeley: Univ. of California Press, 1988], esp. p. 85).

absences that characterize the good wishes in the epithalamium tradition. James W. Fernandez emphasizes that members of a culture participate in it to different extents and in different ways and establishes a vocabulary for recognizing those distinctions.[105] "Cultural consensus" involves agreement on the meaning of shared symbols; "social consensus," in contrast, involves acknowledging the need for social interaction and hence participating in rituals even if one does not agree with other participants about their meaning. The disagreements about marriage that characterized Stuart England encouraged social rather than cultural consensus, and thus the vague good wishes in many epithalamia represent a retreat from controversial issues about wedlock. Fernandez also suggests that societies marked by many tensions often deliberately avoid explaining the meanings of their symbols. The epithalamium, I suggest, indicates that response coexisted with several others. Stuart poets skirt some explanations. But they also react to the uncertainties attending on marriage by emphasizing the meanings of some symbols, such as the threshold of the house, and reinterpreting that of others, such as the feast.

IV

In expressing its visions and re-visions of marriage, the Stuart epithalamium relies not only on the motifs and conventions we have been examining but also on a series of formal patterns. I am not of course suggesting that these rhetorical and prosodic strategies are unique to the Stuart wedding poem or to the epithalamium tradition in general: many of these techniques, such as the deployment of antithesis, are common in classical and Renaissance literature. But the epithalamium tradition often assigns new functions to old devices. Some serve to express the tensions attending on marriage in many cultures; others reflect the nature of wedlock in Stuart England.

Epithalamia are traditionally peppered with syntactical and rhetorical antitheses, with oppositions and contrasts of all kinds.[106] Thus

[105]James W. Fernandez, "Symbolic Consensus in a Fang Reformative Cult," *American Anthropologist*, 67 (1965), 902–929. Other practitioners of his discipline do, of course, also question universalist assumptions. For an important instance see M. Z. Rosaldo, "The Use and Abuse of Anthropology: Reflections on Feminism and Cross-cultural Understanding," *Signs*, 5 (1980), 389–417.
[106]In "Milton and the Epic Epithalamium," *Milton Studies*, 5 (1973), Gary M. Mc-Cown points out that humanist epithalamia often deploy *oppositio* to compare fallen love with the chaster version of that emotion in Eden.

they characteristically use the negative formula, the technique of defining something by saying what it is not. Catullus 61 includes the lines,

> quae tuis careat sacris,
> non queat dare praesides
> terra finibus.
>
> (71–73)

(A land that should want thy sanctities would not be able to produce guardians for its borders.)

Alternatively, epithalamia build in contrasts through other types of negative and antithetical syntactical constructions. Spenser, for instance, does so in his paradoxical declaration "Bvt if ye saw that which no eyes can see" ("Epithalamion," 185). Indeed, his "Epithalamion" is studded with such constructions: "But let this day let this one day be myne, / Let all the rest be thine" (125–126), "Ne thought of thing vncomely euer may / Thereto approch to tempt her mind to ill" (198–199), "Poure not by cups, but by the belly full" (251), "Ne let hob Goblins, names whose sence we see not, / Fray vs with things that be not" (343–344), and so on. And Bartholomew Young's translated epithalamium offers a particularly interesting instance: he rhymes "sadness" and "gladness" in every stanza, a literal rendition of the ways the whole tradition, as it were, rhymes the two.

Stuart poets readily adopt the negative formula. In a passage we examined earlier from a different perspective, Beaumont observes, "*Leander* here no dang'rous iourney takes, / To touch his *Heros* hand" ("An Epithalamium vpon the happy marriage of our Soueraine Lord King Charles, and our gracious Lady Queene Mary," 7–8). Similarly, Carew writes, "Let Tempests struggle in the Ayre, but rest / Eternall calmes within thy peacefull brest" ("On the Mariage of T. K. and C. C. the morning stormie," 13–14). Drayton declares, "and no Girle / Carouse but in dissolved Pearle" ("The Eighth Nimphall," 203–204) rather than "and every girl carouse in dissolved pearl"; in *Argalvs and Parthenia* Quarles prays, "May these Lovers never want / True joyes" (p. 105) instead of "May these lovers have true joys." Jonson's contributions to the genre demonstrate two other forms this predilection for opposites can assume. He uses the disjunctive conjunction "or" in a context in which "and" would have been as apt:

"When look'd the Earth so fine, / Or so did shine" ("Epithala-mion . . . Celebrating the Nvptials of that Noble Gentleman, Mr. Hierome Weston . . . with the Lady Frances Stuart," 21–22). Later in the same poem he delights in commutatio: "Mens Loves unto the Lawes, and Lawes to love the Crowne" (104).

The debate format that we find in many epithalamia outside the English tradition is structured around oppositions.[107] Catullus 62 re-peatedly plays the position of the youths against that of the maidens. The French tradition offers some suggestive analogues. Grévin writes a pastoral dialogue, "Les Pasteurs." The stanzas in Marot's "Chant nuptial du Mariage de Madame Renée, Fille de France, & du Duc de Ferrare" alternate between declaring that the night is cruel and de-claring that it is not, hence internalizing within the single speaker of the poem Catullus's opposition between young men and maidens. Though Catullus 62 inspired few direct imitations in the English Re-naissance, some poets do adapt the amoeban debate form to other speakers. Thus Campion includes dialogues in his *Hayes Masque;* in an epithalamium in Massinger's *The Guardian,* Juno advises the bride and Hymen the groom. Indeed, when antitheses assume the form "not x, but y," they are in a sense syntactically enacting the debate structure.

Why do these related though distinct forms of antithesis and op-position recur so often in the epithalamium tradition? Antithetical tropes are, of course, staples of both classical and Renaissance rheto-ric manuals. And evidence suggests that both Roman and Greek folk epithalamia may have involved alternating choruses.[108] The primary reason, however, is that antithetical patterns express rhetorically the oppositions in which the genre is grounded. It may perhaps be rele-vant here that exogamy by definition involves difference rather than sameness, though one must acknowledge that in many cultures wed-dings are endogamous instead. More to the point, the opposition be-tween and reconciliation of male and female are central to wedlock and to the literary form that celebrates it.

This much is true of most of all epithalamia, but in the case of poems written in cultures where marriage was an especially contro-versial issue, or those composed by poets who considered that state

---

[107]On the amoeban form of the genre and the variations it can involve, see Tufte, *The Poetry of Marriage,* pp. 28, 59, 235–236, 241.

[108]See E. Faye Wilson, "Pastoral and Epithalamium in Latin Literature," *Speculum,* 23 (1948), esp. 36.

highly problematical, rhetorical oppositions serve additional functions. They may, for example, stem from and reflect the author's preoccupation with another opposition: the implicit but deeply embedded contrast between unhappy marriages and the ideal being celebrated, between ostensible Edens overrun with snakes and the happier Eden the couple in question will establish. Furthermore, the rhetorical patterns in question indicate not only the nature of marriage but also the nature of the poet's responses to it: in many cases, I suggest, they represent a projection onto the text of the dissensions and debates within the writer or within his culture. The problems attending marriage in Stuart England were not unique, of course, but some of them were particularly intense. Hence rhetorical oppositions and antitheses, which allow an expression of tensions that are often repressed on the semantic levels of the poem, no doubt seemed especially attractive to many Stuart poets.

Another rhetorical pattern that recurs in the epithalamium tradition is a form of copia. Often adopting a paratactic structure, poets in the genre incorporate catalogues of items: they variously list types of good fortune, evils to avoid, the attributes gracing the bride and groom, and so on. Thus the epithalamium in Sidney's *Arcadia* consists of a list of good wishes; we might assume that Donne's interest in birds does not extend beyond the English slang meaning of that term, but in fact both he and Spenser include long lists of avian species in their wedding poems. The predilection for lists, like the one for oppositions, demands several explanations. Though especially beloved of Renaissance rhetoricians, copia of course attracts both theorists and writers in many other periods. But yet again rhetorical traditions do not provide a complete explanation: we must also note that a pattern poets could well have adopted simply because of those traditions is in fact particularly suited to the epithalamium. An Elizabethan example helps us to understand why. Notice the way Spenser phrases one of his invitations:

> Bring with you *all* the Nymphes that you can heare
> *both* of the riuers *and* the forrests greene:
> *and* of the sea that neighbours to her neare.
> ("Epithalamion," 37–39; emphases added)

In other words, these lists mime syntactically the linear inclusiveness that we examined earlier; epithalamia involve successions not only of participants in the occasion and of anticipated heirs but also of enumerated items.

Paradoxically, then, the epithalamium tradition includes both antitheses and lists of similar items. These contrasting rhetorical patterns embody values and strategies present on other levels of the poems. The two patterns respectively enact the two ways poems in the genre strive to ensure the harmony of the marriage and the larger social order it mirrors: excluding threatening forces and individuals on the one hand, including all other members of the community on the other. From other perspectives these two rhetorical patterns may be said to correspond respectively to banishing and calling forth, or to the play between outside and inside.

The closural and anticlosural devices that characterize the epithalamium tradition similarly demonstrate the intimate relationships between formal decisions and the values and problems that lie at the heart of the genre. Studying these patterns is complicated by the multiple meanings that have been associated with closure, which may variously signify aesthetic or thematic resolution, the termination of a predictable pattern that does not necessarily involve resolution, and so on.[109] The epithalamium tradition, I suggest, incorporates and at times contrasts these several forms of closure.

Closural strategies figure prominently in many wedding poems, but they are singularly marked in the lyric epithalamium. Most such poems terminate at night, a particularly effective mode of concluding a poem because it conjoins several kinds of thematic and aesthetic resolution. Opening the lyric at daybreak and ending it at night creates a sense of harmony and order. Moreover, one often associates night with sleep and silence, which, as Barbara Herrnstein Smith among others has demonstrated,[110] are common closural motifs. Many epithalamia express and attempt to resolve a potential conflict between the natural world and the human world; by going to bed when they do the couple match diurnal patterns and hence strengthen the links between natural and human spheres elsewhere forged by the poems. The closural technique in question is also ef-

---

[109]On these types of closure and the problems of studying them see esp. Frank Kermode, The Sense of an Ending: Studies in the Theory of Fiction (London: Oxford Univ. Press, 1967); Barbara Herrnstein Smith, Poetic Closure: A Study of How Poems End (Chicago: Univ. of Chicago Press, 1968); Marianna Torgovnick, Closure in the Novel (Princeton: Princeton Univ. Press, 1981).

[110]Barbara Herrnstein Smith, Poetic Closure, pp. 172–182.

fective because it dovetails with other methods of resolving the poem: moving from outdoors to within the house is a spatial analogue to the temporal progression from day to night.

These methods of creating closure and a concomitant sense of harmony and order, then, provide yet another explanation for the appeal of the lyric epithalamium. And they provide further evidence for the artistry that so often graces the epithalamium tradition: the signs of tension and discord that are evident elsewhere in the genre, including some of its other ways of attempting closure, do not preclude poetic skill and success.

Forms of closure occur, of course, not only in the lyric epithalamium but also in other versions of the genre. Epithalamia often introduce the idea of conclusion semantically; thus when Peacham writes "The Dores are shut" ("Nuptiall Hymnes," sig. F2^v) or Chapman commands "Shut all doors" ("A Hymn to Hymen," 81), the closing of the doors gestures towards that of the poem itself. Many wedding poems conclude by referring to the couple's death, generally in the form of a wish that they will live long and ultimately die at the same time.

Prosodic and other rhetorical devices also establish the sense of an ending. The refrain is so important and complicated an instance that it demands separate treatment, and we will return to it shortly. Chapman, however, provides a useful example of less ambiguous closural techniques when he ends "A Hymn to Hymen" on the same two lines that opened the poem. Some epithalamia conclude by moving to a different mode of speech: the declaratives that have predominated earlier give way to the optatives expressing the hopes that heirs will appear, that the couple will enjoy happy lives, and so on.

Despite—or because of—all these ways of establishing closure, anticlosural forces also play an important role in the epithalamium tradition. If optatives encourage closure by moving to a different grammatical mode, they also undermine it by introducing uncertainties—will the heirs who are so eagerly anticipated survive infancy? will the bride and groom themselves survive long enough to enjoy the happy marriage the poet is predicting? The emphasis on listing is also potentially anticlosural in that enumeration could often be extended: the poet could pile on yet more good wishes, just as he might name further species of birds earlier in the poem.

We have seen that some devices are closural in one sense and anticlosural in another. One formal strategy by definition includes both poles. Texts, whether they be literary or not, often demonstrate a phenomenon that we might term "closural continuity": paradoxically, they effect an ending by suggesting that something will continue, hence providing both closure and anticlosure at once. Social scientists have observed that encounters often end on—and through—a statement that emphasizes the continuation of the relationship, such as "See you soon" or "I'll call you tomorrow then."[111] Such lines represent a well-established code for terminating the interaction, and yet they suggest as well a continuation or a new beginning for what has just occurred.

Closural continuity occurs in many genres, but nowhere is it more prominent than in the epithalamium. We find it in prayers that the couple will live long and produce heirs. It recurs lexically and semantically. Terms that refer to something unchanging often appear near the end of wedding poems. Thus Wither ends his "Epithalamion" "Thus to wish her good, *for euer*" (sig. D; italics added), and Quarles writes that a son will "*Perpetuate,* and crowne thy name" (p. 120; italics added). Donne concludes his epithalamium on the marriage of Frances Howard and the earl of Somerset on an allusion to a lamp that burns forever.

Aesthetic imperatives lie behind many of the devices we have been examining; we need to remind ourselves that the intimate connections between this genre and its social milieux do not preclude other explanations for its poets' decisions. In one sense, of course, the drive towards closure is an impulse to create an orderly work, to shape a well-wrought urn. For instance, when the authors of epithalamia conflate many different types of closure by alluding to night, they are demonstrating and delighting in their skill as craftsmen.

But the line between aesthetic and social or political motivations quickly blurs: the attraction to orderly endings is in some instances at least a response to the disorder the poet fears may attend on weddings. indeed, both the closural and the anticlosural patterns in wedding poems accord to the nature of marriage itself. Weddings are closural in that they culminate the period of courtship, yet anticlosural in that many of the hopes on which they are based, such as the

---

[111]See two articles by Stuart Albert and Suzanne Kessler, "Processes for Ending Social Encounters: The Conceptual Archaeology of a Temporal Place," *Journal of the Theory of Social Behaviour,* 6 (1976), esp. 164–167 on "the continuity process"; "Ending Social Encounters," *Journal of Experimental Social Psychology,* 14 (1978), esp. 542, 551–552.

longevity of the couple and the production of heirs, are necessarily uncertain. Marriage characteristically punctuates experience with a semicolon, not a period.

In Stuart England, however, both the closural and the anticlosural propensities of marriage were intense. The closural force of that institution must have seemed more marked and more reassuring simply because of the tensions that preceded the event itself. For marriage signaled the conclusion not only to the complex financial negotiations associated with many aristocratic and royal weddings but also to the ambiguous, ill-defined threshold state created by prenuptial contracts. Anticipating modern anthropologists' fascination with liminality, in *Of Domesticall Dvties* William Gouge observes that such arrangements constitute a middle position between the married and single states (p. 199). The uncertainties engendered by prenuptial contracts—did they legitimize sex? under what circumstances were they valid?—could best be resolved by marriage itself.

But if Stuart weddings could seem reassuringly closural, their participants were threatened by as many anticlosural energies as the would-be brides in *The Faerie Queene*. As the treatises on marriage examined in Chapter 1 demonstrate, the very question what constituted a valid marriage, and hence when and how its putative closure is realized, was moot. Contemporary mortality rates also established optatives, not declaratives, as the necessary mode of the genre celebrating weddings. Statistics on this subject, like most subjects, are tricky: longevity varied significantly from one part of the country to another,[112] and figures about life expectancy are skewed by the high incidence of infant mortality. Nonetheless, the premature death of bride or groom or both must have been as haunting a fear at Stuart weddings as divorce is at contemporary ones; Lawrence Stone has shown us that in the late sixteenth and early seventeenth centuries death interrupted over one-third of all first marriages within fifteen years.[113]

The epithalamium tradition itself offers poignant instances of the workings of these statistics. The "conquering Bride" (2) whom Carew celebrates in "On the Mariage of T. K. and C. C. the morning stormie" was not able to conquer her unhappy fate: married on June 29, 1636, she died on New Year's Day 1637/38.[114] Elizabeth

[112]On that variation see Laslett, p. 112.
[113]Stone, *The Crisis of the Aristocracy*, p. 589.
[114]*The Poems of Thomas Carew*, p. 254.

Radcliffe, the bride commemorated in Jonson's *Haddington Masque,* was married in February 1608 and became a victim of smallpox in December 1618; she gave birth to three children in her short life, but none lived very long.[115]

Refrains are common throughout the epithalamium tradition, but they assume different forms. The refrain often consists of an entire line, as in Spenser's "Epithalamion" and "Prothalamion"; alternatively, the poet may repeat a single word at the end of his stanzas, as Heywood does when he plays on "Elizabeth" in a passage from his "nuptiall hymnes" we will examine shortly. The authors of wedding poems must also decide whether to repeat the same basic refrain or several different ones, and if they do opt for the same formula, they have to choose whether to effect variations within it. These decisions, like many of the others we have examined, reflect and illuminate both aesthetic challenges and cultural tensions.

Refrains may serve at once to create and to confound closural patterns and in so doing to comment on the attitudes to marriage latent in those patterns. Obviously, this prosodic device signals the end of a stanza. Yet its role in the final stanza of the poem is more ambiguous: a refrain by definition may recur, just as lists of good wishes are open-ended, so its appearance at the end of the lyric has the capacity to render that conclusion inconclusive. Several Stuart poets, however, skillfully adapt their refrains so that the final one will in fact create a less ambiguous ending. In particular, like some of their predecessors, they set off the final refrain by varying it. Quarles's *Argalvs and Parthenia* is by and large an indifferent poem, but the refrain in one of its epithalamia is a real triumph. Having ended the first three stanzas on "Let *Juno's* hourely blessing send ye / As much joy as can attend ye," Quarles moves to his final stanza:

> Thus to *Hymens* sacred bands,
>   We commend your chast deserts,
>   That as *Juno* link'd your hearts,
> So he would please to joyne your hands;
>   And let both their blessings send ye
>   As much joy as can attend ye.
>   (p. 106)

On one level, of course, Quarles, like the other poets we have enumerated, simply creates closure through variation. But the move-

[115]*Ben Jonson,* X, 487.

ment from mentioning Juno alone in the earlier stanzas to referring to her male counterpart as well in the phrase "both their blessings" also serves to enact the central movements of the wedding itself: the marriage effects the union of bride and groom, just as the poem brings about that of Juno and Hymen.

Refrains may serve other functions too. They involve both the repetition of words that have occurred earlier in the same poem and the repetition of a prosodic technique that has recurred frequently in their genre.[116] The continuity they thus exemplify and symbolize stands in sharp contrast to the uncertainties and potential interruptions that threaten the marriage; and the regular temporal movement they effect is the opposite number to the concerns about untimeliness that we noted earlier. Indeed, as Thomas G. Rosenmeyer has pointed out, refrains are associated with stability.[117] In other words, the poem yet again enacts and embodies an idealized vision that contrasts with the actual conditions of marriage. It substitutes its happier Eden for beleaguered paradise. The poetic processes of the epithalamium are a metaphor for its social vision; the poem itself becomes an icon of order, an exemplar of conservatism. These functions no doubt attracted poets in many ages, but they must have been particularly appealing to writers confronted with the intense and varied uncertainties that attended marriage at the Stuart court.

In a particularly striking instance of such continuity, Heywood repeats the name "Elizabeth" in the final lines of his stanzas:

> But for a Godesse after death
> They had ador'd *Elizabeth*.
>
> . . . . .
>
> Who did but lament the death
> Of that good Queene *Elizabeth*?
>
> . . . . .
>
> For that alone [fame] liues after death;
> So shall the name *Elizabeth*.
> (*A Marriage Trivmphe*, sig. E1ᵛ)

The poem embodies prosodically the rebirth it heralds semantically: the word "Elizabeth" reappears in succeeding stanzas just as the

[116]Compare Thomas G. Rosenmeyer's contention that refrains often involve stasis and stability (*The Green Cabinet: Theocritus and the European Pastoral Lyric* [Berkeley: Univ. of California Press, 1969], pp. 94–95).

[117]Rosenmeyer, *The Green Cabinet*, pp. 118–119.

queen herself is reborn in the person of the princess. Heywood intensifies this emphasis on return and renewal through many lines that comment overtly on this subject; the passage quoted above offers some examples, and the poem is packed with others. But if Heywood's lyric demonstrates the ways refrains can symbolize continuity, it also soberingly reminds us of one reason they need to do so. The repeated rhymes on "death" and "Elizabeth" may be intended to create a contrast between the two—and, as poets might be less embarrassed than literary critics to admit, they serve *faute de mieux,* since the language does not offer many alternative rhymes. But one also suspects that the words rhymed in Heywood's psyche as well, much as "sadness" and "gladness" rhyme in more sense than one in Young's sixteenth-century epithalamium: the recent death of Princess Elizabeth's brother Henry no doubt intensified the usual fears that the bride or groom would not live till old age.

John Hollander has asserted that refrains involve "a dialectic of memory and anticipation,"[118] and this phrase indicates further functions they serve in the epithalamium in general and the Stuart tradition in particular. Memory and anticipation are the very activities that impel and empower the genre: as we will see in Chapter 3, epithalamia typically look backwards nostalgically to an idealized age, and they look forwards as well to the succession of generations that will be initiated by this wedding. In a sense Janus, not Juno, is the presiding deity at weddings, and the refrain pays tribute to him.

The functions we have noted involve similarities between Stuart refrains and their counterparts in many other wedding poems, though sometimes Stuart poets may respond in a more intense way to issues that concern earlier writers as well. In one important respect, however, the refrains in early seventeenth-century wedding poems differ from most of their predecessors: Stuart writers more frequently effect significant variations within a given refrain.[119] By and large the writers of classical and French epithalamia craft wholly unchanging refrains, as Eustache Deschamps does in his "Ballade," or alternate several refrains but without including any significant changes within

---

[118]John Hollander, "Breaking into Song: Some Notes on Refrain," in *Lyric Poetry: Beyond New Criticism,* ed. Chaviva Hošek and Patricia Parker (Ithaca: Cornell Univ. Press, 1985), p. 78.

[119]Tufte draws our attention to the variations that do occur in classical and Continental refrains, but these shifts are relatively insignificant (*The Poetry of Marriage,* p. 26).

them, as Joachim Du Bellay does in his lyric on the wedding of the duke of Savoy and Princess Marguerite, or include minor changes within refrains, as Catullus does when he addresses Hymen in slightly different ways. The sixteenth-century English tradition, however, offers a few precedents for more creative approaches. In his "Epithalamion" Spenser plays on changes in his pronouns ("The woods shall to me answer" [18] changes to "The woods shall to you answer" [55] and so on); and, of course, he shifts at nightfall to "The woods no more shal answere" (314).[120] These changes may have been inspired by the refrains in Young's translation of *Diana*. Similarly, the refrain in the epithalamia in Sidney's *Arcadia* is transformed from "O *Himen* long their coupled joyes maintaine" (9) to "For *Himen* will their coupled joyes maintaine" (99).

Several Stuart poets follow the example set by Young, Sidney, and Spenser. Much as Heywood plays on the name "Elizabeth," so Donne rings the changes on allusions to Bishop Valentine in his epithalamium on the marriage of Princess Elizabeth and the Elector Palatine; they range from the naughty "This day, which might enflame thy self, Old Valentine" (14) to the more respectful "Till which houre, wee thy day enlarge, O Valentine" (112). His wedding poem for the marriage of Frances Howard and the earl of Somerset effects similar variations by repeating the words "eyes" and "heart." Donne's friend Goodyer ends the first two stanzas of his "Epithalamion, of the Princess Mariage" on "This night for w[ch] this Moneth doth gyve awaye twoe dayes" (11, 22) and concludes all the succeeding ones on repetitions of or minor variations on "This night w[ch] to this Moneth, doth recompence twoe dayes" (33); the shift from loss to recovery mirrors prosodically the emphasis on recuperation and renewal that is so central to the whole genre. Phineas Fletcher's "An Hymen at the Marriage of my most deare Cousins Mr. W. and M. R." refers to the god of marriage at the end of each stanza, but these statements include, "Hymen, oh Hymen, here thy saffron garment bring" (7), "Hymen, come holy Hymen, Hymen lowd they sing" (14), "Hymen, come Hymen; here thy saffron coat is rested" (21), and so on.

The example set by Sidney and Spenser no doubt spurred their successors to experiment with changing refrains, and the pleasure in

[120]Many scholars have commented on these changes. See, e.g., Richard Neuse, "The Triumph over Hasty Accidents: A Note on the Symbolic Mode of the 'Epithalamion,'" *MLR*, 61 (1966), 173.

craftsmanship that we have witnessed several times energized these
experiments. Once again, however, formal decisions also encode social values and visions. This type of refrain functions rather like closural continuity in that at once it embodies continuity and change,
often by playing a fixed element like a repeated name against a shifting one. These prosodic instances of orderly and delimited change,
or, to put it another way, change bounded by the unchanging, no
doubt seemed especially attractive in a culture that had witnessed
more abrupt changes, such as the shifts in social status engendered
by James's creation of new peers and the metamorphoses in court
politics sparked by his rejections of erstwhile favorites. Even more to
the point, changing refrains attract Stuart poets in part because this
prosodic strategy symbolizes the values many of these writers wish
to associate with marriage itself. The weddings in the happier Edens
they envision involve not disruption and danger but rather orderly
change from one state to another; the shift from virginity to marital
sexuality, from the closed to the open body, comes to seem as unthreatening as the prosodic shifts effected in these refrains.

V

Stuart epithalamia are grounded in paradox. The occasion they
mark can inspire both admiration for the bride and fear of her potentially uncontrolled sexuality. The anticipation of heirs generates
both hope and anxiety. Weddings celebrate life and renewal, yet they
are glossed by the reminder "Et in thalamos ego."

When poets respond to the tensions involved in these paradoxes,
two related but conflicting responses predominate. Writers in the
genre may attempt to civilize and control the anarchic through the
rhetoric of rites and harmless battles, through the banishing-
of-danger motif, and so on. Or they may deny it through use of core
fantasies, especially the fantasy of an Edenic society.

But that summary needs to be further qualified and refined: each
of the two categories encompasses a wide range of responses to the
influence of anxiety. Freudian paradigms for how people react to
stress can help us anatomize those responses. Sometimes Stuart writers repress fears, as in the instance of concerns about the death of the
children the couple may produce. Elsewhere we encounter a version
of reaction formation: the intense praise of the bride may be in
part—though only in part—a reversal of hostility. The most relevant

model, however, is displacement: fears of uncontrolled sexuality are displaced onto the feast, anxieties about brides and patrons onto such externalized forces as Jealousy and hobgoblins, and so on. Yet these Freudian paradigms, though useful, may encourage a contemporary critical tendency we might term cultural ventriloquism: viewing art as merely the passive vehicle for expressing the will of those in power or, more to our purposes here, for reflecting shared cultural tensions. The epithalamium does at times exemplify both functions; but its poets also achieve more thoughtful and balanced ways of acknowledging and coping with the influence of anxiety. Freudian models, we should remind ourselves, can represent not just neurotic reactions but also successful adaptations.[121]

Even this brief summary suggests the complexities involved in explicating this range of responses. Texts in the genre do sometimes achieve the harmony so often celebrated by earlier generations of critics, but they also exemplify two patterns that more recent critics characteristically emphasize, the eruption of dissonances and the imposition of cultural norms. By and large it is not difficult to distinguish among these and other reactions to tension; for instance, in the banishing-of-dangers motif we typically find traces of partially repressed tensions, whereas many of the closural strategies adopted by the genre achieve a more persuasive serenity. Occasionally, however, the categories elide, reminding us that these classifications may depend in part on the perspective, ideological and otherwise, of the observer. A reader or an author committed to certain patriarchal assumptions may find that descriptions of the bride both advocate and achieve social harmony; someone examining the same passages from the perspective of the bride may see not harmony but its dark underside, suppression. Thus if, as I suggested in Chapter 2, marriage manuals connect ordering in the sense of establishing serenity with ordering in the sense of giving commands, epithalamia problematize that connection.

The issues explored in this chapter, then, demonstrate how and why allusions to cultural anxieties demand critical tact. We should not seesaw between seeing only the serenity that some critics have associated with the genre and seeing only turmoil: both are present. The happiness expressed in Stuart weddings is sometimes but not

---

[121]Compare George E. Vaillant's thesis that many personality patterns in fact represent successful adaptations (*Adaptation to Life* [Boston: Little, Brown, 1977], esp. chaps. 1, 12, and pp. 385–386).

invariably the product of repressed antagonisms or idealized fantasies; though some references to the wedding feast may read like excerpts from an American Heart Association pamphlet on the perils of overeating, many other passages on the subject testify to the genuine happiness associated with weddings. Nor should we skid from emphasizing only the formal to neglecting aesthetic issues in favor of social and cultural considerations: the two are intimately entwined. We have traced some connections between formal and cultural motivations in examining the rhetorical patterns that characterize the genre. And we will encounter further connections as we turn to the literary milieux of the Stuart epithalamium.

CHAPTER 3

Systems and Strategies

When I, whom sullein care,
Through discontent of my long fruitlesse stay
In princes court, and expectation vayne
Of idle hopes, which still doe fly away,
Like empty shaddowes, did aflict my brayne,
Walkt forth to ease my payne.

                    Spenser, "Prothalamion"

I

If epithalamia evoke the fantasy of a stable and unified social system, they also participate in a multivalent and multifarious literary system. Or, rather, they participate in a series of interlocking,
overlapping, and sometimes conflicting literary systems. Their authors are involved—and implicated—in the fluctuating policies that
comprise patronage in Stuart England. And epithalamia play a prominent role as well in a different type of system, the diachronic and
synchronic patterns formed by related genres and modes.

Turning our attention to these topics does not, however, entail as
radical a shift from the concerns explored in Chapters 1 and 2 as one
might anticipate: we are changing routes, not destinations. Studying
patronage raises some of the methodological problems involved in
studying views of marriage, as well as similar substantive issues,
such as the means by which power is both expressed and concealed.
Comparing the epithalamium with other literary forms reveals how
wedding poems respond to the anxieties and the joys of marriage;

patronage in turn represents both a source of and a solution to its own set of anxieties.

Some of the relationships between the poetry of marriage and other genres are predictable and familiar; critics have noted, for instance, connections between the epithalamium and love lyrics. Other relationships, such as the link with the epic, are more subtle though no less significant. These subtle links demonstrate the complexities of analyzing a generic system. We need to look beyond the more predictable parallels on semantic and thematic levels: genres may, for example, also be allied because they fulfill the same functions within their culture or because they involve the same speech acts.[1] Thus the epithalamium is connected with the epic in its values, its plot, its global speech act, and so on, whereas it shares with the pastoral mode a curious affinity in its affective functions and in the fantasy behind those functions. Studying the links between genres is complicated in another way: as Alastair Fowler trenchantly asserts, we need to observe the diachronic relationships that literary types assume as well as the synchronic ones.[2] Some of the most intriguing similarities between the epithalamium and other literary forms are specific to Stuart England. Hence I first introduce the more abstract and ahistorical links between the epithalamium and other genres, then play those potentialities against the ways the wedding poem actually functions in the Stuart period.

II

One of the best means of understanding the epithalamium per se, as well as its relationship to other genres, is to compare it to two modal prototypes, epic and pastoral. On one level, the epic and the epithalamium are opposites, countergenres.[3] One celebrates making love, the other making war. Romantic and sexual liaisons may prevent epic heroes from attaining their goals, whereas such liaisons are

[1]On the functions of genres, compare Heather Dubrow, *Genre* (London: Methuen, 1982), pp. 113–116.

[2]Alastair Fowler, *Kinds of Literature: An Introduction to the Theory of Genres and Modes* (Cambridge: Harvard Univ. Press, 1982), esp. pp. 45–52 and chap. 11. Also compare Dan Ben-Amos, "Analytical Categories and Ethnic Genres," *Genre*, 2 (1969), 275–301; he maintains that we should relate folkloric genres to the particular "network of communication" (291) in which they function.

[3]Throughout this section I use the term "epic" to refer to heroic poetry, not the so-called epic epithalamium.

the goal of wedding poems.[4] In addition to these thematic contrasts, differences of scale may distinguish the two forms: epic is capacious,[5] but the epithalamium, like classical comedy, often focuses on events in one place and on one day. Such contrasts are embodied in the texts of Stuart epithalamia and of their predecessors. In the "Prothalamion," for example, after enumerating Somerset's glorious deeds, Edmund Spenser relegates further discussion of them to other poets: "Which some braue muse may sing / To ages following" (159–160). Thomas Campion contrasts the world of his poem with that of armed conflict: "signes of joy and peace / Fill royall Britaines court while cruell warre farre off doth rage, for ever hence exiled" (*The Hayes Masque*, p. 229).

But generic maps risk misrepresenting circular relationships as linear. Seemingly opposite poles like satire and pastoral may sometimes meet; a genre often resembles its countergenre quite as much as it differs from it. In this case, I argue, the similarities between epic and epithalamium are at least as significant as the obvious distinctions.[6] In particular, the lyric epithalamium may be seen as an epic transposed to a minor key, as a miniaturized epic: it compresses epic action into what happens on one day, and it contracts the cast of thousands found in epic poetry into the couple and their celebrants.

Comparing the plot of the epic genre with that of the epithalamium demonstrates some of these connections. Both the lyric epithalamium and epic involve physical journeys, which are paralleled on the narrative level by linear plots; the vast spatial movement of the epic hero finds its analogue in the movement of the wedding procession, as well as in the temporal progression from day to night. Both genres evoke the forces that threaten the goals of that journey: the temptresses encountered by Ulysses are not unlike the allegorized powers against which the authors of wedding poems warn us, and

[4]Epics may, however, culminate in marriages. As Andrew Fichter has pointed out, in many instances the dynastic implications of wedlock are stressed (*Poets Historical: Dynastic Epic in the Renaissance* [New Haven: Yale Univ. Press, 1982]).

[5]For an important treatment of this and related characteristics of epic, see Northrop Frye, *Anatomy of Criticism: Four Essays* (Princeton: Princeton Univ. Press, 1957), esp. pp. 315–326; Thomas Greene, *The Descent from Heaven: A Study in Epic Continuity* (New Haven: Yale Univ. Press, 1963), pp. 9–12.

[6]Frye notes that Spenser's "Epithalamion" has the range of epic poetry but does not acknowledge the links between wedding poetry and the epic tradition as a whole (p. 324).

the bride's tardiness in awakening reminds us of the dangerous delays that can threaten the epic hero. In many instances both genres culminate in a battle, whether literal or, in the case of wedding poetry, metaphorical. And both move towards similar goals: the result of the battle is the foundation of a city or a family line. Often, too, those goals involve a garden—an earthly paradise, an Eden reclaimed.[7] Such similarities are intensified in the instance of what Andrew Fichter terms "dynastic epic," whose principal theme, he argues, is "the rise of *imperium*, the noble house, race, or nation to which the poet professes allegiance."[8]

The epithalamium also involves more subtle transpositions and transmutations of epic elements. Even the apparent spatial and temporal differences that I noted earlier may be interpreted in terms of similarities. The epithalamium frequently encompasses an entire day from dawn to night and moves as well from allusions to birth to references to death; in so doing it mimes epic inclusiveness within its own more narrow scope. In foreseeing a line of heirs the author of an epithalamium recalls the prophetic role of his counterpart in the epic tradition.

The concern for authority that is so prominent in epic—some epic heroes literally carry their fathers around, others do so metaphorically[9]—is echoed in the epithalamium tradition. Thus it is telling that both often begin with invocations, for that form of appeal establishes a paradigmatic instance of the preoccupation with power and authority that shapes both literary types. This preoccupation is manifest as well in their most characteristic speech acts.[10] The global speech acts (that is, the modes of address that characterize and define

---

[7]On the role of gardens in the epic tradition, see A. Bartlett Giamatti, *The Earthly Paradise and the Renaissance Epic* (Princeton: Princeton Univ. Press, 1966). On comparable elements in epithalamia, see the discussions later in this chapter concerning the relationships of that genre to pastoral in general and the country-house poem in particular.

[8]Fichter, p. 1.

[9]A particularly suggestive commentary on this issue may be found in Greene, *The Descent from Heaven*, pp. 91–92.

[10]Cf. Tzvetan Todorov, "The Origin of Genres," *NLH*, 8 (1976), 159–170; he argues that genres derive from speech acts and traces the ways those acts are transformed. An additional transformation could be added to his system: genres sometimes conceal their original speech act, as in the instance of the sonnet, which one might argue derives from the sexual invitation it often obscures.

a work as a whole)[11] in both genres come from the category that
J. L. Austin terms "exercitives" and John R. Searle, refining and
shifting his predecessor's system of classification, calls "directives."[12]
However it is labeled, this category includes orders, requests, pleas,
and warnings—more to our purposes here, it contains illocutionary
acts that, as Austin puts it, involve "the exercising of powers, rights,
or influence."[13] We have already observed the significance of such
speech acts in the epithalamium and will uncover more roles that
they play. In the epic, too, the principal characters are engaged in
receiving orders, whether from Fate or a god or a military commander, and in giving them; the audience is also implicitly subject to
injunctions to uphold particular values, whether they be military, nationalistic, moral, or, as is sometimes the case, an amalgam that
shrewdly obscures the very possibility of separating those three sets
of values.

But perhaps the deepest connection between the two genres relates
to their roles in their societies and their effects on their readers. Both
are deeply concerned with harmonious cultures; indeed, their unified
plots become metaphors for the unified, purposeful communities
that they variously evoke, advocate, and in some instances problematize. The overt nationalism that marks some epics resembles the covert fantasy we find in epithalamia, their dream of a cohesive and
stable social order. Such parallels direct our attention to one of the
deepest and most central links between these two literary types, their
political agendas: both attempt to instill certain cultural values in
their readers (patriotism, marital fidelity, and so forth), and both do
so not only by offering didactic precepts but also by crafting a myth.

[11]For a useful summary of the concept of global speech acts and of other recent
developments in pragmatics, see Joseph A. Porter, "Pragmatics for Criticism," *Poetics*, 15 (1986), 243–257.
[12]J. L. Austin, *How To Do Things with Words*, ed. J. O. Urmson and Marina Sbisà,
2d ed. (Cambridge: Harvard Univ. Press, 1975), pp. 150–163; John R. Searle, "A
Taxonomy of Illocutionary Acts," in *Language, Mind, and Knowledge*, Minnesota
Studies in the Philosophy of Science, vol. 7, ed. Keith Gunderson (Minneapolis:
Univ. of Minnesota Press, 1975), esp. pp. 355–356. The classification of speech acts
is, however, one of the most controversial issues in pragmatics, and many practitioners of that field would not accept the categories proffered by Austin and Searle.
For a different classification, see, e.g., Stephen R. Schiffer, *Meaning* (Oxford: Clarendon Press, 1972), pp. 99, 102–103.
[13]Austin, *How To Do Things with Words*, p. 151.

These and other connections between the two forms are signaled by the occasional presence of epic motifs in the epithalamium tradition and vice versa. Witness, for instance, the neo-Latin poet George Buchanan's allusions to the history of Scotland in his epithalamium.[14] The wedding poems composed for the marriage of Princess Elizabeth and the Elector Palatine emphasize the political and dynastic implications of their union; thus George Wither is unabashed in his anti-Catholic nationalistic fervor:

> Make this *Rhyne* and *Thame* an *Ocean:*
> That it may with might and wonder,
> Whelme the pride of *Tyber* vnder.
>   (sig. C2ᵛ)

And Spenser's great epic reminds us of the significance of marriage within its own genre: weddings are the culmination, realized or anticipated, of many military conflicts, and even the Thames makes an honest woman of the Medway. Though these emphases might be traced in part to Spenser's conflation of epic and romance, marriages assume a significant role even in epics whose genre is not mixed, such as the *Aeneid*.

The connections I have been citing are essentially synchronic. But they assume an especial significance when we locate the epithalamium within the patterns of literary and political history. We teach students in our survey courses that the seventeenth century witnessed the decline of the epic; *The Faerie Queene* could boast many admirers but few immediate successors. Yet this generalization, like so many, needs to be refined. As the Russian formalists have taught us, generic systems are as restlessly metamorphic as Ovidian landscapes.[15] Many of the cultural functions of the epic, I suggest, are assumed in Stuart England by the epithalamium. In particular, wedding poetry takes on

---

[14]On these passages in Buchanan, see Virginia Tufte, *The Poetry of Marriage: The Epithalamium in Europe and Its Development in England,* Univ. of Southern California Studies in Comparative Literature, 2 (Los Angeles: Tinnon-Brown, 1970), p. 93. Her observations on the prominent patriotic elements in the late-seventeenth-century epithalamium are also germane here (pp. 252–253).

[15]Many members of this school have commented intelligently on generic evolution. See, e.g., Boris Eichenbaum, "The Theory of the 'Formal Method,'" in *Russian Formalist Criticism: Four Essays,* ed. and trans. Lee T. Lemon and Marion J. Reis (Lincoln: Univ. of Nebraska Press, 1965), pp. 132–138.

one of the most central political tasks of epic, celebrating the ideal—
and the ideology—of a unified and stable community.[16]

It is telling, however, that these functions are assumed by a genre
that is more delimited: the achievements it commemorates have resonances for the entire culture, but they focus on microcosmic units, a
single couple and a single day. This diminution reflects a pessimism
about the nationalistic ideal that epics uphold, a pessimism motivated, perhaps, by observations and meditations similar to those that
were to discourage John Milton from casting his own epic as a nationalistic Arthuriad. And it is telling, too, that the vision of the
epithalamium is at least somewhat more private than that of the epic,
even though its primary values are, as I have argued, communal and
social. Not the least reason this literary type is popular in the early
seventeenth century, then, is that it fills a void—and fills it in a way
that expresses contemporary values and fears.[17] Once again we find
that the wedding poem, far from being unsuited to the literary and
social climates of seventeenth-century England, is singularly well
adapted to that era.

The complex relationship between the epithalamium and the epic
demonstrates the need to supplement the principal models through
which students of genre customarily structure the relationships between literary forms. Critics are accustomed to recognize two types
of relationships: opposing literary types, variously termed "countergenres," "anti-genres," and so on, or similar types, labeled "twinned
genres" by Claudio Guillén.[18] Students of genre have, to be sure,
mapped subtle gradations in the landscape of each category; most
notably, Fowler has cited linguistic terminology to describe the dif-
fering ways a form may relate to its countergenre.[19] And counter-

---

[16]Susan Crane argues, "Ideologies inform genres more directly than do economic
and social conditions" ("Alison's Incapacity and Poetic Instability in the Wife of
Bath's Tale," *PMLA*, 102 [1987], 20). These categories may, however, sometimes
prove hard to distinguish; we have already observed many instances in which ideologies are in fact interpretations of economic and social conditions.

[17]Compare Fredric Jameson's emphasis on reading genres as ideological constructs
tailored to particular historical occasions (*The Political Unconscious: Narrative as a Socially Symbolic Act* [Ithaca: Cornell Univ. Press, 1981], esp. pp. 136–145).

[18]On countergenres and twinned genres, see Rosalie L. Colie, *Shakespeare's Living
Art* (Princeton: Princeton Univ. Press, 1974), chap. 2; Fowler, *Kinds of Literature*, esp.
pp. 174–178, 251–255; Claudio Guillén, *Literature as System: Essays toward the Theory
of Literary History* (Princeton: Princeton Univ. Press, 1971), chap. 5.

[19]Fowler, *Kinds of Literature*, p. 252.

genres, like foil characters, resemble their opposite number enough to highlight the differences, whereas twinned genres are obviously separated by some distinctions.

But such paradigms, however subtly constructed, still assume that the relationship between two forms can be readily categorized as one primarily of similarity or of difference. In certain intriguing cases, however, the similarities and differences balance each other or, alternatively, in some cultures the similarities may outweigh the differences whereas other cultures will shift the balance.[20] Thus it is misleading to describe the epithalamium and epic either as genre and countergenre or as twinned genres: they fit both categories and hence in a sense fit neither. Similarly, to label pastoral and science fiction either as opposites or as twins would be to indulge in an arbitrary privileging of some characteristics over others. These forms share a concern with juxtaposing the values of two worlds; yet they differ in several key respects, such as the fact that one locates its utopia or distopia in the past and the other looks towards the future.

To accommodate such cases, we should add another type of classification, "mirror genres," to our lexicon. Mirror genres, like mirror images, are at once similar and yet opposed. And they, like the form of figure skating known as mirror skating, move in opposite directions and yet in so doing precisely reflect each other's patterns. Thus romance and science fiction share strikingly similar quests; yet here, as in the related instance of pastoral and science fiction, one literary type is backward-looking and the other futuristic. Rosalie L. Colie's seminal observations on the relationship of sonnet and epigram prepare us to understand mirror genres;[21] I am in effect arguing that those two forms represent not a sport but rather one instance of a broader pattern. And, as Colie's work suggests, one fruitful way of plotting the generic map of a particular culture or a particular writer is observing whether the similarities between mirror genres are stressed more than the differences.

Epithalamia, like epics, speak in optatives; but the pluperfects of the pastoral tradition are also included in their grammars. Indeed, pastoral elements, particularly the tendency towards the regressive

---

[20]Compare Colie's suggestion that the sonnet and epigram are sometimes seen as twins and sometimes as antithetical forms (pp. 95–96); Fowler also notes that closely related genres can turn into antigenres (*Kinds of Literature*, pp. 251–252).

[21]Colie, *Shakespeare's Living Art*, chap. 2.

and nostalgic that we so often encounter in the mode, are prominent throughout the epithalamium tradition. Catullus 61 refers to a pastoral landscape in its evocation of Hymen. Jacques Grévin casts a wedding poem as a pastoral dialogue, and both of Spenser's contributions to the genre are located in "the realm . . . of Flora, and old Pan." Such literal allusions to pastoral are funded by a deeper connection: as I suggested earlier, wedding poems typically negotiate connections between the raw and the cooked, the natural and the civilized worlds.

Other links between the two literary types involve their shared values and fantasies. We have already identified nostalgic and idyllic elements in the epithalamium: like pastoral, the epithalamium is impelled by the search for a vanished ideal.[22] The rebirth of Elizabeth, or even the return of the refrain, signals an impulse that is closely allied to the pastoral drive to recover the past. In Christian wedding poems that drive is fueled by theological principles that had become commonplaces: as James Grantham Turner has demonstrated in his exhaustive study of Renaissance attitudes towards marriage, Christian writers routinely associate the institution with a return to Eden.[23] Instituted in paradise, wedlock offers fallen man an opportunity to recover at least a moiety of paradisaical happiness. Thus the marriage ceremony in the Book of Common Prayer, like its Catholic antecedents, reminds listeners of the origins of wedlock; the priest is directed to say, "Almighty God, which at the beginning did create our first parents Adam and Eve, and did sanctify and join them together in marriage."[24] We will return to these Edenic elements from another direction when we examine the relationship between the epithalamium and one particular form of pastoral, the country-house poem.

The connection between marriage and pastoral paradises, and between the genres that celebrate them, carries with it an agenda that is political in several senses.[25] Obviously, by stressing that God insti-

---

[22]On the role of that search in Renaissance literature, see Harry Levin, *The Myth of the Golden Age in the Renaissance* (Bloomington: Indiana Univ. Press, 1969).

[23]James Grantham Turner, *One Flesh: Paradisal Marriage and Sexual Relations in the Age of Milton* (Oxford: Clarendon Press, 1987), esp. Introduction.

[24]*The Book of Common Prayer 1559: The Elizabethan Prayer Book*, ed. John E. Booty (Charlottesville: Univ. Press of Virginia, 1976), p. 297.

[25]Louis Adrian Montrose finds different but not incompatible political agendas in pastoral; in particular, he argues that it obscures the actual conditions of patronage ("Gifts and Reasons: The Contexts of Peele's *Araygnement of Paris*," *ELH*, 47 [1980], 433–461; " 'Eliza, Queene of Shepheardes,' and the Pastoral of Power," *ELR*, 10

tuted marriage in Eden, Renaissance writers justify and promote it; indeed, such statements are typically marshaled to rebut the Catholic denigration of marriage. But a similar function is served by any allusions that associate the institution with the natural world, whether or not a Christian Eden is involved: such references imply that wedlock is not a social construct but rather a natural phenomenon. The cultural imperative to marry (rather than, say, to fornicate or participate in a homosexual relationship or become a celibate priest) is mystified. It is not arbitrary but virtually inevitable; it is the dictate not of a particular culture and its potentially fallible or self-serving leaders but of nature itself.[26]

The relationship between pastoral and the Stuart epithalamium exemplifies and complicates these more general and ahistorical connections between the two forms. Stuart wedding lyrics often evoke the beauties of the countryside; even John Donne, a great frequenter of theaters but not, one assumes, of crystalline brooks, bodies forth a group of birds in the wedding poem he composed for the marriage of Princess Elizabeth and the Elector Palatine. Anxieties about the workings of marriage made poets especially eager to naturalize wedlock.

Yet the presence of these pastoral elements in the Stuart tradition makes the absence of others especially striking. Unlike Grévin's epithalamium, only a handful of these wedding poems are pastoral dialogues between shepherds; and, though many laud the beauty of the landscape, few are set entirely in a pastoral milieu. A number of Stuart epithalamia instead satisfy indirectly one of the main impulses behind evocations of the pastoral milieu, the drive to recover a lost paradise: they deflect such a drive onto the allusions to Queen Elizabeth examined in Chapter 2. The primary reason Stuart epithalamia seldom include shepherds and the other accouterments of full-fledged pastoral poetry, however, is that their authors are more interested than many of their predecessors in creating a speaker who can credibly command the courtly participants in the wedding. Even an apparent exception proves this rule. Though Wither's speaker

---

[1980], 153–182). This chapter maintains that while epithalamia sometimes obscure those conditions, they also work out strategies for acknowledging and surmounting them.

[26]For a different but compatible argument about the naturalization of marriage, see Marilyn L. Williamson, *The Patriarchy of Shakespeare's Comedies* (Detroit: Wayne State Univ. Press, 1986), esp. chap. 3.

identified himself as a shepherd and addresses his colleagues in that profession, these references surprise us when they occur, since we encounter little evidence in the poem as a whole that he is a shepherd.

The epithalamium interacts not only with modal forms such as pastoral but also with a whole range of genres. The most obvious connections involve other forms of love poetry. Thomas P. Roche, Jr. and Carol V. Kaske have shown us that the juxtaposition of the *Amoretti* and the "Epithalamion" within a single volume reflects a juxtaposition on the level of the imagination: the genre of the wedding poem and the values it embodies offer solutions to the problems expressed through and represented by the sonnet.[27] Spenser's seventeenth-century successors explore such connections as well. Sir John Beaumont, for example, distinguishes the wedding about which he is writing and the genre in which he is doing so from other forms of love and of love poetry:

> Seuere and serious Muse
> Whose quill, the name of loue declines,
> Be not too nice, nor this deare worke refuse,
> Here *Venus* stirs no flame, nor *Cupid* guides thy lines,
> But modest *Hymen* shakes his Torch, and chast *Lucina* shines.
> ("An Epithalamium to my Lord Marquesse of Buckingham,
> and to his faire and vertuous Lady," 1–5)

And in a line we examined earlier, he boasts, "*Leander* here no dang'rous iourney takes" ("An Epithalamium vpon the happy marriage of our Soueraigne Lord King Charles, and our gracious Lady Queene Mary," 7). Given the popularity of Christopher Marlowe's epyllion, this line seems to allude not only to the myth of Hero and Leander but also to the genre that treats it, the epyllion. Hence Beaumont implicitly contrasts the perilous loves recorded in those Ovidian mythological narratives with the chaster and safer emotions celebrated in epithalamia.

These passages from Beaumont are typical of their genre in their effects: by referring so often to such forms as the sonnet and the epyllion, epithalamia remind us that the kind of love they commemorate is more stable than that evoked in other forms of love poetry.

[27]Carol V. Kaske, "Spenser's *Amoretti* and *Epithalamion* of 1595: Structure, Genre, and Numerology," *ELR*, 8 (1978), 271–295; Thomas P. Roche, Jr., "Shakespeare and the Sonnet Sequences," in *English Poetry and Prose, 1540–1674*, ed. Christopher Ricks (London: Barrie and Jenkins, 1970), pp. 105–106.

Once again, however, a recurrent generic characteristic assumes special functions in a particular period, in this instance Jacobean England. On one level, I suggest, the genres of love poetry that are being condemned metaphorically represent the *liaisons dangereuses* so prevalent in the Jacobean court; here, as in their references to blustery storms and allegorized forces like Jealousy, poets are contriving a way of criticizing that milieu. They are, however, apparently criticizing not only the lovers who participate in such relationships but also the writers who dignify those lovers in their poems: composing epithalamia, their authors seem to be hinting, is a more responsible pursuit.

We are hardly surprised when Stuart epithalamia refer to other forms of love poetry; but we may be more puzzled to discover how often funeral bak'd meats do furnish forth the marriage tables. We uncover allusions to death elsewhere in the tradition, as in the martial passages in classical wedding poems or Spenser's own injunction that the muses sing no more of death, but the subject recurs with unusual frequency in Stuart epithalamia. Sometimes the Stuart poems evoke death only to banish it, isolating it to exclude it from the wedding festivities. The poems written for the marriage of the Princess Elizabeth and the Elector Palatine are studded with such allusions, although they do appear in epithalamia composed for other occasions as well. George Chapman opens and closes "A Hymn to Hymen" with the observation that "Bright Hymen's torches drunk up Parcae's tears" (2, 84), and in the first of his "Nuptiall Hymnes" Henry Peacham declares, "Heauen, the first, hath throwne away / Her weary weede of mourning hew" (5–6). The frequency of such references in poems written for this occasion is not, of course, surprising. Princess Elizabeth's wedding took place shortly after the death of her brother, the beloved Prince Henry, so members of the Jacobean court witnessed an enactment of the generic convention of replacing elegy with epithalamium, mourning with panegyric. Life imitated art.

Death intrudes into the Stuart epithalamium in several other forms. Some poets portray the loss of virginity as a type of demise. Richard Crashaw's "Epithalamion" provides the most extreme instances, but they are not unique. In an extraordinary passage to which we will return in Chapter 5, Robert Herrick commands, "lye / Drown'd in the bloud of Rubies there, not die" ("A Nuptiall Verse to Mistresse Elizabeth Lee, now Lady Tracie," 15–16). And in observing that "a Great Princess falls, but doth not die" ("An Epithalamion, or Mariage Song on the Lady Elizabeth, and Count Palatine," 38), Donne manages his customary trick of having it both ways: he denies the bride's death while at the same time introducing its possibility. Students of the genre have noted that its works often culminate in a reference to heirs; it is equally common towards the end of the poem, however, to allude to the death of the couple. Poets typically express the hope that the bride and groom will die at the same time: "Live in the Love of Doves, and having told / The Ravens yeares, go hence more Ripe then old" (Herrick, "Connubii Flores," 62–63).

References to death are not confined to these categories: other allusions are scattered throughout Stuart epithalamia. Thus Henry Goodyer's wedding poem shows him to be as preoccupied with death as his friend John Donne; he writes,

> and as a well taught soule
> Calls not for death, nor doth controwle
> Death when hee comes.
>
> (46–48)

And in the epithalamium within *Hymenaei*, Ben Jonson refers overtly to a fear that must have haunted many other authors in his genre: "Informe the gentle wombe; / Nor, let it proue a tombe" (543–544).

How can we explain all these allusions to death in the Stuart epithalamium? To begin with, genre theory suggests some fundamental affinities between the epithalamium and the funeral elegy. Celeste Schenck has drawn our attention to the odd amalgam of similarities and differences that characterizes the relationship of the two forms. She points out that these two literary types share central similarities; in particular, both are ceremonial and epideictic.[28] These similarities cast their obvious differences into relief: one concerns life and birth and the other death, one focuses on beginnings and the other on endings, and so on.

Traditional psychoanalytic theory provides a further explanation: the connection between death and sex, so memorably and so frequently expressed in Renaissance wordplay on "die." And, as I suggested in Chapter 2, the authors of epithalamia are preoccupied with

[28]Celeste Marguerite Schenck, *Mourning and Panegyric: The Poetics of Pastoral Ceremony* (University Park: Pennsylvania State Univ. Press, 1988), esp. Introduction.

death because it so deeply threatens the occasion and the values they are celebrating. The bride might produce stillborn children and die herself in the process. The very hopes that epithalamia express might themselves be stillborn. It is no accident that the marriage ceremony in the Book of Common Prayer juxtaposes a reference to heirs with the hope that the couple will enjoy long lives: "We beseech thee assist with thy blessing these two persons, that they may both be fruitful in procreation of children, and also live together so long in godly love and honesty, that they may see their children's children."[29] Pregnancy itself was a liminal state in Elizabethan and Stuart England: the potentialities for life and death, rejoicing and grieving, were inextricably connected.

Death and the genre that memorializes it function in the epithalamium, then, in much the same way as the other anxieties and threats we have analyzed. The authors of wedding poems attempt to tame and control this danger: they refer to the Parcae's tears only to emphasize that the funeral torches have dried them, and they allude to the deaths of the bride and groom only to express the hope that they will occur at some far distant time. Once again, they use negative constructions in order safely to acknowledge the forbidden, in order to say and unsay at the same time. But once again, too, such strategies are not completely successful: the frequency of the references testifies to fears that are not wholly quieted by their expression. And those references are likely to stir, not merely soothe, anxieties about untimely deaths in their readers as well.

All of these explanations could apply to other cultures: they do not tell us why Stuart poets "saw the skull beneath the skin" more frequently than most of their classical and Elizabethan counterparts did. Some of the passages in question reflect general predilections of their authors as much as or more than responses to the epithalamium itself; Donne, for instance, could contrive to allude to death in writing a laundry list. And such allusions may be traced to cultural as well as more idiosyncratic and personal preoccupations: our customary generalizations about the fascination with death in Jacobean England are surely germane to seventeenth-century epithalamia. Further answers, I suggest, lie in the workings of anxiety: the specific tensions and doubts connected with marriage create in some poets the generalized sense of foreboding, of impending doom, that is sometimes termed

[29]Booty, p. 296.

"free-floating anxiety"; this unease is then localized in fears about the worst catastrophe that could befall the couple. The poets proceed variously to express that fear through intrusive references to the possibility of death or to exorcise it by alluding to the long lives and simultaneous deaths that will be granted to the couple.

Recognizing the links that customarily connect the epithalamium and the elegy allows us to approach Crashaw's curious "Epithalamium." One can readily understand why some critics have labeled this poem an anti-epithalamium.[30] It mourns the death of the bride's maidenhead as much as it celebrates the birth of a new union and the potential birth of heirs. It reverses wedding imagery; funeral tapers usurp the place of wedding torches. And the voice recording these reversals and upheavals is ambivalent and uneasily suggestive:

> A froward flower, whose peevish pride
> within it selfe, it selfe did hide,
> flying all fingers, and euen thinking much
>   of its owne touch
>
> This bird indeed the phaenix was
>   late chaced by loues revengefull arrowes,
> whose warres now left the wonted passe
>   and spared the litle liues of sparrowes.
>
>   (21–28)

The first four lines are reminiscent of Shakespeare's procreation poems not only in their overt critique of selfishness but also in their covert hints about masturbation; yet the allusion to the unique and majestic phoenix invests virginity with a kind of grandeur.

No reader of such lines could attempt to argue that Crashaw's poem is a run-of-the-mill epithalamium. But neither is it simply a sport, as the few critics who have analyzed it have suggested. Rather, Crashaw is exaggerating elements present in many other Stuart wedding poems: Herrick himself mourns the death of a maidenhead, Goodyer packs allusions to death into apparently unlikely sections of his poem, and so on. Indeed, we have already seen just how often ambivalences about sexuality characterize the Stuart literature of

[30]See Schenck, chap. 4. A brief discussion of the poem may also be found in Mary Ellen Rickey, *Rhyme and Meaning in Richard Crashaw* (1961; rpt. New York: Haskell House, 1973), pp. 30–31; she notes that Crashaw moves from burlesquing the genre to writing a more conventional epithalamium.

marriage. Moreover, the plot of Crashaw's lyric moves from mourning the maidenhead to celebrating the marriage; in other words, he controls and subdues the elegaic, the very process enacted in so many other wedding poems.

Recognizing these connections between Crashaw's wedding poem and those of his contemporaries encourages us to refine the concept of the anti-epithalamium. To the extent that it implies a radical and systematic rejection of the norms of the epithalamium, the category needs to be discarded: as Crashaw's poem demonstrates, the apparently discordant elements in the so-called anti-epithalamium, such as references to death, are themselves norms that appear even in "straight" versions of the genre.[31] We could, however, usefully affix the label "anti-epithalamium" to this and other works such as Donne's "Epithalamium made at Lincolnes Inne" and Sir John Suckling's parodic "A Ballade. Upon a Wedding" if we redefine it, acknowledging that such lyrics are unusual not because they introduce foreign elements into their genre but rather because they radically shift the balance between familiar ones; in particular, they emphasize the types of discord that more conventional wedding poems attempt to subdue and suppress. Once again an apparently discordant tendency in the seventeenth-century epithalamium represents not a simple decline from or a misunderstanding of the tradition but rather a reinterpretation and redirection of it.

The epithalamium and masque are related in some obvious ways: both flourish in Renaissance England, and many court masques are written for weddings and embed epithalamia within their texts. The process of generic embedding, however, often reflects a deeper affinity (witness, for example, Colie's analysis of the epigrammatic elements within the sonnet), and this instance is no exception. Both forms extol order and hierarchy.[32] That order is exemplified by the wedding procession in the epithalamium and by an analogous

[31]A few classical works do include more straightforward reversals of elements from the epithalamium tradition; these are not, however, wedding poems in their own right but rather works in other genres that describe weddings. For an analysis of these passages, see Tufte, The Poetry of Marriage, chap. 3.

[32]On this aspect of the masque tradition, see Jonathan Goldberg, James I and the Politics of Literature: Jonson, Shakespeare, Donne, and Their Contemporaries (Baltimore: Johns Hopkins Univ. Press, 1983), esp. pp. 122–141; John C. Meagher, Method and Meaning in Jonson's Masques (Notre Dame: Univ. of Notre Dame Press, 1966), chap. 8; Stephen Orgel, The Jonsonian Masque (Cambridge: Harvard Univ. Press, 1965), esp. p. 35.

element in the masque, the dance on which it concludes. Like the masque, the epithalamium is often a tribute not only to the particular couple but also to the courtly culture. The epithalamium celebrates the putative fertility of the couple; the masque, as Jonathan Goldberg has persuasively argued, celebrates the metaphorical generativity of the monarch.[33]

These similarities in values and themes are matched by structural parallels: the antimasque that interrupts the masque functions very like the dangers that threaten to interrupt the ideal world established by the epithalamium.[34] In at least one instance this parallel becomes even closer: the antimasque in Beaumont's "Masque of the Inner Temple and Gray's Inn," written to celebrate the marriage of Princess Elizabeth and the Elector Palatine, numbers among its participants two baboons. The contemporary fascination with exotic creatures of all sorts helps explains their presence, but it is significant as well that apes are often associated with uncontrolled sexuality.[35] In other words, epithalamia typically acknowledge and then attempt to control the anarchic power of desire, and a similar process is enacted through the presence and subsequent suppression of these simian masquers. And often in both genres these threats represent a licensed and regulated form of anarchy that is not really anarchy at all: the authors of epithalamia use their negatives to control the very dangers they are acknowledging, and the authors of masques admit the antimasque in the knowledge that it will be succeeded by the restoration of order. These processes help explain the appeal of the masque in Tudor and Stuart England, as well as the vogue the epithalamium enjoyed in the latter period: both genres write narratives in which disorderly and irregular forces may be successfully ordered and regulated and thus provide reassuring models for readers troubled by the threat of unrest in other spheres, particularly church and state.

The epithalamium and the masque also resemble each other in the roles in which they cast their spectators. In both the external audience views a spectacle while at the same time identifying with its participants. Thus the role of the audience gestures towards yet another similarity: the reflexive, self-conscious mode that characterizes

[33]Goldberg, pp. 60–61.
[34]Compare Goldberg, pp. 122–141.
[35]See H. W. Janson, *Apes and Ape Lore in the Middle Ages and Renaissance* (London: Warburg Institute, 1952), chap. 9.

these literary forms. Both participate in a process that might be termed metamimesis: they call forth a world that mirrors the world viewing them, then draw attention to the artistic acts involved in that calling forth. Wedding poems may also become reflexive by incorporating another wedding poem; the song of the nymphs in Spenser's "Prothalamion" exemplifies this sort of structure, and we find versions of it in the interwoven and embedded narratives of the epic epithalamium.

The most intimate generic relationship that wedding poetry enjoys, however, is also the most neglected. In a few ways the epithalamium differs from the country-house poem; in particular, the linear and temporal narrative that characterizes the former finds no counterpart in the more meditative structure of the latter. In most respects, however, the two genres are extraordinarily close: their relationship is not that of genre and countergenre or even of mirror genres but rather the clearest instance of twinning that Stuart literature offers.

The most significant gene these twins have in common is their drive to recover a lost Edenic world. In the epithalamium the recuperated world is associated with the events of a single day, the occasion of the wedding, whereas in the country-house poem that world is delimited not temporally but spatially: the country house in question is contrasted with others. But this difference is minor—far more important is the social conservatism that links the two genres and emerges most clearly in their vision, at once nostalgic and recuperative, of the lost Eden.

In the epithalamium tradition, this recuperative impulse assumes a range of forms. Most obviously, Stuart poets sometimes construct marriage as the recovery of Eden itself. Thus Augustine Taylor writes, "be thy chosen prize / A faire terrestriall happy Paradize" (sig. C) This motif may be found in both earlier and later wedding poems. When Sir Philip Sidney evokes his own terrestrial happy paradise in the epithalamium in the Third Eclogues of the *Arcadia*, he refers to Eden indirectly: in banishing "vile jealousie" (82), he commands, "Goe snake hide thee in dust" (86). And some four centuries later Edith Sitwell compares the wedding she is celebrating to "the young world before the Fall of Man" ("Prothalamium," 11).[36] I suggest, however, that the readers of Renaissance wedding poems

[36]The citation is to *High Wedlock Then Be Honored: Wedding Poems from Nineteen Countries and Twenty-five Centuries*, ed. Virginia Tufte (New York: Viking, 1970).

responded more intensely to such allusions than Sitwell's contemporaries did, and that Stuart readers were perhaps even more responsive than Elizabethan ones. A Renaissance audience may well have seen in the antiquity of marriage a compensation for and displacement of its potency as a sacrament. And antiquity implies a stability that would render the institution attractive in any culture, but especially so in Stuart England, where ignorant armies were clashing by night.

But epithalamia may refer to the recovery of a lost idyllic world without confining its resonances to the Christian paradise. Sir John Beaumont's poem on the marriage of King Charles and Queen Mary includes two such instances. Like so many Renaissance writers, he relies on the myth of the golden age to suggest the restoration of past glory: the birth of heirs, he announces, "shal change our Ir'n to Siluer, Brasse to Gold" (57). Even more telling is his evocation of a landscape that seems to merge Eden with pagan paradises:

> The Trees with fruite, with Flowres our Gardens fill'd,
> Sweete honey from the leaues distill'd,
> For now *Astreas* raigne appeares to be a Tipe of this.
>
> (52–54)

The reference to Astraea suggests both the return of a glorious past and its surpassing in a still more glorious future. The association of Queen Elizabeth with Astraea is surely germane here, and it reminds us that references to James's predecessor in Stuart wedding poems themselves participate in the nostalgic and recuperative mode that characterizes the tradition. Moreover, in referring to and repeating what has come before, the refrain enacts this preoccupation.

Individual poets also craft idiosyncratic ways of announcing a recuperation. The French tradition offers a particularly marked precedent to Stuart poems: in his "Ballade" Eustache Deschamps tells us that just as Eve caused the fall and another woman repaired it, so a woman caused the division between France and England and another woman is going to repair it. Thus his emphasis on the past builds a vision of a still more glorious future. Similarly, Donne alludes to one of his favorite pets, the phoenix, in his poem on the wedding of the Elector Palatine and Princess Elizabeth, declaring, "And by this act of these two Phenixes / Nature againe restored is" (99–100). His friend Goodyer, as we have already observed, shifts his refrains from statements like "This night for wch this Moneth doth gyve awaye twoe dayes" (11) to "This night wch to this Moneth, doth recompence twoe dayes" (33).

As the example of Deschamps reminds us, nostalgia and recuperation do not definitively distinguish the epithalamia of any period or country from their counterparts: we can find versions of these motifs in a wide range of poems. They appear more frequently, however, in certain instances of the tradition. The connection between marriage and Eden encouraged Christian poets to associate wedlock with loss and recovery more than most of their pagan counterparts did. And, though the Tudor tradition includes too few poems for a thorough comparison, it is fair to say that that association appears to be particularly common in Stuart wedding poems. Witness, for example, the repeated references to the reincarnation of Elizabeth in the person of her niece. This emphasis is hardly surprising. If wedlock is indeed a microcosm of church and state, the perception of discord in those two arenas would naturally lead to treating marriage as a symbol of the restored peace that seemed even more precious—and even more difficult to achieve—in the political and religious arenas.

The country-house poem deploys similar tropes to develop a similarly conservative social and political vision. Poems in this genre typically associate the houses they are celebrating with Edenic order and harmony.[37] In lieu of postlapsarian scarcities, we encounter overflowing orchards and "carps, that runne into thy net" (Jonson, "To Penshurst," 33). Postlapsarian strife and divisiveness are also absent: the farmers love their landlord, the fish even love those who devour them. And country-house poems, like epithalamia, do not confine their paradises to explicitly Christian models. In "A Panegyrick to Sir Lewis Pemberton" Herrick refers to "the old Race of mankind" (38). And when he boasts in "A Country life: To his Brother, M. Tho: Herrick" that "thy wife, by chast intentions led / Gives thee each night a Maidenhead" (41–42), he is invoking paradisaical purity and rebirth in the form of sexual innocence (and demonstrating that a concern with female chastity is yet another link between the two genres).

The Edenic ideals and idylls described in both genres are based on common values. In both instances, man and nature achieve an ex-

---

[37]Many critics have commented on this aspect of the genre. See, e.g., Heather Dubrow, "The Country-House Poem: A Study in Generic Development," *Genre,* 12 (1979), esp. 162–163, 170; McClung, chap. 1.

traordinary harmony. That harmony also characterizes the relationships among the human denizens of the paradisaical communities being evoked. Country-house poems are not consistent, however, in how they achieve this vision. In "To Sir Robert Wroth" Jonson evokes a golden age that, like its prototype, apparently does away with social distinctions: "Freedome doth with degree dispense" (58). More often, though, the peacefulness of country-house poems is rooted not in a return to a classless society but rather in a joyous acceptance of social distinctions; the socioeconomic conflicts that characterized Stuart England are not the least of the tensions that are mystified and apparently resolved.[38] Thus in "To my friend G.N. from Wrest" Thomas Carew assures us that "Some of that ranke, spun of a finer thred / Are with the Women, Steward, and Chaplaine fed / With daintier cates" (37–39). And in "To Penshurst" servants treat others well because they themselves are treated well; nonetheless, they know their place: "He knowes, *below*, he shall finde plentie of meate" (70; italics added). The dining arrangements in these two lyrics synecdochally represent other social arrangements. Similarly, in the epithalamium all members of the community fulfill the roles associated with their stations; indeed, we saw that Michael Drayton's epithalamium is based on questions about who will perform various responsibilities ("By whom must *Tita* married be" [171], and so on). These questions are imperative in several senses, as the repetition of "must" reminds us.

In both genres, too, the ideal of social unity is represented through plots of unification. In the epithalamium, all members of the community typically join in a procession as well as in the standard comedic symbol of harmony, a feast. Similarly, country-house poems portray disparate and potentially antagonistic members of the culture coming together literally just as they come together in their ideals and values: the happy farmers troop to present tributes, the king visits Penshurst, and so forth.[39]

Moreover, the epithalamium and the country-house poem share the pastoral predilection for a dialogic contrast between two opposing spheres. Both genres play their paradisaical world against less

[38]Raymond Williams is among the critics who find a mystification of actual social relationships in the country-house poem (*The Country and the City* [London: Chatto and Windus, 1973], chap. 3).

[39]On the way country-house poems emphasize voluntary participation in the life of the community, compare McClung, pp. 118–122.

happy Edens, whether they be the marriages in which jealousy, early
death, and so on do conquer the couple, or the houses that are "built
to enuious show" ("To Penshurst," 1), or the unhappiness of the
court itself. Thus in Carew's "To Saxham" we learn that less fortunate neighboring houses lack adequate food, much as epithalamia
suggest that less fortunate marriages lack the serenity and good luck
associated with the match at hand. Each of these literary forms may
also adduce such contrasts by alluding to other genres. Just as certain
epithalamia juxtapose their own pacific visions with the martial values of epic, so Carew ends "To my friend G.N. from Wrest,"

> Thus I enjoy my selfe, and taste the fruit
> Of this blest Peace, whilst toyl'd in the pursuit
> Of Bucks, and Stags th'embleme of warre, you strive
> To keepe the memory of our Armes alive.
>   (107–110)

Often the contrasts that characterize both genres involve the use of
the rhetorical device known as the negative formula.[40] We have already observed that in the epithalamium the motif of averting dangers is rooted in this type of construction, and it appears with equal
frequency in the country-house poem. Imitating the opening of "To
Penshurst," Carew boasts,

> here the Architect
> Did not with curious skill a Pile erect
> Of carved Marble, Touch, or Porpherie.
> ("To my friend G.N. from Wrest," 21–23)

Similarly, Herrick precedes the passage on chastity quoted earlier
with the assurance, "Nor has the darknesse power to usher in / Feare
to those sheets, that know no sin" (39–40), lines that may well remind us of the ways the authors of epithalamia deploy the negative
formula as they try to banish their own types of darkness, literal and
metaphoric.

[40]For a valuable general discussion of this trope and of its functions in a range of
literary types, see Howard Rollin Patch, The Other World According to Descriptions in
Medieval Literature (Cambridge: Harvard Univ. Press, 1950), esp. pp. 12–13. Kitty W.
Scoular observes the use of negatives in poems in praise of the country (Natural Magic
[Oxford: Oxford Univ. Press, 1965], pp. 165–166), and Harry Levin relates this rhe-
torical formula to conceptions of the golden age (p. 97).

Both epithalamia and country-house poems delight in tropes playing "outside" against "inside," and in both genres the contrasts assume two forms.[41] First, the outside represents the forces that must
be kept at bay to allow the paradisaical ideal to flourish. When writing in each of these genres, Carew deploys the weather to represent
such forces. Thus he opens "To Saxham" by informing us that
though the weather outside is bad, all is cosy within. Similarly,
when he turns to the epithalamium he assures us, "The cheerefull
Bridegroome to the clouds and wind / Hath all his teares, and all his
sighes assign'd" ("On the Mariage of T.K. and C.C. the morning
stormie," 11–12), a passage that, like so many others in its genre,
acknowledges the existence of tears and sighs at the very moment of
declaring them irrelevant.

But the forces symbolizing outside and inside interact in a second
way as well. Sometimes the outside, whether represented by potentially anarchic natural phenomena or by potentially disruptive individuals, is welcomed within, though in tamed and civilized form.
We find a version of this pattern in "To Penshurst": "all come in, the
farmer, and the clowne" (48). Similarly, in "To Sir Robert Wroth"
Jonson writes, "The rout of rurall folke come thronging in" (53).
And we have observed that epithalamia repeatedly subdue and then
incorporate potential threats to the wedding, such as the bride's sexuality or death.

But in both genres a more significant outsider, or rather potential
outsider, is welcomed within: the poet himself. In one instance he
dines at the lord's table, in the other he directs the lord's wedding; in
both cases, he insists on his presence at an event from which he
might well be excluded in the normal course of events. In the
country-house poem as in the epithalamium, the poet asserts control
and autonomy despite—and because of—the fact that he is often of a
class lower than that of the people to whom his lyric is directed. This
assertion is central to the workings of the epithalamium.

All of these parallels between the two genres indicate it is no accident that they both flourish in the first half of the seventeenth century. If the epithalamium assumes some functions formerly filled by
the epic, it shares other cultural and political work with the country-
house poem. Each form evokes an alternative to the mounting ten-

[41]On the relationship of "inside" and "outside" in the country-house tradition,
compare Rosalie L. Colie, *"My Ecchoing Song": Andrew Marvell's Poetry of Criticism*
(Princeton: Princeton Univ. Press, 1970), Pt. 3, chaps. 3 and 4.

sions in their period. Each speaks to—and helps create—the growing need for an ideal and idealized vision.[42] Each grounds that vision in a myth of a conservative and unified community. In lieu of the socio-economic and religious problems of Stuart England, the country-house poem and the epithalamium enshrine their irenic and Edenic fantasies.

III

In the opening of his epithalamium on the wedding of the earl of Somerset and Frances Howard, Ben Jonson numbers himself among the "true freindes, / That bid, God giue thee ioy, and haue no endes" (5–6). But Jonson did in fact "haue . . . endes": his poem, like the vast majority of Stuart epithalamia, is a bid not only for joy but also for patronage. Most of the lyrics on which this book focuses signal both the culmination of the groom's courtship of his bride and the continuation of the poet's courtship of his patron. Many students of that second mode of wooing have concentrated on masques, but in fact the epithalamium tradition can reveal as much, if not more, about the workings of patronage. In particular, studying the poems produced for the Somerset-Howard wedding and for that of Princess Elizabeth and the Elector Palatine allows us to examine how different poets respond to the same occasion; the lyrics composed for the Somerset-Howard union demonstrate as well the ways poets react to the pressures of praising an event that might seem a fitter occasion for satire.

At first glance, however, the main generalization these groups of poems yield is simply that they resist generalization because their responses to patronage are so varied. For instance, the model of the masque might lead one to predict that the wedding of the king's daughter would inspire unqualified flattery not only of the bride but also of the monarch himself and the entire culture he symbolized. Yet the many poets who celebrate this marriage differ strikingly in the target of their compliments. Thomas Heywood does in fact cram nationalistic and even jingoistic compliments to the Crown and state into his poem:

[42]Romance also filled this role in Tudor and Stuart England. On this and related functions of the genre, see, e.g., Frye, pp. 186–206; Jameson, pp. 110–119; Patricia A. Parker, *Inescapable Romance: Studies in the Poetics of a Mode* (Princeton: Princeton Univ. Press, 1979), esp. Introduction.

May the Branches spread so far,
Famous both in peace and war,
That the Roman eagle may
Be Instated some blest day.
        Despite of Romes proud brags,
        Within our English flags.

                                    (sig. E2)

Wither also celebrates the nationalistic implications of the event.
Goodyer, however, devotes most of his attention to the mysteries of
the occasion rather than the glories of any of its participants ("O
most misterious night" [23], and so forth), whereas Donne acknowledges only in passing that the bride is a princess.

Moreover, the tones of these compliments differ significantly: the
bestowing of praise variously seems a solemn, almost religious ritual
and a light-hearted game. Thus Goodyer invests his observations
with gravity and stateliness:

        Which of you Muses please
    To shew your cunninge soe, as to teache mee
        To devide Loue from Maiestie,
    Where they doe make one bodie, as in these.

                                    (1–4)

On the other hand, Wither's jingly rhythms sometimes deflate the
potential solemnity of his commentary on the court and its achievements, making his tone seem playful and even avuncular rather than
awed and respectful:

        Oh you sleep too long, awake yee,
        See how *Time* doth ouertake yee:

                . . . . .

        Worthies, your affaires forbeare yee,
        For the *State* a while may spare yee.

                                    (sigs. C1, C3)

Moreover, Donne's lyric, like some of the others written for this
wedding, is not wholly adulatory.[43] He peppers his compliments

_____

[43]In "Poets and Patrons: Literary Adulation in the Epithalamium of the Spanish
Golden Age" (*South Atlantic Review,* 53 [1988], 32–33), Thomas Deveny notes that
two Spanish epithalamia include social criticism as well as praise.

with wry observations about the couple; in particular, like so many other poets in the genre, he is concerned with delays:

> And why doe you two walke,
> So slowly pac'd in this procession?
> Is all your care but to be look'd upon,
> And be to others spectacle, and talke?
>   (61–64)

The tone is playful enough, the sentiments conventional enough to avoid real offense; but in a court that delighted so much in processions and spectacles, the monitory message is clear.

The group of poems that Henry Peacham composed for this occasion exemplifies the range of responses to patronage, just as it exemplifies the range of subgenres comprised within the epithalamium tradition: his lyrics are a compendium of different ways of performing the epideictic functions associated with his genre. Thus the first of the "Nuptiall Hymnes" focuses on how the natural world will celebrate the occasion; praise is present (Zephyr presumably would not bother to perfume the air for just anyone), but it is subdued and subterranean. In the second poem, a description of dressing the bride, the approach to the epideictic aspects of the genre is similar: the bride must be a glorious creature to merit this elaborate costuming, but most of the time we are left to infer that fact. The third poem, which is very close to Catullus 61, focuses on the occasion itself. The fourth, modeled on Catullus 64 and other epic epithalamia, does praise the couple but distances the act of doing so: Venus and Cupid, rather than the poet himself, deliver the compliments, and these tributes to the bride and groom are framed by a playful mythological narrative.

If Stuart poets differ in the extent to which they bestow praise, they differ as well in the extent to which they level rebukes. The singularly sordid wedding of Frances Howard and the earl of Somerset is a good test case for the amount of criticism possible under the patronage system.[44] In reviewing the background to this marriage one is tempted to sympathize with the fastidious descendent of the bride who is said to have declared, "Nor shall I dwell on the

---

[44]On the circumstances behind this wedding, see R. C. Bald, *John Donne: A Life* (Oxford: Clarendon Press, 1970), pp. 273–274, 313–314; David Harris Willson, *King James VI and I*, The Bedford Historical Series (1956; rpt. London: Jonathan Cape, 1959), pp. 338–343.

disgusting particulars,"[45] for an account of those particulars makes the *National Enquirer* seem restrained and elliptical. Having established a liaison with Rochester (who subsequently became earl of Somerset) while she was married to the earl of Essex, Frances Howard attempted to dissolve her marriage on the grounds of her husband's impotence and her consequent virginity. When the bishops conducting the hearing did not seem disposed towards a favorable verdict, James, like many sovereigns after him, packed the court with more tractable men of God. Some of the evidence presented to them suggested that Frances Howard had tried to induce impotence with drugs obtained from that dubious character Simon Forman. Whatever the truth of those accusations, shortly after her marriage she was found guilty of a far more serious crime: complicity in the murder of Thomas Overbury, once a confidant of Rochester, who had been thrown into the Tower after opposing the marriage. In short, the sometimes abstract anxieties about female chastity and the dangers of marriage experienced by Stuart poets and their contemporaries seemed to be enacted by the blushing bride: this wedding was a literal, intensified version of many of the fantasies and fears that constitute the dark subtext of the genre.

The bridegroom was James's current favorite, so one might predict an outpouring of congratulatory wedding poetry; but only a few poets mark the event in that way. Evidently the pressures of the patronage system, though great, were not irresistible. And the poems that were written vary significantly in their responses to the sordid events. Jonson contrives to compose a lyric that skirts the oddities of this wedding, as well as two masques that deal with it only tangentially,[46] whereas Donne's responses within a single poem range from blatant sycophancy to trenchant criticism. Chapman's *Andromeda Liberata,* which allegorizes the events preceding the marriage by recounting the story of the rescue of Andromeda, incorporates an epithalamium entitled "Parcarum Epithalamion." Most of this lyric generalizes about weddings and hence moves to a safe distance from the events at hand; and, thanks to Chapman's customary obscurity

[45]Quoted by Edward Le Compte in his account of the marriage, *The Notorious Lady Essex* (London: Robert Hale, 1969), p. 14.
[46]For a thoughtful analysis of those masques and the broader questions about panegyric that they raise, see David Lindley, "Embarrassing Ben: The Masques for Frances Howard," in *Renaissance Historicism: Selections from "English Literary Renaissance,"* ed. Arthur F. Kinney and Dan S. Collins (Amherst: Univ. of Massachusetts Press, 1987).

and vagueness, on the whole the compliments he does include would avoid offending either those who combed through the text for flattery or those with whom open flattery would not sit well on this occasion. But the poem incorporates two lines that are at the very least indiscreet in view of Frances Howard's assertions about her husband's impotence—Perseus is actually described as "you that slew what barren made the shore" (sig. E2^v), much as the narrative of the tale refers to rescuing Andromeda from a "barraine Rocke" (sig. B4^v). If we briefly extend our scope from epithalamia to the masques written for this wedding, we find more allusions to its controversial events, though they are far more tactful than Chapman's odd references: in Campion's masque, for instance, Rumor, Error, Credulity, and Curiosity entrap the participants, but they are soon vanquished.

The works written to celebrate these two weddings, then, vary considerably in the focus and the extent of the praise they bestow or the criticisms they direct at the couple and the court. In so doing they demonstrate that we need to replace our usual generalizations about the patronage system with an emphasis on patronage systems: the institution in question is no more monolithic than marriage itself.[47] The art historian Michael Baxandall has demonstrated that the nature of artistic patronage varies dramatically even in the instance of statues made in the same medium, limewood, in southern Germany over a period of some fifty years: at one extreme, the client controls the process, providing materials and defining the job as day-work rather than piece-work, whereas at the other extreme the craftsman enjoys far more autonomy, contracting for the whole object and subcontracting for particular tasks.[48] This diversity may prepare us for the diverse ways Stuart poets sculpt epithalamia for their patrons.

At any given moment the patronage systems offered poets a range of options. Open sycophancy was one, as some passages from the epithalamium tradition, and from many other Stuart poems, undeniably remind us. But several recent studies, a second-generation response to the new historicist emphasis on patronage, have demonstrated the measure of independence and criticism available to writ-

[47]On this subject I am indebted to discussions with David Harris Sacks and Wallace MacCaffrey.

[48]See Michael Baxandall, *The Limewood Sculptors of Renaissance Germany* (New Haven: Yale Univ. Press, 1980), esp. pp. 102–106.

ers. David Norbrook, for example, traces the techniques through which court poets negotiate some degree of freedom from the pressures of received ideas and the demands of patrons.[49] Susanne Woods describes an analogue to that process which she terms "elective poetics": writers such as Spenser and Milton, who are preoccupied with questions about freedom and choice, develop literary strategies that build those qualities into the texture of their writing and into the process of reading it.[50] Annabel Patterson has argued for a model that involves more active cooperation with the patrons. She maintains that writers and political leaders subscribed to an implicit contract that determined what could and could not be said: ambiguities were skillfully marshaled to facilitate censure.[51] In Donne's epithalamia we will encounter textbook illustrations of that pattern.

But Patterson's model risks implying more control and deliberation than in fact sometimes occurred, and patronage arrangements may permit a degree of criticism for many reasons besides the ones she cites.[52] Adapting the models of reader-response critics, we might argue that those arrangements vary precisely because their participants do *not* agree on a common set of rules. Rather, their perceptions of the relevant codes and, in particular, of the amount of criticism permitted differ enough to problematize the concept of rules and codes: hence there are as many patronage systems as there are poets and patrons continually reading—and hence creating—their texts. Rather than agree to accept criticism, moreover, patrons may simply be unaware of it. Linguists have taught us that we distinguish only phonemes, the sounds that are meaningful in our own language; Westerners have trouble with Chinese pitch. A patron who associates epideictic poetry with the language of praise may simply not notice intrusions of a different, more critical language unless they are so blatant that he realizes he is encountering as it were, a foreign

[49]David Norbrook, *Poetry and Politics in the English Renaissance* (London: Routledge and Kegan Paul, 1984), esp. pp. 11–13.

[50]Susanne Woods has developed this argument in several papers, principally "Elective Poetics and Milton's Prose: *A Treatise of Civil Power* and *Considerations Touching the Likeliest Means to Remove Hirelings Out of the Church*," in *Discourses of Truth: Milton's Prose Works and the Seventeenth-Century Crisis,* ed. David Loewenstein and James Turner (Cambridge: Cambridge Univ. Press, forthcoming).

[51]Annabel Patterson, *Censorship and Interpretation: The Conditions of Writing and Reading in Early Modern Europe* (Madison: Univ. of Wisconsin Press, 1984).

[52]I am grateful to the members of the Carleton College–St. Olaf College Renaissance Colloquium for useful suggestions about this section.

tongue. Criticism may also have been facilitated by the fact that patrons did not read their epithalamia as closely and carefully as literary critics do. Indeed, they may have glanced through these poems as casually as we look at greeting cards, assuming that it's the thought that counts. Casual perusal must have been especially tempting in the busy period surrounding a wedding. And perhaps it is not unduly cynical to suggest that most brides and grooms in the Stuart court were more interested in the lands and jewels they received as wedding presents than in the less material gifts bestowed by poets.

But the range of responses we are uncovering should be traced not only to the nature of patronage but also to the poets participating in it. The contemporary critique of the concept of the individual threatens to obscure intriguing distinctions in how different poets respond to the demands of patronage; the salutary recognition that the self is neither autonomous nor unchanging should not be pushed to the extreme of denying that a discourse is the product of distinct and distinctive voices. In this instance, we have been prone to believe that the primary motivation poets share when they court their patrons, enlightened self-interest, affects these writers in similar, or even identical, ways. But this reading of patronage assumes a rational and consistent response to demands and needs.[53] That assumption is inherently problematical, as anthropologists reacting against similar models in their own disciplines have reminded us.[54] It becomes especially problematical when applied to the demands made by any authority, including a patron, since in many cultures, including Stuart England, responses to authority vary markedly; indeed, one would be hard pressed to construct a better touchstone for distinctions among members of that society. One possible response to authority is passive-aggressive delay; this may be the reason Donne composed his poem on the Somerset-Howard wedding late. Another possibility is to overdo one's task in a way that undermines it; Chapman's aim in referring to barrenness may have been to justify the divorce, but the result emphasizes the unsavory events that

[53]In "When Was the Renaissance?", a paper delivered at the 1986 Modern Language Association convention, James Dean Wilkinson suggests that new historicists, like game theorists, are in danger of attributing to writers and patrons "a knowledge of interests and an ability to achieve them which often seems little short of miraculous."

[54]See Richard A. Shweder, "Anthropology's Romantic Rebellion against the Enlightenment," in *Culture Theory: Essays on Mind, Self, and Emotion,* ed. Richard A. Shweder and Robert A. LeVine (Cambridge: Cambridge Univ. Press, 1984).

preceded it. Thus he imperils the very praise he attempts to bestow—not a totally surprising result once we abandon the preconception that all poets respond with exemplary rationality to the demands of patronage.

We also need to allow for another type of variety in studying the ways those demands affect the epithalamium tradition: historical changes. As I argued earlier, literary critics would do well to imitate the historians who focus on units of decades or even smaller time periods. Patronage systems vary diachronically as well as synchronically. Many historical studies have demonstrated that Elizabethan patronage, which typically offered several routes to favor, differed significantly from Jacobean single-faction patronage, which allowed one to come to the monarch's attention only through the offices of a small group of current favorites.[55] The pattern is further complicated by recent indications that towards the end of Elizabeth's reign her approach to patronage anticipated that of her Stuart successor.[56] But we can and should make even more precise chronological distinctions within the Jacobean period. The death of Prince Henry, for instance, affected the tenor of patronage in many ways; those who had relied on his favor were stranded, and even poets who had invested their hopes in other patrons must have been reminded of the unpredictability of such hopes and such investments. One critic, in fact, has traced some of the changes in Sir Walter Raleigh's *History of the World* to the demise of that exemplary prince.[57] Some of the epithalamia written for Henry's sister praise James so volubly because the death of his son reminded poets of a certain temperament about

[55]On the distinctions between Elizabethan and Jacobean patronage, see two essays by Wallace T. MacCaffrey: "Place and Patronage in Elizabethan Politics," in *Elizabethan Government and Society: Essays Presented to Sir John Neale*, ed. S. T. Bindoff, J. Hurstfield, and C. H. Williams (London: Athlone Press, 1961); and his as yet unpublished article "Patronage and Policy in Sixteenth Century England"; J. E. Neale, *Essays in Elizabethan History* (New York: St. Martin's, 1958), esp. pp. 74–84. I am grateful to Professor MacCaffrey for making the latter manuscript available to me before publication. For a revisionist interpretation, see two studies by Linda Levy Peck, *Northampton: Patronage and Policy at the Court of James I* (London: George Allen and Unwin, 1982), pp. 215–216, and "Court Patronage and Government Policy: The Jacobean Dilemma," in *Patronage in the Renaissance*, ed. Guy Fitch Lytle and Stephen Orgel (Princeton: Princeton Univ. Press, 1981).

[56]See Peck, *Northampton*, and "Court Patronage and Government Policy."

[57]Leonard Tennenhouse, "Sir Walter Ralegh and the Literature of Clientage," in *Patronage in the Renaissance*, pp. 253–258. On the effects of Prince Henry's death, see also Arthur F. Marotti, "John Donne and the Rewards of Patronage," in *Patronage in the Renaissance*, p. 230.

the insecurities of patronage and hence encouraged them to rely on its surest source, its fount. Other poets apparently reacted with increased ambivalence about any bids for patronage; hence they played down the compliments to which the occasion so clearly lent itself.

The relationship of the epithalamium to Stuart patronage systems depends as well on the workings of the genre itself. Some of the variety we have noted reflects the potentialities of the literary type in which it occurs: not the least of the many reasons the epithalamium attracted Stuart poets is that it offered convenient opportunities for negotiating their complex relationships with their patrons. Despite the flexibility I have just indicated, both rhetorical strictures about epideictic poetry and practical pressures about attracting a patron do of course dictate that epithalamia include at least some measure of praise; the epithalamium offered poets strategies for presenting that praise in a form palatable to both the patron and the writer. And whereas the process of wooing his patron may cast the poet in a subservient role, the epithalamium includes some potentialities for shifting the balance of power.

Barbara Kiefer Lewalski has shown us that the verse epistle lends itself to a mode of symbolic praise:[58] Donne in particular crafts the genre to transform what might otherwise have been demeaning praise into a meditation on the symbolic worth of the person he is complimenting—and in so doing guards his integrity. The wedding poem achieves similar results through a different strategy. In addition to all their other similarities, the epithalamium and the country-house poem share a mode of delivering compliments that I have termed "deflected praise":[59] whereas one genre creates the illusion that the poet is praising not the individuals whom he wishes to woo but rather an inanimate architectural structure and the values it symbolizes, so its twinned genre can imply that he is complimenting not the patron he wishes to court but rather someone or something that he admires more dispassionately. This is another reason that most of the poems on the wedding of Princess Elizabeth and the Elector Palatine devote little attention to the bride's father. Deflected praise is psychologically effective, since the poet can maintain the impression—or the illusion—of some degree of autonomy; and the process is rhetorically effective as well, since it creates a sense that the lyric is

---

[58]Barbara Kiefer Lewalski, *Donne's "Anniversaries" and the Poetry of Praise: The Creation of a Symbolic Mode* (Princeton: Princeton Univ. Press, 1973).

[59]See my "The Country-House Poem: A Study in Generic Development," 176.

motivated by genuine enthusiasm, not crass self-interest. Thus praising Princess Elizabeth allows poets indirectly to praise the king who had sired her and hence to avoid open sycophancy. Similarly, the epithalamium permits the poet to focus as much or more attention on the events of the day as on the bride and groom; in this way too he could foster the hope—or create the illusion—that his motivation in writing is a disinterested excitement about the occasion.

The epithalamium permits another type of response to the dangers and the opportunities of patronage: an emphasis on the authority of the speaker and the poet behind him. I have already suggested that the category of directives or exercitives is central to the genre, constituting its global speech act. Thus in epic epithalamia the gods and goddesses may order around the human participants. More to our purposes here, the generic traditions of the lyric epithalamium include a speaker who assumes the role of master of ceremonies at the wedding; in Catullus 61 that figure opens the lyric by invoking Hymen and proceeds to command the other participants as well. The plot of poems in this subgenre is typically impelled by a series of orders and requests: the speaker tells the bride to awake, the women to adorn her, and so on. Moreover, as Julius Cæsar Scaliger reminds us, the *allocutio sponsalis,* an address to the bride and groom that typically involves advice about marriage, constitutes an important convention of the genre. (The marriage ceremony in the Book of Common Prayer resembles the epithalamium tradition in this as in so many other respects; embedded in questions like "Wilt thou obey him and serve him, love, honor, and keep him, in sickness, and in health?"[60] is an indirect speech act of counseling or even ordering.) By miming and modifying the paradigm of the command, then, Stuart poets attempt—with varying degrees of success—to respond to the conditions of patronage in their own milieu.

That paradigm attracts seventeenth-century English writers for two reasons. First, the genre allows them to act out a fantasy that they are important members of a court in which they may have felt marginal. Thus the structure of the lyric epithalamium, as of several of the subgenres that fit neither the lyric nor the epic category, reverses the actual conditions behind writing an epithalamium for a patron. In the process of celebrating an event from which they might well have been absent, poets can draw attention to their presence; the

[60]Booty, p. 292.

repeated allusions to "inside" and "outside" in the genre aptly gloss the poet's own position. Second, and even more to the point, in the very act of acknowledging their dependence on a patron, they can assert their own power, for in the fictive world of the poem they themselves guide the events of the wedding. The speaker is not only a participant in the occasion but also its director: whereas the country-house poem portrays the poet as a guest at the dining table, in a sense in the epithalamium he sits at its head. In short, the persona in the lyric epithalamium provides the poet who creates him with wish-fulfillment, a dream fantasy of potency and authority: it is he who tells the participants what to do, he who marshals the entire community, including courtly participants.

The commanding role that the epithalamium offers its poets gestures towards a salient connection between this genre and other forms of Renaissance literature. The wedding poem enacts more literally and explicitly the relationship between the author and his culture that Louis Adrian Montrose and others have traced in such works as *The Shepheardes Calendar*. Montrose demonstrates how Spenser contrives to become the creator, not merely the creature, of the monarch whom he is celebrating.[61] The epithalamium takes this process even further, for here, unlike other genres, the poet's commands literally call the entire occasion into being.

The imperatives that characterize the genre appeal to Stuart poets and their readers for a further reason. I have argued that the masque and epithalamium are attractive in periods of unrest because the control of the antimasque and of the threats involved in the apotropaic statements in wedding poetry provide a tempting model for a stable social order. Similarly, the epithalamium offers a model for one possible source of such stability: strong and clear leadership. Its persona has no rivals for his role as master of ceremonies; indeed, he speaks for and to the community, in a sense coalescing a whole series of secular and religious authorities in his own person. Like the bride's father—and, in the case of many courtly weddings, like the king—he organizes and oversees the match. Like the priest, he officiates and offers blessings. Not only does the genre present a community in which potential authorities do not vie with one another; in the fantasy world it evokes, commands and requests are willingly obeyed.

[61]Louis Adrian Montrose, "The Elizabethan Subject and the Spenserian Text," in *Literary Theory/Renaissance Texts*, ed. Patricia Parker and David Quint (Baltimore: Johns Hopkins Press, 1986).

The bride may sleep too long, but she soon responds to the poet's remonstrances. And other members of the wedding party willingly follow his injunctions; indeed, by and large the speaker tells them to do what they presumably would wish to do even without his urging. In short, then, the authority of the speaker metaphorically gestures towards a harmoniously hierarchical community, an ideal that stood in telling contrast to Grand Remonstrances, broken sumptuary laws, congregations that asserted the rights of their lecturers over the dictates of their bishops, and so on. In important ways the nostalgic, conservative, and recuperative vision of the epithalamium is, as we have observed before, a political vision.

The role of the speaker in the lyric epithalamium involves another type of reassurance: it implies that, much as there are no rivals vying for authority at the wedding celebration, so there are none vying for a place in the bride's bed.[62] The plot of this subgenre allows the poet to exorcise any desire he may himself have felt for the bride and in so doing to model the ways other participants—her father, the minister, the community as a whole—may subdue their own passions. Common sense offers useful caveats about exaggerating the intensity or even assuming the presence of such desire: writing a poem is not necessarily the most erotic of activities, the brides in question were not necessarily the most attractive of women. Nonetheless, in some instances the poet and other observers no doubt felt some attraction to the bride, whether because of the beauty and chastity she symbolized or because of the social status she represented. And, in any event, since the genre is so preoccupied with controlling potentially anarchic passions, those experienced, if only potentially, by the speaker and the spectators are in fact germane. Suckling's burlesque of the genre again draws our attention to anxieties present even in its "straight" form:

> And did the youth so oft the feat
> At night, as some did in conceit,
>   It would have spoil'd him, surely.
> ("A Ballade. Upon a Wedding," 76–78)

Epithalamia demonstrate the control of such desires and the willing surrender of the bride by one of the groom's potential rivals: the

[62]I am indebted to Janet Adelman and Susan Suleiman for useful suggestions about this section of the argument.

speaker not only accepts but actively encourages the events of the wedding, including its consummation, just as the other participants joyously fulfill their own roles. The potentiality for triangulated desire is resolved into the dyad of bride and groom.[63] But such willingness does not preclude—and may even depend on—a continuing involvement in their union, including its sexual consummation; much as James I was rumored to satisfy his own prurient curiosity by questioning couples about the consummation of their marriages,[64] so the poet is actively involved in the supervision and surveillance of the wedding night. In one sense, of course, he is left outside the bedchamber—the final culmination of the patterns of inside and outside. But in another and more important sense he is not outside. Jonson, for example, writes,

> Why stayes the *Bride-grome* to inuade
> Her, that would be a matron made?
>
> . . . . .
>
> To night is VENVS *vigil* kept.
> This night no *Bride-grome* euer slept;
> And if the faire *Bride* doo,
> The married say, 'tis his fault, too.
> Wake then; and let your lights
> Wake too: for they'l tell nothing of your nights.
> ("Epithalamion," *The Haddington Masque*,
> 415–416, 426–431)

The final lines attempt to reassure the couple about the very privacy that earlier lines have threatened. Carew's observations are even more intimate: "'Tis mercy not to pitty though shee bleed" ("On the Mariage of T.K. and C.C. the morning stormie," 32). In other words, by giving advice that is often quite detailed and personal, the poet inscribes his presence and even his authority at the most private of events, much as he enacts the wish to be present and authoritative at the courtly celebration. In one sense voyeurism substitutes for fulfillment. And perhaps in another sense the lust for authority replaces other forms of lust.

Yet the role of the poet in the Stuart epithalamium is in fact as complex as his role in the Stuart court: assertions of potency are in-

---

[63]The classic study of triangulated desire is René Girard, *Deceit, Desire, and the Novel: Self and Other in Literary Structure*, trans. Yvonne Freccero (Baltimore: Johns Hopkins Press, 1965).
[64]Compare Willson, p. 339.

deed significant, but so too are qualifications to and limitations in the role he assumes. Pragmatics, or speech-act theory, provides a useful tool for examining these issues, as well as for studying many other literary problems; but this mode of analysis has not yet enjoyed the influence it deserves in Renaissance studies. The principal reason is that it is often associated, consciously or not, with the positivism and intentionalism of John Searle and its other architects[65]—not a strong recommendation when so many literary critics are emphasizing the indeterminacies of discourse.[66] But in a sense this is guilt by association: speech-act theory and the related analyses of communication that of late have interested linguists do not necessarily assume determinate and unambiguous utterances. Quite the contrary: these theories can provide a fruitful way of analyzing what goes wrong in communication, literary or otherwise. Some of the most intriguing Gricean speculations, for instance, involve situations in which his Cooperative Principle, which outlines the rules through which conversations occur, break down.[67] Moreover, speech-act theory can be tailored to examine social relationships, including the ways a speaker and listener use and abuse power.

No genre demonstrates the potentialities of this methodology better than the epithalamium. To begin with, lyric epithalamia, and to a lesser extent their epic analogues, are structured around imperatives; but the English imperative, unlike its counterpart in many other languages, can encompass acts as different as commands, requests, pleas, and warnings. To put it another way, the speech acts of wedding poems can confidently be categorized as Searle's directives or

[65]For an influential critique of speech-act theory, see Stanley Fish, *Is There a Text in This Class? The Authority of Interpretive Communities* (Cambridge: Harvard Univ. Press, 1980), chap. 9.

[66]Joseph A. Porter, one of the comparatively few literary critics who has worked extensively with pragmatics, exemplifies its use and argues for its significance in *The Drama of Speech Acts: Shakespeare's Lancastrian Tetralogy* (Berkeley: Univ. of California Press, 1979). Also cf. several of his other works on these subjects: *Shakespeare's Mercutio: His History and Drama* (Chapel Hill: Univ. of North Carolina Press, 1989); "Fraternal Pragmatics: Speech Acts of John and the Bastard," in *King John: New Perspectives,* ed. Deborah Curren Aquino (Newark: Univ. of Delaware Press, 1988); and "Gender Vectors in the Pragmatic Space of Shakespearean Drama," presented at the 1986 International Shakespeare Association meeting in Berlin.

[67]See H. Paul Grice, "Logic and Conversation," in *Speech Acts,* vol. 3 of *Syntax and Semantics,* ed. Peter Cole and Jerry L. Morgan (New York: Academic Press, 1975), esp. pp. 49, 52–56. For a trenchant summary and analysis of Gricean principles, see Mary Louise Pratt, *Toward a Speech Act Theory of Literary Discourse* (Bloomington: Indiana Univ. Press, 1977), pp. 125–132 and chap. 5.

Austin's exercitives (or as the "imperatives," "impositives," and so on that other students of the field have substituted when devising their own systems of classification).[68] Yet when we try to distinguish the subdivisions within those categories, to untangle the orders from the requests, we become less confident. Scholars have delineated characteristics of the social and speech situations that distinguish these types of imperatives, but their tests can be more difficult to apply than they sometimes acknowledge. The status of speaker and hearer may of course indicate that a statement is an order rather than a command—yet it is easier to determine status in one example linguists often provide, the general telling the private to peel the potatoes, than, say, in the instance of a poet addressing a young bride. Other tests—would one say "please"? would one apply the verb "tell" or "ask"?—depend on judgment calls.[69]

The authors of epithalamia differ significantly in the nature of their speech acts, as in so many other aspects of their relationship to their community in general and their patrons in particular, and some tend towards particular types of imperatives. Thus the playful tone of Wither's wedding poem suggests less respect than we encounter in other members of its genre, and his rapid rhythms gesture towards an imperiousness that makes commands seem more likely than pleas—"Oh you sleep too long, awake yee, / See how *Time* doth ouertake yee" (sig. C). Our responses may be complicated somewhat by the discordant suggestion that the speaker is a shepherd, but by and large we read his speech acts as commands or orders.

In many instances, however, judgment is more difficult. The gap between the actual social status of the couple, especially in the case of royal weddings, and that of the poet may lead us to expect requests rather than orders. But that definition of social status is only part of the story. We need to revive the often discredited concept of the persona and admit that the authors of epithalamia create a mask, a figure whose status may be much higher than that of the poet: the speaker in the epithalamium, as we have seen, organizes the event and in a sense speaks for the whole culture. He may even appear to take on the roles of bride's father or priest. For these reasons many

[68]For these alternative systems, see, e.g., Schiffer, esp. pp. 95, 99; Georgia M. Green, "How to Get People to Do Things with Words: The Whimperative Question," in *Speech Acts*, 125.

[69]See Green's tests for distinguishing the speech acts in this category (pp. 120–122).

speech acts in epithalamia seem like commands or orders rather than respectful requests.

Often poets establish a context that further helps us to locate their imperatives on the spectrum between orders and pleas. Thus in the epithalamium in *Hymenaei*, Jonson writes, "Shrinke not, soft *Virgin*, you will loue, / Anon, what you so feare to proue" (453–454). The sexual experience of the speaker compared to the innocence of the bride gives him a type of superiority. Jonson intensifies this gap in status by assuming the role of a tutor who instructs the bride in what to expect of the wedding night and by addressing her as "soft *Virgin*" (453), a phrase that draws attention to her youthfulness. For all these reasons we are likely, I think, to read these lines as a command. In the opening of the Southwell epithalamium Herrick expresses his usual preoccupation with time:

> Then Faire ones, doe not wrong
> Your joyes, by staying long:
> Or let Love's fire goe out,
> By lingring thus in doubt:
> But learn, that Time once lost
> Is ne'r redeem'd by cost.
>
> (3–8)

When we begin to interpret this passage it is hard to be sure whether we are in the presence of orders or requests; but in the word "learn" (7) the speaker more clearly assumes a tutelary function that (at the very least) increases the likelihood that these speech acts are grounded in authority. Similarly, Donne's address to Bishop Valentine, "This day more cheerfully then ever shine" (13), could be a respectful request to a luminary with some status in the Christian calendar. But the next line reads, "This day, which might enflame thy self, Old Valentine" (14). The sly import of the observation, as well as the epithet attached to Valentine's name, increase the odds that the speaker is assuming a authority that is likely to issue in a command. Similarly, the repeated use of "must" in a range of contexts in Drayton's pastoral epithalamium tempts us to read other his imperatives as closer to orders than pleas.

Many of the ambiguous speech acts in the Stuart epithalamium can, then, be interpreted as commands—but this is not to say that all of them can be or that the decision is generally clear-cut. Nor, of course, do the speech acts that the poet favors at one point in the poem necessarily predict those he will employ at another or use when he addresses different personages. Two apparently similar passages illustrate the intriguing difficulties that attend these considerations. Three stanzas after the one we have just examined, Jonson writes, "Haste, tender *lady,* and aduenter; / The couetous *house* would haue you enter" (477–478). And later in the Southwell epithalamium, Herrick declares, "You, you that be of her neerest kin, / Now o're the threshold force her in" (81–82) and proceeds to give detailed directions about the charms that should be employed to safeguard the bride at this difficult moment. For several reasons, I suggest, we tend to read Jonson's statement as a request (he asks her to enter) and Herrick's as a command (he tells them "force her in"). In the differences between the passages we see how a range of forces may interact to produce these distinctions in tone. For one thing, the social gap between poet and participants is greater in Jonson's case. "Tender *lady*" (477) carries with it some of the solicitousness of "soft *Virgin*" (453), but the noun transforms the woman into an adult and also alludes to her social rank. In the Herrick passage, in contrast, the use of "force" (82) in a different but related context, as well as the lengthy and knowledgeable instructions that immediately follow the line, encourage us to read the lines as a command.

But how do the complexities of such passages affect the experience of reading and writing epithalamia? We should preface all analyses with the admission that in some cases their significance is slight; otherwise, we again risk allowing ingenuity to override common sense, a situation not unknown in contemporary criticism. After all, even if the speaker is delivering requests he is doing so under circumstances that ascribe considerable though not unlimited power to him: he is directing the occasion, its participants will eagerly respond to his requests, and so on. Nonetheless, the ambiguities in question are significant. They embed in the grammatical structure of the epithalamium the complexities of the poet's role in Stuart culture: his ability to deliver commands to his superiors, his need to make respectful requests of them, and above all the blurred or absent boundaries between both roles.

These ambiguities have some positive effects: they give the poet space, an opportunity to negotiate his role with his patron in a way that can please both of them. An imperative that can be read variously as a command or a request permits the writer to assert his authority while providing his patron with the illusion that the author is admitting his subordination.[70] In a sense the poet merely subscribes to a fantasy. But in another sense he exemplifies and enacts a way of gaining authority: using language, his tool in trade, at once to assert and to conceal power.

Epithalamia offer other instances of the same process. Jonson and Donne both deploy indirect speech acts in addressing their patrons:[71] they deliver questions whose illocutionary force is really an order or at least a pointed request. Thus in the wedding poem in *The Haddington Masque,* Jonson's speaker speculates, "Why stayes the *Bridegrome* to inuade / Her that would be a matron made?" (415–416). The indirect speech act here is an imperative ("Do not delay consummating the marriage"). The form in which Jonson delivers his imperative, however, has the advantage of politeness, as indirect speech acts so often do,[72] and also of a delicacy that might seem appropriate when discussing sexuality. Similarly, in a passage we examined previously from his wedding poem on the union of Princess Elizabeth and the Elector Palatine, Donne asks, "And why doe you two walke, / So slowly pac'd in this procession?" (61–62). These lines, like the series of similar questions that surrounds them, tactfully urge the participants in the occasion to hasten towards its consummation.

From another perspective, though, Donne's query and the ambiguous speech acts in the epithalamium tradition are more troubling. For the poet is pretending to an authority he does not have; the am-

---

[70]Compare Patterson, esp. p. 18, on the role of "functional ambiguity" in patronage.

[71]The nature of the indirect speech act is a highly controversial issue among linguists. In particular, they disagree on how we recognize the presence of the indirect act within the primary one, ascribing that process variously to the linguistic structure of the statement, to social convention, and so on. See, e.g., Alice Davison, "Indirect Speech Acts and What to Do with Them," and John R. Searle, "Indirect Speech Acts," both in *Speech Acts.*

[72]Though some linguists see politeness as the primary motivation of indirect speech acts, such acts typically serve many other functions. The "whimperatives" in a poem to which I referred above, "My Last Duchess," are really an assertion of power, not of politeness. In certain instances, too, indirect speech acts permit us to say something we would hesitate to express directly for reasons other than social manners. In one such case, not only the message but also the addressee differ from the ostensible one. Witness the father saying to the child, "Stay well." On one level this is a command addressed to the child, ("Put on your galoshes when it rains so you don't catch cold"); on another level, however, it is a prayer directed to a force whose existence the father may doubt enough to preclude more direct modes of address.

biguities of his language reflect the ambiguities of his position. He may indeed be eating at his lord's table, but he is seated far from its head. The principal thrust of the lyric epithalamium is to establish a secure and honored position for the poet in the fictive world of the poem; but in so doing these poems remind us of the insecurities of his position in the world of the court.

The potential contrasts between those two worlds draw our attention to another way in which speech-act theory can help us analyze the social and poetic status of the authors of Stuart epithalamia. One could make a case that the speech acts in those poems are infelicitous in the technical sense. One way of defining the peculiar mimetic world of the epithalamium would be to say that the speech acts of the speaker violate appropriateness conditions in that a poet in the Stuart court has neither the authority nor the opportunity to command a princess to arise, to get dressed. But such an argument naively assumes a simple form of mimesis. It is more logical to suggest that the speech acts of the Stuart epithalamium draw attention to the gap between the fictive world portrayed in and created by these poems and the conditions in which poets lived: in the first they could deliver exercitives of all sorts, whereas in the second pleas are more appropriate than demands.

Stuart epithalamia, like many of their predecessors, sometimes express the social complexities encoded in their speech acts in another way. The speaker is typically a commanding figure, and he is generally a central participant, indeed the key participant, in the festivities. But in a handful of intriguing instances we encounter instead the antitype to that speaker, his negative identity: a figure who draws attention to and laments his own marginality. Several earlier poems foreshadow this kind of persona in the Stuart epithalamium. That curious and moving lyric "Pervigilium Veneris," which manifests many similarities to the epithalamium tradition although is is not itself a wedding poem, includes such a speaker.[73] We find hints of the same pattern in William Dunbar's "The Thrissil and the Rois," which is modeled on the dream vision. Rather than command others to awake, he is told by Aurora and May to get up—and rather than do so, he in effect tries to turn off the alarm: the weather is nasty, he replies, and there aren't enough birds to get excited about. And, of

[73]On this poem, see the introduction to Sir Cecil Clementi, ed., *Pervigilium Veneris: The Vigil of Venus*, 3d. ed. (Oxford: Basil Blackwell, 1936). I am most grateful to Gwynne Blakemore Evans for drawing this poem—and so many other germane texts—to my attention.

course, in the "Prothalamion" Spenser laments his own rejection by the courtly world that is celebrating these betrothals; the poem implicitly contrasts his failures and Somerset's radiant successes. His alienation is also manifest in the ways the structure of this poem differs from that of so many other epithalamia: the nymphs rather than the speaker deliver the primary celebratory lyric, and the speaker observes the events and their participants but does not call them into being through his own commands or requests.

In the seventeenth-century tradition, Wither's "Epithalamion" presents a persona who, though identified as a shepherd, has more in common with the shepherd's bastard brother, the satirist: he actually refers to Wither's collection of formal verse satires, *Abuses Stript and Whipt*:

> I *my selfe* though meanest stated,
> (And in *Court* now almost hated)
> Will knit up my *Scourge,* and venter
> In the midst of them to enter.
>
> (sig. C3)

But he agrees at least to participate, as does the discontented persona in Joshua Sylvester's "Epithalamion"; the speaker in the poem Donne wrote for the Somerset-Howard wedding, as we will see, is reluctant to do even that. An analogous pattern is manifest in Suckling's "Upon My Lord Brohall's Wedding," a dialogue that includes a figure who does not join in the festivities. We also find some instances of the alienated speaker in later poems outside the scope of this study, notably Sir William Davenant's "Epithalamium," written for the wedding of the earl of Barymore and Martha Laurence.

The type of figure I am identifying is relatively uncommon in the epithalamium tradition; but the issues he raises are broad and important. The discontented speaker fills both formal and psychological functions. On one level he is the dramatic enactment of the elegiac elements in his genre. To put it another way, the dangers and discontents that must be controlled or rechanneled for the wedding to succeed are in these instances bodied forth not in allegorized forces like Jealousy or in mythical figures like hobgoblins, but rather in the person of the poet himself.

But this is only half the story: unlike the threatening forces and figures whom they ostensibly resemble, these discontented poets are integrated into the wedding. The extent differs from poem to poem, but integration does occur; Jacques and Malvolio depart before the wedding feast, but their counterparts in the epithalamium tradition get a piece of the cake, as it were, and a piece of the action. Initially a participant in the fundamental structural opposition of outside versus inside, such speakers come to represent towards the end of the poem yet another version of the forces that are welcomed within. Thus Wither emphasizes that he will "enter" (sig. C3).

This summary may hint at a further function assumed by the alienated speakers in question: their metamorphoses contribute to the focus on process and change that characterizes the lyric epithalamium. The diurnal movements that structure the poem parallel the bride's movement from sleeping to waking, from virgin to matron, and so on, while the wedding procession is, as its name suggests, an enactment of such patterns. Similarly, the speaker moves from outsider to insider.

To fully understand the type of speaker we are examining, however, we need to enlarge our perspective: a parallel pattern occurs in allusions to weddings outside the epithalamium genre. The alienated speaker finds his counterpart in Satan's voyeuristic meditations on Adam and Eve and, above all, in "The Rime of the Ancient Mariner." In these instances, he serves to define by contrasts, indirectly emphasizing the joy of the wedding, but also to remind us of the dark underside of the occasion, the issues and emotions that the wedding may tempt us to overlook or that we try in vain to ignore.

The alienated speakers we have identified serve an additional function in the Stuart wedding poem in particular. In other Stuart epithalamia, the poet's potential discontents and anxieties about patronage are exorcised through a fantasy of harmony with the community; in the lyrics that body forth such speakers, however, tensions are instead expressed through a fiction of disunity or of disunity yielding to unity. It is tempting to say that in one case the poet lies to us and to himself by pretending to more power than he has, and in the other he acknowledges his own relative powerlessness. But the truth, as we have seen, is more complex. The patronage systems could encompass both sycophancy and satiric rebukes. Being a poet in the Stuart court, like the specific act of writing an epithalamium, involves potentialities for both power and powerlessness. The insider who assumes the role of master of ceremonies and the outsider who must be coaxed into an even partial connection to the wedding, like several of the genres examined at the beginning of this chapter, are both opposites and twins.

CHAPTER 4

John Donne

A hardy, sharp, insistent

Growing thing that prospers even in this
Barely green and stony place where we live.
John Hildebidle, "For a City Wedding"

I

John Donne's epithalamia have hardly proved "an endlesse moni-
ment." Anthologies seldom include them, and critics seldom analyze them. The most minor lyrics in the *Songs and Sonets* regularly
receive more attention than the best of Donne's wedding poems, as
scholarly bibliographies demonstrate. This neglect is unjustified: his
three epithalamia illuminate both their genre and their author.

Though Donne's "Epithalamion made at Lincolnes Inne" was apparently composed in the 1590s,[1] this lyric can clarify the tensions
associated with Stuart marriage and Stuart marriage poems. Like
Richard Crashaw's "Epithalamium," the "Epithalamion made at Lincolnes Inne" is disturbing in part because it resists our original temp-

[1]On the dating of Donne's epithalamia, see Herbert J. C. Grierson, ed., *The Poems
of John Donne*, 2 vols. (Oxford: Clarendon Press, 1912), II, lxxxi, 91; Helen Gardner,
ed., *The Divine Poems*, 2d ed. (Oxford: Clarendon Press, 1978), p. lxxix; W. Milgate,
ed., *The Epithalamions, Anniversaries, and Epicedes* (Oxford: Clarendon Press, 1978),
esp. p. 110; David Novarr, "Donne's 'Epithalamion made at Lincoln's Inn': Context
and Date," *RES*, 7 (1956), 254–255. As these sources argue, though the phrase "made
at Lincolnes Inne" in theory could refer to the later period when Donne was a Reader
at the Inn, it is much more likely that the poem was written in 1595 during his initial
affiliation with the Inn.

tation to distinguish it from other instances of its genre by labeling it
a mere sport or a parody or an anti-epithalamium: rather, the reader
encounters in both these texts darker, more intense, and hence more
visible versions of the shadows that cloud the otherwise optimistic
and irenic visions celebrated in seventeenth-century epithalamia. And
if the "Epithalamion made at Lincolnes Inne" glosses the anxieties I
catalogued in Chapters 1 and 2, the wedding poem Donne composed
for the nuptials of Frances Howard and Somerset not only exemplifies but also consciously explicates those studied in Chapter 3, especially the problems of patronage.

Donne's epithalamia, then, offer textbook examples of the tensions
associated with their literary type and with marriage in Renaissance
England; they allow us to explore in more depth the conflicts I have
been anatomizing. At the same time, however, these lyrics demonstrate the richness and suppleness of their generic heritage:[2] For, like
other Stuart wedding poems, they typically counter both cultural
and more idiosyncratic personal tensions by deploying the conventions and norms of the epithalamium tradition. In so doing, they
testify to Donne's own skill in adapting literary forms: despite all the
flaws in the "Epithalamion made at Lincolnes Inne" and the "Epithalamion at the Marriage of the Earl of Somerset," both works contain some striking passages, and "An Epithalamion, or Mariage Song
on the Lady Elizabeth, and Count Palatine" is a real triumph.

Yet the very vocabulary I have just used to praise the achievements
of these poems—the linguistic register that encompasses words like
"richness," "skill," "triumph," or, indeed, "works" rather than
"texts"—is now rare in many professional circles: our sanative reaction against the New Critical adulation of the text, justified and intensified by our recognition that valuation is not objective but
culture-linked,[3] has made many critics more willing to scrutinize the

---

[2]Some recent critics have countered the older emphasis on Donne's iconoclasm by
stressing his indebtedness to literary traditions. See, e.g., Donald L. Guss, *John
Donne, Petrarchist: Italianate Conceits and Love Theory in "The Songs and Sonets"* (Detroit: Wayne State Univ. Press, 1966); M. Thomas Hester, *Kinde Pitty and Brave Scorn:
John Donne's "Satyres"* (Durham: Duke Univ. Press, 1982); and my own article, "Tradition and the Individualistic Talent: Donne's 'An Epithalamion, or Mariage Song on
the Lady Elizabeth . . . ,' " in *The Eagle and the Dove: Reassessing John Donne*, ed.
Claude J. Summers and Ted-Larry Pebworth (Columbia: Univ. of Missouri Press,
1986).

[3]One of the most influential statements of this position is Barbara Herrnstein
Smith, "Contingencies of Value," *Critical Inquiry*, 10 (1983), 1–35.

tensions that texts inscribe than to celebrate the resolutions they achieve. Donne's epithalamia do testify, as unmistakably as the marriage manuals, to the uncertainties and conflicts attendant on weddings in Renaissance England. But much as his combative speakers typically turn an antagonist's threats to their own advantage, so his wedding poems at their best skillfully marshal aesthetic and other resources to resolve cultural and idiosyncratic threats connected with marriage, sexuality, and gender. Hence these lyrics encourage us one again to bridge the positions of older and more contemporary critics: Donne's epithalamia are both an arena for conflicts and a storehouse of carefully crafted solutions to those conflicts.

II

Even a brief survey of his other works reminds us of the problems Donne confronts when he attempts to write epithalamia. Though his preoccupation with love and sexuality no doubt made the genre attractive to him, on the whole wedding poems did not come naturally to him. For one thing, as we have seen, typically that literary type is intensely communal in its values. The sermons and *Devotions upon Emergent Occasions* remind us that communal values are not totally alien to Donne; but by and large his secular poetry constructs the social order not as a harmonious unit but rather as an arena where opponents—who can often be classified simply as "us" (or, more often, "me") and "them"—stage their battles.[4]

In particular, Donne's telling preoccupation with intrusion signals his predilection for seeing the community as a source of entrapment rather than support. It is no accident that two of his satires imitate Horace's Satire I.ix, a poem that depicts an encounter with a bore, despite the number of other plot models offered by Horace, Juvenal, and Persius. For the Horatian narrative enacts his recurrent fantasy of intrusion, whether by a "Busie old foole"[5] of a sun, by an eavesdropper,[6] or, most ominously, by a political spy. The actual danger of

[4]Compare Clay Hunt, *Donne's Poetry: Essays in Literary Analysis* (New Haven: Yale Univ. Press, 1954), pp. 146–148, 176–177; this critic emphasizes Donne's self-centeredness and asserts that he lacks a sense of community.

[5]All citations from the *Songs and Sonets* and elegies are to *The Elegies and the Songs and Sonnets,* ed. Helen Gardner (Oxford: Clarendon Press, 1965).

[6]Anne Ferry (*All in War with Time: Love Poetry of Shakespeare, Donne, Jonson, Marvell* [Cambridge: Harvard Univ. Press, 1975], p. 112) notes that the reader of the *Songs and Sonets* frequently eavesdrops.

spies at court reminds us of the interplay between psychological patterns and the cultural events that in part—but only in part—shape
those patterns; it is as risky to neglect one in favor of the other as it
is to neglect the ways texts surmount tensions in favor of anatomizing the ways they succumb. This tendency to view the outer world
as a collection of antagonistic intruders is related as well to Donne's
preference for addressing an individual or a coterie rather than the
larger public audience to whom epithalamia are generally directed.[7]

"For that first mariage was our funerall," Donne observes in "An
Anatomy of the World" (105),[8] and many of his works testify to
ambivalent attitudes to women, sexuality, and wedlock that further
confound his approach to the epithalamium.[9] In particular, Donne
embodies especially intense and complicated versions of some of the
pressures I analyzed in Chapter 2. The notion that he wrote poems
like "The Canonization" for his wife is, as Northrop Frye said about
generic definitions, "chiefly interesting as [an] example . . . of the
psychology of rumor";[10] but whatever their source, such lyrics demonstrate that their author's responses to women are often assured,
respectful, and joyous. At the same time, however, both the major
and more minor works repeatedly reveal a misogyny intense enough
to recall some of the patristic writers whom Donne knew so well.
Thus, anticipating the passage from the *Anniversaries* that I just
quoted,[11] *Metempsychosis* emphasizes Eve's responsibility for the fall
in terms that are not likely to cheer a prospective bridegroom:

[7]Many critics have commented on Donne's private voice. See, e.g., Anthony Low,
"The Compleat Angler's 'Baite'; or, The Subverter Subverted," *John Donne Journal*, 4
(1985), 1–11. Arthur F. Marotti's important study of Donne as a coterie poet reinterprets and renders more precise the conventional wisdom about his private voice (*John
Donne, Coterie Poet* [Madison: Univ. of Wisconsin Press, 1986]).

[8]Citations from the funeral poems are to *The Epithalamions, Anniversaries, and Epicedes*, ed. W. Milgate.

[9]Many critics have of course attempted to trace these issues. For a recent poststructuralist interpretation of them, see Thomas Docherty, *John Donne, Undone* (London:
Methuen, 1986), esp. chap. 2. Kathryn R. Kremen's analysis of Donne's attitudes
towards marriage stresses the connections between human wedlock and divine unions,
such as that between man and God (*The Imagination of the Resurrection: The Poetic
Continuity of a Religious Motif in Donne, Blake, and Yeats* [Lewisburg: Bucknell Univ.
Press, 1972], pp. 96–98).

[10]Northrop Frye, *Anatomy of Criticism: Four Essays* (Princeton: Princeton Univ.
Press, 1957), p. 13.

[11]The parallel is also discussed in Milgate, *Epithalamions*, pp. 134–135; as he points
out, in these passages Donne is relying on Ecclesiasticus 25.24, but the orthodox
position of the church ascribes the Fall to Adam.

Man all at once was there by woman slaine,
And one by one we'are here slaine o'er againe
By them. The mother poison'd the well-head,
The daughters here corrupt us, Rivulets.

$$(91-94)^{12}$$

For Donne as for the authors of the marriage tracts, the coexistence
of such divergent attitudes is itself a source of tension.

A related and sometimes neglected source of tension is the problem of interpreting the nature—or natures—of women: Donne's
works not only invite but also themselves perform and problematize
hermeneutics. His fear of inconstancy is in part a fear of not recognizing it for what it is.[13] Interpretation, like so much else, is combative and competitive in many of the *Songs and Sonets*: their subtext
is often the assertion "I will guess what you're really like before you
can fool me." Both Donne's lyrics and his prose refer often to this
and other interpretive challenges. Thus in "The Primrose" the
speaker traces the need to establish some middle ground in his responses to women, and, similarly, the sermon Donne delivered at the
marriage of Margaret Washington talks about the necessity—and the
difficulty—of achieving a golden mean between contempt and worship: "Between the denying of them souls, which S. *Ambrose* is
charged to have done, and giving them such souls, as that they may
be Priests, as the *Peputian* hereticks did, is a faire way for a moderate
man to walk in. To make them Gods is ungodly, and to make them
Devils is devillish; To make them Mistresses is unmanly, and to
make them servants is unnoble" (III, 242). Donne argues for that
"faire way" with such intensity in part, at least, because he finds it
hard to walk in it.

These and other problems are deepened when Donne focuses specifically on wedlock. Later in the Washington sermon, he asserts that
we should avoid the difficulties he is outlining by seeing women as
wives; but that advice is not persuasive or reassuring, for so many of
his statements about wives are ambiguous or contradictory. Donne's
attitudes to marriage in general and to the loss of virginity in particular are ambivalent, as we saw in Chapter 1, even though his own

---

[12] *The Satires, Epigrams and Verse Letters*, ed. W. Milgate (Oxford: Clarendon Press,
1967).

[13] Docherty's observation that Donne often sees woman as displaced and lacking a
stable identity is germane here (see esp. pp. 61–71).

marriage may well have been a happy one.[14] Thus, for example, the text on which one sermon celebrating a marriage is based focuses on the assertion that angels do not themselves marry (VIII, 94–109). Another of his sermons emphasizes that vestal virgins were as good as wives but not better and in so doing invites the obvious comparison with virgins and matrons in Donne's own culture (VIII, 101); yet another, however, as firmly declares that virginity is "the proper, and principal chastity" (III, 68).[15] Similarly, in praising Elizabeth Drury's "Virgin white integrity" ("A Funerall Elegie," 75), he proffers a paradoxical generalization: "For mariage, though it doe not staine, doth dye" (76).[16]

But the best introduction to these and other problems that Donne's two Stuart epithalamia confront and often surmount is his first attempt at the genre, the "Epithalamion made at Lincolnes Inne." Though written in the 1590s, this curious lyric deserves attention from students of the seventeenth-century versions of its genre, for it conveniently demonstrates several of the challenges that the authors of Stuart wedding poems were to encounter and that Donne himself was to resolve more successfully in his later wedding poems. In some passages, to be sure, the lyric merely offers unproblematical instances of generic characteristics. It conflates and reconciles the natural and human worlds, for instance, when the attendants are told to assign "fit place for every flower and jewell" (20); and the use of "fit" in that line and in the one that follows it immediately exempli-

---

[14]J. B. Leishman, however, reminds us that it is hard to be sure what Donne's attitudes to his family really were (The Monarch of Wit: An Analytical and Comparative Study of the Poetry of John Donne, rev. ed. [New York: Harper and Row, 1965], pp. 41–43).

[15]The latter passage is also discussed in John Carey, John Donne: Life, Mind and Art (New York: Oxford Univ. Press, 1981), p. 11; his argument differs from mine, however, in that rather than see continuing inconsistencies in Donne's approach to the issue, Carey argues that Donne becomes a defender of virginity.

[16]Similar allusions occur in some problematical passages in Donne's prose. E.g., we may encounter related ambiguities in the twenty-third prayer of Devotions upon Emergent Occasions: "O God, let mee never put my selfe aboard with Hymeneus" (Devotions upon Emergent Occasions, ed. Anthony Raspa [Montreal: McGill-Queen's Univ. Press, 1975], p. 127); as Raspa (p. 187) points out, however, the line may refer either to the god of marriage or to Antigone's fiancé. In Paradox 12, addressing the question of whether virginity is a virtue, Donne relies on the paradox form to avoid committing himself on the issue; it is not clear, however, whether this work is in fact canonical (Helen Peters lists it among the "dubia" in her edition of Donne's work in the genre, Paradoxes and Problems [Oxford: Clarendon Press, 1980]). In any event, Donne's other writings offer ample proof of his ambivalence about virginity.

fies the emphasis on order that we have encountered so often in the epithalamium tradition. But by and large this lyric is far from unproblematical: it compares the attendants to "Golden Mines" (14), the church's burial area to a "hunger-starved wombe" (40), the consummation of the marriage to ritualistic sacrifice, and so on.

David Novarr attempts to explain these and other peculiarities.[17] Discovering in this epithalamium "a number of puzzling elements which disturb the conventional epithalamic attitude" (250), he argues that its wit and imagery are cruder and blunter than their analogues in Donne's other wedding poems. Such a poem, he asserts, could not have been written for the wedding of an aristocratic patron or even for the marriage of one of Donne's own acquaintances; rather, this lyric is in fact a parody of Edmund Spenser's "Epithalamion," intended for mock nuptials performed at Lincoln's Inn.

Novarr's thesis justifies some of the oddities of a problematical poem; yet several of his presuppositions are themselves problematical.[18] If the rhetoric in the "Epithalamion made at Lincolnes Inne" is less successful than in the other epithalamia, one possible explanation is that the earliest of the three poems is a parody—but surely a more likely explanation is that its author was more liable to occasional blunders in 1595 than in 1613 and more likely to have trouble with a new genre on his first attempt than on his second or third. Moreover, the argument that this poem is parodic assumes that it is puzzling to find a seriously flawed poem in the canon in question: lapses in taste must represent deliberate strategy, not unwitting error. But the quality of Donne's lyrics varies considerably, and we certainly find signs of carelessness and haste elsewhere in his work.

The claim that the poem is parodic must, however, be evaluated primarily through a reading of the text. Our examination of the genre has demonstrated that many of the characteristics Novarr considers inappropriate in an epithalamium, such as Donne's emphasis

---

[17]Novarr, "Donne's 'Epithalamion made at Lincoln's Inn': Context and Date." I attempt to rebut his argument at greater length than this chapter allows in my article "Donne's 'Epithalamion made at Lincolnes Inne': An Alternative Interpretation," *SEL*, 16 (1976), 131–143; I still argue that the poem is not primarily or consistently written as a parody, but I now acknowledge more parodic elements than my earlier study of this lyric admitted.

[18]A few critics have challenged presuppositions other than the ones I cite. In *John Donne: A Life*, Bald questions whether revels were in fact held during the summer (p. 77); in *The Poetry of Marriage*, Tufte expresses doubts about whether the poem is parodic but does not explore the issue (p. 218).

on death,[19] the neglect of the groom, and the licentious rhetoric, do in fact occur elsewhere in the tradition. Other apparent oddities and inconsistencies find their counterparts in Donne's later and indisputably unparodic wedding poems if not in the tradition as a whole; for instance, just as he links the bride with the male symbol of the sun here, so he reverses normal gender in his other epithalamia, variously comparing Princess Elizabeth to a sun and her groom to a moon and praising the "manly courage" (122) of Frances Howard.

What Donne does not do is, moreover, as revealing as what he does. Spenser's alliterative sound effects and densely textured language render his work a prime candidate for stylistic parodies, much as Algernon Charles Swinburne's style tempts the impulses expressed in his self-parody "Nephelidia." Yet Donne avoids the rhetorical exaggeration and mockery that, one assumes, he would have enjoyed writing and his clever friends at the Inns would have enjoyed reading.[20] Donne has many extraordinary virtues, but understatement and restraint are not normally among them; had he set out with the firm intention of writing a parody, one would have expected a bolder and funnier one.

Indeed, the poem often reads not like a satire on Spenserian lyricism but rather like an assay at satire by some minor seventeenth-century Spenserian. Witness, for example, the opening stanza:

> The Sun-beames in the East are spred,
> Leave, leave, faire Bride, your solitary bed,
>   No more shall you returne to it alone,
> It nourseth sadnesse, and your bodies print,
> Like to a grave, the yielding downe doth dint;
>   You and your other you meet there anon;
>   Put forth, put forth that warme balme-breathing thigh,
> Which when next time you in these sheets wil smother,
>   There it must meet another,
>   Which never was, but must be, oft, more nigh;
>   Come glad from thence, goe gladder then you came,
> *To day put on perfection, and a womans name.*
>   (1–12)

---

[19]Gayle Edward Wilson has argued that etymological wit may explain one of the references to death in this poem ("Donne's Sarcophagal Imagery in 'Epithalamion made at Lincolnes Inne,' vv. 37–42," *American Notes and Queries*, 18 [1980], 72–73).

[20]On the influence of his coterie at the Inns, see Marotti, *John Donne, Coterie Poet*, chap. 1.

Though it is risky to trace sources in a genre that relies so heavily on stock motifs, the first line may echo Spenser's "His golden beame vpon the hils doth spred" ("Epithalamion," 20). In any event, the careful alliteration throughout and the stress on the polysyllabic "perfection" (12) build an unmistakable impression of Spenserian dignity.[21] To be sure, the stanza contains passages more characteristic of the author of "The Canonization" than the author of the *Amoretti*: for all his frank sensuality, for instance, Spenser would not have referred to the bride's thigh in this way. But read in the context of the rest of the stanza, such lines appear to be signs not of parody but rather of the emergence of Donne's own voice in the course of a generally respectful imitation of his predecessor.

But if one questions Novarr's categorization of the poem, how can one explain its peculiarities? The bride's attendants are indisputably mocked:

> Daughters of London, you which bee
> Our Golden Mines, and furnish'd Treasurie,
>   You which are Angels, yet still bring with you
> Thousands of Angels on your mariage daies.
>
> (13–16)

Despite—or more likely because of—the shakiness of his own claims to gentility, Donne cannot resist gibes at the wealthy bourgeoisie. Perhaps, too, in these passages he is externalizing and hence distancing himself from his own ambivalent and ultimately unrealized ambitions of, as the splendidly revealing phrase has it, "marrying well."[22] In any event, his desire to prove that he is a gentleman prevents him from acting like one, and whatever its genesis the resulting passage certainly undermines the Spenserian vision established in the preceding stanza. Nor are the groom's attendants spared jokes about their writing abilities ("barrels of others wits" [27]), their sexual proclivities ("who but your beasts love none" [28]), and so on. And how do we interpret other odd passages, notably the rendition of the bride as a sacrificial lamb?

[21]This tone is all the more striking because, as Hunt points out (pp. 126–127), Donne's poetry normally lacks the type of ceremoniousness and solemnity we find in Spenser's "Epithalamion."

[22]Compare Marotti, *John Donne, Coterie Poet* (esp. p. 134), on Donne's conflation of love and economic success.

The answer to these and other questions about the poem is that
Donne is not consistently and systematically parodying Spenser, yet
the poem does certainly contain parodic elements.[23] The author of
the "Epithalamion made at Lincolnes Inne" is pulled between his
primary aim, writing a "straight" imitation of Spenser and his
genre, and an impulse to undermine that imitation with parody, or,
to put it another way, a characteristic impulse to view Spenser as
not a model to emulate but a rival to challenge. Donne typically
responds to threats from rivals and other enemies with a satirical
counterattack, as "The Sunne Rising" and many other poems demonstrate. Thus at key moments here, notably the second and third
stanzas, parody and other types of satire interrupt respectful evocation of the Spenserian vision, a stylistic counterpart to the uninvited
and unwelcome wedding guests who so often threaten the festivities
celebrated in this genre. But Donne then returns to a more straightforward imitation of the "Epithalamion": parody is deflected by an
impulse towards serious, "straight" imitation, rather in the way that
parody itself is deflected from the bride and groom themselves towards their attendants. This lyric is so disturbing not merely or primarily because it mocks the conventions of its genre and the values it
represents but because parody and imitation usurp and decenter each
other.[24]

The rest of Donne's canon offers some analogues. Both "The
Baite" and *Metempsychosis* shift back and forth between satire and
parody on the one hand and an unmediated imitation of a more solemn lyricism on the other;[25] in this important respect these three
works are companion pieces. But explanations for the uneasy juxtaposition of parody and imitation I attribute to the "Epithalamion
made at Lincolnes Inne" lie not only in Donne's sensibility but in

[23]While I part company with Milgate's assertion that the poem is primarily satiric,
his observation that it is "neither consistent satire nor committed celebration" (*Epithalamions*, p. xxii) resembles my own interpretation.

[24]Many critics have, of course, mapped the multiple types of instability that char-
acterize Donne's texts. See, e.g., Judith Scherer Herz, " 'An Excellent Exercise of
Wit That Speaks So Well of Ill': Donne and the Poetics of Concealment," in *The
Eagle and the Dove*.

[25]This reading of "The Baite" is substantiated in my article "John Donne's
Versions of Pastoral," *Durham University Journal*, 37 (1976), 33–37. For different inter-
pretations of this unduly neglected lyric, see, e.g., Guss, pp. 82–84; Low, "The
Compleat Angler's 'Baite' "; Patricia Garland Pinka, *This Dialogue of One: The
"Songs and Sonnets" of John Donne* (University: Univ. of Alabama Press, 1982), pp.
42–43.

parody itself.[26] Critics are sometimes prone to interpret that literary mode in a binary fashion: a poem either is or is not a parody. This method of categorization is successful in defining the relationship between, say, *Pamela* and *Shamela;* but it is less successful when we turn to works that bear a more complex relationship to their heritage. Often parody is not a subgenre of satire that authors either select or reject but a modal potentiality in which they may sporadically participate. Texts may well shift back and forth between a serious and an ironic response to their literary models, much as they may shift in their responses to their subject matter.

Adapting Frye's anatomies,[27] we can acknowledge these shifts by locating individual texts and entire genres on a spectrum that runs from a "straight" to an ironic response to both form and content. At one pole we find an unqualified and unironic vision, at the other what might, to borrow the rhetoric of contemporary thrillers, be termed the Autolycus Factor. One important position on this spectrum is the changing and inconsistent combination of straight and ironic reactions to a model exemplified not only by Donne's "Epithalamion made at Lincolnes Inne" but also by *The Rape of the Lock* and *Don Quixote*. Recognizing such patterns rather than seeing parody as a simple, binary option allows us to describe texts more precisely and also to classify, and in so doing to note the connections among, a variety of strategies that express an ironic distance: stylistic parody, the incorporation of elements from a countergenre, juxtaposition with another text in the same volume,[28] and so on.

Formal contexts illuminate the "Epithalamion made at Lincolnes Inne" in other ways. It is no accident, I suggest, that this epithalamium, like several other works that shift back and forth between parody and imitation, involves love and, in some cases, seductiveness. The body of the text, like the more literal bodies in these narratives, is itself the site of a dual pattern of seduction: in turning to

[26]For discussions of that form, see, e.g., Gilbert Highet, *The Anatomy of Satire* (Princeton: Princeton Univ. Press, 1962), chap. 3; John D. Jump, *Burlesque* (London: Methuen, 1972), chaps. 1, 4.

[27]In *Anatomy of Criticism,* Frye suggests a scale ranging from pure convention to experiments that purport to reject convention (pp. 103–104); the scale I am proposing is similar but encompasses issues besides convention. His comments (e.g., p. 177) on the axis of irony and romance are also germane.

[28]For a useful though brief discussion of the connections among Renaissance texts published together, see William Shakespeare, *The Sonnets and "A Lover's Complaint,"* ed. William Kerrigan (Harmondsworth: Penguin, 1986), pp. 14–15.

parody, the author shows himself immune to the seduction of the
style he is rejecting, while in returning to that style he is seduced,
willingly or not, by lyricism or heroic grandeur. Such works are often mimetic in another, related sense: they may approach the literary
models behind them with the same unstable combination of awe and
antagonism that characterizes the approaches of their authors—and
their male protagonists—to their Belindas.

The competitive and mutual decentering of parody and imitation
that I attribute to this lyric, then, accounts for some of its oddities;
but we still have not explained away the frequency of the references
to death or the extraordinary trope on which they culminate:

> Ev'n like a faithfull man content,
> That this life for a better should be spent,
>   So, shee a mothers rich stile doth preferre,
> And at the Bridegroomes wish'd approach doth lye,
> Like an appointed lambe, when tenderly
>   The priest comes on his knees t'embowell her.
>   (85–90)

Critics have alluded to these lines only in passing, but the passage
deserves sustained attention.[29] For here is the nexus of the most disturbing elements in the poem, the core fantasy that shapes its darker
vision. As Donne says of a word he explicates in one of his sermons,
this passage is "the hinge upon which all this Text turns" (III, 241)—
and several of Donne's other texts as well.

To be sure, the opening of the quotation does gesture towards a
type of rebirth and renewal grounded in the cycles of a Christian's
life, thus anticipating the emphasis on cyclical regeneration in
Donne's two later epithalamia. But the succeeding lines more trou-
blingly suggest that the bride is willingly appropriated for and destroyed in a sacramental ritual. In so doing they conflate cultural
anxieties connected to marriage with Donne's more idiosyncratic
constructions of the sexual and the sacred. The bride's willing submissiveness is a fantasy that attempts to compensate for fears of female equality so tellingly revealed in some of Donne's sermons, such
as the one he delivered at Sir Francis Nethersole's wedding. In the
behavior of the priest we encounter peculiar slippages between dom-

---

[29]Many critics have been troubled by this passage, though they have generally referred to it only in passing. See, e.g., Maurice Evans, *English Poetry in the Sixteenth
Century* (London: Hutchinson's University Library, 1955), p. 173.

ination and respect and between violence and tenderness. Thus "on his knees" (90) may, as one critic argues, allude to a sexual position;[30] but it is even more unsettling than that interpretation suggests, for it conflates that sexual position with the priest's reverential stance at the bloody ritual he is performing. Despite that reverence, the primary thrust, so to speak, of Donne's trope is an act of violation, with "t'embowell" (90), rather than "to disembowell," characteristically casting sexual intercourse as yet another instance of intrusion. For these and other reasons, one suspects that the passage is impelled by the same psychological dynamic that lies behind the repeated allusions to sacrifice in Sons and Lovers: an impulse to dominate and even violate generates guilt about the resulting violence and hence a need to mystify and sanctify that violence by constructing it as a religious ceremony. At the same time, the sacramental focus of the passage lends itself to a cultural explanation: the ritual the lines evoke is a religious analogue to the colonialized appropriation of the bride implied by describing the "Daughters of London" (13) as "Golden Mines" (14) and the bride herself as "rich as Inde" (22). To put it another way, the allusion to the priest mystifies and implicitly justifies the ways other men take possession of her. We need not and indeed should not choose between these psychological and cultural interpretations: the two etiologies coexist and interact, just as psychological and cultural interpretations should do. In short, the consummation of the marriage is constructed as a disturbing interplay of sanctioned male aggression, willing female submission, holy violence, and unholy bawdiness.[31]

This trope cannot be dismissed as a mere sport, any more than the poem in which it appears: it is so revealing precisely because we find many of its constituent elements in Donne's other works. In the Songs and Sonets, Eros and Thanatos enjoy a relationship as intimate as that of many of the lovers being portrayed. Throughout his canon Donne links other varieties of creation and destruction ("Therfore that he may raise the Lord throws down" ["Hymne to God my God, in my sicknesse," 30]),[32] though the connections are particu-

---

[30]Carey, p. 143.

[31]Compare René Girard's observation that sacrifice often "assumes two opposing aspects, appearing at times as a sacred obligation to be neglected at grave peril, at other times as a sort of criminal activity entailing perils of equal gravity" (Violence and the Sacred, trans. Patrick Gregory [Baltimore: Johns Hopkins Univ. Press, 1977], p. 1).

[32]Divine Poems, ed. Gardner.

larly disturbing when applied to the consummation of a marriage. "The Flea" is one of many poems that connect "mariage bed[s]" (13) with "mariage temple[s]" (13). The *Holy Sonnets* of course reflect another predilection that is germane here: Donne's tendency to map relationships in terms of domination and submission.[33] And throughout the *Songs and Sonets* the speaker responds to threats, real or putative, through violent aggression; witness among many instances "The Apparition."[34]

Both the description of the bride as a sacrificial lamb and the rest of the poem in which it appears anticipate the problems and conflicts that Donne confronts when he returns to the epithalamium roughly eighteen years after composing his "Epithalamion made at Lincolnes Inne." First of all, he needs to work out the tension between lyrical and satirical impulses that destabilizes his first wedding poem. And that generic conflict is in turn closely connected to other decisions enjoined by the genre: will his speakers, like their analogues in other Stuart wedding poems, be active and enthusiastic participants in the festivities, or will they be detached, even cynical, outsiders? how will he balance his attraction to private poetry with the public voice of the epithalamium? how will he reconcile his drive towards self-assertion with respect for authorities, whether patrons or literary predecessors? Above all, however, the return to the epithalamium challenges Donne to resolve the problems inherent in his trope of the sacrificial lamb by untangling the knots between sexuality, violence, death, and religion.

III

If Donne's "Epithalamion made at Lincolnes Inne" is one of the clearest instances of the problems and tensions associated with the Stuart epithalamium, "An Epithalamion, or Mariage Song on the Lady Elizabeth, and Count Palatine" is one of the best examples of their resolution. This is not to say that the tensions manifest in his "Epithalamion made at Lincolnes Inne" disappear totally: at several telling junctures we are in fact reminded of the problems inscribed in that earlier poem. But such moments are relatively rare, and in any event the tensions in question are generally cauterized while still *in situ*. Whereas other wedding poems, including those by Donne him

[33]Many critics have noted his preoccupation with domination. See, e.g., Carey, esp. pp. 106–130.
[34]Donne treats threatening male figures in a similar way as well. See, e.g., Ferry, *All in War with Time*, p. 79.

self, often merely repress, here Donne more frequently resolves: in this epithalamium he works through many of the problems stemming from his attitudes to wedlock and, in particular, those revealed by his earlier image of the bride as a sacrificial lamb.

These achievements are all the more striking because the circumstances surrounding this epithalamium may have intensified Donne's ambivalence about the genre. On the one hand, as we have already seen, this wedding was widely viewed as an antidote to the grief occasioned by the recent death of the bride's brother. The political significance of the wedding further heightened its importance for many observers. Though she had been courted by a number of suitors, including King Philip of Spain, Elizabeth was marrying a Protestant.[35] Moreover, that marriage strengthened James I's position with the Protestant German princes. Although, as John Carey has maintained, Donne's publicly avowed commitment to Protestantism may have concealed some regrets about his apostasy,[36] his concern for the maintenance and extension of royal power surely led him to welcome the apparent political ramifications of this match.[37] On the other hand, Donne's longstanding ambivalence about the court and about his own role in celebrating its achievements is likely to have been heightened by the extravagance of the occasion: the marriage cost the bride's father £93,294. It is conceivable, too, that Donne had reservations about the match despite the obvious advantages of the princess' marrying a Protestant; his close associate Robert Drury publicly and tactlessly expressed his disapproval of the bridegroom.[38]

The primary focus of this lyric is, however, sexual and marital politics, not courtly politics. We encounter hints of the threats that cloud the treatment of sexuality in "Epithalamion made at Lincolnes

[35]On Elizabeth's previous suitors and the political consequences of her match, see G. P. V. Akrigg, *Jacobean Pageant, or The Court of King James I* (Cambridge: Harvard Univ. Press, 1962), p. 142 and chap. 27; David Harris Willson, *King James VI and I*, The Bedford Historical Series (1956; rpt. London: Jonathan Cape, 1959), pp. 282–283, 286–287, 408–431. Though he exaggerates the influence of his apostasy on Donne, Carey does provide a valuable reminder that his responses to a strengthening of Protestantism may well have been mixed (see esp. chap. 1).

[36]Carey, *John Donne: Life, Mind and Art*, esp. chaps. 1 and 2.

[37]Those benefits proved more apparent than real: James had cause to regret his alliance with the Protestant Germans when, participating in an ill-fated rebellion, the Count Palatine assumed the title king of Bohemia. On these events, see Akrigg, chap. 27.

[38]See R. C. Bald, *Donne and the Drurys* (Cambridge: Cambridge Univ. Press, 1959), pp. 102–103, 122.

Inne," but here those threats are typically controlled and subdued. Thus one telling line appears in the otherwise lighthearted evocation of a parliament of fowls on which the poem opens: "The Sparrow that neglects his life for love" (7). This reference unmistakably gestures towards the potential destructiveness of sexuality and the connections between marriages and funerals to which Donne alludes elsewhere. Yet his playful tone warns the reader against taking such dangers too seriously. After all, his reference to the legendary lustfulness of sparrows would have read more ominously had he written, say, "gives up" or "destroys" rather than "neglects." Indeed, the main effect of this and the other allusions to birds is to rejoice in sexual vitality. And, more to the point, throughout the epithalamium Donne constructs marriage as a source of rebirth and renewal rather than a harbinger of death. For that obvious position, of course, he could find ample precedent in his genre; but his expression of it is singularly felicitous and, one suspects, singularly hard won.

The principal way Donne connects the marriage in general and its consummation in particular with rebirth rather than death and destruction is by replacing the linear narrative structures that characterize many other works in his genre with a series of cycles. He hints at this strategy early in the poem when he links the presiding deity of the poem, Bishop Valentine, to natural cycles: each February 14, Donne reminds us, that character officiates at the weddings of birds ("Thou marryest *every* yeare" [5; italics added]). And the poem itself proceeds to enact a series of cycles. Most epithalamia move from day to night; the plot of this one circles around from day to night and then back again to day. Indeed, it does so lexically: the first and last lines of the poem include the word "day." Prosodic devices also contribute to these cyclical patterns: here, as elsewhere in the genre, the refrain conveys a sense of continuity.

The primary way Donne emphasizes the cyclical, however, is by invoking one of his favorite pets: he portrays the couple as a pair of phoenixes.[39] The legend of the phoenix intrinsically celebrates an immortality achieved through repeated cycles of death and rebirth. In this context, however, the mythical bird suggests a second type of cyclical rebirth. Donne's references to the "Phoenix Bride" (29)

---

[39]Don Cameron Allen points out that Donne alludes to a longstanding debate about whether or not the ark included a phoenix ("Donne's Phoenix," *MLN*, 62 [1947], 340–342.

indirectly but unmistakably effect a comparison between Princess Elizabeth and Queen Elizabeth, who was often associated with the phoenix.[40] Several other authors who composed epithalamia for this event connect the princess with her namesake to suggest both nostalgia and rebirth; Donne makes the same point more subtly through his allusions to the phoenix. That bird conveys rebirth in another way: Donne writes, "Where motion kindles such fires, as shall give / Yong Phoenixes, and yet the old shall live" (25–26). These lines perform the transformation that is so often the praxis of the Stuart epithalamium: potential danger is acknowledged but averted, in this case by portraying the "fires" (25) of passion as not a source of destruction, but a stage in the regenerative life cycle of the phoenix.

The poem addresses several problems connected with sexuality in the "Epithalamion made at Lincolnes Inne" in particular and the rest of the canon in general. Donne resolves those dilemmas in part by rendering the sexual union of his phoenixes as a natural process: in relating the consummation of this marriage to the mating of sparrows and larks, he preserves the event from the unnaturalness and violence with which it is associated in his earlier epithalamium. He accomplishes the same ends by reinterpreting gender. Elsewhere in the canon his ambivalences about sexuality are manifest in his recurrent habit of celebrating it by suggesting its disappearance. Donne typically praises sex by praising sexlessness: "So, to one neutrall thing both sexes fit" ("The Canonization," 25). At the most emotionally and physically ecstatic moments in his poetry, the man and woman are typically degendered. This epithalamium performs a similar process: it variously confounds gender through the opening of the seventh stanza, which we will examine shortly, and, more to our purposes now, denies it through the image of the phoenix, a "neutrall thing." Admittedly, here, as in the instance of Donne's lecherous sparrow, the tensions he is attempting to still are only imperfectly suppressed: as I have suggested, it is telling that he can celebrate sexuality only by denying gender. Yet in so doing he does manage to escape and reject the dichotomy of submissive female victim and respectful yet aggressive male attacker which is latent in the "Epithalamion made at Lincolnes Inne."

[40] On the association between Queen Elizabeth and the phoenix, see Frances A. Yates, *Astraea: The Imperial Theme in the Sixteenth Century* (London: Routledge and Kegan Paul, 1975), pp. 58–59, 65–66, 78.

An analysis of the seventh stanza of the poem demonstrates how Donne deploys his reinterpretations of gender, and several additional strategies, to avoid other problems he encountered—and created— when writing the "Epithalamion made at Lincolnes Inne." Throughout this section of the poem, Donne effects the move that we have traced so often in this book: he introduces potentially threatening energies in a form that renders them less threatening.

> Here lyes a shee Sunne, and a hee Moone here,
>   She gives the best light to his Spheare,
>   Or each is both, and all, and so
> They unto one another nothing owe,
>   And yet they doe, but are
> So just and rich in that coyne which they pay,
> That neither would, nor needs forbeare, nor stay;
> Neither desires to be spar'd, nor to spare,
>   They quickly pay their debt, and then
> Take no acquittances, but pay again;
> They pay, they give, they lend, and so let fall
> No such occasion to be liberall.
> More truth, more courage in these two do shine,
> Then all thy turtles have, and sparrows, Valentine.
>   (85–98)

The opening lines work out some of the tensions to which we have just referred: they shift from an emphasis on female power ("a shee Sunne" [85]) to a reactive emphasis on male domination ("She gives the best light to his Spheare"[86]) to the eradication of sexual difference ("Or each is both, and all" [87]). The final line quoted contrives to resolve the tension between equality and mutuality on the one hand and submission on the other by claiming that she is not merely a woman rather than by claiming that she is not subordinate. Donne's restless intellectual movements are mirrored in the restlessness of his language throughout the stanza. Thus his characteristic reliance on the tellingly named disjunctive conjunction "or," as well as his asyndeton ("They pay, they give, they lend" [95]), mime the rapid shifts in the argument and in so doing may even recall the sexual energies that the passage describes. Yet the destabilizing effect of all of these intellectual and syntactical shifts is limited: Donne steadies the passage with several rhetorical devices. The epanalepsis in line 85—"*Here* lyes a shee Sunne, and a hee Moone *here*" (italics added)—creates a sense of balance and stasis that literally and meta-phorically encases the subversive ideas contained between the two words. And the antitheses that structure the line intensify its sense of balance.

Like many other Stuart writers, Donne relies on the concept of due benevolence to transform marriage and married love from a danger to a desideratum. The construction of the marriage debt serves to control sexuality, masking the potentially anarchic or de-structive powers of Cupid and presenting the consummation of the marriage and the bride's own loss of virginity as the fulfill-ment of a responsibility. But Donne goes further, wittily portraying what might otherwise be interpreted as threateningly intense sexu-al appetites on the part of both bride and groom as generosity and benevolence: "Neither desires to be spar'd, nor to spare" (92). The continuing slippage between the normally separate roles of lender and borrower, which recalls the slippages in gender roles earlier, emphasizes the mutuality of this love, suggesting that the woman fully shares both the passion and the pleasure in its ful-fillment.

The poem implies and advocates respect for sexuality in another way. Just as its narrative structure separates procreation from the consummation of the marriage, referring to them in the second and in the seventh and eighth stanzas respectively, so the poem as a whole implies that sexuality is not a mere means to an end but rather an end in itself. And in the reference to heirs Donne, un-like other practitioners of the genre, emphasizes the survival of the couple themselves: "Where motion kindles such fires, as shall give / Yong Phoenixes, and yet the old shall live" (25–26). This em-phasis anticipates the final stanza, which portrays the bride and groom, not their heirs, as the source and symbol of regeneration: "And by this act of these two Phenixes / Nature againe restored is" (99–100).

The "Epithalamion made at Lincolnes Inne," as we saw, connects sexuality and spirituality through its disturbing and heavyhanded evocation of the priest and lamb, as well as through its lengthy de-scription of the church. In the wedding poem for the union of the Count Palatine and Elizabeth, Donne does not undo the knot tying the two realms in question. Rather, he refastens it more gracefully: he cleverly contrives to associate the marriage with spirituality while at the same time emphasizing the autonomy and power of bride and groom. He achieves this in part through his evocation of Bishop Valentine, the figure who, displacing the pagan Hymen, presides over the poem. Based on a martyr—or possibly two conflated martyrs—from the Christian calendar,[41] Donne's Valentine assumes a key role in the lyric: in tribute to his day, each stanza is fourteen lines long, and the lyric literally opens and closes on references to him, a pattern mirrored in the repetition of his name in the initial and final lines of the first stanza.

Yet Valentine, like so many other potential authorities in Donne's poems, is approached lightheartedly, even at times mockingly. The opening stanza stresses his connections with the natural world more than his supernatural significance.[42] In declaring "All the Aire is thy Diocis" (2) and "all the . . . other birds are thy Parishioners" (3–4), assertions that signal the commonplace link between the figure from the Christian calendar and the legend of birds mating on St. Valentine's Day, Donne at once celebrates and circumscribes the power of the figure: he is the bishop of everything and of nothing. Moreover, the stanza ends on a note of goodhumored raillery: "This day, which might enflame thy self, Old Valentine" (14). Donne is, as it were, having his wedding cake and eating it too: he is retaining the invocation characteristic of his genre and the linkage between sexual and spiritual realms characteristic of his own temperament while at the same time he prevents us from taking too seriously the leading representative of the spiritual realms.

The treatment of Valentine is also germane to Donne's resolution of another generic problem. I have suggested that Stuart epithalamia, like many of their predecessors, typically emphasize the communal and public implications of the wedding, whereas Donne is more prone to stress the privacy of love and of lovers. Throughout this epithalamium, he mediates between public and private worlds but characteristically gives his own preference, the latter, the edge. Although the poem devotes considerable emphasis to the figure of Bishop Valentine, the actual bishop who marries the couple—no less

[41]On the background to this figure and the debate about whether two martyrs named Valentine are conflated, see. F. L. Cross and E. A. Livingstone, *The Oxford Dictionary of the Christian Church*, 2d ed. (London: Oxford Univ. Press, 1974), p. 1423; Herbert Thurston, S.J., and Donald Attwater, eds., *Butler's Lives of the Saints*, rev. ed., 4 vols. (New York: P. J. Kenedy and Sons, 1956), I, 47, 332–334.

[42]For a trenchant commentary on the ways Donne moves between the natural and supernatural realms throughout the poem, see Milgate, *Epithalamions*, pp. xxiii–xxiv.

a dignitary than the archbishop of Canterbury[43]—and the religious
institutions he represents are treated almost offhandedly:

> Goe then to where the Bishop staies,
> To make you one, his way, which divers waies
> Must be effected.
>
> (51–53)

Other epithalamia devote as much as an entire stanza to the church
ceremony; Donne's vague reference to that event occupies only one
and one-half of the fourteen lines in its stanza. And his writing
"Goe" (51) rather than "Come" is also revealing. Consistently em-
ploying proximal deictics such as "here" and "this," he stresses elsewhere in the poem his speaker's proximity to the happening being
described; "*Come* forth, *come* forth" (43), "Staies he new light from
these to get?" (59), "*Here* lyes a shee Sunne, and a hee Moone *here*"
(85; italics added in all quotations), and so on. Hence the word
"Goe" (51) represents a significant deviation, rendering the church
ceremony more distant from the speaker's vision and from that of the
reader.

Donne further emphasizes the private aspects of the wedding by
playing down—indeed, apparently ignoring—its courtly context.
The delightful opening of the poem is worth quoting at length. Following the rhetoricians' strictures about relating the wedding at hand
to other marriages,[44] Donne writes:

> Haile Bishop Valentine, whose day this is,
>   All the Aire is thy Diocis,
>   And all the chirping Choristers
> And other birds are thy Parishioners,
>   Thou marryest every yeare
> The lirique Larke, and the grave whispering Dove,
> The Sparrow that neglects his life for love,
> The household Bird, with the red stomacher,
>   Thou mak'st the Blackbird speed as soone,
>   As doth the Goldfinch, or the Halcyon;

---

[43]See Margaret M. McGowan, " 'As Through a Looking-glass': Donne's Epithalamia and Their Courtly Context," in *John Donne: Essays in Celebration*, ed. A. J.
Smith (London: Methuen, 1972), p. 185. This important article anticipates by some
ten years many of the emphases of the new historicism.

[44]See e.g., *Menander Rhetor*, ed. and trans. D. A. Russell and N. G. Wilson (Oxford: Clarendon Press, 1981), pp. 136–139.

> The husband Cocke lookes out, and straight is sped,
> And meets his wife, which brings her feather-bed.
> This day more cheerfully then ever shine,
> This day, which might enflame thy self, Old Valentine.
>
> Till now, Thou warmd'st with multiplying loves
> Two larkes, two sparrowes, or two Doves;
> All that is nothing unto this,
> For thou this day couplest two Phoenixes.
>
> (1–18)

Epithalamia typically mediate, as we have observed, between the natural and the civilized realms. Donne, however, here devotes more attention to the former than most of his counterparts in the genre, evoking a pastoral scene whose details are precisely, even lovingly, observed. That evocation is all the more striking when one remembers how urban his vision is elsewhere. On one level this denial of the courtly is in fact the courtliest of stratagems: Donne, as it were, naturalizes an extravagant and showy event, implying that all of the negotiations and celebrations surrounding this marriage resemble nothing so much as the mating of birds. But in another sense the pastoral setting allows him to avoid the respectful, even sycophantic, awe that this occasion generates in some of the other poets who celebrate it, such as George Wither; indeed, as the lyric progresses, it nowhere mentions the king and only once alludes to the fact that the bride is a "Great Princess" (38).

Donne's privileging of a pastoral setting in lieu of a courtly one relates to another decision he makes. His contemporaries typically draw attention to the political and dynastic implications of the wedding. "Happy they, and we that see it, / For the good of *Europe* be it" (sig. C2ᵛ), Wither rhapsodizes and proceeds to devote the rest of the stanza to a nationalistic attack on Rome. By disregarding the issues that Wither and other poets raise, Donne again implies that what is most important is the union of the couple.

He establishes that point later in the poem as well. Like the authors of many other epithalamia, he laments the delays that interfere with the consummation of the marriage; unlike some of those authors, he blames those delays on communal festivities:

> The feast, with gluttonous delaies,
> Is eaten, and too long their meat they praise,

The masquers come too late, and'I thinke, will stay,
Like Fairies, till the Cock crow them away.
                    .   .   .   .   .
    What meane these Ladies, which (as though
They were to take a clock in peeces,) goe
        So nicely'about the Bride;
A Bride, before a good night could be said,
Should vanish from her cloathes, into her bed.
                                        (65–68, 73–77)

In the comment on the masquers we may detect an undertone of
criticism of the lengthy and lavish festivities occasioned by this wedding, the very criticism Donne had sidestepped earlier by deploying
pastoral motifs. But the poet's customary commitment to the privacy of love is surely the impetus behind these passages: the celebrations of the masquers and the ministrations of the matrons, he
implies, are not central to an occasion that should center on the relationship, especially the sexual union, of the couple themselves.[45] Ben
Jonson's epithalamia typically celebrate weddings in part because
they provide communal festivities. In contrast, here, as elsewhere in
his writings, Donne constructs the outside world as a source of intrusion and entrapment rather than of solace and pleasure.

Composing this epithalamium invites Donne to resolve not only
the couple's relationship to the public world but also his own. In
particular, the genre, like the formal verse letter, challenges him to
develop strategies for bestowing the praise that the occasion and the
genre enjoin on him without descending to the cloying sycophancy
that mars so many other wedding poems composed for the event. To
put it another way, he confronts the cluster of problems we examined
in Chapter 3: participating in ritualistic compliments without surrendering his independence and self-respect.

One solution lies in the conceit of the phoenix, which conveys tacit
yet intense praise. It suggests the uniqueness and mystical power of
both bride and groom. And it allows Donne to effect between Princess Elizabeth and Queen Elizabeth the link that is forged in many
other epithalamia written for this occasion—but to do so only implicitly, thus avoiding the obtrusive flattery of, say, Thomas Heywood's rendition of the same compliment.

---

[45]Compare Milgate, *Epithalamions,* p. xxiii, on Donne's omission of minor wedding customs such as the fight over the garters.

The third stanza demonstrates several other strategies for delivering praise while preserving one's self-respect:

> Up then faire Phoenix Bride, frustrate the Sunne,
>   Thy selfe from thine affection
>   Tak'st warmth enough, and from thine eye
> All lesser birds will take their jollitie.
>   Up, up, faire Bride, and call,
> Thy starres, from out their severall boxes, take
> Thy Rubies, Pearles, and Diamonds forth, and make
> Thy selfe a constellation, of them All,
>   And by this blazing, signifie,
> That a Great Princess falls, but doth not die;
> Bee thou a new starre, that to us portends
> Ends of much wonder; And be Thou those ends.
>   (29–40)

Once again we encounter a hint of tension: the conceit of the falling star does not completely explain away "falls" (38), which, evoking the commonplace connections between sexuality and the Fall, reminds us of the uneasy responses to the loss of virginity we find elsewhere in Donne's canon.[46] By and large, however, this passage resolves rather than reflects tensions, especially those stemming from its author's ambivalence about his genre and the epideictic role it enjoins on him. The phrase "frustrate the Sunne" (29) signals the first of those resolutions. Other epithalamia generally enjoin the bride to rise because the sun has already done so. Donne reinterprets that generic norm in terms of his predilection for viewing relationships as combative and competitive. Thus he reshapes conventional compliments to the demands of his own temperament.[47]

---

[46]Brief comments on the appearance of this word here and in the Somerset-Howard epithalamium may be found in Doniphan Louthan, *The Poetry of John Donne: A Study in Explication* (New York: Bookman Associates, 1951), p. 79; he argues the term refers to a fall from virginity. Also cf. Marotti, *John Donne, Coterie Poet*, p. 273; McGowan, p. 207.

[47]Only a few lines later, however, we encounter a tribute that involves a more conventional nod to literary tradition: the word "jollitie" (32) appears nowhere in Donne's poetic works save this passage and a similar one in the "Epithalamion made at Lincolnes Inne" (see Homer Carroll Combs and Zay Rusk Sullens, *A Concordance to the English Poems of John Donne* [Chicago: Packard, 1940], s.v. "jollity"): he is echoing—and perhaps self-consciously alluding to as well—a line from Spenser's "Epithalamion," "With ioyance bring her and with iollity" (245).

The imperatives through which Donne commands the bride to dress are also telling. Linking courtly jewels and heavenly stars, these lines once again conflate the natural and human worlds and in so doing praise the princess as a paragon in both spheres. At the same time, however, these imperatives function in the way we traced in Chapter 3: they assert the poet's own potency and centrality at an occasion at which he may in fact have felt a marginalized outsider.[48]

The commands to the bride also serve at once to intensify and to modulate the very praise they are bestowing. "Make / Thy selfe a constellation, of them All" (35–36) and "Bee thou a new starre" (39) indisputably compliment Princess Elizabeth: she is gifted not only with the potentiality of being a star but also with the power of transforming herself into one. At the same time, the lines draw attention to elements of play and of pretense—and, indeed, of self-fashioning—in the process of the bride's dressing up. A lyric that is concerned with transformations of all types (people turn into phoenixes, jewels into stars, and so on) here focuses on the metamorphoses that the bride performs. And as she is adorning and thus transforming herself, we are reminded, the poet is adorning and thus transforming her rhetorically: in the line "Bee thou a new starre" (39) the poet turns her into one.

The final stanza can help us summarize the workings of the whole poem, for it reintroduces both the tensions and the solutions we have encountered throughout the lyric, much as the final act of a play brings the characters back on stage:

> And by this act of these two Phenixes
> Nature againe restored is,
> For since these two, are two no more,
> Ther's but one Phenix still, as was before.
> Rest now at last, and wee
> As Satyres watch the Sunnes uprise, will stay
> Waiting, when your eyes open'd, let out day,
> Onely desir'd, because your face wee see;
> Others neare you shall whispering speake,
> And wagers lay, at which side day will breake,

---

[48]Marotti, *John Donne, Coterie Poet*, pp. 271–272, also notes that the speaker is presented as a participant in the festivities in this epithalamium. Ann Hurley makes a similar point about the Somerset-Howard epithalamium in "The Elided Self: Witty Dis-Locations in Velázquez and Donne," *Journal of Aesthetics and Art Criticism*, 44 (1986), 357.

And win by'observing, then, whose hand it is
That opens first a curtaine, hers or his;
This will be try'd to morrow after nine
Till which houre, wee thy day enlarge, O Valentine.
(99–112)

The reference to satyrs is curiously inappropriate and puzzling, especially since Donne's editors have been able to glean no definitive information about the custom to which he is apparently alluding.[49] The satirical energies that disrupt the "Epithalamion made at Lincolnes Inne"—that is, the drive to undermine a calm lyrical vision and the preoccupation with uncontrolled and possibly excessive sexuality—here emerge through what is a more literally satirical vision. The poem is bracketed by its opening reference to libidinous sparrows and its concluding allusion to lecherous satyrs.

This stanza is troubling in another way. Donne's curiously voyeuristic reference to guests outside the bedchamber is grounded in both historical practice and literary convention. James I delighted in asking married couples for details of their wedding night, as we saw earlier, and the very term "epithalamium" reminds us that the genre is rooted in folk epithalamia that were apparently delivered outside the bedchamber.[50] But this background does not fully explain why a poem that has elsewhere been so concerned to stress the privacy of love and to downplay the communal festivities associated with the marriage here emphasizes the presence of visitors at the most private of moments. One answer is that Donne wishes to end the poem, as he began it, on an intimate note. But the principal explanation for these lines is personal as well as political. Though in certain sections of the "Epithalamion made at Lincolnes Inne" the speaker establishes a satirical distance from the events, elsewhere in that lyric he is eager to insist on his own presence and participation. Like his analogues in other epithalamia, he repeatedly delivers commands; and he reinforces the immediacy of his vision through such usages as "*This* Bridegroom," and "*our* amorous starre" (31, 62; italics added). The apparent oddities of the final stanza of the epithalamium written for

[49]For instance, Milgate (*Epithalamions*, p. 117) merely defines satyrs and notes that they were given to revelry; Grierson does not explicate the line; John T. Shawcross suggests that the satyrs "would not be glad to see the sunrise and thus end their pleasure-filled night" (*The Complete Poetry of John Donne*, The Stuart Editions [New York and London: New York Univ. Press and Univ. of London Press, 1968], p. 177).

[50]See, e.g., George Puttenham, *The Arte of English Poesie*, ed. Gladys Doidge Willcock and Alice Walker (1936; rpt. Cambridge: Cambridge Univ. Press, 1970), p. 51.

the Count Palatine and Princess Elizabeth can be explained in a similar way. Donne, who was at this point in his life trying hard to
secure preferment, is eager to indulge in fantasies of his own presence
and importance at court: the voyeuristic observers act out his own
desire to see and be seen. These lines represent, then, an uncommon
response to the common tensions traced in Chapter 3.

Primarily, however, the tone of this stanza is positive. Here, as in
so much of the poem, Donne transforms potential disruption into a
vision of restored and recuperated order: "Nature againe restored is"
(100). He effects that move in the characteristic way we noted earlier: throughout this stanza, as in previous sections of the poem, he
emphasizes cyclical processes. The word "againe" (100) is telling,
and, as I pointed out above, the poem ends on two of the words on
which it began, "day" and "Valentine." Characteristically, of course,
Donne expresses through linguistic instability the social stability created by the restoration of nature. "For since these two, are two no
more, / Ther's but one Phenix still, as was before" (101–102), lines
rendered even more complicated by the fact that "still" could mean
"always" in Renaissance English,[51] paradoxically declares that the
two phoenixes are reunited and that they were never separated in the
first place. A source of sacramental violence in Donne's earliest epithalamium, the consummation of the marriage is here instead a
source of the restoration of nature itself.

Throughout this poem, we find traces of the problems and anxieties typically inscribed in Stuart epithalamia. At the same time,
however, Donne delimits those tensions through a series of restora-
tions, renewals, and reconciliations. Thus in lieu of connecting sexuality and death, he evokes a vision of rebirth through prosodic and
semantic allusions to cycles. Instead of the troubled conjunctions of
sexuality, violence, and submission that emerge in the "Epithalamion
made at Lincolnes Inne," he lauds equality and mutuality. And the
poem involves another kind of resolution. Elsewhere in his canon
Donne often shifts uneasily between celebrating his submissiveness
to secular and spiritual powers on the one hand and constructing a
loaded adversarial relationship with them on the other; here he circumscribes the significance of those powers and thus reconciles his
vision of the wedding and his own role within it with the literary
authority of his generic tradition, the religious authority of the
bishop who married the couple, and the political authority of the
king and the court.

[51]*OED*, s.v. "still."

IV

Having triumphantly met so many challenges when commemorating the wedding of Princess Elizabeth and the Count Palatine, Donne was confronted with trickier versions of those same challenges and a series of new ones a few months later when he composed an epithalamium for the marriage of Frances Howard and Somerset.[52] (Robert Carr was created viscount of Rochester in 1611 and earl of Somerset in 1613.) The dubious events surrounding this marriage rendered its celebration problematical for any poet; the occasion was better suited for a Jacobean tragedy than an epithalamium. In particular, the fears of sexuality, especially female sexuality, that attended on weddings found their objective correlative in the reputation of the bride. The anxieties embodied in Donne's image of the sacrificial lamb suggest that he would have responded especially intensely to the moral ambiguities of this event: he did not need much encouragement to associate marriage with violence and destruction.

The moral problems posed by this wedding generated literary ones: adapting generic norms to celebrate the union of Somerset and Frances Howard was a perilous undertaking. For instance, the prayer for children, so central in other epithalamia, was a potentially explosive motif since it drew attention to the alleged impotence of Frances Howard's first husband. Nor could poets celebrating this occasion readily posit a reconciliation of sexual urges and social values: the events behind this particular wedding exemplified an intensification of that conflict, not its resolution. Similarly, the convention of portraying a community happily celebrating the wedding was inappropriate: the marriage certainly occasioned lavish festivities, but contemporary reports of scandalized gossip suggest that the court hardly responded with uncritical enthusiasm to the celebrations.[53] Some of the more obvious solutions to such problems were not feasible. In particular, as Barbara Kiefer Lewalski has shown, Donne had developed what she terms "symbolic praise" as a strategy for preserving his integrity while complimenting patrons and patronesses.[54] But that technique was not accessible to him or his con-

---

[52]I am indebted to Richard Strier for several useful suggestions about this section of the book.

[53]See, e.g., Thomas Birch, ed., *The Court and Times of James the First,* 2 vols. (London: Henry Colburn, 1848), I, 269–289.

[54]Barbara Kiefer Lewalski, *Donne's "Anniversaries" and the Poetry of Praise: The Creation of a Symbolic Mode* (Princeton: Princeton Univ. Press, 1973).

temporaries when they came to celebrate this wedding: "symbolic praise" depends on building up the subject of the poem into an ideal, a process difficult in this case.

The circumstances of the wedding made composing an epithalamium singularly unattractive, but the circumstances of Donne's own career made doing so virtually unavoidable. The poem was probably written early in 1614, when his need to please a patron was acute.[55] He had been trying without success for several years to obtain an attractive appointment; Sir Robert Drury at first seemed a promising avenue to preferment but had recently proved a liability to those associated with him. Donne's tract *Pseudo-Martyr* inspired the king to recommend religious appointments for its author, not the secular ones he had been so sedulously and so unsuccessfully pursuing. Though actively considering the church, Donne remained hesitant. Under these circumstances, Somerset may well have seemed his last hope for secular preferment.

He was also in some senses Donne's best hope. After initially attracting the king's attention by injuring his leg in a tournament, Somerset had become James I's favorite. The significance of that fact emerges when we contrast the Jacobean and Elizabethan courts. For most of her reign Elizabeth skillfully juggled favorites and permitted several factions, so there were many paths to royal patronage. James I, in contrast, indulged in single-faction rule: it was through the support of his favorite of the moment that one could attract the king's interest and secure his largesse. At the time Donne was courting the favor of Somerset, then, that nobleman was in a singularly good position to obtain for Donne the preferment he had been seeking. Hence the pressure to please him was particularly intense.

Yet Donne no doubt recognized the fragility of Somerset's power. The shelf-life of courtly favorites, after all, was not always long, as Somerset's own fall was soon to demonstrate. Recent shifts in the center of power at court, notably those occasioned by the death of Prince Henry in 1612,[56] testified to the slipperiness of courtly ladders as eloquently as Sir Thomas Wyatt's extraordinary lyrics on the

[55]On this period in Donne's life and on Drury's own professional problems, see Bald, *John Donne: A Life*, p. 238 and chap. 11.
[56]On the significance of this death, see Arthur F. Marotti, "John Donne and the Rewards of Patronage," in *Patronage in the Renaissance*, ed. Guy Fitch Lytle and Stephen Orgel (Princeton: Princeton Univ. Press, 1981), p. 230.

subject a century earlier. Such perceptions did not prevent Donne from seeking to please Somerset, but they do help explain aspects of the resulting epithalamium.

Donne's letters suggest that he felt ambivalent about composing an epithalamium under these circumstances. "I deprehend in my self more then an alacrity, a vehemency to do service to that company," he writes, "and so, I may finde reason to make rime."[57] One denotation of "deprehend" is to "to catch . . . in the commission of some evil or secret deed,"[58] a meaning underscored by "vehemency," with its suggestion of a loss of reason and balance, and by the denigration of the artistic process implied by "make rime." A similar ambivalence about patronage in general and his relationship to this patron in particular creates a strong undertow in an apparently complimentary letter Donne addresses to Somerset himself: "After I was grown to be your Lordships, by all the titles that I could thinke upon, it hath pleased your Lordship to make another title to me, by buying me" (p. 290).

Donne responds to the clash between his reluctance to celebrate the wedding and the pressures to do so in two principal ways. Using many of the same devices he had deployed in his poem on the marriage of Princess Elizabeth and the Count Palatine, he attempts to resolve the tensions associated with wedlock in general and this union in particular; thus, for example, once again he transforms linear patterns into cyclical ones. But his second response distinguishes this epithalamium from "An Epithalamion, or Mariage Song on the Lady Elizabeth, and Count Palatine." There he deployed proximal deictics to emphasize the immediacy of the event and his own involvement in it ("And by *this* act of *these* two Phenixes" [99; italics added]); here he devises a whole range of strategies to distance his speaker and his audience from the events being described.

Both responses testify to his indebtedness to generic conventions: if they are part of the problem in the instance of this wedding, they are also part of the solution. For all of Donne's originality, in no sense are his epithalamia sui generis. To borrow a phrase that Annette Kolodny uses in a different context, it is in part by adapting

[57]John Donne, *Letters to Severall Persons of Honour* (London, 1651), pp. 180–181. Also cf. the letter on pp. 270–271. Subsequent citations to this edition will appear in my text.
[58]*OED*, s.v. "deprehend."

generic norms that Donne performs the feat of "dancing through the minefield."[59]

The results of that perilous dance are mixed.[60] The problems involved in writing this epithalamium are greater than those Donne had confronted when composing "An Epithalamion, or Mariage Song on the Lady Elizabeth, and Count Palatine," and at several points the solutions he attempts are less successful. Nonetheless, he responds to such problems with more skill than he had been able to bring to their counterparts in his "Epithalamion made at Lincolnes Inne"; in particular, he subtly but trenchantly sandwiches criticism of the couple between his compliments to them. Many critics have ignored those criticisms: they do not see what they do not expect to see, the same psychological pattern that no doubt affected the way Donne's patron read the poem, if indeed he did more than glance at it. Yet Donne's criticisms of the bride and groom deserve far more attention than they have received, for they once again demonstrate his skill at solving the problems attending on the epithalamium.

One such problem is the connection between marriage and death. In his seventh stanza that connection appears to be troubling Donne:

> Live, till all grounds of wishes faile,
> Till honor, yea till wisedome grow so stale,
> That, new great heights to trie,
> It must serve your ambition, to die.
>
> (173–176)

This passage is, of course, a version of the conventional prayer for a long life, but its length is surprising and its wit strained. Such flaws reflect some of the tensions that generated the description of the sacrificial lamb in the "Epithalamion made at Lincolnes Inne."

[59]Annette Kolodny, "Dancing through the Minefield: Some Observations on the Theory, Practice, and Politics of a Feminist Literary Criticism," *Feminist Studies*, 6 (1980), 1–25.

[60]For a more positive evaluation of this poem, see, e.g., Joseph H. Summers, *The Heirs of Donne and Jonson* (London: Chatto and Windus, 1970), p. 33. William A. McClung and Rodney Simard argue that many criticisms of the poem may be traced to critics' prejudices about the homosexuality at James's court ("Donne's Somerset Epithalamion and the Erotics of Criticism," *Huntington Library Quarterly*, 50 [1987], 95–106). I am grateful to the authors for making their manuscript available to me prior to publication.

Yet the epithalamium for Frances Howard and Somerset resolves
some of those tensions by transforming death into one stage in a cyclical process of renewal. Donne substitutes the resurrection of the
year for the diurnal resurrection in his second wedding poem—
"Thou art repriv'd, old yeare, thou shalt not die, / Though thou
upon thy death bed lye" (105–106)—and proceeds to suggest that the
fire from the couple will rescue the failing year. These references to
rebirth have broader resonances. They remind us of the praxis of the
genre, which so often transforms anxieties and threats, and of
Donne's own aim of rescuing the couple themselves from the death
of their reputations. And since these allusions to renewal follow directly after the speaker, Idios, asserts that he himself is dead, Donne
may be hinting as well that the poem represents a kind of resurrection for its speaker as well as for the year.

Symmetrically, this epithalamium closes on a reference to avoiding
death:

> Now, as in Tullias tombe, one lampe burnt cleare,
>   Unchang'd for fifteene hundred yeare,
>   May these love-lamps we here enshrine,
> In warmth, light, lasting, equall the divine.
>   Fire ever doth aspire,
> And makes all like it selfe, turnes all to fire,
> But ends in ashes, which these cannot doe,
> For none of them is fuell, but fire too.
>
>   (215–222)

These lines mention the possibility of destruction, of "ashes" (221),
only to deny its relevance, a move we have often encountered in the
genre.

The main challenge Donne faces in writing this lyric, however, is
constructing marriage and sexuality in general and that of this couple
in particular as a source of social and personal rewards rather than of
risks. The problem is that such a challenge involves different and
often conflicting pressures. Most obviously, the pressures of the patronage system enjoin defending and celebrating the match; moral
pressures encourage criticism. Some of the apparent contradictions in
the poem stem from Donne's attempt to serve a variety of masters—
and to turn at least some of them into his servants instead.

We saw that in the epithalamium composed for Princess Elizabeth
and the Count Palatine, he skillfully deployed generic conventions to

shape praise that never crosses the line between tactfully crafted compliments and cloying sycophancy. That line is sometimes crossed in his third epithalamium. A victim of his increased desperation about patronage, Donne often seems primarily concerned with the political advantages the poem could bring him. Moreover, he festoons this epithalamium with particularly fulsome compliments—perhaps in an attempt to overcompensate for the distaste for the Somerset wedding implied in some of the covert criticisms he incorporates in the lyric.

Thus it is striking that the flattery here is much more blatant and extensive than the compliments to the Princess Elizabeth and her bridegroom. The Palatine epithalamium devotes less space to praising the couple; its first stanza evokes a natural scene, for example, ignoring the wedding itself until the final two lines, whereas the corresponding stanza of the Somerset poem culminates on a compliment to the bride and bridegroom:

> The passage of the West or East would thaw,
> And open wide their easie liquid jawe
> To all our ships, could a Promethean art
> Either unto the Northerne Pole impart
> The fire of these inflaming eyes, or of this loving heart.
>
> (7–11)

The differences between these opening stanzas point to a distinction that continues to demarcate the two lyrics: the compliments in the Palatine poem are more playful and more restrained.

Many of the flattering tributes in the Somerset epithalamium are directed to the king himself. At first this tactic appears curious: the wedding of James I's daughter Elizabeth would have seemed a more obvious opportunity for such compliments, and yet the Palatine epithalamium contains very few of them. Only once in the entire poem are we even reminded that the bride is a princess. One reason the Somerset wedding poem includes such tributes is that the king himself was indirectly implicated in the dubious events behind the wedding, having favored the bridegroom and supported his attempts to marry the notorious Frances Howard. To praise him was to acknowledge and implicitly accept his responsibility for the marriage. In addition, it is likely that when he wrote the Somerset epithalamium Donne was even more desperate about patronage than he had been a year earlier and hence more eager to scatter compliments as widely as possible. Perhaps, too, his nervousness about the political longevity of James's favorites encouraged him to flatter the ultimate source of bounty rather than simply devote the poem to praising its conduit.

Donne responds to the demands of the patronage system in a second and more subtle way. In the interests of lending respectability to this match and defending Somerset and Howard from the accusations that had been leveled against them, he repeatedly develops the generic convention of presenting sexuality as tamed, controlled, and rechanneled. This task was not an easy one in the instance of this particular marriage, but Donne's wit serves him well. For example, one image in the lyric cleverly implies that this wedding does indeed involve the conventional reconciliation of social and sexual forces:

> Our little Cupid hath sued Livery,
> And is no more in his minority,
> He is admitted now into that brest
> Where the Kings Counsells and his secrets rest.
> (87–90)

In more ways than one, these lines civilize the god of love. By describing him as "Our little Cupid" (87), an epithet that may suggest fondness or condescension or both, the passage effectively tames him; sexuality becomes not an enemy of the court and its values but rather its pet ("*Our* little Cupid" [87]). The assertion that he "hath sued Livery" (87) also lessens the threats Cupid might otherwise represent. One editor interprets this image as a statement that Cupid, no longer a minor, has filed a legal application to leave the system of wardship; another glosses "Livery" (87) as the clothes of a retainer, worn to indicate that he is in Somerset's service.[61] Both readings are possible, and both make Venus's son seem less menacing than readers of Renaissance texts—or readers of the cultural text at hand, the wedding of Somerset and Howard—might otherwise assume. If Cupid is petitioning the legal system, he is not an opponent of society but rather a participant in it. Furthermore, he is petitioning it because he "is no more in his minority" (88); this phrase suggests he has traded the childish fecklessness and recklessness normally associated with him for adulthood. And it is an adulthood presented in

---

[61]See, respectively, Milgate, *Epithalamions*, p. 121; Shawcross, *The Complete Poetry of John Donne*, p. 180.

terms of legal rights and and political responsibility, not the irre-
sponsibility manifested by the adults to whom this poem refers.
Alternatively, if we read the lines as an affirmation that Cupid is—
by choice—clothed, then the image is a literalized version of one way
Donne defends the couple throughout the poem: here and elsewhere
Donne indicates that the raw forces of sexuality choose to wear the
vestments of society, of respectability. Our impression that this Cupid will not threaten society is intensified by "is admitted" (89),
where the passive implies that Cupid did not shove or shoot his way
into the hearts of the bride and bridegroom but rather entered po-
litely, at their pleasure.

The epithalamium deploys other generic norms to suggest that
sexuality is controlled and subdued even—or especially—in the instance of this scandalous match. In many wedding poems the speaker
urgently anticipates the wedding night and complains about the
events that delay it. In the Palatine poem Donne himself writes, "and
night is come; and yet wee see / Formalities retarding thee" (71–72);
the implication is not that the bride is hesitant about going to bed
but that the events of the day are impeding her. In the Somerset epithalamium, in contrast, the speaker chastises the bride for her apparent reluctance to consummate the marriage:

> What mean'st thou Bride, this companie to keep?
> To sit up, till thou faine wouldst sleep?
> Thou maist not, when thou'art laid, doe so.
> (193–195)

On a subterranean level this passage acknowledges one tension associated with the wedding; it posits a clash between the demands of
society, of "companie" (193), and the demands of sexuality. But of
course Donne is reversing the way that tension actually functioned in
the events behind the marriage: he suggests that Frances Howard is
prone to fulfill her social duties at the expense of her sexual drives,
not vice versa. Thus the passage serves to obfuscate and even deny
her actual behavior. These and subsequent lines attribute to Frances
Howard a singularly improbable maidenly modesty—a point made
more explicitly in what is undoubtedly the most outrageous lie of the
poem: "Their soules, though long acquainted they had beene, /
These clothes, their bodies, never yet had seene" (210–211).

Similarly, this poem, like "An Epithalamion, or Mariage Song on
the Lady Elizabeth, and Count Palatine," plays down the conven-

tional prayer for children; but Donne's motivations here are significantly different. "Raise heires, and may here, to the worlds end, live / Heires from this King, to take thankes, you, to give" (177–178), he writes in the epithalamium addressed to Frances Howard and Somerset. The syntax is knotty, but the main point seems to be that the heirs of the couple will serve those of the king; the lines devote more attention to courtly service than to the offspring as such. In so doing they allow Donne again to compliment the king, hence cutting his losses if Somerset himself proved a less helpful patron than Donne hoped. But the passage serves other functions more germane to our purposes: it permits Donne to touch only lightly on a subject rendered delicate by Frances Howard's accusations against her first husband and to deflect attention from the sexual act necessary for the production of heirs.

Another way Donne develops generic conventions to lend respectability to the couple is by playing up the church ceremony. He spends very little time on that episode in his Palatine wedding poem, as we saw, and hence implies that the emotional and physical union of the couple is far more important than the way the priest joins them together. In the Somerset epithalamium, in contrast, the church service becomes as central as it is in Spenser's "Epithalamion," though it is central for different reasons: Donne is stressing that the church blesses this marriage and hence sanctions it. In so doing he also defies the bishops who had in fact opposed the match.[62]

In Donne's first epithalamium, religious references serve primarily to justify the violent consummation of the marriage. In his second sortie into the genre, the references to Bishop Valentine render the events sacred while preserving the autonomy of the couple and distancing them from the court. And here, in his third epithalamium, Donne in a sense circles back to one of the purposes impelling his "Epithalamion made at Lincolnes Inne": he again uses religious references to lend respectability to otherwise dubious events. But in this instance his aim is to defend not the consummation of the marriage but rather the prior behavior of the couple, as well as the actions of the speaker who celebrates them. Thus the act of writing the poem is repeatedly described as sacerdotal: "this poore song, which testifies / I did unto that day some sacrifice" (103–104), "I will lay'it upon / Such Altars, as prize your devotion" (234–235), and so on. Such a

---

[62]On Donne's allusions to the bishops, cf. Carey, p. 87.

claim deepens the implication that this wedding is a sacred event, not a sordid one.

Besides whitewashing the behavior of the couple, the lines in question attempt to perform the same service for their writer: the imagery of priests and altars suggests that his art is not a token in the demeaning financial transactions of patronage but rather a ritual in the holy ceremony of matrimony. Similarly, in "To the Countesse of Huntingdon" ("Man to Gods image"), Donne depicts himself as a priest, hence dignifying and mystifying his own role as suppliant in the more mundane negotiations associated with patronage. Yet, as is so often the case in the Somerset epithalamium, excuses are undermined even as they are proffered: "sacrifice" (104) hints that his devotion to his patron is not without its price.

Donne attempts to defend the couple in another way. Much as the conceit of the phoenix implied the unity and virtual identity of the couple, since we all know there is only one phoenix, so here Donne emphasizes the indivisibility of his lovers:

> Be try'd by beauty, 'and than
> The bridegroome is a maid, and not a man.
> If by that manly courage they be try'd,
> Which scorns unjust opinion; then the bride
> Becomes a man. Should chance or envies Art
> Divide these two, whom nature scarce did part?
>
> Now from your Easts you issue forth, and wee,
>   As men which through a Cipres see
>   The rising sun, doe thinke it two,
> Soe, as you goe to Church, doe thinke of you,
>   But that vaile being gone,
> By the Church rites you are from thenceforth one.
>   (120–125, 160–165)

These passages serve several ends. Most obviously, they justify the bride's divorce and subsequent remarriage. Lines 124–125 state explicitly what the rest of these passages imply: those events are natural and, indeed, virtually inevitable. It is telling, too, that Donne again associates harmony between man and woman with the destabilization of gender. But it is equally telling that in this quotation, unlike the comparable passage about the Princess Elizabeth and the Count Palatine, traditional assumptions about gender, though questioned, are ultimately supported and maintained. Courage is in this instance associated with the woman and beauty with the man, but the poem does not deny that these generally are and should be male and female qualities respectively; notice in particular the implications of the phrase "manly courage" (122). Here, as in American politics of the 1980s, anxieties generate a reassertion of conventional and conservative values.

But defenses of the couple are not the sole purpose of the poem, which at other points slips back and forth between praising or defending them and criticizing them. Such passages may recall the slippage between lyrical and satirical voices in the "Epithalamion made at Lincolnes Inne": the events behind this occasion reactivated Donne's conflicting drives both to celebrate and to criticize the participants in the wedding. Thus his refrains repeatedly refer to the couple's "inflaming eyes."[63] This is yet another tribute to the charms of Frances Howard and Somerset; but when we remember the Renaissance notion that the eyebeams of lovers become entangled when they fall in love, we sense that the lines in question contain a subterranean rebuke, a reference to the illicit passion that lies behind this wedding. This criticism is limited, however, subdued by the fact that the refrains are fourteeners. The resulting languorous movement lessens the sense of passion contained in the imagery of flames: "Since both have both th'enflaming eyes, and both the loving heart" (126). On the prosodic level, as on so many others, the poem attempts to contain the fires ignited by this wedding, to turn a conflagration into a hearthside glow.

Even more suggestive are the lines that invite the bride to weep because the spectators cannot otherwise look safely on her sunlike glory:

> For our ease, give thine eyes, th'unusuall part
> Of joy, a Teare; so quencht, thou maist impart,
> To us that come, thy'inflaming eyes, to him, thy loving heart.

V

Her Apparelling
Thus thou descend'st to our infirmitie,
Who can the Sun in water see.

(146–150)

---

[63]Compare Hurley, 365; she suggests the references to fire throughout the poem may allude to the sins of the couple.

In one sense, this is simply a tribute to the bride's radiant charms, a compliment intensified by adducing the Platonic passage that lies behind this image: she is, the lines imply, like the Idea that cave-dwellers would find it difficult to look upon.[64] Yet just as Plato's imprisoned characters would be hurt by looking at the light, so, Donne's image hints, looking directly at Frances Howard could blind us. One implication is that in general it is dangerous to be too close to the powerful, too much in the sun; another, that we dare not gaze at this particular woman, whether because what we see would be frightening or because we might be burned by the fire emanating from her. This second implication most obviously connects her power with that of male sun-gods, but an allusion to Medusa may be present also[65]—an especially telling resonance when we recall Freud's argument that Medusa is associated with sexual threats. Yet these suggestions remain subdued, ambiguous. And so the lines at once allude to and embody one way the poem works: it handles sensitive issues indirectly and hence renders them safe for the poet to touch and safe for the audience to observe, like a sun in water. By indirection he—and we—find direction out.

Donne responds to the clashes between the demands of patronage, the dark vision exemplified by his trope of the sacrificial lamb, and the values and imperatives of his genre in another way as well: at several points in the poem he offers uncompromising criticisms of the couple. Thus one of the speakers' injunctions to Frances Howard is less ambiguous than the lines we have been examining:

> Pouder thy Radiant haire,
> Which if without such ashes thou would'st weare,
> Thou, which, to all which come to looke upon,
> Art meant for Phoebus, would'st be Phaëton.
> (142–145)

On one level, these lines merely refer to a common method of adorning the hair, but it is surely no accident that ashes are traditionally associated with penitence. This passage subtly but unmistakably

---

[64]Plato, *Republic*, VII, 515–516.

[65]For a discussion of Medusa-like women, see Marjorie B. Garber, *Shakespeare's Ghost Writers: Literature as Uncanny Causality* (London: Methuen, 1988), chap. 5. It is suggestive that, as she reminds us, the Medusa is related to fears of castration, since disapproval of Frances Howard's sexual license may well have involved a sense that she was sexually threatening.

warns the bride that only repentance will preserve her from danger: she must control her passions (and also, perhaps, beware of her desire to be too close to the sun in the sense of the powerful members of the court) lest she destroy and be destroyed as tragically as that arrogant young astronaut Phaëton.

Both the facts behind this wedding and the traditions behind Donne's genre intensify the force of this warning to the bride. Hair often represents sexuality, so a statement that the bride's beautiful hair is potentially dangerous acquires troubling resonances when one considers the circumstances of the particular marriage. Furthermore, at the wedding Frances Howard wore her hair flowing down her back, the sign of a virgin;[66] hence the lines comment as well on her deceptive semiotics, suggesting that the predilection for falsehood represented by her hair needs to be controlled, chastened.

Moreover, if generic traditions lie behind the praise of the bride at other points in the poem, here they implicitly contribute to yet another rebuke. Stuart epithalamia, like their predecessors, frequently suggest that the bride's chastity controls lust: "That's hir *Vertue* which still tameth / Loose desires: and bad thoughts blameth," as Wither puts it ("Epithalamion," sig. C2). Elsewhere in the genre the bride controls the fires of passion emanating from others; here the fires emanating from her might endanger those around, just as Phaëton's flight through the skies kindled a conflagration. Thus the allusion to Phaëton is the dark side, the demonic parody, of the earlier compliments that suggest Frances Howard's eyes inflame the rest of the court.

Donne further criticizes the wedding by writing,

> Plenty this day
> Injures; it causes time to stay;
> The tables groane, as though this feast
> Would, as the flood, destroy all fowle and beast.
> (182–185)

These lines may be playful, but they also hint at a negative judgment on the lavishly expensive festivities associated with the wedding. In another sense, too, this allusion to the destructiveness of gluttony has a sharp and somber edge to it, reminding us of the destructiveness of the other deadly sin in which the couple has indulged. We

---

[66]See Carey, p. 87.

have traced connections between gustatory and sexual appetites earlier. In this instance the excesses of the feast recall the excesses of the bride and bridegroom—and perhaps those of the poet when he bestows hyperbolic praise.

Witness, too, Donne's curious evocation of the bride as a fallen star:

> As he that sees a starre fall, runs apace,
> And findes a gellie in the place,
> So doth the Bridegroome hast as much,
> Being told this starre is falne, and findes her such.
>
> (204–207)

Relating this trope to a particular type of alga supposed to be part of a fallen star, John Carey points out that Donne aptly conveys the way the bridegroom is disconcerted.[67] But the lines also serve to convey some doubts about Frances Howard. In this poem, like Donne's second epithalamium, the suggestion of a fall is troubling; and in this poem, unlike Donne's second epithalamium, the context, especially the earlier critical notes and the references to a "gellie" (205), intensifies the disturbing connotations that attend on the allusion to the Fall.

But it is above all through numerology that Donne censures the wedding. Most readers have ignored this aspect of the poem, in part because they have not anticipated and hence have not found any negative commentary on the couple and also perhaps in part because the extreme claims of some numerological studies have made many critics suspicious of the whole enterprise. Alastair Fowler, the one scholar who has paid any attention to the numerology of the poem, interprets it only positively, finding triumphal forms in the ordering of the stanzas.[68] But it is no accident, I suggest, that eleven stanzas, each consisting of eleven lines, comprise the poem. For as St. Augustine, whose work Donne knew well, declares, "surely then the number eleven, passing ten as it does, stands for trespassing against the law and consequently for sin."[69] Mystical philosophers of

---

[67]Carey, p. 144.

[68]Alastair Fowler, *Triumphal Forms: Structural Patterns in Elizabethan Poetry* (Cambridge: Cambridge Univ. Press, 1970), pp. 71–73.

[69]Augustine, *The City of God against the Pagans*, trans. George E. McCracken et al., 7 vols. (Cambridge and London: Harvard Univ. Press and Heinemann, 1957–1972), IV, 535.

the Middle Ages develop this connection between eleven and sin.[70] Writers, too, pick it up; for instance, as one scholar demonstrates, some of the measurements of Dante's hell are based on multiples of eleven.[71]

How, then, does Donne himself play on the significances of eleven? In the Palatine epithalamium, the fourteen-line stanzas remind us that the wedding takes place on Valentine's Day, February 14, with the beneficent Bishop Valentine as its presiding deity. When we turn to the Somerset epithalamium, in contrast, we find that the length of the stanzas invokes the concept of trespass; just as the number goes beyond the decalogue and hence represents sin, so the couple have gone beyond the decalogue, especially its seventh commandment, in committing their own sins. And the allusion also involves an autobiographical reference: Donne is violating his own moral dictates in praising bride and groom.

Donne relies on another strategy to address the conflict between moral and political imperatives: he develops techniques to distance himself and his audience from the occasion he is forced by the constraints of patronage to celebrate. Jonson too uses distancing devices in one of his epithalamia, but there they serve to evoke an awed contemplation of the event. In Donne's poem these devices function differently, in part because his epithalamium draws our attention to the dangers of contemplating the couple. The distance he creates expresses yet another response to the imperatives of patronage and the vagaries of patrons: if you can't beat 'em, don't join 'em.

In most epithalamia, including Donne's other contributions to the genre, the speaker actively participates in the events, acting as both master of ceremonies and guest at the festivities. In the Somerset-Howard wedding poem, in contrast, Donne generally assumes the more removed stance of observer: "let me here contemplate thee" (129), "wee which doe behold" (152), and so on. Only at a few points does he issue the type of command that recurs so often in other epithalamia. Similarly, in other works in the genre, members of the community participate actively in the events. Here, however, they do not fill many of the functions customarily assigned to them. Attendants surround the bride in Donne's first epithalamium, and

[70]See Vincent Foster Hopper, *Medieval Number Symbolism: Its Sources, Meaning, and Influence on Thought and Expression* (New York: Columbia Univ. Press, 1938), p. 101.
[71]Hopper, p. 152.

matrons undress her in his second; no such figures are present in the "Epithalamion at the Marriage of the Earl of Somerset." When this lyric alludes to members of the community, it does so in terms so vague and general as to play down the presence of the personages they ostensibly evoke: "to all which come to looke upon" (144), "For every part to dance and revell goes" (188).

The responses of Donne's audience mime those of the fictive audience at the festivities, for the reader, too, is distanced from the events. Donne adopts the unusual strategy of prefacing each stanza with a title: "The time of the Mariage," "Raysing of the Bridegroome," and so on. His friend Christopher Brooke, who was writing his own epithalamium at the same time, may have borrowed this technique from Donne.[72] But the conventional wisdom that leads us invariably to ascribe innovation to the more distinguished writer in a pair is, like other conventional wisdom, debatable: it is quite possible that Donne borrowed from Brooke. Whatever the etiology, however, the very existence of such titles frames the action, removing the reader from it so that we, too, feel like detached observers. Similarly, the final stanza of the poem celebrating the marriage of Princess Elizabeth and Count Palatine ends on a vision of the united, or reunited, phoenixes; here, in contrast, Donne concludes on his meditations on Tullias's tomb, a passage that directs some of our attention away from the marriage at hand.

These distancing strategies help us understand one of the most surprising ways Donne approaches his generic heritage. The "Epithalamion at the Marriage of the Earl of Somerset" differs from most Stuart instances of its genre, including Donne's other wedding poems, in that the epithalamium proper is encased within a curious pastoral dialogue. A character named Allophanes rebukes one called Idios for absenting himself from the wedding and retiring to the country in the worst season, "Whilst Flora'herselfe doth a freeze jerkin weare" (8). Idios rejoins that he was not in fact absent since the country is an epitome of courts. Answering that objection, Allophanes proceeds to sing the glories of James's court and, in particular, of the wedding that has just taken place there. Idios declares it is precisely because he agrees that he left the court:

[72] The Brooke poem cannot be dated with certainty since it is not clear whether it was written for a particular wedding; its terminus ad quem is 1614, the publication date of the edition of *England's Helicon* in which it appears.

> I knew
> All this, and onely therefore I withdrew.
> To know and feele all this, and not to have
> Words to expresse it, makes a man a grave
> Of his owne thoughts.
>
> (91–95)

As this passage suggests, the pastoral world in the poem exemplifies the pathetic fallacy; its deathlike coldness and barrenness mime the mental landscape of Idios, who was referred to in the opening line of the poem as "statue of ice." That character proceeds to explain that after retiring to the country he did in fact write an epithalamium, which he then apparently shows Allophanes. Idios attempts to burn the poem, but in the final line of the eclogue Allophanes declares he himself will present it at court.

The few critics who comment on the eclogue at all tend to interpret it as a straightforward apology for the absence from court and from the wedding occasioned by illness, a seventeenth-century version of the greeting cards that apologize for tardiness in commemorating an event.[73] Such readings typically adopt Sir Herbert Grierson's interpretations of the personages in the poem: Idios (the "private man") is Donne himself, and Allophanes ("in another voice") is probably Sir Robert Ker, a friend of Donne's with the same name as the bridegroom.[74] But Donne could have apologized for missing the wedding and submitting his epithalamium late merely by adding a few lines to the poem. The eclogue in fact serves far more complex functions, and the identification of its characters is correspondingly more complex than we have acknowledged. In the course of this eclogue, in brief, Donne is working out—which entails acting out—his relationship to the event. Always intensely self-conscious, he incorporates into the poem an examination of his own participation in the courtly milieu that inspired it and, in particular, a critique of courtly praise.[75] Thus the eclogue reinterprets and at-

---

[73]See, e.g., Bald, *John Donne: A Life*, p. 274.

[74]*The Poems of John Donne*, II, 94.

[75]Several critics have commented on the uses of pastoral in courtly poetry. See esp. Frank Whigham, *Ambition and Privilege: The Social Tropes of Elizabethan Courtesy Theory* (Berkeley: Univ. of California Press, 1984), p. 128. Also cf. Lewalski's observation that Donne's exploration of the process of praise distinguishes his verse letters and epicedes from those of his contemporaries (*Donne's "Anniversaries" and the Poetry of Praise*, esp. pp. 43–44).

tempts with varying degrees of success to resolve many of the problems and challenges we have been tracing throughout this chapter, as
well as in Chapter 3.

One of the roles of the eclogue is to intensify the distancing that
the poem achieves in so many other ways. The pastoral framework
offers a strategy, though a transparent one, for excusing the distaste-
ful act of composing the poem: it was presented at court against Idios's will. Like the other alienated speakers catalogued in Chapter 3,
he distances himself from the festivities; Idios's geographical separation from court provides a metaphor for the psychological separation
he—and Donne himself—wishes to achieve. In a sense, too, Donne
is separating himself from the community of writers who have composed epithalamia, an act reminiscent of the defensive satiric stance
he assumes in the "Epithalamion made at Lincolnes Inne."

But the main function of the eclogue is to express and embody the
problems of courting a patron. Some of that commentary is autobiographical. To the extent that Idios represents Donne, his problems in
writing the epithalamium evidently mirror the poet's own; indeed,
Donne's characteristic self-involvement is reflected in the fact that
even when composing an epithalamium, one of the most public of
forms, he opens and closes with allusions to his own situation. To
put it another way, the relationship between the eclogue and epithalamium responds to Donne's ambivalences about public poetry: he
inserts a public poem in a private framework.

Though references to death and icy coldness recur throughout
Donne's poetry, they may have a more local significance here, representing metaphorically a sense of sterility or perhaps an actual writing block.[76] The "inexpressibility conceit" is a common literary
convention, and one might make a case that Donne is mechanically
adducing it; but all of his other allusions to his ambivalences about
the poetry suggest instead that he is using that conventional conceit
to express his own responses to the problems of praising Somerset
and his blushing bride.

Yet why should we assume that only Idios represents Donne? An-

---

[76]In a prose letter he declares that he could write an epithalamium for the occasion
were his Muse not dead (*Letters to Severall Persons of Honour,* p. 270), but it is hard to
be sure that this reference substantiates his difficulties in writing rather than merely
excuses his failure to do so. One of his verse letters refers less ambiguously to unpro-
ductive periods ("To Mr. Rowland Woodward" ["Like one who'in her third wid-
dowhood"], 1–3).

other interpretation of Allophanes's name is that he is an alternative side of Idios, an alter ego.[77] The fact that each speech ends on a half-line that the other character completes hints at this relationship between them.[78] And Donne's biography confirms that hint: the conversations between these two characters do enact dialogues that may well have taken place within their creator. In so doing they enact as well many of the broader cultural tensions that I traced in Chapter 3. Thus Allophanes stands for the attraction to the court that motivated so many of Donne's actions, whereas Idios bodies forth the reluctance to participate in that world to which Donne's verse letters often testify. Allophanes's insistence on bringing the epithalamium to court represents the willingness to please a patron that led Donne to write the poem, whereas Idios's desire to burn it expresses the poet's doubts about that task.[79] Allophanes is the successful courtier Donne wanted to be, Idios the failed courtier he sensed he really was.[80] And in another interpretation these conflicting voices mirror a specific period in Donne's career: during the Mitcham years he seesawed between living at court like Allophanes and eschewing that world like Idios.[81] These autobiographical dichotomies are in turn mirrored by generic categories: Allophanes adopts the respectful attitude towards the writing of epithalamia that characterizes most poets and speakers in the tradition, whereas Idios

[77]Virginia Tufte touches on the possibility that the speakers may represent Donne's internal debates but then limits the significance of this insight by asserting that Idios states Donne's real opinions and Allophanes argues against them (*The Poetry of Marriage: The Epithalamium in Europe and Its Development in England*, Univ. of Southern California Studies in Comparative Literature, 2 [Los Angeles: Tinnon-Brown, 1970], p. 227). After completing my work on this section of the book, I heard the paper that Annabel Patterson presented at the 1985 MLA convention, "Donne: The Self and the Other"; she too acknowledges that Allophanes may be a mask for Donne himself. For a different but not incompatible reading of these names, see Jonathan Goldberg, *James I and the Politics of Literature: Jonson, Shakespeare, Donne, and Their Contemporaries* (Baltimore: Johns Hopkins Univ. Press, 1983), p. 132: he suggests that the play on the names implies that being at court involves surrendering one's own identity and being totally controlled by the king.

[78]I am grateful to Gwynne Blakemore Evans for this insight.

[79]Milgate (*Epithalamions*, "Introduction," p. xxiv) rightly observes that this epithalamium was written "with an odd mixture of willingness and reluctance"; I am arguing that this mixture is dramatized through Donne's dialogic eclogue.

[80]On the ways courtiers attempted to cope with failure, cf. Whigham, p. 22. Many other critics have commented on Donne's own ambition; see, e.g., Carey, chaps. 3 and 4; Marotti, "John Donne and the Art of Patronage"; Patricia Thomson, "The Literature of Patronage, 1580–1630," *Essays in Criticism*, 2 (1952), 280–284.

[81]See Bald, *John Donne: A Life*, chap. 8.

exemplifies the disaffected outsider whose counterparts appear in Spenser's "Prothalamion" and Wither's "Epithalamion."

In any event, the author who delights in yoking together disparates on the linguistic level here does so on a dramatic level, through the evocation of two characters who are different yet the same. In many respects the relationship between them was anticipated in "Satyre IV," where Donne displaces his own attraction to the court onto the satiric antagonist: that character is his negative identity, the representative of the values in himself that Donne fears and wants to reject.[82] And we find analogues to the relationship between Idios and Allophanes elsewhere in the "Epithalamion at the Marriage of the Earl of Somerset" itself. Donne's references in lines 79 and 176 to the ambitions or lack of ambitions of others externalize and displace the ambitions that motivate his composition of this poem, just as his evocation of Allophanes displaces his own desire to succeed at court. Similarly, the contradictions that are bifurcated into the conflicting figures of Allophanes and Idios emerge in Idios's paradoxical and ambiguous statements about whether or not his own ambition motivates this epithalamium:

> Reade then this nuptiall song, which was not made
> Either the Court or mens hearts to invade,
> But since I'am dead, and buried, I could frame
> No Epitaph, which might advance my fame
> So much as this poore song.
>
> (99–103)

The dialogue between Allophanes and Idios illuminates Donne's relationship to generic patterns as well as psychological ones. The epithalamium is, as we have seen, a fundamentally dialogic medium: the dialogue that occurs explicitly in Catullus 62 and imitations of it is manifest in the paired opposites we find in other versions of the genre: nature against society, male against female, and so on. Once again the reactions of an idiosyncratic writer to an idiosyncratic wedding find apt expression in well-established generic conventions: in the Somerset epithalamium Donne adapts this dialogic predilection of his genre to express the personal tensions he brings to it.

[82]In *John Donne, Coterie Poet*, pp. 105–106, Marotti suggests that the emphasis in "Satyre IV" on the internalization of the court reflects Donne's own ambivalence about it; Hester argues that the bore "figures forth also the satirist's own generic sinfulness as fallen man" (p. 80).

The presence of some of those tensions in Donne's other poems, particularly the verse epistles composed in the decade before he wrote the "Epithalamion at the Marriage of the Earl of Somerset," helps us explicate their workings in this eclogue. His criticisms of the court and of London, though frequent, are contradictory: sometimes he dismisses the apparent alternatives to those milieux with equal antagonism, at other points he ambivalently praises country life. Thus in "To Sir Henry Wotton" ("Sir, more then kisses") he criticizes both "Countries dulnesse" (61) and "Courts hot ambitions" (60),[83] advocating in their place a version of neo-Stoicism.[84] "To Mr. E.G." ("Even as lame things") deserves more critical attention than it has received for many reasons, not least its revealing ambivalences about pastoral and its alternatives. The poem ostensibly condemns London and praises the country life of its recipient, but the terms in which it does so are telling:

> fill not like a Bee
> Thy thighs with hony, but as plenteously
> As Russian Marchants, thy selfes whole vessell load,
> And then at Winter retaile it here abroad.
>
> (15–18)

Even while defending the country, Donne rejects a bucolic metaphor in favor of mercantile economies ("Russian Marchants" [17], "retaile" [18]). He attempts to reconcile the two worlds in his final references to "hive and warehouse" (20), but the sense of strain remains. The same type of strain recurs in the dialogue between Idios and Allophanes.

That dialogue raises another question about patronage: whether it is indeed possible to escape the court and its patronage system. The poem does not offer a clear or definitive answer; the paradoxes in Idios's responses (as we have seen, he variously claims he is away from court and he is there, he was unable to write an epithalamium and he in fact did so) reflect, one suspects, the contradictions in Donne's own reactions. Despite these paradoxes and contradictions,

[83]Citations are to *The Satires, Epigrams, and Verse Letters,* ed. W. Milgate.
[84]Ted-Larry Pebworth and Claude J. Summers explain some of the ambivalences in Donne's verse letters to Wotton by relating them to political problems at court and Donne's own complex relationship with Wotton ("'Thus Friends Absent Speake': The Exchange of Verse Letters between John Donne and Henry Wotton," *MP*, 81 [1984], 361–377).

however, the primary implication of the eclogue is that it is difficult and painful to distance oneself, literally or metaphorically, from the court. The poem goes back repeatedly, if not obsessively, to the problems and perils of doing so even as it attempts to establish its own distance from the court through criticisms of the wedding and through rhetorical strategies we have already charted, such as appending titles to its stanzas.

Thus the apparent alternatives to the court, the poem reminds us, are unattractive; the "world elsewhere" to which Idios retreats is not the *locus amoenus* of many other pastorals but rather a wilderness. Indeed, the imagery of the poem associates that wilderness with barrenness, with death itself; rather than tending his flocks while melodious birds sing madrigals, Idios becomes a "statue of ice" (1). To describe leaving the court as a type of death is on one level to offer a tribute to that world but on another, of course, to remind us that leaving the court could in fact involve the death of one's political hopes. (Being banished from court was in fact a punishment to which courtiers were liable for many types of infractions, such as breaking the law against dueling.)[85]

Throughout the poem, moreover, attempts to escape the court are subverted, whether by internal or by external forces. Idios, a master (and a slave) of occupatio, writes a courtly poem that is in part devoted to his unwillingness to write a courtly poem. His own attitudes to that text are also revealing. At one point he declares, "As I have brought this song, that I may doe / A perfect sacrifice, I'll burne it too" (226–227). On their primary level, of course, these lines are merely a witty joke, Idios's clever way of opposing Allophanes, and yet, as we have already seen, they are not without other resonances. His language suggests at once a desire to destroy the poem (like its creator, it will be dead once it has been burned) and hence not participate in the event—and a desire to assume that sacerdotal role we examined earlier. In any event, whatever Idios's attitude to the poem may be, Allophanes triumphs: he wrests the text from its author and lays it on those "Altars" (235).

These ambiguities and tensions reflect the fact that Donne was pulled between the moral necessity to condemn the wedding and the financial necessity to praise it—and also, perhaps, between his desire to absent himself from the court and his urge to participate in

[85]Linda Levy Peck, *Northampton: Patronage and Policy at the Court of James I* (London: George Allen and Unwin, 1982), p. 163.

courtly rituals, even morally dubious ones. In any event, it is clear that he—and, by implication, other courtiers—do not find it easy to achieve that world elsewhere. As Donne puts it in one of the most revealing lines of the poem, "And yet I scap'd not here" (97). In short, in this epithalamium Donne reactivates and reenacts a dialogue that appears in the "Epithalamion made at Lincolnes Inne" in less dramatic form: the conflict between the role of satiric outsider who comments wryly and at times sharply on the events of the wedding and the role of the participant who directs and joins in them.

That is but one of many ways in which this poem addresses the conflicts about marriage that shape the Stuart epithalamium in general and those that shape Donne's own epithalamia in particular. In so doing, it implicitly addresses our own interpretive decisions when we read poems in this tradition. For the "Epithalamion at the Marriage of the Earl of Somerset" demonstrates yet again that we need not and should not neglect formal considerations, especially generic patterns, in studying either cultural or psychological anxieties. It is through such artistic strategies that anxieties are variously repressed and resolved. And it is in large measure through his aesthetic achievements and skills that Donne, though a "statue of ice," contrives to play with fire without being melted.

CHAPTER 5

Ben Jonson and Robert Herrick

Whence for some universal good
The priest shall cut the sacred Bud.
Marvell, "Upon Appleton House"

I

Joseph H. Summers, one of the most acute readers of Cavalier poetry, remarks that Robert Herrick is "the most devoted (and the
most single-minded) of the Sons of Ben."[1] But, like many devoted
sons, Herrick differs from his father. One anticipates distinctions, of
course, even in the instance of very similar poets; but those we encounter in this case run surprisingly deep, especially when each
writer turns to the epithalamium.

In one sense contemporary critical methodologies provide the perspectives we need to understand these distinctions: the questions
about gender and sexuality that feminists have addressed and the political emphases of the new historicism together direct our attention
to many of the salient differences that separate this particular father
and son. Yet at the same time some of the winds blowing in the
current critical climate might tempt scholars to neglect or underestimate the dissimilarities in question. The principal contrasts between
Jonson and Herrick emerge most clearly when we scrutinize linguistic nuances and aesthetic decisions; these types of close attention to
literary texts are out of fashion in some circles.

[1]Joseph H. Summers, The Heirs of Donne and Jonson (London: Chatto and Windus,
1970), p. 52.

But if we must study the tones of individual poems to understand
the relationship between Herrick and Jonson, so too must we scrutinize the tonalities of their individual temperaments: as I have argued
in Chapters 1 and 4, generalizations about cultural anxieties should
regularly be qualified with a close and detailed examination of the
radically dissimilar forms those anxieties may assume. Some, though
by no means all, new historicists are prone to underestimate the differences among poets:[2] describing a culture in terms of its dominant
and subversive elements can encourage us to hear only two voices,
and the current onslaught on liberal humanism often involves a rejection of the concept of the individual subject. But that assault typically blurs some important distinctions: oversimplifying the position
it is condemning, it may synecdochally assume that any discussion of
the individual necessarily posits a consistent and unified personality
virtually uninfluenced by historical and cultural forces. Contemporary critics can and should preserve their recognition that the subject is neither autonomous nor ahistorical nor static—while at the
same time acknowledging the extent of the distinctions among such
subjects.

Paradigms borrowed from other critical schools could offer salutary correctives to such attitudes. As practitioners of reader-response
criticism have maintained, the meaning of a text resides not in the
words on the page but rather in the interplay between those signifiers and their readers. In an important sense cultural anxieties, like
patronage systems, are a text that is continually being read—and
hence created in new and distinctive forms—by different members of
the culture. Nor, as I have argued, can we elide the dissimilarities
among those readers by asserting that they are all part of a homogeneous interpretive community: witness the contrasts among the authors of the marriage manuals, or some of the differences between
John Donne and other authors of epithalamia. Or we might derive
another apt analogy from the Russian formalists and their heirs: the
anxieties are the story, their interpretations by various poets the plot.
This chapter, then, contrasts the ways Jonson and Herrick plot the
story of gender and marriage in Stuart England.

Even a preliminary comparison of their epithalamia demonstrates
why critics should concentrate on not only the similarities that

[2]See the brief but thoughtful comments on this topic in Richard Helgerson's review of Leah S. Marcus, *The Politics of Mirth: Jonson, Herrick, Milton, Marvell, and the
Defense of Old Holiday Pastimes, RQ,* 40 (1987), 827.

connect the two poets but also the differences that distinguish them—and in so doing demonstrates the importance of attending to details of language and of tone. A superficial comparison of "An Epithalamie to Sir Thomas Southwell and his Ladie" with the wedding poem in Jonson's *Hymenaei* might well tempt us to conclude that Herrick is not Jonson's son but his twin. On the surface it would be hard to find two more similar epithalamia. Their verse forms are very close, as one of Herrick's editors has observed.[3] Many seventeenth-century poets either terminate each stanza with the same refrain or effect significant variations within that refrain; but here both Herrick and Jonson adopt the classical practice of using one or more refrains intermittently.[4] And they allude to classical and other antiquarian wedding customs more frequently than most of their contemporaries: Jonson's notes as well as his text testify to his interest in this sort of folklore, and Herrick in turn crams his poem with references to the bride's yellow veil, threshold rites, and so on.

Linguistic echoes also resonate between the poems. Thus Jonson's lyric opens, "Glad *time* is at his point arriu'd, / For which *loues* hopes were so long-liu'd," lines paralleled in Herrick's own opening, "Now, now's the time; so oft by truth / Promis'd sho'd come to crown your youth." The early draft of Herrick's epithalamium indicates that his poem was originally even closer to Jonson's, since in his preliminary version he adopted his predecessor's battle imagery as well.[5] And just in case we had any remaining doubts about these debts, Herrick borrows the word "adventer," writing "Tel them, now they must adventer" (99); Jonson had declared, "Haste, tender *lady*, and aduenter" (477).

Yet these similarities may distract us from the more telling differences between the poems. Jonson merely refers briefly to the bride's reluctance to consummate the marriage in one stanza whereas Her-

---

[3]L. C. Martin, ed., *The Poetical Works of Robert Herrick* (Oxford: Clarendon Press, 1956), p. 510.

[4]On this and other classical influences on Jonson's epithalamia, see James A. S. McPeek, *Catullus in Strange and Distant Britain*, Harvard Studies in Comparative Literature, 15 (Cambridge: Harvard Univ. Press, 1939), pp. 191–207; Virginia Tufte, *The Poetry of Marriage: The Epithalamium in Europe and Its Development in England*, Univ. of Southern California Studies in Comparative Literature, 2 (Los Angeles: Tinnon-Brown, 1970), pp. 209–210.

[5]That draft is reprinted in Martin, Appendix B. I include subsequent citations to it within my text.

rick focuses on that subject throughout the poem.[6] Six of his first
seven stanzas emphasize it through their refrain, "come, Hymen
guide / To the bed, the bashfull bride" (9–10, 19–20, 29–30, 39–40,
49–50, 69–70); later the bride's relatives "force her in" (82; italics
added), and Venus is implored to encourage her not to be afraid.

The bride's emotions, I argue, echo Herrick's own. We will need
to look at other poems fully to substantiate my suggestion that Herrick is himself experiencing reservations about the consummation of
the marriage; but for now we can at least observe a curious passage
in this lyric:

> Deare, is it this you dread,
> The losse of Maiden-head?
> Beleeve me; you will most
> Esteeme it when 'tis lost.
> Then it no longer keep,
> Lest Issue lye asleep.
>   (13–18)

The intended meaning of "you will most / Esteeme it when 'tis lost"
(15–16) is surely "you will not regret abandoning your maidenhood"; but the lines seem to warn her that her regrets about the loss
of virginity will intensify when it is too late. One can well understand why a bride hearing such advice would wish to delay her marriage, and, more to the point, Herrick's own reservations about the
consummation of the marriage emerge in these peculiar lines. Jonson
is not, of course, free of ambivalence about sexuality; but his doubts,
unlike Herrick's, do not center on the loss of virginity, and their effects on his epithalamia are less profound because of his insistent
strategies for resolving and subduing them.

Herrick's treatment of sex differs from Jonson's in another way. If
Jonson chooses not to dwell on the bride's reluctance, neither does he
emphasize the power of erotic desire. Described as "chaste, and holy
loue" (503) earlier in the poem, sex does indeed sound chaste when
Jonson describes it. Even an adolescent boy would find it hard to be
titillated by lines like, "Now, free from vulgar spight, or noyse, /
May you enioy your mutuall ioyes" (509–510) or "And, looke, be-

---

[6]Other critics have noted Herrick's emphasis on the bride's delays, though most of
them treat it only in passing. See, e.g., Gordon Braden, The Classics and English Renaissance Poetry: Three Case Studies (New Haven: Yale Univ. Press, 1987), esp. p. 223;
Roger B. Rollin, Robert Herrick (New York: Twayne, 1966), p. 112.

fore you yeeld to slumber, / That your delights be drawne past number" (517–518). Herrick, in contrast, eroticizes the bed itself, giving
new meaning to the witticism that wives should look to their linen:

> And now, Behold! the Bed or Couch
> That ne'r knew Brides, or Bride-grooms touch,
>   Feels in it selfe a fire;
>   And tickled with Desire,
>   Pants with a Downie brest,
>   As with a heart possest:
>   Shrugging as it did move,
>   Ev'n with the soule of love.
>   (131–138)

These lines are more overtly and directly erotic than anything in Jonson—and yet at the same time more covertly and indirectly erotic
than the epithalamium in *Hymenaei* in that they deflect desire from
the bed's inhabitants to the bed itself.

The poets differ not only in their treatment of sex but also in their
approach to one of its consequences, procreation. Herrick is overt:

> O! give them active heat
> And moisture, both compleat:
> Fit Organs for encrease.
>   (125–127)

Jonson, in contrast, manages the peculiar feat of expressing a similar
prayer while distracting our attention away from the people it most
concerns, the bride and groom:

> And VENVS, thou, with timely seed
> (Which may their after-comforts breed)
>   Informe the gentle wombe;
>   Nor, let it proue a tombe:
>   But, e're ten *moones* be wasted,
>   The *birth*, by CYNTHIA hasted.
>   (541–546)

The one direct allusion to the couple, the pronoun "their" (542), occurs in what is literally and metaphorically a parenthetical aside. Its
marginalization is confirmed by Jonson's writing "the. . . . wombe"
(543) rather than "her womb," as well as by the curious syntax in

the two final lines, which focuses on the birth itself at the expense of the woman giving birth. Contemporary physiological theories that underestimated the role of the woman in procreation may in part explain this passage;[7] but the lines are shaped as well by Jonson's approach to agency, which is, as we will see throughout this chapter, one of the most distinctive—yet one of the most neglected—qualities of his poems.

Herrick's description of the marriage bed exemplifies another difference that separates his lyric from that of Jonson. The tone of the epithalamium in *Hymenaei* is essentially monochromatic and stable. Elsewhere in its author's canon, to be sure, we encounter a pull between frantic movement and calmness;[8] but in his epithalamia stasis prevails. Herrick's poem, in contrast, is restless: just as the objects in it move about, "Shrugging" (137), so too does its tone.[9] The lyric shifts from the magisterial cadences of the opening lines ("Now, now's the time; so oft by truth / Promis'd sho'd come to crown your youth"), to the melancholy allusions to weeping virgins, to the energies evoked in this description of the wedding bed. In these rapid shifts as in several other ways, Herrick's epithalamium is more reminiscent of the work of Donne than that of Jonson.[10]

In drawing attention to the relative stability of Jonson's tone, my aim is not to posit an Apollonian Jonson and a Dionysian Herrick; those tendencies coexist in both poets. Nor do I intend to assign New Critical stability to Jonson's texts and poststructuralist instability to Herrick's; that reading is not without its grain of truth, but its oversimplified dichotomy underestimates the conflicts, resolved and unresolved, that generate Jonson's assertions of order. Rather, I want to suggest that tensions about marriage emerge in the epithalamia of both writers; but, as even our preliminary comparison of

---

[7]For a useful summary see Jay L. Halio, "*Perfection* and Elizabethan Ideas of Conception," *ELN*, 1 (1964), 179–182.

[8]Compare Arthur F. Marotti's analysis of the Apollonian and Dionysian elements in Jonson in "All about Jonson's Poetry," *ELH*, 39 (1972), 208–237.

[9]Rollin also notes shifts in mood in Herrick's wedding poems (*Robert Herrick*, p. 115).

[10]Tufte observes a specific parallel between Donne and Herrick, their focus on the marriage bed (*The Poetry of Marriage*, p. 243). Anthony Low argues for a parallel between two specific works by these poets ("The Gold in 'Julia's Petticoat': Herrick and Donne," *Seventeenth-Century News*, 34 [1976], 88–89); J. Max Patrick attempts to rebut the case in "The Golden Leaves and Stars in 'Julia's Petticoat': A Reply to Anthony Low," in the same issue (89–91).

them has implied, their responses—generic, linguistic, psychological, and moral—to those tensions are different.

To understand the sources and the consequences of the differences in question, we need to examine each of the two poets in more detail. It has become a cliché to comment that in several respects Jonson is the bricklayer and Herrick the goldsmith. But an analysis of these two poets will lead us to revise that critical commonplace and many others: if Jonson's medium is brick, Herrick's is quicksilver.

II

Most literary critics have taken Jonson at his word in one important respect. Accepting the assertions in "Why I write not of Love," a poem whose polemical import is emphasized by its placement as the initial lyric in *The Forrest*, otherwise persuasive critics have enumerated Jonson's reasons for ignoring romantic and sexual love.[11] But the conventional wisdom is dangerous, not because it is totally wrong but rather because the half-truths embedded in it can so easily tempt us to believe it is totally right. To be sure, Jonson avoids the plots of romantic comedy, variously ignores and mocks his Petrarchan inheritance, and composes far fewer love poems than most of his contemporaries. Yet he does indeed write of love more often and more tellingly than we have acknowledged. In fact, Anne Ferry has pointed out that five of the fifteen poems in *The Forrest* involve that very subject, and, classifying the lyrics differently, Claude J. Summers and Ted-Larry Pebworth maintain that as many as seven concern love.[12]

In writing of love Jonson sometimes enacts a version of occupatio. Thus "Why I write not of Love" is a poem about the very topic it

---

[11]See, e.g., Richard Helgerson, *Self-Crowned Laureates: Spenser, Jonson, Milton, and the Literary System* (Berkeley: Univ. of California Press, 1983), pp. 110–116; Lawrence Venuti, "Why Jonson Wrote Not of Love," *Journal of Medieval and Renaissance Studies*, 12 (1982), 195–220. An important exception to the general critical consensus on the subject, however, is Anne Ferry, *All in War with Time: Love Poetry of Shakespeare, Donne, Jonson, Marvell* (Cambridge: Harvard Univ. Press, 1975), chap. 3; though we base our arguments on different poems, I am at several points indebted to this illuminating study.

[12]Ferry, *All in War with Time*, p. 153; Claude J. Summers and Ted-Larry Pebworth, *Ben Jonson* (Boston: Twayne, 1979), p. 158.

claims to ignore.[13] Similarly, the Charis sequence and "My Picture left in Scotland" are important sorties into the subject their author asserts he is avoiding; these lyrics often concern failed and rejected love, but that in itself hardly distinguishes them from the poems many of Jonson's contemporaries were writing in the 1590s. Such works, then, exemplify the habit of saying and unsaying that characterizes so many of its author's lyrics: "Ile tell you of more, and lye, so you will come" ("Inviting a friend to supper," 17); "Alas, but *Morison* fell young: / Hee never fell, thou fall'st, my tongue" ("To the immortall memorie, and friendship of that noble paire, Sir Lvcivs Cary, and Sir H. Morison," 43–44), and so on.[14] The habit may be traced in part to Jonson's career in the duplicitous world of the court and, in particular, to the exigencies of praising patrons whatever their actual worth; like those other victims and students of duplicity, the Jesuits, Jonson adopts a version of equivocation. But whatever its origins, the tendency to say what one denies saying recurs throughout his work.

It is the masques, however, that most clearly demonstrate that Jonson on occasion wishes not only to address the subject he claims to eschew but also to write about writing about it. A striking number of them are involved with literally or figuratively recuperating love. Most obviously, in *The Haddington Masque* Cupid is lost, then rediscovered. Similarly, in *Love Freed From Ignorance and Folly* the first of the three title characters is imprisoned by the sphinx but on his release helps Beauty to celebrate the king. The plot of *Love Restored* involves a false and usurping Cupid who criticizes masquing; he is displaced by the genuine article, who (predictably) approves of masques. Echoes of this plot of recovery appear in other Jonsonian masques; for instance, in *Lovers Made Men* not love but lovers are assumed dead but prove to be alive and well. Admittedly, Love assumes a range of significances, including adulation of the king, in many of these courtly entertainments; this range on occasion offers Jonson another convenient way of pretending to avoid romantic and sexual love. But it is only a pretense: Cupid is explicitly present in

---

[13]Venuti claims that Jonson chooses to write not about love but about its resistance to representation ("Why Jonson Wrote Not of Love"); I am in effect arguing we should shift the balances and see that resistance to representation as one of the many issues Jonson explores when writing about love.

[14]Several critics have commented on this habit. See, e.g., Stanley Fish, "Authors-Readers: Jonson's Community of the Same," *Representations*, 7 (1984), esp. 28.

several masques, and even in others he remains one of the most important components in the abstraction Love. Reflexive in so many other senses, these masques, I argue, enact an autobiographical allegory: in them as in Jonson's own career, love is lost or hidden or disguised, only to keep emerging in new form. Jonson is plotting his own development when he plots his masque.

The contours of these courtly entertainments, then, can help us map those of Jonson's career. He does not avoid the subject of love early on, only to turn to it abruptly in his final work, as many though not all readers have assumed. Rather, throughout his life he devises strategies for writing of love in forms that he considers acceptable, tempering the subject with the skill of the alter ego, Vulcan, he invokes in two masques.

Jonson's approach to one putative form of love, the marriages celebrated in epithalamia, substantiates and complicates these patterns. His wedding poems demonstrate both his ambivalence about and his attraction to the occasion they commemorate; by reinterpreting the generic norms he inherited, Jonson attempts to write about wedlock in a way that will not threaten him or his readers. In so doing he provides us with our best example of the ways the Stuart epithalamium tries to ward off the snakes that threaten its happier Eden.

In certain respects the type of love celebrated in epithalamia, married love, was peculiarly congenial to Jonson, more so than to many other writers of his period, notably Donne. The lyric epithalamium, I have argued, celebrates the community in the course of praising its principal protagonists. This characteristic alone would have drawn Ben Jonson to the genre: his commitment to communal values matches an equally deep preoccupation in the epithalamium tradition. And he develops techniques for emphasizing those values.[15] Some of them we will encounter only when we look more closely at each of his epithalamia, but for now we can observe a few recurrent strategies. Jonson, as we have already seen, deploys the first person plural pronoun to suggest that the couple belong to their society: "Place you our *Bride* to night" ("Epithalamion," *Hymenaei*, 495), "And such ours bee" ("Epithalamion," *The Haddington Masque*, 391). Similarly, in the poem written for the wedding of Hierome Weston

---

[15]Many critics have traced the attitudes to community elsewhere in Jonson's canon. See, e.g., Fish, "Authors-Readers: Jonson's Community of the Same"; Katharine Eisaman Maus, *Ben Jonson and the Roman Frame of Mind* (Princeton: Princeton Univ. Press, 1984), chap. 5.

and Frances Stuart, he rejoices that the earth is festooned with flowers "To welcome home a Paire" (24); marriage is less a new beginning than a homecoming, a reentry into the community. The antiquarian references crammed into his poems establish another type of community: they link these celebrants with those who attended weddings in earlier eras, much as the imitativeness of the genre links its current practitioners with earlier writers.

Jonson is also attracted to marriages in the literal sense because they can so conveniently symbolize some of the metaphorical marriages it was politic for him to celebrate. D. J. Gordon's reading of *Hymanaei* acutely traces the connections between marital union and the union of England and Scotland.[16] Similarly, the conclusion of *Loves Triumph Through Callipolis* conflates human marriage with the connections between the rose and the lily and between two kingdoms.

In other respects, too, the values celebrated in epithalamia correspond to Jonson's own ideals as well as to his political needs. Influenced by the Roman moralists, he emphasizes the filial and familial at many points in his dramatic and nondramatic works;[17] distorted families such as that comprised of Volpone and his house staff recur throughout the plays, and Jonson's evil characters often signal their unreliability by their neglect of parental or filial duties. The norms of the epithalamium readily lend themselves to this preoccupation; Jonson plays up the dynastic prophecies of his genre, devoting far more attention to the heirs whom the marriage will produce than many other poets, including Herrick, are prone to do. The Weston-Stuart epithalamium, for example, culminates on a vision of "a race to fill your Hall" (169), and the wedding poem in *Hymenaei* devotes three of its fifteen stanzas to the subject of heirs.

So far we have been concentrating on the more obvious affinities between Jonson's temperament and the epithalamium. In addition, one of the most fundamental drives impelling that genre accords to one of the most fundamental drives in Jonson himself: the impulse to acknowledge threats in a form that subdues them, or, to put it an-

---

[16]D. J. Gordon, "*Hymenaei:* Ben Jonson's Masque of Union," *Journal of the Warburg and Courtauld Institutes,* 8 (1945), 107–145.

[17]Compare Maus, esp. p. 116; also see Thomas M. Greene's comments on Jonson's fear of domestic invasion ("Ben Jonson and the Centered Self," *SEL,* 10 [1970], 334–336). A substantially revised version of this essay appears as chap. 13 in *The Light in Troy: Imitation and Discovery in Renaissance Poetry* (New Haven: Yale Univ. Press, 1982).

other way, the impulse to assert one's control over the potentially uncontrolled and uncontrollable. "Inviting a friend to supper" suggests one important source of that drive. The fear of court spies, Jonson's "Pooly" and "Parrot," clouds even, or especially, the conviviality of friends; the intrigues of the Jacobean court no doubt intensified, and perhaps even sparked, Jonson's preoccupation with threats.

Jonson demonstrates that preoccupation in both his linguistic mannerisms and his narrative formulas. His dramatic and narrative works are peppered with negative syntactical patterns of all sorts. The negative formula recurs explicitly throughout "To Penshurst," as it does in so many other poems in its genre ("That neuer failes to serue thee season'd deere" [20] and so on);[18] but it appears as well when Jonson works in other literary types, as when he celebrates Morison and Cary by observing, "No pleasures vaine did chime, / Of rimes, or ryots, at your feasts" (102–103). In addition, the contrasts between good and evil characters around which such poems as the "Epistle. To Katherine, Lady Avbigny;" and the Morison-Cary ode are structured in effect enact a version of that formula. Elsewhere, too, Jonson deploys negatives in following the rhetoricians' strictures about defining by contrasts. In "Inviting a friend to supper," for instance, he writes not "a coney is to be hoped for" but rather "a coney / Is not to be despair'd of " (13–14).

Jonson's grammar of negatives has been parsed in many ways by his readers: the habit has been variously traced to his tendency to undercut his ostensible purposes, to his attraction to the Roman habit of defining qualities through their opposites, to his Baconian predilections.[19] Fair enough, but the primary function of these neg-

---

[18]This habit recurs in "To Penshurst" in a different form as well. I am grateful to Carol Ann Johnston for the observation that the fish who are willing to be caught represent an extreme version of Jonson's negatives: the suggestion that they are not unwilling to be caught is exaggerated into the assertion that they are eager to be.

[19]See respectively Fish, "Authors-Readers: Jonson's Community of the Same," esp. 28–30; Maus, pp. 100–101; Richard C. Newton, "Ben./Jonson: The Poet in the Poems," in Two Renaissance Mythmakers: Christopher Marlowe and Ben Jonson, Selected Papers from the English Institute 1975–1976, ed. Alvin Kernan (Baltimore: Johns Hopkins Univ. Press, 1977). Newton's argument that these negatives involve rejection is particularly germane to my own, though in relating that rejection to patterns of fragmentation rather than to insistent control he moves in a very different direction. For a related argument, also see Gail Kern Paster, "Ben Jonson's Comedy of Limitations," SP, 72 (1975), 51–71; her contentions about Jonson's interest in limitations are relevant to his negatives.

atives in and out of his epithalamia returns us to our analyses of the role of the banishing-of-dangers motif in the genre as a whole: Jonson's negatives serve above all to express potential threats in a delimited and controlled form. The assertion that a coney "is not to be despair'd of" reminds us of the possibility of not obtaining it—while reassuring us that it will indeed be obtained.

This defensive strategy[20] finds its analogues throughout Jonson's canon. The syntactical predilection for controlled negatives is enacted in the fundamental narrative structure of the masque: the antimasque functions as the danger that is controlled, the negative that is acknowledged but held in check. And a similar pattern occurs in the plays. Robert N. Watson has persuasively anatomized the "parodic strategy" by which literary positions that Jonson wishes to reject, plots that he condemns, are associated with unfavorably presented characters;[21] this too is a version of caging what is potentially threatening or destructive.

Some works contain more specific versions of this pattern of delimiting threats in the process of acknowledging them. For instance, the negatives in "To Penshurst" remind us that its genre is structured around contrasts between modest and ostentatious country houses—again a dialogue with a winner clearly assumed. Defining a threat in a form that muzzles it resembles setting up a debate while assuring the victory of one side, and this is precisely what Jonson does in the evidently unfair contest between Truth and Opinion in *Hymenaei*. Notice, too, the emphasis on obedience and control in a telling phrase from the same masque: "These, these are they, / Whom *humour* and *affection* must obey" (259–260).

The Haddington Masque is packed with instances of controlling potential threats. Thus Cupid's antimasque is defined in a way that allows it to coexist with the main masque; similarly, when Vulcan describes the zodiac of marriage he tells us that Leo is tempered by the Virgin, and the *"stings"* (299) of wedlock are removed when the archer inflicts new wounds. Moreover, the central allegory of this work involves an acknowledged but subdued source of energy. Vulcan himself represents *calor naturae*, the heat of nature that is neces-

---

[20]Maus notes that the Roman moral attitude that influenced Jonson so much is defensive, though she does not relate this observation specifically to his negatives (p. 109).

[21]Robert N. Watson, *Ben Jonson's Parodic Strategies: Literary Imperialism in the Comedies* (Cambridge: Harvard Univ. Press, 1987).

sary for generation, as one of Jonson's own notes tells us;[22] but the plot of the masque sublimates the sexual significance of that character, focusing on his creative rather than procreative energies. Vulcan's peculiar reassurance that fresh wounds will remove the stings of love reminds us that the strategy of transforming dangers into a more benign form is not always persuasive in its reassurances. But whether or not it succeeds, that strategy recurs frequently enough throughout Jonson's canon to demonstrate his deepest affinity to the epithalamium: the genre's emphasis on banishing dangers and controlling threats accords to one of the most fundamental patterns in Jonson's own behavior.

Despite such affinities, Jonson remains ambivalent about marriage and the literary type that describes it, as he is about so much else: the cultural pressures enumerated in Chapter 1 coincide with and intensify more idiosyncratic reservations and tensions. Speculations about the marriages of writers who died some centuries ago should be approached cautiously, since they are likely to be no more reliable—and no more resistible—than similar speculations about the marriages of our acquaintances; but some evidence does suggest that Jonson's own union may not have been happy.[23] And, though he chooses to "write to love" more frequently than we sometimes acknowledge, his distrust of sexual desire is evident throughout his work. He repeatedly connects passion with the unstable and even the chaotic; "Epode" contrasts the "continuall tempest" (43) of desire with the "calme, and god-like vnitie" (53) of true love, and the unhappy lovers in *Loves Triumph Through Callipolis* are associated with giddy motion.[24] In *Volpone*, as many readers have observed, romantic and sexual love are represented not by a marriage between Celia and Bonario but by the title character's perverse courtship of Celia and Corvino's willing agreement to that ordeal. Other works suggest that the principal way love destroys harmony and breaks the compass is by emphasizing the individual's needs and drives at the expense of those of the community; this assumption is one of many links between his work and that of the Roman moralists who influ-

[22]VII, p. 257. On this allegory also see D. J. Gordon, "Ben Jonson's 'Haddington Masque': The Story and the Fable," *MLR*, 42 (1947), esp. 184–186; though otherwise valuable, this article does not acknowledge the ways the text distracts attention from the procreative and sexual.

[23]See Summers and Pebworth, *Ben Jonson*, p. 26.

[24]Compare Helgerson's observation that the villains in the plays are the characters least comfortable with stasis (p. 160).

enced him so deeply.[25] Thus, to return to *Loves Triumph Through Callipolis,* it is not surprising that Jonson so carefully distinguishes from each other the unfortunate lovers who comprise the antimasque: one of his points is that love itself makes such distinctions. And we can now understand one of the principal reasons he is more comfortable writing about romantic love in masques than in romantic comedies: the masque can emphasize the relationship of one set of lovers to their community and the links between one version of union and other versions, whereas the plot of romantic comedy stresses the conflicts between a younger and an older generation, one lover and his rival, and so on.[26]

Jonson's reservations about marriage are further complicated by his sporadic attraction to the very issues he finds it so difficult to discuss. We have seen some evidence of that attraction in his work outside the epithalamium genre; but the most striking evidence occurs in the wedding poem in *Hymenaei.* The epithalamium ostensibly delivered at the bedchamber is but one of many subgenres, and certainly not among the most popular in the English tradition, but this is the form Jonson selects. The choice is odder because this wedding, the union of Frances Howard with her first husband, the earl of Essex, was not immediately consummated because of the youth of the couple.[27] Jonson, then, variously responds to his ambivalences about sexual love by repressing that subject and by resolutely attempting to demonstrate to others and to himself that he can confront it; the epithalamium in question, as we will see, exemplifies both responses.

Edmund Wilson's justly discredited attack on Jonson warns us to tread cautiously when we essay psychoanalytic criticism.[28] Nonethe-

---

[25]Cicero's *De Officiis* is a paradigmatic expression of the Roman emphasis on one's duties to the community. The relative valuation of various ties and obligations in this work is also telling. Cicero argues that nature endows men with love for their family, and he emphasizes the strength of kinship ties (I.iv, xvii); but in ranking duties he writes, "there are gradations of duty so well defined that it can easily be seen which duty takes precedence of any other: our first duty is to the immortal gods; our second, to country; our third, to parents; and so on, in a descending scale, to the rest" (*De Officiis,* trans. Walter Miller [London and New York: William Heinemann and Macmillan, 1913], p. 165).

[26]For an alternative but not incompatible explanation, see Maus, p. 110.

[27]See David Lindley, "Embarrassing Ben: The Masques for Frances Howard," in *Renaissance Historicism: Selection from "English Literary Renaissance,"* ed. Arthur F. Kinney and Dan S. Collins (Amherst: Univ. of Massachusetts Press, 1987), p. 250.

[28]Edmund Wilson, "Morose Ben Jonson," in *The Triple Thinkers: Twelve Essays on Literary Subjects,* rev. ed. (New York: Oxford Univ. Press, 1948); reprinted in *Ben*

less, passages in Jonson's work do invite us to describe his hesitations about sexuality in psychological as well as intellectual terms. In particular, it seems likely that Jonson felt insecure about his own capabilities as a lover. The figure of the old and unattractive lover who appears in such poems as the Charis sequence and "My Picture left in Scotland" cannot of course be directly associated with Jonson: he is evoking a literary convention, and the concept of the persona, though unpopular in many circles today, is never more apt than in this case. But explaining Jonson's attraction to the unappealing lover by merely saying that he is following a convention is as inconclusive as explaining the bitterness in many of his epigrams (or, indeed, in Herrick's) in such terms: it is at the very least probable that he is attracted to those conventions because they offer him an excuse to write about subjects that interest him deeply while also allowing him to mask that interest as mere adherence to literary norms.[29] Further substantiation for his concern with the effects of age on love may be found in the epithalamia themselves: other poets only occasionally allude to the subject, but Jonson includes it in two of his four wedding poems, emphasizing it through its position in the pivotal final lines of the poems:

> So eithers strength out-liue
> All losse that *Age* can giue:
> And, though full yeares be told,
> Their formes grow slowly old.
> ("Epithalamion," *Hymenaei*, 561–564)

> And when your yeares rise more, then would be told,
>   Yet neyther of you seeme to th'other old.
> That all, yᵗ view you then, and late; may say,
>   Sure, this glad payre were married, but this day.
> ("To the most noble, and aboue his
> Titles, Robert, Earle of Somerset," 23–26)

Jonson: A Collection of Critical Essays, ed. Jonas A. Barish (Englewood Cliffs, N.J.: Prentice-Hall, 1963). For an intelligent critique of Wilson, see E. Pearlman, "Ben Jonson: An Anatomy," *ELR*, 9 (1979), 364–394; he substitutes a more subtle psychoanalytic reading, emphasizing in particular Jonson's ambivalences about power.

[29]Compare the sensitive treatment of this issue in Ferry, pp. 156–163. Also see John Lemly's brief but trenchant suggestion that the persona Jonson is creating is "almost formulaic" ("Masks and Self-Portraits in Jonson's Late Poetry," *ELH*, 44 [1977], 249).

But whether or not we agree that Jonson's attitudes to his own sexuality are complicated, his attitudes to the epithalamium certainly are. Throughout his canon he enthusiastically endorses many of the values often associated with the genre, notably its emphasis on communal activity; and yet he remains ambivalent about desire itself, even when it is sanctioned by marriage. The country-house poem is one of his two principal responses to that dilemma. In a sense Jonson would have preferred to write epithalamia that culminate at the dining table rather than at the bridal chamber—and in a sense he has his wish, for the country-house poem incorporates a vision of an idealized marriage, playing up the types of communal responsibilities and social harmonies lauded in epithalamia yet playing down the sexual union (or, in the case of "To Sir Robert Wroth," a lyric closely related to the country-house poem, presenting that union in a singularly unthreatening form). This potentiality is one of the many reasons for Jonson's attraction to the genre he pioneered in "To Penshurst": if the epigram did not exist, Jonson would have invented it, and since the country-house poem did not exist, he did invent it. But he also responds to his conflicting attitudes to marriage in a second way: he reshapes a genre in response to his reservations about the occasion it celebrates, as a detailed reading of each of his epithalamia will indicate.

The marginal notes that encase the wedding poem in *Hymenaei* insistently emphasize its debts to antiquarian wedding customs; and the lyric is just as deeply indebted to literary traditions. The basic structure of this work is a song outside the wedding chamber as night approaches, a type for which, as we have seen, Jonson could cite classical and Continental analogues. He borrows more specific traits from his predecessors, too, such as the Catullan habit of using a series of different refrains intermittently. One of his most creative adaptations of literary traditions involves the pattern of inside versus outside that we traced in Chapter 2. Jonson literally brings the outside inside:

> Whole showers of *roses* flow;
> And *violets* seeme to grow,
> Strew'd in the chamber there.
> (487–489)

The poem is indebted as well to a different context, its own position within a masque. It develops some of the tropes that Jonson evokes in that entertainment; for instance, *Hymenaei* envisions marriage as a constellation, and the wedding poem focuses on Hesperus and compares the bride to the evening star. The central plot of the masque is the banishing of the forces that threaten marriage, the Humours and the Affections, and Jonson's epithalamium, like so many other representatives of its genre, itself effects that type of banishing.

But this epithalamium is shaped by the pressures as well as the potentialities associated with its literary type. Rather than ignore those pressures, Jonson acknowledges them, even at times emphasizes them, in the course of the poem. Witness his decision to locate his poem outside the marriage chamber rather than select another version of the genre less connected with the consummation of the marriage. And this epithalamium focuses not only on the potentially unruly force of desire but also on several other sources of discord. Jonson is, for example, the only Stuart poet who adapts the tradition of the bride seized from her mother; this is one of several ways in which he introduces allusions to discord into his epithalamium. Similarly, he devotes considerable attention to the battle imagery that he inherited from his classical predecessors.

In selecting antiquarian wedding customs from the vast number available to him, moreover, Jonson chooses two that draw attention to the threats associated with weddings. Thus he orders the matrons to "snatch" (496) the light from the bride, a verb which reminds us that the bride herself has been snatched from the side of her mother; by using that word rather than, say, "take," he introduces a hint of tension into the relationship he describes. Tensions become far more explicit when he proceeds to explain the reason for his order:

> That shee not hide it dead
> Beneath her *spouse's* bed;
> Nor he reserue the same
> To helpe the *funerall flame*.
> (497–500)

And while the text merely advises the bride to lift her feet high as she crosses the threshold, Jonson's marginal notes explain that this custom serves to avoid the drugs that witches might bury at that perilous place. Thus the threats associated with weddings are included, though in literally marginalized form.

Those explanatory notes prepare us for Jonson's strategies elsewhere in the poem. Throughout the lyric he metaphorically margin-

alizes threats: though this poem repeatedly evokes tensions, it repeatedly controls and subdues them as well. This pattern is, as I have
maintained, central to the Stuart epithalamium; but some of Jonson's
applications, notably his treatment of agency, are original. First of all,
since both the masque form and his own poetry are prone to celebrate royal power, it is hardly surprising that in this lyric various
allusions to authority and to willing obedience serve to control the
evils attempting to invade the happy Eden represented by the wedding. In many other epithalamia, Hymen is merely encouraged to
attend the festivities; Jonson's appeal is phrased in a telling way,
"*Lead,* HYMEN, *lead* away" (3; italics added). Notice, too, the choice of
auxiliary: "To place her by that side / Where shee *must* long abide"
(465–466; italics added).

   In addition, the poem contains the threats Jonson associates with
sexuality by presenting the subject in indirect and guarded language.
Though he draws on a classical formula that emphasizes the erotic
significance of the wedding, the epithalamium delivered outside the
bedchamber, he interprets the formula in ways that play down the
erotic. The actual consummation is described chastely enough to
pass muster in a family magazine: "And, looke, before you yeeld to
slumber, / That your delights be drawne past number" (517–518),
and so on. But Jonson's evocations of sexuality are indirect in another and more telling way: he plays down, even denies, the agency
of the bride. Early in the poem a passive construction hints at that
process: "When (like to him) her *name* / Is chang'd, but not her
flame" (475–476). Those hints are realized in the description of her
anticipated maternity: here, as in the passage from Sir John Beaumont we examined in Chapter 2, motherhood is not a state she
achieves but a condition determined by others. As I suggested earlier
in this chapter, the use of the definite article rather than the pronoun
"her" is telling: "Informe the gentle wombe" (543). Here, as in
other wedding poems, such constructions delimit the sexual threat
the woman might otherwise represent. They relate as well to Jonson's curious approaches to agency elsewhere in his epithalamia.

   Jonson also counterbalances the potential disruptions associated
with the wedding, such as infidelity and jealousy, by turning his
poem into an icon of balance and stability, an exemplar of the values
he wishes to associate with the occasion. He relies on couplets and
on a stanza form that is simple and regular—and looks that way on

the page. And no other Stuart epithalamium establishes closure as insistently as this poem. The final stanza is a textbook example of techniques for doing so: the youths and virgins are told to "Cease" (557), the door is closed, and the poet's wishes for the couple's future enumerated.

In effecting closure, the final stanza also repeats the word "perfection," thus demonstrating the principal way Jonson calms the tensions associated with his subject. With slight variations, three refrains read, "So may they both, e're day, / Rise perfect euerie way" (547–548), a pattern culminating in the reference to perfection in the last stanza. To develop this concept, Jonson characteristically draws on several sources, ranging from neo-Platonic philosophy to proverbial lore.[30] A popular expression assures us that women are perfected by men, and Aristotle's influential theory of conception holds that the embryo is imperfect until the male imparts the sensitive soul.[31] Pythagoras inspired numerological interpretations of perfection on which Jonson sometimes draws in his masques. As Jonson notes in *Hymenaei* itself, for example, five is a perfect number and is produced from the male and female numbers two and three. (This note implies that perfection involves the coming together of otherwise disparate forces, yet another hint of Jonson's emphasis on the communal.) The source that best glosses Jonson's discussion of perfection, however, is the allegorical figure of Perfectio explicated in Cesare Ripa's *Iconologia*.[32] Associated with the zodiac, a circle, and an—unbroken—compass, she represents perfect order and unity. To put it another way, she represents the polar opposite of the chaos that Jonson elsewhere connects with sexuality.

When Donne refers to perfection in his "Epithalamion made at Lincolnes Inne," he associates it primarily with the bride. Jonson sometimes genders the concept in a similar way; in his *Masque of*

[30]Useful summaries appear in Allan H. Gilbert, *The Symbolic Persons in the Masques of Ben Jonson* (Durham: Duke Univ. Press, 1948), pp. 189–192; *Ben Jonson,* ed. C. H. Herford and Percy and Evelyn Simpson, 11 vols. (Oxford: Clarendon Press, 1925–1952), X, 475–476. For a more detailed analysis, see two studies by D. J. Gordon, "*Hymenaei*: Ben Jonson's Masque of Union," esp. 120; "The Imagery of Ben Jonson's *The Masque of Blacknesse* and *The Masque of Beautie,*" *Journal of the Warburg and Courtauld Institutes,* 6 (1943), esp. 136–137.

[31]On these theories cf. Halio, "*Perfection* and Elizabethan Ideas of Conception."

[32]This work went through numerous editions. See, e.g., Cesare Ripa, *Iconologia* (Padua: Donato Pasquardi, 1630), pp. 564–565.

Beautie, for instance, perfection is an attendant of beauty, and the *Masque of Blackness* refers to women attaining perfection. Here, however, Jonson suggests that both the groom and the bride achieve perfection through sex. For in this epithalamium, as in many other passages in his work, he is concerned less with the destructiveness of female sexuality than with the way desire may cripple men as well as women. In other poems he responds to that threat with prosodic or linguistic strategies, but here he draws on the complex intellectual traditions that converge in his figure of Perfection. That notion is his key to reinterpreting the results of sexuality: the consummation of the marriage generates order, rather than producing the anarchy that he and so many other Stuart writers associated with desire. Pythagoras, not Ursula, presides over the consummation of this union, and the semiotic system of sexuality is transformed from damp and wrinkled sheets to circles, zodiacs, and perfect numbers.

It is no accident that this poem, like the epithalamium in *The Haddington Masque,* juxtaposes conventional allusions to the battles of love with Jonson's more idiosyncratic focus on perfection. He is again acknowledging potential discord in the process of disarming it. The resolution of the restless movement of battles into the calm harmony of perfection exemplifies the tension between intense energy and stasis that characterizes so much of his work;[33] and in his epithalamia, unlike many of Herrick's, that tension is resolved by asserting the victory of stasis. No reader of these wedding poems would be surprised to learn that alchemists, those enemies of stasis, are the villains in one of Jonson's best and most characteristic plays. Nor would a reader of these lyrics be surprised to find how often their author's verse praises the monarch: his royalist conservatism is the political analogue to his support for other types of stasis.

The epithalamium in *Hymenaei,* then, provides a fitting culmination to a masque in which Reason presides over the defeat of the Humours and the Affections. Jonson keeps a tight rein on the horses

[33]On this pattern elsewhere in his canon, see Marotti, "All about Jonson's Poetry"; Greene, "Ben Jonson and the Centered Self," and *The Light in Troy,* chap. 13. On stasis in Jonson, also cf. Mary Thomas Crane's unpublished article " 'His Own Style': Voice and Writing in Jonson's Poems"; she comments on his habit of turning living beings into inanimate objects. Her observations on Jonson's tendency to present his poems as impersonal inscriptions also substantiate my arguments about agency.

Plato evokes in his speculations on desire: the forces threatening order and reason, particularly passion, are subdued throughout the lyric.

In crafting the plot of *The Haddington Masque,* in contrast to that of
Hymenaei, Jonson does not consider it necessary to banish his antimasque. Instead, the characters in it, playful spirits known as the Ioci
and Risus, are permitted to attend on Love. This is not to say the
masque celebrates sexuality as unrestrainedly as Herrick does; in particular, it is telling that though the figure of Vulcan may represent
the heat necessary for procreation, the plot of the masque deflects
attention from this significance onto his role as artisan.[34] We find a
similar pattern in the epithalamium within this masque: its mood is
more energetic than that of the wedding poem in *Hymenaei,* though
the energies this lyric both celebrates and embodies are still controlled, much as Jonson controls the connotations of the figure of
Vulcan. Stephen Orgel has suggested that Jonsonian masques change
after 1609; their author comes to see the antimasque not as a simple
alternative to the masque but as a world that can be accommodated,
though in revised form, within it.[35] *Hymenaei* was performed in 1606
and *The Haddington Masque* in 1608; the epithalamium in the second
work effects an accommodation that anticipates the accommodation
within the masque itself.

The opening of the epithalamium in *The Haddington Masque* demonstrates Jonson's continuing skill at adapting generic conventions to
the predilections of his own temperament: "Vp *youthes* and *virgins,*
vp, and praise / The *god,* whose nights out-shine his daies." The
command is closely modeled on the beginning of Catullus 62, in
which the chorus of young men declares, "The evening is come, rise
up, ye youths." But in Jonson's classical model the youths rise up
to pursue an argument with their opposite numbers, the maidens.
Jonson, in contrast, reshapes the generic norm to emphasize the
communal values to which he is so committed.[36] He transforms
combative debating into communal eulogizing: the youths and maidens are united in their celebrations just as they are united in the

[34]Though D. J. Gordon's learned analysis of the sexual significance of Vulcan indubitably aids our understanding of the masque, he neglects the ways Jonson distracts
our attention from that significance ("Ben Jonson's 'Haddington Masque': The Story
and the Fable," *MLR,* 42 [1947], 180–187).

[35]*Ben Jonson: The Complete Masques,* ed. Stephen Orgel (New Haven: Yale Univ.
Press, 1969), "Introduction," pp. 12–14.

[36]As McPeek (pp. 201–203) points out, however, the debate between Truth and
Opinion does echo the one in Catullus 62.

opening phrase of his poem. And elsewhere in the poem he emphasizes the sharing of values and experiences. For instance, he implies that the youths and virgins should themselves marry:

> And what they are,
> If you'll perfection see,
> Your selues must be.
> (378–380)

Compare, too, his habit of using the first personal plural pronoun to refer to the couple: "And such ours bee" (391).

The enthusiasm implied and encouraged by the opening command to arise also anticipates patterns that we find throughout the lyric: though Jonson maintains the dignity that characterizes his earlier epithalamium, here his mood is more jubilant and playful. Here, in fact, he explicitly celebrates the festive, literally and figuratively incorporating the spirits termed Ioci and Risus into his epithalamium just as they have been incorporated into, not banished from, the masque itself:

> *Loues* common wealth consists of toyes;
> His councell are those *antique* boyes,
> *Games, laughter[s], sports, delights,*
> That triumph with him on these nights.
> (404–407)

As this quotation would lead us to expect, Jonson treats sexuality more overtly and more enthusiastically here than in the epithalamium in *Hymenaei*. "But there are *rites* behind / Haue lesse of state, but more of kind" (395–396), he reminds the couple, and when he comes to describe those rites, for a moment his tone verges on the ribald:

> This night no *Bride-grome* euer slept;
> And if the faire *Bride* doo,
> The married say, 'tis his fault, too.
> Wake then; and let your lights
> Wake too: for they'l tell nothing of your nights.
> (427–431)

We observed earlier, however, that the word *"rites"* (395) can serve to sanctify sexuality. And, as his usage of the term here suggests, Jonson's celebration of the sexual union of the couple is neither unqualified nor unmediated: in this epithalamium, as in its counterpart in *Hymenaei,* he stabilizes and socializes even, or especially, the consummation of the marriage. For example, he emphasizes perfection even more than he did in the epithalamium in *Hymenaei:* here the word appears in the refrain of every stanza. In each instance, too, he suggests its connection with the wars of love; thus at one point he writes,

> Speed well in HYMEN's warre,
>   That, what you are,
> By your perfection, wee
>   And all may see.
>
>   (421–424)

In the literal sense, "warre" rhymes with "starre" in this and other stanzas, but in another sense it rhymes with perfection: Jonson's response to the tensions and discords connected with the wedding is again to resolve them through the concept of perfection.

His second mode of resolution occurs in one striking passage of the poem: "Tomorrow, rise the same / Your *mother* is" (419–420). The lines can, of course, simply be paraphrased, "Tomorrow you, like your mother, will be a matron," but they resonate with other implications. For Jonson describes becoming a wife in terms of bridging the gap between parent and child. In so doing he foreshadows an assertion that will find clearer expression in the epithalamium written for Hierome Weston and Frances Stuart: marriage closes the divisions between the generations, much as the endings of romantic comedy typically resolve conflicts between parents and their offspring.

Even Jonson's grammatical choices serve to convert desire from a privatized and anarchic impulse to a social and stabilizing force; thus he develops idiosyncratic strategies to fulfill a common goal of the Stuart epithalamium, the taming of Cupid. The refrains in Jonson's earlier wedding poem vary, but here in each stanza ends, "Shine, HESPERVS, shine forth, thou wished *starre*." Contrast this line with the way Herrick evokes the anticipation of the wedding night:

                              let thy Torch
                     Display the Bridegroom in the porch,
                              In his desires
                More towring, more disparkling then thy fires.
                     ("A Nuptiall Song, or Epithalamie, on Sir
                     Clipseby Crew and his Lady," 33–36)

Herrick locates desire in the bridegroom; Jonson diffuses—and de-
fuses—it though the generalizing word "wished." Once again he
confounds agency, in this case deflecting attention away from the
couple's own desires while at the same time suggesting that the entire community shares their anticipation of the wedding night. Notice, too, the contrast between Herrick's present participles and
Jonson's past participle: "wished" renders even the process of wish-
ing, which we normally associate with excitement and uncertainty,
as a passive state rather than an activity.[37]

The grammatical patterns we are tracing—and the psychological
patterns that they in turn trace—recur elsewhere in Jonson's work.
His predilection for past participles is striking; he refers, for example, to "mowed meddowes" ("To Sir Robert Wroth," 39), and the
titles of his masques include *Love Freed From Ignorance and Folly, Love
Restored, Lovers Made Men*, and so on. These participles serve not
only to establish stasis but also to deflect or disguise agency: who is
variously freeing and restoring love or making lovers men? Similarly,
the fish in "To Penshurst" jump willingly into the net, absolving
fishermen of the guilt of catching them. But nowhere does Jonson
confound agency more systematically than in his ostensibly autobiographical works, suggesting that one function of the process of denying volition is to assuage guilt. Thus he blames his muse for
betraying him "to a worthlesse lord" ("To my Mvse," 2), and in
"Why I write not of Love" he first implies that he is forced to write
about love ("Some act of *Loue's bound* to reherse" (1; italics added on
"bound"), then proceeds to insist that he wishes to talk about love
but cannot.

The strategies we have identified thus far in the epithalamium in
The Haddington Masque, especially its emphases on disguising agency
and constructing desire as a force that binds the community, deepen
our understanding of Jonson, but they do not shake any of our as-

---

[37]Greene offers a different but related observation about the way Jonson's adjectives
create "an unassailable stability" (*The Light in Troy*, p. 276).

sumptions about him. In one surprising passage, however, that pro-
ponent of regal and aristocratic power, that celebrant of authority
and even authoritarianism, observes,

> What joy, or honors can compare
> With holy *nuptialls,*
>
> .   .   .   .
>
> When, in the happy choyce,
> The *spouse,* and *spoused* haue the formost voyce!
> (382–383, 386–387)

The relationship between the potential couple's choice and the wishes
of their parents was a vexed issue in Elizabethan and Stuart England,
as the marriage manuals attest. Many sources try to skirt the conflict
by having it both ways: the parents have the right to select their
children's mates, these books declare, but they should attend to the
requests of the future bride and groom—a paradigm that can work
smoothly only when the wishes of both generations conveniently
coincide.[38] Here, however, Jonson urges the primacy of the couple's
desires. He does not deny the significance of other opinions—they
have the "formost" (387), not the only, voice—but he does stress the
rights of the bride and groom. The satiric attacks on unhappy marriages, especially January-May misalliances, that we encounter in
Volpone and other plays may be the product not only of literary conventions but also of observations of the consequences of matches in
which the couple do not have the foremost, or even any, voice.

The poem that Jonson composed for the unfortunate marriage of
Somerset and Frances Howard does not seem to have detained its
author long, nor is it likely to detain its readers: its list of best wishes
and of hopes for the future is mechanical and predictable. The aesthetic failures of this lyric, as of Donne's lyric about the same occasion, no doubt reflect its author's discomfort with the task of
praising the unpraiseworthy. Its length, too, is telling. The epithalamium is only twenty-six lines long, whereas the epithalamia in *Hymenaei* and in *The Haddington Masque* are one hundred twenty and
seventy-seven lines respectively, and the one written for the marriage
of Hierome Weston and Frances Stuart extends to one hundred
ninety-two lines; Jonson's decision to write so short a lyric in a genre

[38]Compare Perkins's insistence that three actions, performed respectively by the
parents, the minister, and the couple, constitute a marriage (*Christian Oeconomie*
[London, 1609], p. 82).

in which he is usually more expansive substantiates one's impression that his heart was not in the task.

Nonetheless, the poem is not without interest: it encourages us to extend our investigations into the influence of patronage on the Stuart epithalamium. This work does not wholly avoid the sycophancy and prevarication that mark and mar so many of its author's other addresses to the nobility: he calls Somerset "vertuous" (7) and claims, as we observed earlier, that genuine love rather than pecuniary need motivates his poem. But we encounter less flattery than Jonson's other poems might lead us to expect. This epithalamium deploys the optatives that characterize its genre to stress wishes for the future rather than observations about the past: "So, be there neuer discontent, or sorrow, / To rise wi'h eyther of you, on the morrow" (15–16). Thus Jonson is able to skirt discussions of the couple's behavior, as well as of the odds for their avoiding discontent and sorrow.

The poem also exemplifies the subversion we have encountered in other Stuart epithalamia. In this lyric, as in so many others that employ that defensive maneuver, it is impossible to be sure whether the poet is consciously including a clever but subtle critique or whether his own psychological ambivalences generate textual ambiguities of which he may not be fully aware. In particular, Jonson expresses the wish that the bride will resemble the model celebrated in "The Wife," a poem by Somerset's former friend Thomas Overbury: "May she, whome thou for spouse, to day, doth take, / Out-bee y^t Wife, in worth, thy freind did make" (11–12). Sent to the Tower for opposing the match, Overbury had died there a few months before the wedding; Frances Howard was subsequently implicated in poisoning him.[39] Jonson may not have known at this point that Overbury's death was suspicious, but a reference to Somerset's erstwhile friend was somewhat tactless under the circumstances. And a reference to this particular poem was more than somewhat tactless, for Overbury's didactic lyric focuses on the dangers of lust and the importance of chastity; a wife should be "Phisicke for our lust,"[40] he

---

[39]On Overbury, see R. C. Bald, *John Donne: A Life* (Oxford: Clarendon Press, 1970), pp. 313–314; David Harris Willson, *King James VI and I*, The Bedford Historical Series (1956; rpt. London: Jonathan Cape, 1959), pp. 341–343. The echo is noted in Herford and Simpson, XI, 138.

[40]Thomas Overbury, *The Overburian Characters, To which is added "A Wife,"* ed. W. J. Paylor, The Percy Reprints, 13 (Oxford: Basil Blackwell, 1936), p. 101.

assures us, and we should select her not for her beauty but for her moral worth. The notorious and widely discussed liasion between Somerset and Frances Howard rendered Jonson's apparently innocuous comparison with Overbury's paragon monitory at best; in fact, some have even speculated that Overbury composed the poem as a warning against the marriage.[41] Like the peculiar allusions to barrenness in George Chapman's *Andromeda Liberata,* then, this reference reminds us that Stuart poets often juxtapose compliments and criticisms and that, indeed, the process of bestowing one may intensify the drive to bestow the other.

The lyric that Jonson composed for the wedding of Hierome Weston and Frances Stuart is connected in many ways to its authors' other works. The enthusiastic evocation of the wedding here may be a palinode to the more cynical reference to such occasions in the Charis sequence; for instance, in this epithalamium he delights in the ways the wedding is a public spectacle, whereas in the Charis lyrics he implicitly criticizes that very aspect of the occasion—Jonson's habit of saying and unsaying characteristically takes place between poems as well as within them. In any event, this epithalamium is closely related to its author's other works in the same genre. Though it was written in 1632, some nineteen years after the epithalamium for Somerset and twenty-six years after the one included in *Hymenaei,* its values are consistent with those of the earlier lyrics; in particular, it enacts linguistically some of the social attitudes articulated in Jonson's other wedding poetry. And, indeed, those attitudes ally it not only with his epithalamia but also with the major poems in his canon. Although it lacks the poetic skill and complexity of, say, "To Penhurst," "Epode," or the Cary-Morison ode, no poem of Jonson's offers us a surer insight into its author's social vision.

That vision emerges when we identify the two central stances in the poem, observation and exclamation. Jonson repeatedly enjoins the sun and by extension human viewers to watch the events: "See, the Procession!" (9), "See, how she paceth forth in Virgin-white" (41), "See, now the Chappell opens" (121), and so on. In fact, the word "see" and its cognates appear no fewer than seventeen times; and even that statistic is deceptively low, for "Harke" (33) and "Search" (79) perform a similar deictic function. These usages are

---

[41]See Paylor, p. 98.

reminiscent of the Charis sequence, in which we are repeatedly commanded to "See the Chariot at hand" ("Her Triumph," 1) and so
on.[42]

But Jonson's allusions to observation extend beyond his injunctions to the sun and other viewers. Originally a spectacle, the couple
themselves will become spectators: "Till you behold a race to fill
your Hall" (169), he writes, rather than "Till you create a race. . . . "
And one member of that anticipated band of descendants is engaged
in the same activity of gazing:

> And 'tweene their Grandsires thighes,
>   Like pretty Spies,
> Peepe forth a Gemme.
>   (173–175)

(Notice, too, that the "Gemme" [175] occupies the position of its
grandsire's genitals; if the authors of other epithalamia attempt to
displace passion with one of its consequences, generation, here Jonson does so literally.) Only a stanza later Jonson intensifies his emphasis on observation, expressing the hope that these descendants
will continue the family tradition by serving as "*watchfull* Servant[s]
for this State" (178; italics added).

If intense observation is the visual mode the poem recommends,
enthusiastic exclamation is the verbal mode it practices. In many instances where declarative constructions might have been used, Jonson instead composes such lines as, "O happy bands! and thou more
happy place, / Which to this use, wert built and consecrate!" (129–
130) or "With what full hands, and in how plenteous showers / Have
they bedew'd the Earth" (65–66).

In short, this epithalamium emphasizes our gazing in admiration at
a series of tableaux. Two of Jonson's other wedding poems are situ-
ated within masques, and the twin modes of observation and exclamation connect this lyric to the traditions of masques and theatrical
spectacles.[43] Thus the poem exemplifies the process of generic modulation that Alastair Fowler so acutely traces in relationship to liter-

---

[42]For acute comments on this pattern in the Charis poems, see Ferry, pp. 131–133.

[43]Greene makes a related but different point when he observes Jonson's tendency to
turn poems into performances (*The Light in Troy*, p. 286). Also cf. Wesley Trimpi's
observation that the poem is like a royal progress (*Ben Jonson's Poems: A Study of the
Plain Style* [Stanford: Stanford Univ. Press, 1962], p. 285).

ary types other than these;[44] in this instance the Stuart epithalamium slides towards the masque, one of the dominant forms in its age and one to which it is in any event closely allied.

This lyric offers, then, a textbook example of the interest in theatricality towards which the new historicism has directed our own critical gaze. And it is a textbook example, too, of the central impetus behind that theatricality: establishing and celebrating power. The poem focuses on the grandeur of the court and of its king and queen; the marriage itself is not mentioned directly until the fourth stanza. And even when it does come into focus, Jonson emphasizes the power and the glory of those whom the bride and groom metaphorically represent rather than the couple themselves or the occasion: he insistently reminds us that she is the daughter of a duke and he the son of one of Charles's most respected ministers. In other words, the ostensibly central figures in this pageant become signifiers, not signifieds, a semiotic pattern closely related to the problem of agency. Jonson aptly glosses his perspective when he writes, "All is a story of the King and Queene!" (91). In this instance the epithalamium is indeed an Althusserian ideological state apparatus.

Jonson's emphasis on seeing and viewing serves as well to remind us of a pressure that intensified and complicated courtly praise: the intrigue that threatened the denizens of that world. The reference to spies quoted above jars a little, and the allusion to a "watchfull Servant for this State" (178) reminds us that surveillance is a strategy for controlling, not merely for celebrating. These hints are slight ones, yet they are indubitably present.

But, as we have noted throughout this book, new historicist emphases are often most useful when they supplement, not supplant, other readings. The masquelike quality of this poem is overdetermined. It serves to fulfill one of the most traditional of rhetorical principles, teaching through exempla: the repetitions of "see" in effect invite us, like the sun, not only to wonder at but also to learn from what Jonson terms "Our Court, and all the Grandees" (73).[45] He is, so to speak, putting the deictic back in epideictic verse. And recognizing the emphasis on wonder in this poem in turn invites us to relate its fascination with spectacle not only to cultural history and

[44]Alastair Fowler, *Kinds of Literature: An Introduction to the Theory of Genres and Modes* (Cambridge: Harvard Univ. Press, 1982), chap. 11.
[45]On this rhetorical commonplace, see, e.g., *Rhetorica ad Herennium,* IV.i–vii.

rhetorical principles but also to a more idiosyncratic practice in its author's canon: his focus on engendering wonder in both his dramatic and his nondramatic works.[46]

Jonson's emphasis on exclamation and observation relates in other ways to the social vision of the poem. In two of his other epithalamia Jonson evokes the concept of perfection to suggest that marriage is an alternative to, not an intensification of, the restless movement associated with other types of love. Here, in lieu of asserting that the wedding will lead to stability, he repeatedly mimes that value within the poem. The emphasis on process and motion in other lyric epithalamia makes Jonson's attraction to stasis here especially revealing. Thus his exclamations serve to evoke not the movement of the procession or of the events of the day but rather static tableaux: "See, how with Roses, and with Lillies shine . . . The bright Brides path" (57, 59), Jonson writes, although other poets in the genre would be more likely to stress strewing those flowers or leading the bride through them. And even when Jonson does incorporate a verb into his exclamations, the syntax focuses our attention on gazing rather than on whatever process is involved in the verb. Contrast the emphases in "With what full hands, and in how plenteous showers / Have they bedew'd the Earth" (65–66) with those in the alternative that Jonson might have selected, "They have bedewed the earth with full hands and plenteous showers." This privileging of the static is articulated and acted out in the dramatic fiction behind the poem, Jonson's dialogue with the sun: though he does at one point urge that celestial body to depart so that evening will commence, for much of the poem this latter-day Joshua instead commands it to stand still.[47]

Jonson's modes of observation and exclamation serve not only to evoke a stable world but also to express some political and cultural sources of that stability. One is the poet's own authority. As readers of the Charis poems have noted, an emphasis on seeing establishes

---

[46]Many critics have commented intelligently on this aspect of Jonson's work. See L. A. Beaurline, *Jonson and Elizabethan Comedy: Essays in Dramatic Rhetoric* (San Marino, Calif.: Huntington Library, 1978), esp. chaps. 2 and 4; D. Heyward Brock, " 'Mirrors of Man's Life': The Masques of Ben Jonson and Social Order," *RE: Artes Liberales*, 3 (1976), 49–60.

[47]On stasis in the poem also cf. Richard S. Peterson's observation that Weston is presented like a statue in a niche (*Imitation and Praise in the Poems of Ben Jonson* [New Haven: Yale Univ. Press, 1981], pp. 102–103).

the potency of the poet who directs our gaze;[48] in the epithalamium at hand, similar commands serve a similar end. Speakers in other lyric epithalamia tell the participants what to do; Jonson instead tells spectators what to see. Thus the poet remains in command and in control, though he assumes that position less by directing the events of the wedding than by displaying the ensuing tableaux.[49]

The poem implicitly advocates another source of social stability. It relies not only on observation and exclamation but also on a range of other strategies to emphasize the primacy of the community over that of the individual. Adumbrated in Jonson's other epithalamia, this vision is fully and coherently established only in this poem, his final contribution to the genre. Thus he describes the bride and groom less as active participants in the events of the day than as puppets. We have already seen that the syntax of his exclamations plays down what actions they do perform. And their agency and volition are further limited. In particular, even when consummating the marriage they are directed by others. In lieu of portraying a threateningly forceful bridegroom as Herrick does, Jonson writes, "let him freely gather Loves First-fruits" (186), in effect bestowing permission for passion rather than acknowledging its uncontrollable urgency. Admittedly, Jonson proceeds to refer to the groom as "Master of the Office" (187), but this is clearly a master who is himself mastered. And at the conclusion of the poem a few lines later Jonson writes, "Night, and the sheetes will show / The longing Couple, all that elder Lovers know" (191–192). The lines echo a passage in *Hero and Leander*, but their sentiment is wholly characteristic of Jonson himself: even at this culminating moment, the lovers are students rather than graduates, objects rather than subjects.

The description of sexuality in the line just quoted demonstrates yet another way Jonson emphasizes the primacy of the community: he constructs even the consummation of the marriage as a source of social cohesion rather than individual pleasure. His intense need to establish this point is manifest in its repetition. It appears not only in the final section of the poem but in an earlier passage:

[48]See Ferry, pp. 131–132.

[49]Though they focus on works other than this one, several critics offer acute observations about Jonson's drive to be, and to be seen to be, in control. See esp. Fish, "Authors-Readers: Jonson's Community of the Same"; Douglas M. Lanier, "Brainchildren: Self-representation and Patriarchy in Ben Jonson's Early Works," *Renaissance Papers*, ed. Dale B. J. Randall and Joseph A. Porter (Durham: Duke Univ. Press, 1986), esp. p. 53.

> There is a Feast behind,
>   To them of kind,
> Which their glad Parents taught
> One to the other, long e're these to light were brought.
>
>   . . . . .
>
>   that these may know
> All that their Fathers, and their Mothers might
> Of Nuptiall Sweets
>
> (141–144, 146–148)

Another way Jonson develops his communal vision is by extending the service that Weston's father performs for the king into a metaphor for the appropriate relationship of all individuals to the culture. That relationship, he implies, involves willingly accepting one's place within a larger social unit and choosing to serve its ends. His rendition of the dynastic preoccupation that characterizes the Stuart epithalamium is telling: "each [heir] playes his part, of the large Pedigree" (176). Notice, too, his characteristic emphasis on authority and service even when describing participation in the wedding: "The Month of youth, which calls all Creatures forth / To doe their Offices in Natures Chime" (26–27).

But the most subtle and most intriguing proof of Jonson's drive to privilege the community over the individual is found in one of his linguistic habits. Evoking the heirs whom he hopes the couple will produce, he writes,

> A *Richard,* and a *Hierome,* by their names
> Upon a *Thomas,* or a *Francis* call;
>   A *Kate,* a *Frank,* to honour their Grand-dames.
>
> (170–172)

In celebrating the marriage of Honorius and Maria, Claudian expresses the hope that a little Honorius will sit in his grandfather's lap. But this classical borrowing, like most of those we encounter in Jonson's epithalamia, is tailored to a particular vision. The passage aims, of course, to flatter the current members of the family by suggesting that their descendants will immortalize them, and in so doing it also reinforces Jonson's emphasis on stasis by indicating that relationships between Richards and Thomases will continue uninterrupted from one generation to the next. Yet it demonstrates the price of that continuity as well: its indefinite articles drain those descen-

dants of their individuality, much as the bride and groom themselves
surrender their autonomy at other points in the poem.

The Weston epithalamium both demonstrates and develops the
predilections we have encountered throughout its author's wedding
poems. His works in the genre are no more free of discordant intrusions than his masques are free of the threats represented by the
antimasque: antiquarian wedding customs remind us of the circumstances that may preclude a happy marriage, and negative syntactical
formulations repeatedly recall the problems they deny. But Jonson
responds to these threats by performing his own alchemical metamorphoses, transforming agency into passivity, flux into stability,
and, above all, transforming individuals into willing members—and
servants—of their community.

III

Whereas Jonson claims not to write of love, Herrick just as firmly
and far more reliably asserts his intention of writing of its cousin,
marriage. "I sing . . . Of *Bride-grooms, Brides,* and of their *Bridall-
cakes*" (3–4), he declares in that deceptively simple poem "The Argument of his Book," and in this instance, unlike many others, he
proves as good as his word. *Hesperides* includes no fewer than seven
poems that we would classify as epithalamia. "An Epithalamie to Sir
Thomas Southwell and his Ladie," which was written in 1618, and
"A Nuptiall Song, or Epithalamie, on Sir Clipseby Crew and his
Lady," composed seven years later, are his two principal contributions to the genre. But his work in it is also represented by shorter
lyrics: "A Nuptiall Verse to Mistresse Elizabeth Lee, now Lady Tracie," "The Entertainment: or, Porch-verse, at the Marriage of Mr.
Hen. Northly, and the most witty Mrs. Lettice Yard," "An hymne
to Juno," "Connubii Flores, or the well-wishes at Weddings," "The
delaying Bride." A few other poems are closely connected to weddings even though one would hesitate to label them epithalamia.
Thus in "To Anthea" ("Lets call for *Hymen* if agreed thou art") the
speaker proposes to his eponymous beloved and in so doing incorporates conventions from the epithalamium, such as allusions to Hymen and to the wedding tapers. In "To the Maids to walke abroad"
young girls anticipate and describe their prospective marriages. And
in "The Bride-Cake" Herrick concocts a series of compliments that

are in a sense only marginally related to the wedding per se ("Or kisse [the cake] thou, but once, or twice, / And for the Bride-Cake ther'l be Spice" [5–6]); but his decision to connect his tributes to Julia to a wedding again demonstrates his interest in, or even his preoccupation with, that event.

In addition, however, Herrick "sing[s] of *Bride-grooms, Brides,* and of their *Bridall-cakes*" in a harsher voice. Several of his epigrams are cynical comments on marriage; in some of them, such as "His Comfort," the speaker congratulates himself on having avoided that state.[50] "The Tythe. To the Bride" implies that brides may well blush for more reasons than one:

> If nine times you your Bride-groome kisse;
> The tenth you know the Parsons is.
> Pay then your Tythe; and doing thus,
> Prove in your Bride-bed numerous
> If children you have ten, Sir *John*
> Won't for his tenth part ask you one.

The same joke could have been addressed to a wife rather than a bride; in shaping the poem as he does, Herrick demonstrates his preoccupation with weddings. We also find here an impulse to counterbalance the celebrations of marriage with a more cynical vision, a point to which we will return.

Why, then, is Herrick so interested in marriage and in the literary genre that describes it? Most obviously, that genre invites him to explore love and sexuality, subjects that dominate *Hesperides.* The epithalamium also accords to many other predilections of his own sensibility, as it does to Jonson's, though the predilections in question are different. Herrick's critics have disagreed on such fundamental issues as the relationship of paganism to Christianity in his work and the significance, or lack of significance, of the way he arranges the lyrics in *Hesperides*[51]—but, *pace* Stanley Fish, no one is likely to de-

---

[50]Many recent critics have observed Herrick's habit of fashioning companion poems that comment on one another. See, e.g., A. B. Chambers, "Herrick and the Trans-shifting of Time," *SP,* 72 (1975), 85–114.

[51]For a useful summary of scholarship on these and other issues, see Joseph A. Glaser, "Recent Herrick Criticism: Sighting In on One of the Most Elusive of Poets," *CLAJ,* 20 (1976), 292–302; Elizabeth H. Hageman, "Recent Studies in Herrick," *ELR,* 3 (1973), 462–471.

bate whether Herrick is interested in time.[52] The lyric epithalamium, as we saw in Chapter 2, is itself grounded in temporal patterns; witness its emphasis on diurnal changes and on the orderly progress of the wedding day, as well as its concern about events that may slow down the festivities. Similarly, Herrick is intrigued, even entranced, with the interpenetrations of human and natural worlds (in "Corinna's going a Maying," a young woman sports foliage, boys and girls bud, and so on); and, as we have observed, the epithalamium itself typically effects a reconciliation of those domains.[54]

Another affinity between Herrick and the epithalamium is even more central. The Stuart wedding poem is shaped by a drive to return to an Edenic past, and so too is Herrick's own sensibility. As one of his critics points out, the very title *Hesperides* suggests "a golden age on an edenic island,"[53] and many of the lyrics within the collection testify to his attraction to happier Edens. That attraction is at its most overt in poems like "A Country life: To his Brother, M. Tho: Herrick," but it emerges in many other instances. Surely the fairy world is itself a type of displaced paradise. Herrick's delight in folklore is in part a delight in an idealized past. And the childlike tone of many of his poems, notably some of the religious ones, is illuminated when we recall that an attraction to childhood, to pastoral, and to the paradisaical can all be modes of the same impulse. In short, if Jonson finds in the epithalamium a strategy for stabilizing the present and future, Herrick turns to the genre to recuperate the past.

Our analyses of the wedding poems that spring from Herrick's interest in their genre, like many other questions about the author of *Hesperides,* need to be hedged with cautions: one of the many ways he resembles Andrew Marvell is that inconsistencies and ironies mock any pat generalizations that might tempt us.[54] The primary

[52]Many critics have explored this facet of Herrick's work. See, e.g., T. G. S. Cain, "*Times trans-shifting:* Herrick in Meditation," in "*Trust to Good Verses*": *Herrick Tercentenary Essays,* ed. Roger B. Rollin and J. Max Patrick (Pittsburgh: Univ. of Pittsburgh Press, 1978); Earl Miner, *The Cavalier Mode from Jonson to Cotton* (Princeton: Princeton Univ. Press, 1971), chap. 3.

[53]Ann Coiro, "Herrick's *Hesperides:* The Name and the Frame," *ELH,* 52 (1985), 315. Also cf. Peter Stallybrass's comments on Merrie England as a second Eden (" 'We feaste in our Defense': Patrician Carnival in Early Modern England and Robert Herrick's 'Hesperides,' " *ELR,* 16 [1986], 239).

[54]The critical response to this aspect of Herrick's canon provides a convenient microcosm of shifts in literary tastes and methodologies. Earlier critics found philosophical consistency and aesthetic order in *Hesperides* (see, e.g., Robert H. Deming,

reason critics have contradicted one another on such issues as Herrick's putative attraction to moderation is that the poems contradict one another: like statistics, they can conveniently be read to support one's preconceptions. Thus Herrick criticizes excess in his epigram "The Hony-combe"—yet elsewhere he both celebrates and exemplifies it, whether it be represented by hyperbolic language, by repeated words, or notably by drunkenness.[55] In such instances the contradictions seem to emerge from emotional ambivalences rather than artistic policies; but in other cases Herrick deliberately invites and even delights in contradictions. Thus, in arranging the poems in *Hesperides,* as several recent readers have observed, he typically juxtaposes ones with diametrically opposed visions.[56] He speaks in many voices; his use of multiple choruses in "Connubii Flores" enacts a predilection that emerges more indirectly elsewhere. And we find contradictions not only between but also within poems, as the self-defeating observation in the Southwell epithalamium reminds us: "you will most / Esteeme it when 'tis lost" (15–16).

Indeed, that curious advice to the bride demonstrates one of the principal sources of inconsistency in Herrick: paradoxes and contradictions that cannot be comfortably resolved. It is far easier to explain, say, Jonson's "allowed warre" ("Epithalamion; or, A Song: Celebrating the Nvptials of that Noble Gentleman, Mr. Hierome Weston," 31) than Herrick's "cleanly-*Wantonnesse*" ("The Argument

---

Ceremony and Art: Robert Herrick's Poetry [The Hague: Mouton, 1974]). Richard L. Capwell observes the variety of that collection but reads it as a sign not of inconsistency and tension but rather of aesthetic skill ("Herrick and the Aesthetic Principle of Variety and Contrast," *South Atlantic Quarterly,* 71 [1972], 488–495). In the 1980s however, many readers have emphasized the unresolved contradictions and the dissonances in Herrick's work, the position to which I subscribe. For examples of that position, see, e.g., Coiro, "Herrick's *Hesperides:* The Name and the Frame"; Harold Toliver, "Herrick's Book of Realms and Moments," *ELH,* 49 (1982), 429–448. I am grateful to Carol Ann Johnston for drawing my attention to another type of irony in Herrick; as she points out, the very title of *Noble Numbers* involves a self-conscious process of distancing.

[55]Paul R. Jenkins notes the shifts in Herrick's treatment of moderation and excess but attempts to reconcile some of them by arguing that he is in favor of restraining desire because the process of doing so intensifies pleasure ("Rethinking What Moderation Means to Robert Herrick," *ELH,* 38 [1972], 49–65).

[56]See Capwell, "Herrick and the Aesthetic Principle of Variety and Contrast"; also see John L. Kimmey's argument that the order in *Hesperides* reflects the changing moods of the speaker ("Order and Form in Herrick's *Hesperides,*" *JEGP,* 70 [1971], 255–268).

of his Book," 6) or "wilde civility" ("Delight in Disorder," 12)—
though critics committed to finding stability in Herrick's vision
have devoted considerable space to attempts at such explanations.[57]
Similarly, the infamous ending of "The Hock-Cart"—"Not sent ye
for to drowne your paine, / But for to make it spring againe" (54–55)
may suggest either a diminution or a renewal of the pain, contradictory interpretations that cannot be yoked together even by
violence.[58]

Though these tendencies complicate the process of generalizing
about Herrick, a reading of his epithalamia reveals several salient
characteristics. One difference that emerged from my preliminary
comparison of Herrick and Jonson appears throughout their epithalamia: Herrick is far more interested in the bride's, and to a lesser
extent the groom's, delays. The Southwell lyric, as we have already
observed, focuses on this issue, as does the lyric entitled "The delaying Bride." In "A Nuptiall Verse to Mistresse Elizabeth Lee, now
Lady Tracie," the speaker chides, "Indeed you are too slow" (5). The
Crew wedding poem touches on the same topic in its lines, "though
you slow- / ly go, yet, howsoever, go" (59–60); by hyphenating his
adverb, Herrick mimetically enacts the hesitations he is describing.[59]
Moreover, a concern with delays recurs in poems that involve weddings even though they would not be classified as epithalamia. In
"To Anthea" ("Lets call for *Hymen* if agreed thou art") the speaker
declares, "*Delays in love* but crucifie the heart" (2); as the poem
progresses it becomes clear that this emphasis is motivated both by
the sexual energy he feels and by her own countervailing reluctance.
And one of Herrick's religious poems, entitled "Mora Sponsi, the
stay of the Bridegroome," focuses on Christ's delays, a common
theological topic.

[57]See, e.g., Rollin, *Robert Herrick,* chap. 4. Alastair Fowler relates Herrick's paradoxes to his predilection for disorder ("Robert Herrick," *Proceedings of the British
Academy,* 66 [1980], 261–262).
[58]Many readers have commented on this curious conclusion. See, e.g., A. Leigh
DeNeef, *"This Poetick Liturgie": Robert Herrick's Ceremonial Mode* (Durham: Duke
Univ. Press, 1974), p. 49.
[59]Delays are further stressed in the tenth stanza of a variant version of this poem.
The variants, which include some striking alterations, are reprinted in L. C. Martin's
edition, pp. 476–479. The variant stanzas are also reprinted and discussed in *The
Complete Poems of Robert Herrick,* ed. Alexander B. Grosart, 3 vols. (London: Chatto
and Windus, 1876), I, cxliv–cl. Although one cannot definitively prove that these
stanzas are authorial, Grosart's presupposition that they represent Herrick's earlier
versions is clearly highly probable, and my analysis proceeds on that assumption.

Literary decisions are, as we have observed, often overdetermined. In this instance, one aesthetic factor contributes to Herrick's emphasis on delays: the contrast between the bride's hesitations and the speaker's urgings adds a touch of excitement and dramatic tension to the narrative. And Herrick's customary preoccupation with *"Times trans-shifting"* ("The Argument of his Book," 9) is germane here: drawing attention to the bride's hesitations leads him to emphasize the concern with time and the untimely that runs throughout the epithalamium tradition.

Moreover, by playing the speaker's impatient urgings against the bride's delays, Herrick colors his primary genre with the tones of the persuasion poem, thus effecting yet another generic modulation. Hence these lyrics become mirror images of "Corinna's going a Maying," in which traces of the conventions of the epithalamium survive and flourish within a persuasion poem.[60] And we also encounter a similar pattern in the lyric to which I referred earlier, "To Anthea" ("Lets call for *Hymen* if agreed thou art"): here the persuasion poem is decked with the trappings of the epithalamium. Renaissance poets, of course, typically enjoy the virtuosity involved in generic experimentation, especially the mixing of literary types, but Herrick's own pleasure in that process stems as well from his tendency to blur lines, collapse distinctions, push down fences. We encounter many instances in Herrick's best-known poems: the title character is enjoined to "put on your Foliage" (15) in "Corinna's going a Maying," and "The Argument of his Book" moves in curious ways between physical and supernatural objects.[61] His slippages between the human and the animal, the civilized and the natural, find their generic analogue in the slippage between epithalamium and persuasion poem. In that melding of literary types Herrick blurs the division between the communal order and stability usually associated with Stuart wedding poetry and the amoral, naturalistic, and personal vision of the persuasion poem, a point that anticipates the peculiar treatment of sexuality we find in his wedding poems.

We might perhaps be tempted to argue that the motif of the delaying bride represents a genuine concern for that character's feelings. Herrick is indulging his habit of writing palinodes to earlier poems,

[60]On the connections between that poem and the epithalamium, see Phyllis Brooks Toback, "Herrick's 'Corinna's Going a Maying' and the Epithalamic Tradition," *Seventeenth-Century News*, 24 (1966), 13.
[61]On that process in "The Argument of His Book," see DeNeef, pp. 6–7.

so the case would run: he is reacting against his tendency to treat the women he evokes with, as it were, Cavalier indifference. But this argument does not survive scrutiny. The speaker is neither precise about the brides' emotions nor acute about the reasons a woman might fear the loss of virginity. The doubts of these characters, though evoked repeatedly in Herrick's wedding poems, are typically described in stereotyped fashion, then dismissed.

Herrick is really interested in his own doubts about marriage, not those of the bride. This is the primary reason for his preoccupation with her procrastination. He displaces onto these young women his own hesitations about celebrating weddings; the tension between the brides who wish to delay their marriage and the speaker who urges them on externalizes a debate within the poet himself. We encounter this pattern in the treatment of brides in other epithalamia, but nowhere is it as clear or as interesting as in Herrick's.

The ambivalence about the consummation of the marriage—and about sexuality and marriage in general—that I attribute to Herrick is both substantiated and explicated by the ways his epithalamia treat sexuality. Here the distinction between Herrick and Jonson (and, indeed, between Herrick and many other writers) is one of degree, not of kind. Herrick is not the only Stuart poet to dwell on the threats as well as the pleasures of consummating the marriage: those threats are central to the Stuart epithalamium, and Jonson in particular addresses them. But the tensions that arise when Herrick moves from singing of bridal cakes to singing of wedding nights are deeper and darker than those in Jonson's lyrics or in most other epithalamia of the period; and the resolutions he attempts are more uncertain and unstable. Like many other high priests of sex, Herrick is ambivalent about the deity he claims to serve.

Thus the concern about the loss of virginity on which we briefly touched in comparing him with Jonson occurs often in his epithalamia. Some of his other lyrics prepare us for his treatment of this subject in his wedding poems. In particular, several passages in *Hesperides* hint at the attraction to celibacy that is, as I have argued, more powerful in Protestant England than critics usually acknowledge. "A Country life: To his Brother, M. Tho: Herrick," includes a curious tribute to the poet's sister-in-law: "by chast intentions led, / [She] Gives thee each night a Maidenhead" (41–42). The point, of course, is that she remains pure; but the impulse to describe married chastity in terms of virginity and its surrender gestures towards

the same tensions we encountered in the conduct book by Daniel
Rogers. Herrick's characteristic search for a lost Edenic past is here
rechanneled into a search for a lost sexual innocence. Similar assertions—and similar tensions, too—emerge in the curious poem
"Julia's Churching, or Purification":

> All Rites well ended, with faire Auspice come
> (As to the breaking of a Bride-Cake) home:
> Where ceremonious *Hymen* shall for thee
> Provide a second *Epithalamie.*
> *She who keeps chastly to her husbands side*
> *Is not for one, but every night his Bride:*
> *And stealing still with love, and feare to Bed,*
> *Brings him not one, but many a Maiden-head.*
>
> (9–16)

If we encountered the word in isolation, we might be persuaded that
"*feare*" (15) simply refers to a healthy fear of God or of the abuses of
sexuality against which the marriage manuals so sedulously warn us;
but when read in the context of the ambivalent connotations of
"*stealing*" (15), as well as of so many other poems in the canon, we
have reason to suspect that the word reflects Herrick's own fears.[62]

The epithalamia themselves offer further evidence of Herrick's
deep ambivalence about the loss of virginity, an ambivalence that, as
I have argued, lies behind his preoccupation with the bride's own reluctance to consummate the marriage. The allusions in the Southwell epithalamium that we encountered earlier might conceivably be
explained away as demonstrating the bride's, not the poet's, responses; but the contradictions in the twelfth stanza in the poem
more clearly demonstrate that the bride's impulse to delay the marriage both displays and deflects Herrick's own reservations about it:

> Virgins, weep not; 'twill come, when,
> As she, so you'l be ripe for men.
>   Then grieve her not, with saying
>   She must no more a Maying:
>   Or by Rose-buds devine,
>   Who'l be her Valentine.

[62]For a psychological analysis of the tensions in this and Herrick's other poems to
Julia, see Ann Baynes Coiro, "Herrick's 'Julia' Poems," *John Donne Journal*, 6 (1987),
esp. 81–82.

> Nor name those wanton reaks
> Y'ave had at Barly-breaks.
> But now kisse her, and thus say,
> Take time Lady while ye may.
>
> (111–120)

The word "ripe," which is echoed at the conclusion of the poem ("Be ye to the Barn then born, / Two, like two ripe shocks of corn" [169–170]), suggests that marriage is as natural and joyous as the maturation of a harvest,[63] In this one respect, then, the stanza skillfully fulfills its ostensible purpose of urging both the other young women and the bride to abandon their reservations and participate joyously in the occasion. In other respects, however, the lines testify to Herrick's doubts about the abandonment of virginity and, indeed, do little to assuage those doubts. Reading the stanza in the context of its generic tradition demonstrates its oddity. In the lyric epithalamium the young women attending the bride normally do not weep; instead, they occupy themselves by scattering flowers and in other ways happily celebrate the occasion. The only significant analogues to the unhappy attendants Herrick describes appear in Catullus 62 and in the handful of works that imitate or translate it; as we have seen, most Stuart poets reject this model. These attendants, then, are echoing the bride's own doubts, and in so doing rendering those doubts more prominent in the poem. Similarly, by devoting six lines (113–118) to enumerating what they should not say, Herrick is in fact saying those things and so effecting a version of occupatio.

The end of the stanza is odder still. The apparent meaning of "Take time Lady while ye may" is "Marry while ye may"; in other words, Herrick is appropriating *carpe diem* traditions for the epithalamium genre, much as he blends the persuasion poem and the wedding poem elsewhere.[64] In this sense the line exemplifies the process that Leah S. Marcus and others attribute to Herrick: containing potentially subversive energies through social institutions such as marriage.[65] But lines 113–118 also invite us to read the final couplet as "Enjoy the pleasures of girlhood while you may, before you are forced into marriage." These two readings cannot be reconciled:

[63]See Martin, p. 511, on the Virgilian echo here.
[64]On the parallel use of the phrase in other *carpe diem* poems, see Martin, p. 511.
[65]Leah S. Marcus, *The Politics of Mirth: Jonson, Herrick, Milton, Marvell, and the Defense of Old Holiday Pastimes* (Chicago: Univ. of Chicago Press, 1986), chap. 5.

they grate against each other, like the alternative interpretations of "Beleeve me; you will most / Esteeme it when 'tis lost" (15–16) we examined in our preliminary reading of this poem.

We find similar evidence of Herrick's own reluctance about the loss of virginity in a related passage from "A Nuptiall Song, or Epithalamie, on Sir Clipseby Crew and his Lady":[66]

> Strip her of Spring-time, tender-whimpring-maids,
> Now *Autumne's* come, when all those flowrie aids
>   Of her Delayes must end.
>
>   (91–93)

Once again the attendants are bemoaning the occasion rather than rejoicing in it; and the description of its consequences as autumnal suggests yet again that Herrick himself is sympathetic to their sorrows because he shares these responses.

This passage indicates one reason Herrick is so ambivalent about the loss of virginity: he associates it with the transience and mutability that preoccupy him throughout his career. Herrick envisions marriage not as the blooming of the bud but as its decay, as spring collapsing into autumn and even winter. The telling verb in "Strip her of Spring-time" (91) anticipates the sexual undressing to which the rest of the stanza later alludes and in so doing links the wedding in general and the consummation in particular with loss. This interpretation suggests another reason for Herrick's ambivalence about the abandonment of virginity: to him it is an abandonment of "Spring-time." It is not surprising that Herrick's epithalamia are so divided, for his very interest in the genre is grounded in a paradox: the attraction to Edenic innocence that impels him to write epithalamia impels him as well to mourn the loss of virginity celebrated in the genre.

If the assertion that Herrick's delaying brides reflect his own reservations about marriage and sex is supported by his treatment of virginity, it is at the same time complicated by his recurrent hints that the brides are laying claim to a modesty they do not really have. The title character in "The delaying Bride" is admonished with one

---

[66]Thomas R. Whitaker comments intelligently though briefly on the "paradox of decay and fruition" in these lines ("Herrick and the Fruits of the Garden," *ELH*, 22 [1955], 21).

of Herrick's characteristic italicized axioms: *"Coyness takes us to a measure; but o'racted deads the pleasure"* (5–6). Herrick also alludes to acting in his advice to Sir Clipseby Crew's bride:

> and a price
> Set on your selfe, by being nice:
> But yet take heed;
> What now you seem, be not the same indeed.
> (53–56)

And "A Nuptiall Verse to Mistresse Elizabeth Lee, now Lady Tracie" reads "Then feast, and coy't a little; then to bed" (8). "Coy" could of course assume a range of meanings in the Renaissance; but the *Oxford English Dictionary* associates a denotation very germane to our purposes, "to affect shyness or reserve," with the expression "to coy it."[67] If Herrick is, as all his ironies indicate, something of an actor himself, he enlists the brides in his troupe. In so doing he, like his counterparts in the genre, acknowledges the power of female sexuality: these women are pretending to doubts they do not really experience. But these allusions to hypocrisy also offer yet another context for Herrick's own attraction to the delays and ambivalences that he shares with the brides he is evoking: a woman who lays claim to the modesty and hesitation expected of a bride even if she does not really feel them may well indulge in other forms of pretense and hypocrisy after the occasion.

But however we interpret such allusions, many other passages in the epithalamia also serve to reinforce the argument that Herrick shares with his delaying brides an ambivalence about sexuality and marriage; in particular, the attraction to celibacy that I have attributed to Stuart culture is intensified by certain characteristics of Herrick's own temperament. Thus he typically associates the consummation of the marriage with violence. That association is hardly unknown in the genre—witness the commonplace allusions to the battles of love—but in several key passages Herrick moves beyond convention to evoke unusually vehement assaults. As one reads such lines one wonders, indeed, to what extent he is attracted to visions of fairyland and childishness as alternatives to the violent fantasies that haunt him.

[67]OED, s.v. "coy."

In one of the best readings Herrick has received, Gordon Braden
scrutinizes the poet's nervousness about sex, citing among other evidence the reluctant brides and bridesmaids whom we have been
analyzing.[68] Many of his conclusions about Herrick's responses to
that nervousness are sound; for instance, he recognizes that Herrick
associates eroticism with dreams and wishes, and his arguments
about a drive to retreat from sexuality into childishness are supported by Herrick's treatment of virginity, as well as by many other
passages in the epithalamia. Less persuasive, however, is his assertion
that Herrick retreats from aggressive, adult sexuality.[69] Quite the
contrary: his response to doubts and hesitations bifurcates into a gen-
dered dichotomy, an identification with the reluctant maidens on the
one hand and a celebration of masculine aggression that extends to
the point of violence on the other.

We find hints of that violence even in passing allusions. The
Southwell epithalamium, for example, includes the injunction, "You,
you that be of her neerest kin, / Now o're the threshold *force* her in"
(81–82; italics added). The wedding poem composed for Sir Clipseby
Crew and his bride repeatedly presents desire as violent to the point
of destructiveness:

> Display the Bridegroom in the porch,
>   In his desires
> More towring, more disparkling then thy fires:
>   Shew her how his eyes do turne
> And roule about, and in their motions burne
>   Their balls to Cindars: haste,
>   Or else to ashes he will waste.
>
>   (34–40)

In an earlier version, his eyes are "besparkling" (p. 477); the change
to "disparkling" (36) serves to intensify the sense of threat. And,
similarly, Herrick edited "Or like a firebrand he will waste" (p. 477)
to "Or else to ashes he will waste" (40); the final version emphasizes
destruction and loss.

But the most intriguing example of the violence and aggression
that Herrick associates with sexuality occurs in his deceptively simple lyric "A Nuptiall Verse to Mistresse Elizabeth Lee, now Lady
Tracie." At the beginning of the poem balanced couplets convey a

---

[68]See Braden, pp. 217–232.
[69]See esp. pp. 223–224.

sense of emotional stability and assurance: "Spring with the Larke, most comely Bride, and meet / Your eager Bridegroome with *auspitious* feet" (1–2). As the epithalamium progresses, the poet speaks of the wedding night playfully. The bridegroom is, he assures the bride, "an Easie Foe" (11), who "will if you yeeld, lye down conquer'd too" (13). The first fourteen lines of this sixteen-line lyric, then, are urbane and graceful. But Herrick's conventional tropes of battle culminate in a most unconventional conclusion: "Fall down together vanquisht both, and lye / Drown'd in the bloud of Rubies there, not die" (15–16). Concerns about sexuality and the loss of virginity intrude in the poem like uninvited wedding guests. In a sense, indeed, we are encountering a poetic analogue to the fantasy of the interrupted wedding that we explored earlier. The image not only describes but also effects a kind of violence, itself deflowering a lyric that has opened on pastoral evocations of larks and sunbeams.

Herrick's language intensifies the violence. "Drown'd" is emphasized by its initial position in the line and by the trochaic inversion in which it participates. And the recurrence of the word in Herrick's canon—together with its cognates it appears thirty-six times, whereas, say, "mead," "meadow," and their cognates appear only nineteen times[70]—invites us to scrutinize its appearance even more closely. In so doing, we discover that broader concerns about sexuality lie behind and intensify the anxieties about defloration that more obviously emerge in this curious trope. Herrick often uses the verb "to drown" in its literal sense to refer to death and desolation. For Herrick as for Sir Thomas Browne, water is the surest grave. But elsewhere he associates sensual pleasure of all sorts with drowning: he refers to being "Drown'd in Delights" ("Julia's Petticoat," 18) or "in Oyle of *Roses* drown'd" ("To Dewes. A Song," 7), and even his strawberries are "halfe drown'd in Creame" ("Upon the Nipples of Julia's Breast," 6). In other words, he connects pleasure with being overwhelmed, as does Shakespeare's Troilus (III.ii.18–29)—and ultimately, given the negative meanings of drowning, Herrick connects pleasure with destruction.[71] At the same time, however, his fantasy

---

[70]See Malcolm MacLeod, *A Concordance to the Poems of Robert Herrick* (New York: Oxford Univ. Press, 1936), s.v. "drown," "mead," "meadow," and their cognates.

[71]Paul R. Jenkins suggests that Herrick rejects those excesses which threaten him while embracing those which do not ("Rethinking What Moderation Means to Robert Herrick," *ELH*, 39 [1972], esp. 52–53); I am arguing for a more ambivalent and less reasoned response.

of drowning is not only a symptom of perceived danger but also a weapon against it: Herrick seems to respond to his frequently expressed fears of mutability and loss by evoking the immoderation that drowning suggests, much as victims of a financial depression may amass goods. Jonson counters threats through strategies of exclusion, Herrick through strategies of excess. This apocalyptic vision of sensual delight, then, helps us explicate the fears that generate the extraordinary reference to drowning in the blood of rubies.

That reference is further complicated by its incorporation of something precious, rubies.[72] Their solidity may represent Herrick's attempt to contain the flux associated with "bloud" and "Drown'd." Similarly, he seems to be adducing not only the positive connotations of gems in general but also the symbolism of rubies in particular in order to delimit the violence expressed in these lines. The ruby, a seventeenth-century lapidary assures us, "is good against poison, and against the plague, and to drive away sadnesse, evil thoughts, terrible dreams, and evil spirits,"[73] and Herrick's delight in antiquarian lore and folk customs makes it probable that he knew about such connotations. If so, once again an epithalamium concludes on an allusion to controlling dangers: Herrick characteristically yokes together disparates, referring to his rubies in an attempt to transform the violence associated with blood into the protection associated with those precious stones ("not die"). Yet that attempt is largely unsuccessful: the clash between the connotations of "rubies" and those of the other words in the line merely intensifies its tensions. In short, just as the balanced couplets we encountered earlier may be a failed effort to control the anxieties that emerge in the final line, so that unsuccessful containment is enacted here within the line itself. In this extraordinary concluding passage our son of Ben is once again a son of John Donne as well. It is a wise writer who knows his own father.

Even a brief survey of the other poetry in *Hesperides* uncovers further sources for Herrick's reservations about the social institution he is so concerned to celebrate. He frequently alludes to adultery, especially in epigrams like the one I quoted earlier, "The Tythe. To the

---

[72]I am grateful to Mary Thomas Crane for useful comments about the reference to "rubies" here, as well as for other stimulating insights into Herrick's canon.

[73]Thomas Nichols, *Lapidary or, The History of Pretious Stones* (Cambridge, England, 1652), p. 58.

Bride." As many readers have noted, he often deflects eroticism from human bodies and human beings onto such inanimate objects as petticoats. That deflection might signal an enthusiasm about sexuality that fantasizes its extension to the whole world or, alternatively, a nervousness about sexuality that fantasizes its deflection from human beings—but the ambivalences and ironies that so often characterize Herrick's vision make it likely that he is pulled between those two poles. And, of course, many of the epigrams signal a disgust with the human body. Resisting a psychological interpretation, some readers might maintain that such disgust is a by-product of the epigram genre, not of the psyche of the author; but as always such arguments beg the question why the poet repeatedly selects a genre that enjoins such attitudes.

To be sure, Herrick, like Jonson, does attempt to control and delimit the tensions he associates with marriage by imposing harmonies of various types on his vision of the institution and on the poetry that celebrates it. But unlike Jonson, Herrick is only fitfully successful in these attempts. Herrick flirts with order, whereas Jonson espouses it. In his wedding poetry as in so much of his other verse, for example, Herrick's couplets can create a mood of harmony and restraint. But in several instances, notably Herrick's evocation of defloration in terms of gemlike blood, that prosodic stability clashes with the sentiments being conveyed.

Most of the critics who have attributed a harmonious vision to the author of *Hesperides,* however, have located its primary source elsewhere: in the ceremoniousness manifest largely, though by no means entirely, in his evocation of pagan and other antiquarian rites and rituals. Tracing critical responses to that ceremoniousness would be a useful exercise for a graduate seminar: the shifts in opinion reflect changing critical tastes as surely as do shifts in Shakespeare criticism. Readers in the 1960s and early 1970s predictably emphasized the orderly and ordering elements in Herrick's verse; thus Robert H. Deming's study is aptly entitled *Ceremony and Art: Robert Herrick's Poetry,* and A. Leigh DeNeef maintains that "the ceremonial mode" unites Herrick's apparently disparate speakers.[74] Equally predictable is the reaction against such readings: in the 1980s many of Herrick's readers have devoted far less attention to that ceremonial mode, and critics such as Ann Baynes Coiro have emphasized the dissonances in

[74]See DeNeef, *"This Poeticke Liturgie,"* esp. chap. 1.

their poststructuralist Herrick.[75] More recently, new historicist ideologies have sparked a return to the ceremonious Herrick. But the
Herrick of Leah S. Marcus and Peter Stallybrass[76] wears his rites
with a difference: his aim is to stabilize a political world, not a poetic
one, to impose authoritative and even authoritarian control through
the careful management of rituals and festivals. In the instance of the
epithalamia, the truth lies somewhere between the last two positions.
Herrick is indeed preoccupied with the ceremonious and festive, and
these concerns contribute to the emphasis on communal experience
that marks particularly the epithalamium written for Sir Clipseby
Crew. But his treatment of ceremonies and their putative authority is
less consistent and less respectful than recent new historicists have
maintained.

To begin with, in their approach to the ceremonious, as in other
ways already noted, Herrick's epithalamia differ considerably. Thus
"The Entertainment: or, Porch-verse, at the Marriage of Mr. Hen.
Northly, and the most witty Mrs. Lettice Yard" and "An hymne to
Juno" focus on rites, whereas "A Nuptiall Verse to Mistresse Elizabeth Lee, now Lady Tracie" barely mentions them. Herrick's two
longer wedding poems allude to antiquarian wedding customs, some
of his shorter lyrics omit them. Despite these differences, however,
one salient similarity unites his epithalamia: though ceremonies do
sometimes bring order, more often he evokes those ceremonies in a
form designed to destabilize, not stabilize, the poems and the ceremonies themselves. In theory all rituals and rites could serve a function very like the one assumed by perfection in Jonson's canon; in
practice, they generally do not.

One telling though neglected passage in "A Nuptiall Song, or Epithalamie, on Sir Clipseby Crew and his Lady" introduces the patterns in question: "If needs we must for Ceremonies-sake, / Blesse a
Sack-posset; Luck go with it" (131–132). The first line unmistakably
renders the reference ironic, in effect placing it within quotation

[75]For instance, in chap. 8 of *Robert Herrick's "Hesperides" and the Epigram Book Tradition* (Baltimore: Johns Hopkins Univ. Press, 1988), Ann Baynes Coiro emphasizes
the ambivalences in "The Hock-Cart" and traces them to Herrick's doubts about his
own social position. I regret that this study appeared after I had completed my work
on the epithalamium. Also see her article "Herrick's *Hesperides:* The Name and the
Frame."

[76]See Marcus, *The Politics of Mirth,* chap. 5; Stallybrass, " 'Wee feaste in our Defense,' " 234–252.

marks. And the omitted stanzas from the earlier draft of this poem
contain another reference that performs a similar function:

<blockquote>
If
a prayer must be said, be briefe;
The easy Gods
For such neglect, have only Myrtle rodds.

(p. 478)
</blockquote>

This stanza ascribes a measure of significance to the pagan gods
merely by dwelling on them, then undermines their potency through
the lines in question.

Herrick also destabilizes the ceremonious by his emphasis on the
pagan: it is difficult for a Christian audience to know quite how seriously to take references to threshold gods and sacrifices.[77] A poem
like "An hymne to Juno" courts the possibility of being read as a
playful sortie into an alien world:

<blockquote>
Stately Goddesse, do thou please,
Who art chief at marriages,
But to dresse the Bridall-Bed,
When my Love and I shall wed:
And a *Peacock* proud shall be
Offerd up by us, to thee.

(1–6)
</blockquote>

In other words, the rituals that Herrick evokes here function rather
like the indefinite articles whose presence in phrases like "an
Oberon" is shrewdly analyzed by Gordon Braden:[78] the pagan world
is distanced from the reader, bracketed. To put it another way, the
pagan and antiquarian customs on which Herrick relies often locate
his lyrics not in the realms of the numinous but rather in a milieu
closely allied to the dream and fairy worlds he evokes elsewhere.
Harold Toliver notes that the references to fairy land serve "to put

---

[77]Many critics have commented on the relationship between pagan and Christian
elements in Herrick's poetry. For trenchant arguments that he juxtaposes the two, see
esp. H. R. Swardson, *Poetry and the Fountain of Light: Observations on the Conflict between Christian and Classical Traditions in Seventeenth-Century Poetry* (London: George
Allen and Unwin, 1962), chap. 2; Whitaker, "Herrick and the Fruits of the Garden."
S. Musgrove, in contrast, deemphasizes the pagan elements in *Hesperides* ("The Universe of Robert Herrick," *Auckland University College Bulletin*, 38 [1950], 3–34).
[78]Braden, pp. 163–164.

common objects in a foreign light";[79] Herrick effects the same type of defamiliarization when he writes of religious customs, and the result is a kind of distancing and, again, destabilization. Indeed, given the ambivalence that characterizes Herrick's temperament, perhaps he is attracted to pagan ceremonies because they allow him to have it both ways, to evoke and apparently participate in rituals while at the same time not take them completely seriously.

Herrick's attitudes towards the ritualistic aspects of marriage are reflected in what he does not say as well as in what he does. Reading his epithalamia in the context of their genre allows us to identify telling omissions ignored by critics attempting to substantiate his allegiance to ceremony. I have maintained that Stuart epithalamia vary greatly in their responses to the religious ceremony, ranging from poems that devote considerable attention to that event to others that virtually ignore it. The parish priest of Dean Prior, the ostensible adherent to rites and rituals of all sorts, is located near the far left of that spectrum: in some poems he makes a passing allusion to the religious celebration of the marriage, and in others he does not even mention it. Nor can we explain this pattern by citing the difficulties of combining pagan and Christian allusions: Herrick surmounts those difficulties successfully in several other poems, as many readers have noted,[80] and had he wished he could at least have addressed them in his epithalamia. Similarly, the wedding feast, another type of ritual in many Stuart epithalamia, is downplayed in Herrick's own wedding poems. And, finally, like other Stuart poets he could have responded to the threats he associates with sexuality by constructing it as a rite; but this too he chooses not to do.

We should not, then, take Herrick's sorties into the ceremonious at face value, any more than we should read the passing allusion to the priest in "Corinna's going a Maying" as seriously as some critics have done.[81] Herrick's antiquarian leanings, yet another manifestation of his search for a golden age, encourage him to refer to pagan rituals; and those references are motivated as well by the impulse towards stability that we find in his prosodic strategies. But his

---

[79]Toliver, 431.

[80]See, e.g., two studies by Robert H. Deming, *Ceremony and Art* and "Robert Herrick's Classical Ceremony," *ELH*, 34 (1967), 327–348; Alastair Fowler, "Robert Herrick," 262–263.

[81]See, e.g., Marcus, pp. 156–157, for a reading that emphasizes the brief allusion to marriage in the poem.

blessed rage for disorder is often more powerful than its opposite drive: reading his wedding lyrics demonstrates the limitations of his ceremoniousness, just as it demonstrates the limitations of the celebratory mode that is submerged in the bloody conclusion of "A Nuptiall Verse to Mistresse Elizabeth Lee, now Lady Tracie."

Herrick's treatment of the ceremonious is related to a more general pattern in his canon, the illusion of representation. He approaches the material world much as Jonson approaches the verbal: each poet performs a sleight of hand in which something both is and is not present, is and is not said. Herrick's habit of evoking and then undermining a ceremony is paralleled on the narrative level by his tendency to locate poems in the world of fairy or dream, on the visual level by his preoccupation with clouds and gauzelike fabrics,[82] and, finally, on the syntactical level by his reliance on the disjunctive conjunction "or" in key passages. The opening of "A Nuptiall Song, or Epithalamie, on Sir Clipseby Crew and his Lady" exemplifies several of these habits:

> What's that we see from far? the spring of Day
> Bloom'd from the East, or faire Injewel'd May
>   Blowne out of April; or some New-
>   Star fill'd with glory to our view,
>   . . . . .
> Say, or do we not descrie
> Some Goddesse in a cloud of Tiffanie
>   To move, or rather the
>   Emergent *Venus* from the sea?
>   (1–4, 7–10)

Perhaps one reason Herrick is so preoccupied with perfumes is that odors, like the fabric tiffany, are at once material and intangible, present and yet absent.

But yet again this book, like the poets it treats, must strive to balance its emphasis on tensions, especially sexual tensions, with the acknowledgment that they are only one strand, however important, in the texture of the Stuart epithalamium. The threats I am underscoring are certainly present in Herrick's vision of marriage; but they

---

[82]Hugh Maclean also notes Herrick's attraction to transparencies and veils, but his interpretation emphasizes the ways they permit, not prevent, representation (" 'Wit and new misterie': Herrick's Poetry," in *Familiar Colloquy: Essays Presented to Arthur Edward Barker,* ed. Patricia Bruckman [n.p.: Oberon Press, 1978], p. 41).

are not omnipresent. All the ambivalences we have detailed do not preclude enthusiastic and moving celebrations of wedlock. The best of his wedding poems, his lyric for the marriage of Sir Clipseby Crew and Jane Pulteney, is complex enough to demand—and repay—detailed and lengthy scrutiny. A close reading of this poem substantiates my emphasis on the tensions in Herrick's vision and on his largely unsuccessful attempts to control them, while at the same time demonstrating their relationship to the more positive notes we hear in his wedding poems.

This epithalamium opens on the description of the bride as "the spring of Day . . . or faire Injewel'd May" (1–2) just quoted. Though the use of "or" here and later in the stanza in some ways destabilizes the vision, it is still an ecstatic one, and the ambivalences and tensions that emerge so strongly as this lyric progresses will be played against this initial moment of rapture.

Herrick's use of "or" introduces us to another characteristic of this epithalamium: the conjunction produces an impression of movement, the syntactical version of the many other types of energy and restless movement that we encounter throughout his works. Herrick's physical world is Dickensian; witness its bed, which, like its counterpart in the Southwell wedding poem, swells, "brusle[s]" (114), and hugs. Similarly, whereas Jonson locates his Weston epithalamium in a grammar of past participles, the wedding poem composed for Sir Clipseby Crew is alive with the energies of present participles: "Reaching" (5), "Perspiring" (24), "sprinkling" (46), and so on. Jonson typically aims for perfectly composed stills, whereas Herrick shoots with a hand-held camera.

The first stanza differs from many of its generic counterparts in the speaker's stance. Though Herrick's emphasis on communal festivities does not create the ceremonious order that some have found in his poems, it does effect a reinterpretation of the speaker. By using the first person plural pronoun at the beginning of the lyric, he plays down his individual role and vision in favor of a communal one: "What's that we see from far?"[83] As the poem progresses, he assumes the traditional role of giving commands, but at several junctures he also repeats this use of "we"; thus he limits his authority

[83]Compare DeNeef's commentary on the anonymity of the speakers in Herrick's epithalamia (p. 104); although the curious reference to jealousy in the poem written for Sir Clipseby Crew qualifies this assertion, by and large it is persuasive.

and emphasizes that the occasion is communal, just as the antiquarian customs he cites establish a community that includes both the celebrants of previous weddings and those attending the current occasion. Jonson submerges the bride and groom in their community but maintains the autonomy of the poet; Herrick does the reverse in this opening stanza, as at several other points in his wedding poems.

In the third stanza the pattern of allusions to fire that will dominate the whole poem emerges: "As a fir'd Altar, is each stone" (23). Here burning evokes the precious and the holy. Shortly afterwards, however, it comes simultaneously to suggest both ecstatic pleasure and destruction, the very oxymoron embedded in many of Herrick's allusions to drowning:

> The Phenix nest,
> Built up of odours, burneth in her breast.
> Who therein wo'd not consume
> His soule to Ash-heaps in that rich perfume?
> Bestroaking Fate the while
> He burnes to Embers on the Pile.
> (25–30)

This passage is quickly succeeded by a description of the bridegroom that we earlier examined from a different perspective. In adapting the generic convention of the impatiently waiting groom, Herrick associates him with fire and ashes; if in so doing he creates a bond between burning spectators and self-consuming groom, at the same time he suggests that the fire is spreading uncontained:

> Display the Bridegroom in the porch,
> In his desires
> More towring, more disparkling then thy fires:
> Shew her how his eyes do turne
> And roule about, and in their motions burne
> Their balls to Cindars: haste,
> Or else to ashes he will waste.
> (34–40)

In both passages Herrick again associates pleasure, especially sexual pleasure, with excesses that are as attractive as they are destructive, and in both he again makes no effort to contain the chaotic energies he is unleashing. Where id was, there id shall be. We have come a long way from the epithalamium in *Hymenaei*.

A canceled stanza that appeared in the original version at this point intensifies the tensions in the poem. The bride is described as "guilty of somewhat" (p. 477). The lines are, of course, ambiguous. Do they refer to her own desires? As I argued in Chapter 1, the doctrine of due benevolence fanned tensions about such desires in Stuart culture. If the passage does allude to the bride's lust, then the emphasis on her bashful chastity may represent a kind of reaction formation, an impulse to attribute to her the maidenly modesty that the poet fears she does not really possess. Or is she being blamed for stirring up male lust? The rest of the stanza alludes to her doing so, though apparently to justify it: Herrick's readers are informed that she must "begett lust and temptation / to surfeit and to hunger" (p. 477). If she is being blamed, the bridegroom's—and the poet's—male guilt about the consummation of the marriage is being displaced onto the bride, not the first time we have encountered that pattern. In any event, it is telling that Herrick was uncomfortable enough with these ideas about guilt (or with his awkward expression of them) to cancel the lines—but telling as well that he experimented with them.

Yet once again we need to warn ourselves against noting only tensions: the poem moves to a graceful pastoral vision. The bride is surrounded by roses and grass; even—or especially—the "younglings" (43) sing to her. "Drown yee with a flowrie Spring" (44) is not free of the threatening associations that, as we have seen, adhere to the idea of drowning in Herrick's work; but in this instance the threats are very mild.

Having emphasized communal values earlier in the poem, in its seventh stanza Herrick particularizes the community more than his cohorts in the genre generally do: the characters in his poem include not only the conventionalized young girls but also in this instance a cook and butler who are eager to impress and welcome the bride. The inclusion of these figures again demonstrates Herrick's tendency to merge a range of different worlds and different moods; this poem encompasses within a handful of stanzas the numinousness exemplified by the opening passages, the wry knowingness with which the speaker addresses the bride, and the touches of domestic drama in the seventh stanza. And this stanza serves, too, to add a more playful note to the poem, warning us once more against dwelling only on its darker side.

The eighth stanza again develops a familiar convention from an original angle:

> this the longest night;
> But yet too short for you: 'tis we,
> Who count this night as long as three,
>   Lying alone,
> Telling the Clock strike Ten, Eleven, Twelve, One.
>   (72–76)

In a sense, I would argue, the figure of the alienated speaker lies behind this passage—but Herrick is transforming that character in two ways. On the one hand, the alienation is associated with the most personal of emotions, sexual jealousy. But the same impulse to disguise, deflect, and distance that we have encountered throughout his canon is at work even—or, more to the point, especially—here: not the speaker but rather a generalized "we" experience the jealousy.

In drawing attention to that emotion, Herrick renders overt a potential tension that, I have argued, lies behind the genre: the speaker's and the community's envy about the consummation of the marriage. Thus he adds yet another source of anxiety to his poem. But he moves quickly to another topic, a description of wedding customs, and in so doing demonstrates again the rapid shifts in mood and perspective that characterize his lyric.

It is telling, however, that his description of those customs, like certain comparable passages in Jonson's epithalamia, is cast in terms of the threats that must be averted:

> O doe not fall
> Foule in these noble pastimes, lest ye call
>   Discord in, and so divide
> The youthfull Bride-groom, and the fragrant Bride.
>   (85–88)

In this passage we find a playful analogue to the banishing-of-dangers motif that runs throughout the genre, as well as yet another reminder that Herrick himself associates weddings with dangers. More serious types of violence are at once acknowledged and displaced, the dual process we so often encounter in Stuart epithalamia.

The poem proceeds to describe the events immediately preceding the wedding night, as well as the consummation of the marriage. We have already examined several passages from this section of the lyric, notably the description of the "tender-whimpring-maids" (91) and of the halfheartedly blessed *"Sack-posset"* (132), but the extraordinary evocation of the wedding bed demands further attention:

> And to your more bewitching, see, the proud
> Plumpe Bed beare up, and swelling like a cloud,
>   Tempting the too too modest; can
>   Yee see it brusle like a Swan,
>   And you be cold
> To meet it, when it woo's and seemes to fold
>   The Armes to hugge you? throw, throw
> Your selves into the mighty over-flow
>   Of that white Pride, and Drowne
> The night, with you, in floods of Downe.
>   (111–120)

The first two lines establish the bed as not only erotic but phallic (notice the use of "swelling" and of "proud", whose meanings can include "sensually excited");[84] the point is not so much that Herrick is denying adult sexuality but that he is dispersing it. The association of the swan briefly complicates the treatment of sexuality by infusing associations of the Leda story—once again Herrick is introducing, not avoiding, aggressive adult sexuality—but these negative resonances are controlled by the more positive image of the embracing bed that soon follows. Similarly, "Drowne" (119) has, as usual, disturbing implications, but to some extent they are drained from the trope by the allusions to "Downe" (120). This drowning, in other words, is very like Marvell's falling on grass: the threat is at once emphasized and controlled. And Herrick controls the threats he is introducing in another way: the reference is to throwing oneself on the bed reads more like an invitation to a children's game than to adult intercourse.[85] In short, in this stanza we find strategies for containing and controlling sexuality that are characteristic of the genre, though they do not predominate throughout Herrick's wedding poems or even elsewhere in this one.

The poet then deploys abstractions to distance us from the imme-

[84]*OED*, s.v. "proud."
[85]In this instance, though not others, Braden's assertion about a retreat from adult sexuality is persuasive (see esp. p. 223).

diate and intense physicality of his description of the bed: he describes sexuality in terms of "hieroglyphick[s]" (126) and invites his lovers to

> teach
> Nature and Art, one more
> Play, then they ever knew before.
> (128–130)

Both the sentiments and the vocabulary here ally Herrick more with Donne than with Jonson.

Herrick's ambivalences emerge even more clearly in the succeeding stanza, which focuses on the consummation of the marriage. It involves "hells" (134), he emphasizes, but these are hells "of such Torture as no one would grutch / To live therein forever" (136–137). The reassurance does not, however, still the resonances of words as loaded as "hells" and "Torture". Similarly, reverting to his imagery of fire the speaker commands his lovers to "Frie / And consume" (137–138)—and in so doing to "Love the confusion of the place" (140). "Confusion" aptly describes the anarchic sexual energies that Herrick is evoking, and to some extent they are attractive—but the tensions in the passage point as well to confusions in the mind of the poet composing it.

Such tensions also emerge in the description of the consummation of the marriage on which the poem culminates. The authors of other Stuart epithalamia allude to arcane and surprising wedding customs, but Herrick is the only one to incorporate the ritual of sewing the bride in a sheet. Like so many innovations in this genre, however, this one is also related to generic traditions and norms. For Herrick is developing the inside-outside pattern that we have traced and in so doing effecting a new and more extreme version of the fantasy of the safely enclosed woman. These curious and idiosyncratic lines also remind us of another generic predilection, the association of sexuality and death, for the sheet cannot help but remind us of a shroud.[86]

The description of the sewn-up bride is succeeded by a trope that yet again emphasizes the aggressive masculinity of her groom:

---

[86]Compare Whitaker, pp. 26–27, on the fusions of death and consummation that he finds elsewhere in Herrick's canon. Also cf. John T. Shawcross's observations about the connections between intercourse and death elsewhere in Herrick ("The Names of Herrick's Mistresses in *Hesperides*," in *"Trust to Good Verses,"* p. 99).

> but like a
> Bold bolt of thunder he will make his way,
>   And rend the cloud, and throw
>   The sheet about, like flakes of snow.
>   (147–150)

The winter scene on which the stanza terminates in part subdues the references to violence,[87] as does the emphasis on silence in the next and concluding stanza, but, as in the allusions to frying and to hells, they do not disappear completely. In short, in lines 147–150, as elsewhere in the poem, Herrick celebrates erotic energies with an enthusiasm that is rare even in his genre. But at the same time he can never forget, or let us forget, the dangers inherent in those energies. While Jonson constructs his dams, Herrick is drowning in a tidal wave.

[87]Compare the observations about the snowflakes in Braden, p. 160.

CHAPTER 6

Conclusion

Now welcome night, thou night so long expected,
That long daies labour doest at last defray,
And all my cares, which cruell love collected,
Hast sumd in one, and cancelled for aye.
                                    Spenser, "Epithalamion"

D edicated to celebrating harmony and order, the Stuart epithalamium is a product and symptom of conflict. John Donne's evocation of the bride as a sacrificial lamb is extreme but not unique in
its linkage of marital sexuality and violence; in a sense this book has
mapped the mined terrain of a war zone. Such problems as the significance of prenuptial contracts and the relevance of parental consent
could render the actual wedding a source of tense negotiation as
well as joyous celebration. Once married, the couple confronted another series of controversial issues, particularly those focusing on the
status of husband and wife. Contemporary texts such as marriage
manuals and sermons variously stressed the wife's power and responsibility or advocated her submissiveness—or, more often, did both.
Another source of tensions, I have argued, was the relative valuation
of celibacy and marriage, which was far more complex in Protestant
England than most scholars have acknowledged. And Renaissance
debates about the nature of women fueled the fires ignited by these
disagreements about marriage.

Many of the tensions associated with wedlock stemmed from the
presence of competing and changing models and values. Neither of
the two primary theories advanced to explain marriage in sixteenth-

and seventeenth-century England, the Restricted Patriarchal Nuclear Family and the Puritan art of love, can adequately encapsulate that institution. Intellectual history, like literary history, typically involves not a paradigm shift but a continuum; rather than one system of thought unseating and usurping another, the relative significance of coexisting ideas gradually changes.

The best analogy to this process lies in an ostensibly different realm, the decorative arts. As the authors of a perceptive study of American furniture remind us, actual homes, unlike the period rooms in some museums, typically juxtaposed, say, William and Mary, Queen Anne, and even Chippendale furniture: "American furniture forms, details and cabinetmaking traditions persisted long after the period in which they were first developed had passed. Few people threw away the old to embrace completely the new. Within a home, styles were commonly intermixed; even individual pieces of furniture frequently mixed stylistic features. The past should be viewed through complex layers of overlapping and interpenetrating styles, national and regional preferences, differences of economic position, diverse personalities, and the willingness to change or cling to old attitudes. In this vein, an evolutionary analysis of artistic currents in the American colonies seems forced or somewhat arbitrary."[1] The furniture of one's mind may resemble the furniture of these houses, and "an evolutionary analysis" of intellectual and social history, especially when it addresses a subject as complex as the family, risks the error represented by those artificial period rooms.

Stuart poets confronted not only common cultural concerns but also a series of issues related to their own work: if the pressures to celebrate marriage were insistent, so too were the doubts that complicated that enterprise. Commemorating weddings was an obvious route to advancement at court, and the potential rewards must have seemed especially tempting in the instances of the marriage of Princess Elizabeth and the Count Palatine and that of Frances Howard and Somerset. Nor, of course, was self-interest the only motivation encouraging poets to write epithalamia. The impressive models represented by earlier works in the genre, the technical challenges and opportunities offered by such formal devices as the refrain, and the potentiality for exploring such values as communal harmony all rendered this literary type attractive. Yet reservations about marriage

[1]Jonathan L. Fairbanks and Elizabeth Bidwell Banks, *American Furniture, 1620 to the Present* (New York: Richard Marek, 1981), p. 82.

and about patronage at the very least delimited that attractiveness. In particular, the authors of Stuart epithalamia, like the speaker in Shakespeare's neglected but intriguing Sonnet 125, knew that "dwellers on form and favor" (5) were likely to "Lose all, and more, by paying too much rent" (6)—especially if they were paying it to landlords as dubious as Frances Howard and her groom.

The interaction between these cultural pressures and generic norms is, as we have seen, complex and varied. In a few respects the wedding poem is not well tailored to the conditions of marriage in Stuart England; its poets do discard some conventions. Thus Stuart writers in general choose to avoid the compliments to the bridegroom that characterize many earlier works, and by and large they do not join such predecessors as Jacques Grévin in composing pastoral dialogues. Particular weddings could also pose special problems; at the union of Frances Howard and Somerset, for example, the convention of praying for heirs was at best a potential embarrassment. On the whole, however, the relationship between generic and cultural norms, like many human relationships, typically involves neither total equanimity nor total warfare but rather a process of accommodations and negotiations.[2] Those negotiations do not always lead to a resolution of the problems associated with wedlock in Stuart England: repressed anxieties often emerge in troubled and troubling guises. Yet in many other instances Stuart epithalamia reinterpret the conflicts attending on marriage in a form that renders them less threatening, thereby testifying to the skill of their authors and the suppleness of their generic inheritance.

Those authors often respond to similar problems in different ways: many dialects and even idiolects comprise the language of cultural anxieties. For instance, one challenge facing Stuart poets is the conflict between the imperative to celebrate marriage and the lingering attraction of celibacy. Donne's doubts about the relative merits of celibacy and marriage emerge initially in his uneasy trope of the lamb, only to be resolved in his subsequent celebrations of mutuality.

[2]Stephen Greenblatt has recently suggested negotiations as a model for cultural poetics. See esp. his *Shakespearean Negotiations: The Circulation of Social Energy in Renaissance England* (Berkeley: Univ. of California Press, 1988), "Introduction." As the rest of this chapter indicates, however, I take issue with him on some aspects of how such negotiations work, notably the degree of independence the writer can assume. A different model of negotiation, which emphasizes some of the types of flexibility that this book has identified in the epithalamium tradition, may be found in Theodore B. Leinwand, "Negotiation and New Historicism," *PMLA,* forthcoming.

Robert Herrick's poems, like some others in the tradition, displace the attraction to celibacy onto the bride and, even further, onto a vision of paradisaical innocence. Ben Jonson, in contrast, develops the concept of perfection as an attractive alternative to celibacy.

Despite these significant differences, certain strategies for responding to tensions reappear with telling frequency. Displacement is one of the most common responses: the poet's concerns may be displaced onto the bride, the violence associated with the consummation of the marriage displaced onto meteorological phenomena, and so on. Above all, however, control in its many manifestations is central to the praxis of the genre. Earlier we observed the connections between order in the sense of stability and orders in the sense of commands; now we are in a position to recognize that commands are significant because they are a means to effect the many types of control in which the genre is grounded. Controlled or at least directed by the demands of patronage, poets in the genre respond by asserting their own control over the fictive weddings they are evoking. And epithalamia, like the social institution they celebrate, are dedicated to controlling sexuality, especially that of the bride. Finally, the most fundamental aim of these poems is the control of disorder; the house towards which the procession moves represents the stability and stasis towards which the lyric as a whole is directed.

Recognizing these and other characteristics of the Stuart epithalamium demonstrates that this genre is not sui generis: the patterns we find in it occur suggestively in other literary types as well. Thus many genres are engaged in combating the forces that threaten their values, whether those forces be the elegaic elements in pastoral or the satiric voice that complicates romantic comedy. Just as we could anatomize genres by situating them on a spectrum ranging from an unironic presentation of their vision to an ironic undermining of it, so we could create other axes indicating the extent to which they subdue the types of disorder that threaten their vision and the forms that disorder takes. Such a system reinforces the connections between the epithalamium and the masque, as well as between the epithalamium and the country-house poem, all of which, as we have seen, battle unruly intruders in similar ways.

Acknowledging the workings of tensions in the epithalamium also indicates the connections between that genre and romantic comedy. If in one sense the epithalamium celebrates the event on which comedy culminates, in another, less obvious sense it compresses basic patterns found earlier in the structure of comedy: the forces that interfere with the consummation of the marriage in the epithalamium find their analogues in such figures as the senex iratus and the rival lover, and the banishing-of-dangers motif is paralleled by the disappearance or control of the Malvolios who reject comedic festivities. These similarities are especially evident when we play the works examined in this book against *Much Ado about Nothing*, a drama in which the fears haunting the authors of epithalamia are expressed, confronted, and then rejected by being localized in discredited characters. And William C. Carroll has recently drawn our attention to the ways *A Midsummer Night's Dream* incorporates and then subdues violence;[3] recognizing these patterns in the play prepares us for its deep affinity to the epithalamium tradition. The fairy world in the woods, for instance, corresponds to the forces that threaten the marriage and must be banished before its realization; Shakespeare complicates this pattern in his final act by transforming the fairies into beneficent forces that protect the marriage. Oberon, Titania, and Puck then deliver an epithalamium, a fitting conclusion to a play that incorporates elements from that tradition throughout.

Though the primary focus of this book is neither theoretical nor polemical, my work raises methodological issues as well as generic ones. An examination of the Stuart wedding poem is likely to be implicated in several of the problems most central to current Renaissance criticism. Hence studying that literary form clarifies some of the directions in which our discipline has moved and invites us to consider new directions.

The professional promoters who delight in organizing boxing matches between new historicists and feminists often distinguish these ostensible opponents by declaring that the latter group lacks a historical sense. This claim is problematical for two reasons: new historicism is typically ahistorical in certain respects, whereas feminism, especially as practiced in the 1980s, often deploys historical methods and focuses on historical phenomena.[4] But in one limited yet important sense the distinction does hold: certain feminists still construct patriarchy as a stable, essentially unchanging, and, above all, ahistorical entity. Studying the Stuart epithalamia invites us to revise that

---

[3]William C. Carroll, *The Metamorphoses of Shakespearean Comedy* (Princeton: Princeton Univ. Press, 1985), chap. 5.

[4]See, among other instances, Marilyn L. Williamson, *The Patriarchy of Shakespeare's Comedies* (Detroit: Wayne State Univ. Press, 1986).

approach by recognizing that the term "patriarchy," like the term "patronage system," should be declined only in the plural. The range of ways the marriage manuals discuss the putative submission of the wife, like the range of ways Stuart epithalamia variously (and even simultaneously) elevate and subjugate the bride, demonstrates the variety and flux in Renaissance patriarchy.

Both the deepest debts and the deepest quarrels of this book, however, involve not feminism but the new historicism. The important contributions of earlier historical studies to this and other contemporary books should not be neglected or discredited in some Oedipal struggle for territory.[5] But certainly my emphasis on the interplay between literary and other cultural texts can be traced primarily to new historicism. In more specific ways, too, this study is derived from and attempts to contribute to the new historicist project; witness, for instance, its emphasis on the anxieties associated with marriage and on the workings of patronage. So many of the books that have appeared in the 1980s owe a great deal to that project, and this one is no exception.

But its relationship to the new historicism is as complex and ambivalent as many of the literary and human relationships it traces: my aim is both to extend and to interrogate the ways that movement has influenced Renaissance studies. Though contemporary critics generally regard ideas as cultural constructs rather than universal truths, we, like previous generations of critics, are prone to exempt a few of our own fundamental principles from that mode of scrutiny. Relativism, like other people's rights, stops at our nose. Earlier critics practiced their own versions of this habit of mind; in its current manifestation, Renaissance scholars sometimes behave as though current dogmas were handed down on stone tablets from a high mountain on the California coast. Representations, as it were, are transformed into unimpeachable realities. As a result, many methodological premises of the new historicism have been accepted without enough debate; and ideological principles such as the Althusserian concept of literature as a state apparatus have profoundly influenced new historicists despite, or perhaps because of, the fact that such critics have never fully explicated the assumptions behind them.

A careful reading of the Stuart epithalamium, however, invites

[5]On the significance of older historicist studies, cf. Heather Dubrow and Richard Strier, eds., *The Historical Renaissance: New Essays on Tudor and Stuart Literature and Culture* (Chicago: Univ. of Chicago Press, 1988) "Introduction," pp. 2–3, 4.

us to modify some new historicist assumptions while embracing others.[6] In particular, the interpretation of literature as an ideological state apparatus has encouraged some though by no means all critics to ignore the degree of independence poets can wrest for themselves even in a culture as restrictive as the Stuart court. As the seventeenth-century epithalamium reveals, this neglect is one of the most problematical legacies of contemporary scholarship. The eclogue attached to Donne's "Epithalamion at the Marriage of the Earl of Somerset" testifies to the difficulty of achieving that independence—but the poem it encases, like other epithalamia by Donne and his contemporaries, demonstrates strategies and potentialities for doing so.

Above all, by both precept and example this study of the Stuart epithalamium advocates a more capacious and tolerant approach to literary methodology.[7] Literary scholars are often more seismic than systematic and more rebellious than rational in their evaluations of previous modes of criticism. New movements in our field, as in many others, typically establish themselves by asserting that their ideology is the only tenable position rather than one of several valid though competing possibilities.[8] This claim typically invites combative responses to any opposition: if the new movement represents the only correct approach, its proponents must variously attribute ignorance, bad faith, or even evil to their predecessors. Thus, again like previous generations of scholars, we have thrown out the fathers with the bath water.

Pluralism is frequently dismissed as an unsophisticated and illogical attempt to turn back the clock, and in certain instances the claim is quite true; for example, the bland assumption that the nature of the text will guide us towards the best of several critical methods neglects the fact that our methodological presuppositions may gov-

---

[6]New historicism is in fact more varied than either its critics or its practitioners sometimes acknowledge. On that variety, see two essays in *ELR,* 16 (1986): Jean E. Howard, "The New Historicism in Renaissance Studies," 37; Louis Montrose, "Renaissance Literary Studies and the Subject of History," 6–7. Also cf. Dubrow and Strier, "Introduction," pp. 4–5.

[7]On the intolerance that sometimes marks the relationships between literary movements, cf. Gerald Graff, *Professing Literature: An Institutional History* (Chicago: Univ. of Chicago Press, 1987). This important study considers several of the professional issues discussed in this conclusion, though from perspectives different from my own.

[8]I am grateful to James Dean Wilkinson for some trenchant comments on this polemical process.

ern our definitions of its nature. Moreover, advocates of pluralism
may attempt to blur the distinctions among methods. Some principles, of course, simply cannot be reconciled, unless we are willing to
yoke disparates together by violence; after all, language is or is not
opaque and multivalent, and so on. Nonetheless, a more reasoned
and limited pluralism would be valuable for many reasons, not least
because it could variously enrich and challenge the new historicism.
Many critical methodologies are compatible with historicist practices—and at the same time might usefully modify them. Thus this
book has demonstrated that the interplay between texts and their
cultures can best be explicated through another kind of interplay, the
dialogue between some of the questions posed by the new historicism and some of the methods employed by New Criticism, linguistics, and formalism.

I do not of course advocate a return to an ahistorical interpretation
of literature; but certain New Critical techniques of reading are germane even as one acknowledges that texts are rooted in history. Nuances of tone convey nuances of meaning; a detailed and painstaking
scrutiny of language is helpful in explicating the complexities conveyed both by nonliterary texts like the marriage manuals and by
epithalamia. We saw, for instance, that Jonson expresses the communal implications of marriage through his use of the pronoun "our"
and the indefinite article and that Herrick's repetition of the verb "to
drown" reveals his sexual politics. In scrutinizing language in these
ways, we do need to acknowledge the incompatibilities to which I
have just referred; for instance, the New Critical premises about objective interpretation cannot and should not be reconciled with the
theories about language and about cultural conditioning that have
dominated criticism in the late 1970s and the 1980s. But, as the history of deconstruction itself indicates, it is more than possible to
borrow the New Critical attentiveness to language and tone without
borrowing the ideological assumptions which encouraged that attentiveness.

Similarly, as I briefly suggested in Chapter 3, speech-act theory
deserves more attention from Renaissance critics than it has received;
in particular, pragmatics could enrich new historicist projects because, like the systems theory that has proved so fruitful in family
therapy, it could provide tools for analyzing discordant systems as
well as those that run smoothly. This potentiality has thus far been
constrained or even ignored, in part because many linguists view the

infelicitous speech act or the flouted conversational rule as the marked case rather than the norm and devote comparatively little attention to such acts and rules. These violations of linguistic regulations could, however, be mined to study the types of conflict and tension that currently interest many Renaissance critics.

According to the basic tenets of pragmatics, each speech act is associated with what have been termed "appropriateness conditions" or "felicity conditions": a promise, for example, assumes that the hearer wishes the promised event or act to occur, and a command carries with it the presupposition that the speaker enjoys a measure of power or authority over the hearer. In infelicitous speech acts, one or more of these conditions is missing. This, then, is one type of situation new historicist critics, and others, could fruitfully study. If, for example, an appropriateness condition for promising is that the speaker believes the hearer desires the promised act, what happens if the speaker is ambivalent or self-deceptive in that belief, as when Venus attempts to persuade herself that Adonis really desires her? We might also turn our attention to instances in which social complications can fruitfully be expressed as complications in speech-act rules. What happens when several communities coexist, including one in which the speaker has the authority necessary for, say, an illocutionary act of naming and one in which she or he does not? In many of these situations the breakdown of linguistic rules synecdochally demonstrates other types of social and psychological breakdown as well. Speech-act theory can teach us how to undo things with words.

We could expand the scope of both pragmatics and new historicism by emphasizing the social dynamics behind the rules of speech-act theory and even the values and assumptions behind such terms as "appropriateness conditions"; in particular, by seeing linguistic regulations as no less of a construct than other political and rhetorical rules, we could pursue the contemporary concern for the workings of power. For example, the appropriateness conditions in certain situations are not only a precondition that makes discourse possible but also in a sense the covert political aim that discourse attempts to enact. Thus one may give commands not because one has the prior authority to do so but rather because one lacks it, or fears one lacks it, and wishes to lay claim to it; when the speaker in the epithalamium delivers commands he is not only displaying authority but also attempting to establish it.

Linguistics could, then, prove germane to contemporary critical projects, especially those involving the new historicist concern with power. Above all, however, this book has both advocated and demonstrated the continuing relevance of formalist questions to historicist and other modes of inquiry. Formalism occupies a complex and fraught position in contemporary criticism. In many circles it is dismissed with nervous and determined contempt. Such comments often err in assuming that formalism is necessarily both adulatory and ahistorical. Other scholars who might question formalism in theory adduce it in practice. Thus feminists regularly talk about the connections of gender and genre, and many other critics deploy sophisticated modes of rhetorical analysis that owe more to Aristotle than Althusser.[9] Much current criticism could in fact sail under two flags, new historicism or feminism on one mast and what we might term "the new formalism" on another. Nor have theoretical defenses of formalism been wholly absent from contemporary literary theory; but in most instances they are perfunctory prefaces to very different critical modes.

A few theorists have, however, championed formalism more persuasively. Fredric Jameson both asserts and demonstrates the continuing significance of genre. As he puts it, "it would seem necessary to invent a new, historically reflexive, way of using categories, such as those of genre, which are so clearly implicated in the literary history and the formal production they were traditionally supposed to classify and neutrally to describe."[10] Similarly, having argued that semiotics is a "science of forms," Roland Barthes proceeds to offer a broad defense of formalism: "the more a system is specifically defined in its forms, the more amenable it is to historical criticism. To parody a well-known saying, I shall say that a little formalism turns one away from History, but that a lot brings one back to it."[11]

---

[9]Instances of the interest in rhetorical figures and methods that survives in contemporary criticism include Patricia Parker, "Shakespeare and Rhetoric: 'Dilation' and 'Delation' in *Othello*," in *Shakespeare and the Question of Theory*, ed. Patricia Parker and Geoffrey Hartman (London: Methuen, 1985); Joel Fineman, "Shakespeare's *Will*: The Temporality of Rape," *Representations*, no. 20 (1987), 25–76.

[10]Fredric Jameson, *The Political Unconscious: Narrative as a Socially Symbolic Act* (Ithaca: Cornell Univ. Press, 1981), p. 107. The second chapter of this book exemplifies a Marxist approach to genre.

[11]Roland Barthes, *Mythologies*, trans. Annette Lavers (New York: Hill and Wang, 1972), pp. 111, 112.

How, then, should we address the issues raised by Jameson and Barthes and the conflicts and contradictions associated with formalism? To begin with, we might look further at what the rhetoric directed against it reveals about the polemics and the politics of literary criticism. Above all, given that a revisionist formalism is already being to some extent practiced, we need now to acknowledge, systematize, and extend its potentialities, focusing particularly on its relationship to other types of criticism.

The new formalism can view aesthetic issues as related, not inimical, to history, as Jameson indicates. It can explore the dynamic interplay between aesthetic decisions and social conditions, asking, for instance, why a genre flourishes at a particular historical moment or how its conventions perform cultural work that in another period might be done by a different genre or, more intriguingly, by a different product of the culture, such as a myth or a holiday. (Consider, for instance, my suggestion that the cult of Elizabeth and certain literary genres serve the same end: expressing an attraction to virginity in an acceptable form.) Another aim of this new formalism, then, should be to pursue the links between so-called literary and extraliterary texts in new ways. Thus rather than assume that formal considerations are irrelevant to the latter mode of discourse, it will tailor those considerations to the material in question; genre theory might be adapted to political speeches, narrative theory to processionals, and so on. Similarly, one might explore the analogues to the refrain that appear in "nonliterary" texts or examine the ways such texts effect closure.

My aim in proposing the term "new formalism" is not arrogantly to add yet another entry to those compendia of critical terminology which are being so rapidly and often so carelessly revised. Rather, I believe the recognition that contemporary critical methodologies can, should, and do deploy certain traditional formalist techniques would be sanative in several ways: it would help us bridge the gap separating schools and hence often generations of scholars, counter the intolerance that often characterizes the relationships between them, and train graduate students in methods, such as the study of genres, that they might otherwise be tempted to neglect.

But if our current interest in cultural and historical conditions can fruitfully reshape formalist questions, the reverse is true as well. The revisionist formalism that I am describing would serve some current

Idols of the Tribe but also challenge others. Thus it would remind us that though formal decisions cannot and should not be isolated from cultural pressures, neither do those pressures in and of themselves determine such decisions, as certain critics sometimes imply. Literary choices, as I have argued thoughout this book, are typically overdetermined. Moreover, the new formalism could modulate the contemporary tendency to read texts with neither pleasure nor respect. One certainly would not wish to advocate a return to an uncritical worship of literature; but by drawing our attention to literary techniques that we might otherwise ignore, the new formalism could prevent critics from veering too far in the other direction.

No literary form better demonstrates the continuing significance of formalism than the Stuart wedding poem: as we have seen throughout this book, lyrics in this tradition often respond to the anxieties associated with marriage by artfully deploying their poetic resources. For when the authors of these poems "speke of wo that is in mariage," generic conventions are their nouns and formal techniques their verbs.

APPENDIX

Julius Cæsar Scaliger, "On the Epithalamium"

Book III, chapter 101 of *Poetics*, translated with notes by
JACKSON BRYCE

for J. T. W. and R. J. H.

TRANSLATOR'S NOTE

Dispossessed nobleman, brilliant soldier and athlete, noted physician, indefatigable antiquarian, philologist, man of letters, and controversialist, Julius Cæsar Scaliger (1484–1558) was one of the most remarkable of the Renaissance humanists.[1] His writings, especially his monumental *Poetics,* or in Latin *Poetices libri septem,* first published at Lyons in 1561,[2] exercised a decisive influence on the

---

[1]Vernon Hall, Jr., *Life of Julius Caesar Scaliger (1484–1558),* in *Transactions of the American Philosophical Society,* n.s. 40 (1950), 87–165, is concise and engaging, with a thorough bibliography on 163–165.

[2]Subsequent editions were produced at Geneva in 1581, at Lyons in 1586, and at Heidelberg in 1591, 1594, 1607, and 1617. A facsimile of the first edition is available with introduction by August Buck (Stuttgart–Bad Cannstatt: Friedrich Frommann Verlag, 1964). Certain passages are translated by Frederick Morgan Padelford, *Select Translations from Scaliger's Poetics,* Yale Studies in English 26 (New York: Henry Holt, 1905). On the *Poetics,* see Vernon Hall, "Preface to Scaliger's *Poetices Libri Septem,*" *Modern Language Notes* 60 (1945), 447–543; the latest full study is Rose Mary Ferraro, *Giudizi critici e criteri estetici nei Poetices libri septem (1561) di Giulio Cesare Scaligero rispetto alla teoria letteraria del rinascimento* (Chapel Hill: Univ. of North Carolina Press, 1971), with full bibliography on pp. 195–200.

271

neoclassical literary production of the sixteenth, seventeenth, and eighteenth centuries. He also fathered and educated one of the most brilliant scholars of the next generation, Josephus Justus (or Joseph Juste) Scaliger (1540–1609).[3]

The chapter of the *Poetics* translated here[4] begins by placing the genre epithalamium within the species of eulogistic poetry and offers a basic precept about this type of composition. Then an outline is given, with brief instructions for each section of the poem. But the bulk of Scaliger's text provides the would-be poet with actual ancient material drawn from his vast store of antiquarian knowledge.[5] This lore is frequently outlandish and obscure and is presented in Latin just as difficult, full of ellipses and puzzling, only partially parallel structures, rather in the manner of Tacitus. Another Tacitean feature is Scaliger's frequent alterations in tone: now elevated, now down to earth (even earthy); now oratorical, now chatty; now direct, now challengingly abstract and obscure. (The present translation attempts to some extent to reproduce these turns.) His style is marked also by sudden changes in subject and direction and by a use of transitional particles that is persistent without being very helpful.

The frequent etymological material presents special challenges to translator and reader alike; I hope the device of a column of annotation will be helpful. In this column appear transliterations and translations of Greek terms and translations of such Latin terms as have been kept in the original in the main column to reproduce Scaliger's philological procedure. The footnotes are intended not as an exhaustive account of Scaliger's references and sources but rather to assist

[3]See Anthony Thomas Grafton, *Joseph Scaliger: A Study in the History of Classical Scholarship* (Oxford: Oxford Univ. Press, 1983).

[4]Chapter 101 in the first (Lyons) edition; others have it as chapter 100.

[5]His principal sources are Plutarch's *Life of Romulus* 14–15 and *Roman Questions* (= *Moralia* 263D–291C; on marriage-customs see questions 1, 2, 6–8, 29–31, 65, 86–87, 105, and 108); the epithalamia of Catullus (*Carmina* 61, 62, and 64); the *Onomasticon* of Julius Pollux (second–third century), book III, sections 30–45, for Greek terminology; Menander the Rhetorician, of Laodicea (third–fourth century), *Treatise II*, 399–412 (topics VI and VII, on the Epithalamium and the *Kateunastikos* or Bedroom Speech); Isidore of Seville's *Etymologies* (or *Origins*), book IX, chapter vii (*De coniugiis*). On Scaliger's use of Menander, whom he found in the Aldine *Rhetores Græci* (Venice, 1508), see the pioneering article of Francis Cairns, "The *Poetices Libri Septem* of Julius Cæsar Scaliger: An Unexplored Source, "*Res Publica Litterarum* 9 (1986), 49–57 (I am indebted to Nita Krevans for this reference); a text, translation, and commentary appear in D. A. Russell and N. G. Wilson, *Menander Rhetor* (Oxford: Clarendon Press, 1981), pp. 134–159, and 309–323.

readers with some of the more obscure material.[6] Dates in the footnotes are to be understood as A.D. unless B.C. is specified.

Thanks are due to many for assistance, but especially to Nita Krevans of the University of Minnesota and Carmela Franklin of St. John's University, Collegeville, Minnesota, for tenaciously careful reading and many helpful suggestions.

TEXT

Perhaps it would seem best to someone that the principles of eulogistic composition should be set forth, since the evocation of nature is congenial to some, whereas others would celebrate a place, person, deed, or piece of fortune; in consolation also there is ample scope for eulogy. But instruction of this sort must be sought from the masters of rhetoric and from their writings. Let me state only one law, by observation of which you may be able to complete any kind of verse of whatever eulogistic type: have an eye for necessity, utility, and delight, either drawing your material from actuality or composing from verisimilitude. You must choose what is especially splendid, seeking farther afield if what is close to hand seems less noble; all else must be either veiled in shade or wrapped in silence. In sum, then, the foregoing is the chief point to follow, whether you try epithalamion or genethliacon, or essay propempticon,[7] or embark upon the genre of consolation.

Now then, to epithalamion. It is poetry in which a wedding is celebrated, named from *thalamus*. For θάλαμος also, in its first meaning, is the bridal chamber, derived from θάλειν ἅμα, that is, to lead married life together. By the Greeks this genre of

'bridal chamber' *thalamos*, 'bridal chamber'—*thalein hama*, 'to thrive together'

[6]Further research on Roman wedding customs might best begin with J. P. V. D. Balsdon, *Roman Women: Their History and Habits* (London: Bodley Head, 1962), pp. 173–189, and Herbert Jennings Rose, *The Roman Questions of Plutarch* (Oxford: Clarendon Press, 1924), especially pp. 101–108.
[7]A genethliacon celebrates a birthday, a propempticon anticipates a successful journey.

poetry is also called γαμήλιον, since the word for *gamelion, 'nuptial'*
'wedding' would be γάμος, derived from γάνυσθαι *gamos, 'wedding'—*
ἅμα (the expressions sound alike)—unless you pre- *ganusthai hama, 'to beget together'*
fer the derivation γεννᾶν ἅμα. *gennan hama, 'to beget together'*

The argument of the poem commences from the
mutual desire of bride and groom.[8] Of his pursuit,
his heartaches, his celebrations of her in songs,
sport, and deeds of arms, all done for the sake of
the maiden, you will write explicitly. But do not
expose *her* feelings in this way; rather subtly indicate them, leaving telltale signs and misgivings
veiled, thus: "her most chaste breast, taken captive
by devotion to the languishing youth." (By focusing
on his virtues you will provide her excuse.) Sometimes you will describe how by Venus or Cupid she
was forcibly compelled who previously had held
their realm in contempt.

In the next place the praises of both will be un-
folded with regard to fatherland, lineage, intellectual pursuits, and physical beauty. The third section
explains the favorable omens that attend upon their
union. Playfulness and dalliance occupy the entire
fourth section, with blandishments addressed to
each individually or both together. With greater de-
corum will you treat the maid, and yet tease her
about certain matters in a style not altogether modest: note her fear of the coming wrestling-match
and victory,[9] how from tears come laughter and
from hope, assured felicity.

---

[8]This and the five following paragraphs, in which Scaliger addresses the form of
the epithalamium and the content of its various sections, show a good deal of influence from Menander Rhetor's treatment of the Epithalamium and *Kateunastikos* (or
Bedroom Speech), the sixth and seventh topics of *Treatise II*, at 399–412. I am confident that a detailed analysis such as Cairns, 51–46, offers on Scaliger's use of
Menander in chapters 104 and 107 of *Poetics III* would lead to a similar conclusion:
Scaliger is dependent upon Menander but does not hesitate to rearrange, reclassify,
and substitute material from alternative sources.

[9]Latin literature frequently describes lovemaking in such terms; graphic examples
can be found at Apuleius, *Metamorphoses* 2.17, and Ausonius, *Nuptial Cento* (poem
17), vv. 101–131; Menander Rhetor also speaks in such terms at 406 in *Treatise II*,
topic VII on the Bedroom Speech.

In the fifth section the poem promises offspring, makes vows, and engages in prophecy. The final part contains the exhortation to sleep—that is, for the others actual sleep, but for them wakefulness. Meanwhile the nuptial couch itself may be either lauded or merely described, or else the nuptial coverlet or παστός, that is, the spread upon the marriage couch, under the cover of which the sacred rites are accomplished more modestly. Jests of a somewhat brazen character are also mixed in, such as were once called by the ancients Fescennine verses. Their name and style come from the town of Fescennium in Campania or, as others prefer, in the Sabine region.[10] (This is the judgment of Festus.[11] But what he adds, namely that one can also derive the name from *fascinum,* the words themselves do not support very well; they are not only wanton but also often verge upon the disgraceful in the hearing—indeed, you would discern in them something other than incantation!—unless you prefer to joke and recognize a derivation not from βάσκανος but from the Horatian sense of the word *fascinum.*[12] Moreover, this sort of spell [i.e., an incantation to promote fertility, like the Fescennine verses] does have a place in weddings and is willingly sought after as a real necessity. But there is the opposite sort of spell, which is warded off by counterspells, votive offerings, and drugs. This is why the grooms used to protect their houses by decorating the doors with woollen fillets and smearing them with oil or pig or wolf fat.)

Now if in this final exhortation you wish to praise the nuptial rites themselves, you will proceed with examples from legend and scatter principles drawn from natural history. On this wise will you

pastos, 'bedspread'

'incantation'

baskanos, 'sorcerer'
'phallus'

[10]According to Pliny, *Natural History* 3.52, the place was Fescennia in Etruria.

[11]Sextus Pompeius Festus (grammarian, late second century) s.v. *fescennini versus* in Wallace M. Lindsay, *Sexti Pompei Festi De Verborum Significatu quae supersunt cum Pauli Epitome* (1913; rpt. Hildesheim: Georg Olms, 1965), p. 76.

[12]Horace uses the word in the sense of "phallus" at *Epodes* 8.18.

sing of the felicitous union of Peleus and Thetis,
which all the gods dignified by their presence: this
was the gathering that the Fates themselves made
more august by their singing; this the union from
which Achilles, bravest of all mortals, was born.
Into this splendid setting you will bring the nuptial
couch of Father Liber and Ariadne, with the sport-
ing of Satyrs and Sileni.[13] It will be fitting to
mention the union of Hercules and Hebe, at which
no less than the entire assembly of the gods was
present, when Mars danced the pyrrhic, Mercury
demonstrated his gymnastics, Apollo sang the
hymn to Hymen, Venus was the attendant matron,
the Graces raised the torches, the Muses made mel-
ody, the Sun was majordomo, and Diana strewed
the blossoms.[14]

You will be able to add further eulogistic material
from the history of nuptial rites. For example, the
Roman high priest of Jupiter, upon the death of his
wife, used to abdicate his priesthood. From the
realm of cosmology you will introduce Love and
Friendship out of the actual primordial elements of
the cosmos.[15] Or else you will describe the time
when, after Chaos was brought to order, the wedding of Heaven and Earth was celebrated, and how
from their union all species were produced and, being engendered according to their example, were
propagated; and how, despite the fact of their material nature, they attained immortality through the
ordained succession of the species.[16] Moreover,
much matter for the praise of love may be sought

[13]The foregoing matter is from Poem 64 of Catullus; Liber is a Roman name for
Bacchus.

[14]Although most of these divinities dance together in the *Homeric Hymn to Apollo*,
III, vv. 194–206 (cf. Horace, *Odes* 1.30), their connection to the wedding of Hercules
and Hebe must have another source; cf. also Apuleius, *Metamorphoses* 6.24.

[15]The cosmological system of Empedocles of Acragas (fifth century B.C.) pro-
posed the primal elements of Earth, Air, Fire, and Water disposed by the operations
of Love and Strife. The cosmological material here appears to be derived from
Menander Rhetor at 401 (*Treatise II*, topic VI on the Epithalamium).

[16]This material is akin to Hesiod, *Theogony* 116–159, and Lucretius, *De Rerum
Natura* 5.780–836.

from Plato's *Symposium,* but in such a way that the poet will prudently vary his own treatment from what is said in that source.[17] (For indeed, whatever precepts individual poets fetch for themselves from this storeroom, all will likely say one and the same thing.)

Through *epiphonemata* let us also address Hymen, who being the god of marriage is invoked from time to time in the refrains of the verse; in fact, sometimes at the very outset of the poem we add his praises as we mix in our conceits. (His name is derived from that protective membrane which naturally occurs in young women. In Latin he was called Talassius; an explanation is given from the rape of the Sabine women, the story of which is found in Plutarch.[18] There is a question whether that is the actual source of the name, or whether the word is derived from wool-production. For Plutarch[19] says that τάλαροι, that is, the baskets in which wool was contained, were also called τάλασοι, whence also ταλασιουργοί, 'wool-workers'—appropriately enough. Now, he continues, a sheepskin with the fleece was spread beneath a new bride; and the doorposts, as we noted above, were covered with wool; and a strainer, as we will note below, was carried in the procession—as if indeed brides were being led off to labor rather than to give up their maidenhood, or indeed because by demonstrations of that sort the diligence of the future mother of the family was indicated, just as among the Greeks a sieve was also carried, and a pestle tied in front of the nuptial couch. Not so at Rome. For when peace was made after the Rape of the Sabine women, it was mutually agreed that the wives should neither grind grain nor cook. Thus also the ritual cry *talassio* is derived from wool. On

epiphonema, 'address, ejaculation' (rhetorical terminology)

talaroi, 'baskets'

talasoi, 'baskets'

talasiourgoi, 'wool-workers'

(ritual wedding-cry)

[17]In proposing prudent variation, Scaliger may well be thinking of the pervasive homoerotic atmosphere in the *Symposium;* on the other hand, it is clear that he envisions variation and adaptation from all ancient sources.

[18]Plutarch, *Life of Romulus* 14–15.

[19]Plutarch, *Roman Questions* 31; *Life of Romulus* 15.

the other hand, it may be that this is a piece of obscure erudition rather than a true derivation. The ancients used an expression τάλις ἡ μελλονύμφη, that is, 'espoused maiden,' which evidently has a very great affinity with the word *talassio* in certain respects. But on this subject there is more in the *Origins*.[20] Sophocles used the word in the *Antigone*,[21] and indeed in this very way.) [*talis hē mellonymphē*, 'espoused maiden']

However, since a variety of evidence can be taken from many passages, we shall describe the institution itself, as it was practiced among the Romans and among foreign peoples. There were officially three days of a wedding. The first was called προαύλια by the Greeks, and not so ineptly *desponsalia* by us in Latin, since on that day the maiden was betrothed. The second day, on which the marriage took place, was called ἀπαύλια. In Latin you would call it *decubatio*, for thus was it said in the laws of the Flamen Dialis:[22] "Let him not lie apart from his own bed for three nights." And in fact the groom would go away to the house of his father-in-law, where the marriage would take place. The one who used to lead him there was called *paranymphus*. The Greeks called the third day ἐπαύλια, and Latin speakers *repotia*, when the groom's friends would hold a feast at their expense. Then indeed was the bedchamber finally adorned for the groom, in the house of his father-in-law, where the wedding used to take place if the bride was previously unmarried. She would then give presents to her husband, called for that reason by the same term ἐπαύλια. Among these gifts was a garment also named from the same word, the ἐπαυλιστήρια. If she were a widow, however, she was brought to the bridegroom's house. The one who brought her was called *nymphagogus*. (Among the Rhodians it was [*proaulia*, 'before chambering' 'betrothal'] [*apaulia*, 'chambering apart' 'lying apart'] ['groomsman'—*epaulia*, 'after chambering' 'drinking afterwards'] [*epaulia*, 'things for chambering' *epaulistēria*, 'wedding garment' 'bride-guide']

[20]I have found no such discussion in the *Origines* or *Etymologiae* of Isidore of Seville; Scaliger appears to be following Festus (Lindsay, pp. 478–480).

[21]Sophocles, *Antigone*, v. 629.

[22]High priest of Jupiter.

the custom for brides to be summoned through a herald; the groom, sitting at home, received her when she arrived.)

On the first day, in fact, when the marital promises were to be made, the more noble families did not assemble without taking omens. The best auspices[23] were from the turtle-dove and the crow, but only if the pair had in fact appeared together; to have observed single birds was considered worst of all. Therefore, Horapollo says that custom in the ancient rites was to sing these words at a marriage, ἐκκόρει, κόρη, κορώνην,[24] by which a slave-girl *ekkorei, korē, korōnēn,* was commanded to preserve the good luck of the 'sweep out the crow, house by driving out the lone, that is, widow crow. girl' (For this reason the plural κορώνας found in com- *korōnas,* 'crows' mentaries on Pindar[25] is not correct, since a pair would be most auspicious. Indeed, both the crow and the turtle-dove are so devoted to their mates that should one die the survivor seeks no subsequent union. In fact the crow is so chaste that it has been believed to avoid the foulness of copulation, conceiving rather in the mouth. Yet this opinion has been rejected in the third book of *On the Generation of Animals.*[26]) No little charm will be added to your poem through these birds.

After the auspices, they [i.e., the wedding party] would perform sacrifices and immolate a pig to *teleia,* 'having power to Juno, whose proper ritual epithet was τελεία. And fulfill' after her, they would invoke Jupiter τέλειος, Venus, *teleios,* 'having power Diana Cinxia, and Persuasion. Now it is with some- to fulfill'—*Cinxia,* 'of the girdle' thing less than exactitude that both Ζεὺς τέλειος *Zeus teleios* and Ἥρα τελεία have been interpreted as 'adult' *Hēra teleia*

---

[23]Auspices were taken by watching in prescribed quarters of the sky for the appearance at prescribed times of particular birds flying in particular directions.

[24]Horapollo was a grammarian of the fourth or fifth century. At *Hieroglyphica* 1.8 he quotes the proverb in dialect, but Scaliger reproduces it here in perfect Attic.

[25]At least four editions of Pindar with commentaries had appeared by the time Scaliger was writing: Aldus Manutius (Venice, 1513); Callierges (Rome, 1515); Ceporinus (Basel, 1526); and Petrus Brubacchius (Frankfurt, 1542).

[26]Aristotle's *De Generatione Animalium* 756b.

Jove and 'adult' Hera.[27] Why? Because it is proper
only to marry adults and to take a wife in marriage? Others have said that προτελεῖν, a term that
Pollux[28] attributed to the nuptial sacrifices, is
equivalent to *initiari* in Latin; for initiations were
called τελεταί. But this is hardly the explanation.
The ancients say that τέλος was equivalent to
γάμος, because it is marriage that brings the per-
petuation of human life to fulfillment. Therefore
they called both the nuptial sacrifice and the wedding day alike τέλειον; and so, as the same Pollux
says, they called the nuptial sacrifice ἡρατέλεια after the names for both the marriage and the gods of
marriage. The sacrifice on the previous day was in
fact the προτέλεια; you have this word also in Lu-
cian's *On Salaried Posts in Houses.*[29] Therefore Ζεὺς
τέλειος will be none other than *Jupiter Nuptialis.* To
the gods and goddesses mentioned above they offered a portion of the virgin's hair in the manner of
first fruits.[30] (Also they cast bile,[31] extracted from
the gall-bladder of a sacrificial victim, about the altar.) But they let the rest of her hair grow, so that
this might bring expectation of future tranquillity
between the spouses.

With the sacrifice of the wedding day complete,
the groom would be led to his father-in-law's house
by the one whom the Greeks called παράνυμφος, as
it were his attendant. (Some also used to call him
νυμφευτής, some πάροχος, just as the woman who
attended the bride was called προμνήστρια by
them, *pronuba* by us.) These persons, too, may furnish material for your poem. And when the festiv-
ity is celebrated towards evening, or especially at

protelein, 'to instruct
beforehand'

'to be initiated'
teletai, 'initiations;
mysteries'
telos, 'fulfilling,
consummation'
gamos, 'marriage'

teleion, 'fulfilling'
hērateleia, 'Hera's
fulfilling'

proteleia, 'before
fulfilling'
Zeus teleios, 'fulfilling
Zeus'
'nuptial Jupiter'

paranymphos,
'groomsman'
nympheutēs,
'groomsman'
parochos, 'one who sits
beside another in a
chariot'
promnéstria, 'bride's
woman'—'bride's
woman'

---

[27]Another meaning of the word is "complete, fulfilled."

[28]Pollux, *Onomasticon* 3.38.

[29]Lucian of Samosata (second century), Περὶ τῶν ἐπὶ μισθῷ συνόντων or *De Mer-
cede Conductis* 14.

[30]Scaliger compares this offering to the consecration of the first-born (cf. Abel's
sacrifice at Gen. 4:4); but it is not clear that Roman virgins in fact kept their hair
uncut until marriage.

[31]Symbolic of bitterness and acrimony.

night, the poets have not been wont to neglect the suitability of that hour. From the tardiness of sluggish night, your argument will turn towards the constellations, to the Morning Star, to the moon.

And since the ancients thought that water was the prime matter of all things,[32] whereas fire was the form, so both, placed at the threshold, were touched by both hands; and the bride herself was purified by being sprinkled with the same water. Then from the same fire torches would be lit by the aediles, five in number (that there were so many Varro affirms, as Plutarch writes;[33] also that they called these torches *cerei*. Plautus in fact mentions only one taper.)[34] 'wax tapers' Other races cut them from the wood of the pine or pitch-pine, and at the Rape of the Sabine women the Roman herdsmen made them from the thorn-bushes they chanced upon; and their descendants sought out the same material. Some prefer to explain the number of torches from the number of conjugal deities, since the aediles were only three, not five. From this source, then, you will enkindle your wit unto the delight of poesy; you will touch upon the nature of the thorn-bush, noting that its fire is not at all oily and smoky as is that from a torch (though I am aware that only a rather wretched flame can be coaxed from a thorn-bush).

Immediately thereafter the bride was adorned and her hair done; they would divide her hair with the point of a spear (Plutarch gives the reason).[35] And then was the head and face of the bride unveiled; *obnubere*, 'to unveil' the term 'nuptial' comes from unveiling. By the

---

[32]The theory of Thales of Miletus (sixth century B.C.). See Festus under *facem*, Lindsay, p. 74.

[33]Plutarch *Roman Questions* 2; I can find no such discussion in the extant works of Varro.

[34]Plautus, *Curculio* I.i, v.9.

[35]Plutarch, *Roman Questions* 87; *Life of Romulus* 15. Actually Plutarch suggests various possible symbolisms: that Roman marriage originated in the context of the Sabine wars; that wives of brave warriors must accept simple and unaffected adornment; that the marriage can be dissolved only by steel; that the spear is sacred to Juno, goddess of marriage.

Greeks that veil was called ἐανός and καλύπτρα, by   *heanos,* 'fine fabric'
Latin speakers *flammeum,* because it was flame col-   *kaluptra,* 'veil'—
ored, in order to safeguard the modesty of the   'flame-colored'
bride: for if some redness were noticed in her face,
that color might be thought to shine out from the
veil, not her cheeks.

Her husband would give her an iron ring without
a gemstone; the stone was absent in order to denote
the simplicity of the act. The material stood for
constancy and the form of the ring for perpetual
bonding. The bride for her part would carry three
brass coins, one in her hand, another on her foot,
the third in a pocket. She gave the first to her
groom, as if having bought him at that price, she
would keep him to her; the second she would de-
posit on the hearth for the household gods—and
she would also honor the hearth, as Plautus says,[36]
with a bright fire and garlands woven by her own
hand (for indeed, another's was not permitted); the
third she buried at a nearby crossroads.

They used to offer roasted *far* also, if not at all   *far,* 'spelt'
weddings, at least at those when the bride was
given to her husband for usufruct only but not into
his possession; and so the rite of that sort of mar-
riage was called *confarreatio.* There was in fact   'wedding with spelt'
another sort of marriage, when the bride was
given into the possession of the groom by her
matron. By this rite she would pass into the family
of her husband and thus take the name of the
mother of his family; for she was given not only
for usufruct but also into possession. Lucretius also
alludes to these rites in the verse, "and life is given
to no one in possession, but for usufruct to all."[37]
The type of marriage just described was called
coemptio.   'purchase'

---

[36]Plautus, *Aulularia* 385–387.
[37]Lucretius, *De Rerum Natura* 3.971. In Roman law, "usufruct" was the right to
enjoy the use and fruits of a thing owned by another; so that a woman married by
usufruct would still be legally owned by her father or other legal guardian rather
than by her husband.

What remained was to begin the order of the banquet. When the wedding feast was prepared in the Etruscan manner, they would slaughter a pig. In order to sharpen the sexual appetite, they would serve onions, pine-nuts, nuts, cabbages, and pepper, besides other dishes. This was the custom in Etruria; other customs prevailed elsewhere, as we will relate. Then the marriage-hymn was sung chorally, in this fashion: first a soloist sang, adding the *epiphonema;* this done, the entire chorus would take up the refrain, singing back the address to Hymen in identical verses. [*'address' (to Hymen)*] Meanwhile as many as we indicated above [i.e., five youths], having their fathers and mothers still living, would stand by with the torches. When there was enough both of singing and of dancing, then the bride's woman would grasp the bride's hand and lead her to the *lectus genialis;* [*'nuptial couch'*] for thus was the bed called by no less than Catullus—I believe from 'begetting.' [*generandum, 'begetting'*] By the Greeks that couch was called παράβυστος, for the reason [*parabustos, 'stuffed'; 'ottoman'*] that it was covered by the veil that we mentioned above.[38] A woman whom the Greeks called both νυμφεύτρια and θαλαμεύτρια had adorned that bed [*nympheutria, 'bridesmaid'*] [*thalameutria, 'bridesmaid'*] with two mattresses. Led to it by her groom, the bride would be unveiled; and for the unveiling she received from him gifts that were called both ἀνακαλυπτήρια (for that reason) and also ὀπτήρια [*anakalyptēria, 'unveiling things'*] (because then she was seen by him as if for the first [*optēria, 'things upon seeing'*] time); and the words he said to her were called προφθεγκτήρια. (For rightly in Callimachus[39] the [*prophthenktēria, 'utterances in advance'*] name ὀπτήρια is given to the gifts of friends and [*optēria (as above)*] relatives upon first viewing infants, just as the sort [*maiōstra, 'midwife things'*] of gifts given to midwives are called μαίωστρα, [*sōstra, 'things for saving'*] those given to saviors σῶστρα, to liberators λύτρα [*lutra, 'ransom'*] or ἄποινα, to instructors δίδακτρα.) [*apoina, 'ransom'*] [*didaktra, 'teacher's fee'*]

Also the δᾳδοφόροι (or torchbearers) would lead [*dadoforoi, 'torchbearers'*] the bride to bed, and two others besides, who as we

---

[38]Scaliger seems in error here, since his Greek term has to do with the stuffing rather than the covering of upholstery.

[39]Callinachus, *Hymn* 3 (to Artemis), v. 74.

said carried a strainer with wool and a spindle with
thread—signs, as it were, of the labor in which she
was to be engaged. (Of the sieve and pestle belong-
ing to the Greek rite enough was said above.) Besides these items, other attendants would carry a
woman's adornments: gold, bracelets, earrings, ba-
sins also, combs, a mirror, shoes, and more things
of this sort, which are called by legal scholars "par-
aphernalia beyond the dowry." (It has been handed   *praeter dotem parapherna*
down to memory that this luxury was reduced by
Solon[40] to the limit of three dresses only and to ves-
sels of a modest price.) There (at the bedside) the
bride's woman would take one of the torches and
light the conjugal vigil lamp, which was to burn
through the night; and at that point the torches
were customarily extinguished (but it was not considered the most auspicious practice for them to be
put under the bed or kept to make a bonfire).[41]
With two fingers the bride's woman loosened the
girdle of the hesitant virgin, which she would consecrate to Diana, who was titled λυσιζώνη, or by   *lusizōnē,*
Latin speakers *Cinxia,* for that reason. Now the gir-   'girdle-loosening'—
dle was woven of sheep's wool, and tied with a   'of the girdle'
knot called Herculean, since he was regarded by the
ancients as the most prolific of heroes—indeed, sev-
enty children survived him, and once within seven
days he made women of the fifty virgin daughters
of Thestia.[42] There is a dispute about the bride's
girdle: for some say that it belonged specifically
to the bridal regalia, but this opinion is nullified
by the authority of Catullus. For in his hendeca-
syllabics[43] he indicates that the virgin Atalanta had
not been girdled at her wedding by her matron but
on some other occasion. The evidence is the line

[40]Poet and archetypal lawgiver of Athens, seventh–sixth century B.C.; Plutarch reports his marriage-legislation at *Life of Solon* 20.

[41]See Festus under *rapi,* Lindsay, p. 364.

[42]This version of the story is at Athenæus, *Deipnosophistæ* 13.4; but this text gives
the parent's name as Thestios.

[43]The hendecasyllabic or eleven-syllable verse was a favorite of Catullus; the reference here is to poem 2, line 13.

"she loosened her girdle that had long been tied": thus the custom must have been for virgins never to go out ungirdled.

When all had departed, the groom would close the doors, having placed guards outside the chamber to keep the young married women away despite their pleas, sympathy, and ploys in case the bride should cause a disturbance by crying out when she endured the thrust within. Meanwhile the young men would make an uproar, shouting and singing while they threw the nuts that are mentioned both in Virgil and in Catullus's Epithalamium.[44] Various explanations are offered. Some say that because nuts protect their kernel with shell, skin, cover, and hide, throwing them provides a good omen of the parents' sheltering their offspring with equal protection. Others have thought that the cries of the violated bride could be smothered, pointing out that the ancient commentators were so minded. But our opinion is less conventional. It is clear that the ancients used to play with nuts, just as we also did in childhood. So Persius, by the line "whatever we do when we've given up our nuts,"[45] indicates growing out of childhood. So the nuts were thrown as a sign of giving up mindless diversions and entering upon the new pursuits of family life.[46]

The next day, which we called in Greek ἐπαύλια, *epaulia*, 'after chambering' meaning as it were "appendix to the wedding," was called *repotia* in Latin because the feasting was re- 're-drinking' peated. On that day the groom's relatives provided the banquet. That was the day on which the bride began to exercise her rights over her family; and so a key would be given to her, to symbolize authority and possession (rather than to insure ease in

[44]Vergil, *Eclogues* 8.30; Catullus 61.121, 124, 126, 128, 133.
[45]Persius, *Satires* 1.10.
[46]Scaliger could have supported his position with Catullus 61.124–127, where the poem addresses the groom's catamite, soon to be cast aside: "Give the boys nuts, idle catamite! You have played long enough; let it now be your delight to worship the marriage-god with nuts."

childbirth,[47] as some assert). Some have thought,
and indeed this is quite likely, that the procession
we mentioned earlier was held not when the bride
went to the bridal chamber but rather on the day of
the *repotia*, when she was brought from her father's   're-drinking'
house to her groom's. For the custom was that she
would go forth on that occasion with gifts in order
to bring them herself to her husband. (Now the
Greeks used to call these φερνή, and those which   *phernē*, 'dowry'
the groom gave her were ἕδνα.) Indeed, along with   *hedna*, 'bride-price'
those gifts the groom was given a covered box by
his father-in-law containing little accessories,[48] and
also his bride's baby toys. The vessel was called a
camillus, for that was what the ancients called their   'servant' (see footnote)
servants.[49] And after they were in the husband's
house, there were more gifts, from his father now,
which they called ἐπαύλια δῶρα.   *epaulia dōra*, 'after-chambering gifts'

Now let us note also the custom that we have observed being kept in certain places in Italy, where in
leaving her father's house the bride lifts her feet in
order not to touch the threshold. Various explanations have been assigned to this. To me what follows seems closest to the truth: thus she would
avoid the possibility of harm from the magical
charms that sorcerers used to bury under the
threshold, to destroy either the harmony of the
spouses or their procreative powers.

From all of the foregoing you see the number and
amplitude of the passages that can be furnished to
you and your poem, material that you will be able
to sprinkle on with a varied and far from contempt-
ible erudition. Now in simple narration, now in
apostrophe, fitting your verses now to this, now to
that, you will be able to add something even concerning the season. For Plutarch says that originally

[47]However, Carmela Franklin notes that in her native Calabria a spell of "unlock-ing" is still customary when childbirth is imminent.

[48]*Minuta supellectilis* may actually mean "miniature furniture."

[49]Scaliger seems to have confused the term for "servant" with the name of the box, *cumera;* Varro, *De Lingua Latina* 7.34, says that the *camillus* carries the *cumera.*

brides were not married in May; Ovid, that only
wicked women were married then, and from this,
he writes, came the well-known proverb.[50] He reports also that it was customary for widows to be
married on public feast days, but not virgins. The
reason was that, with the people occupied in a public festival, there would be no interest in watching
the marriages of widows; but because there was
need for spectators at virgins' weddings,[51] it would
have been unfair to allow the distractions of greater
festivities. Also on days of ill omen marriages were
forbidden, namely the days following the Calends,
Nones, and Ides,[52] and also the day on which Re-
mus was killed, when sacrifices to dead ancestors
were performed (this feast was first called the Re-
muria after him, later the Lemuria).

Much additional lustre could be provided your
poem from other rites of the ancients which were
observed among diverse nations; we have under-
taken to explain some of the more noteworthy as
follows. Marriages among Persians were not legiti-
mate except at the beginning of spring. The Greeks,
Macedonians, Thracians, Triballians, and Paeonians
had a custom that when the bride and groom met
they tasted a piece of cake that had been cut by a
sword. The Greek custom was that the torches be
held not by young people but by the mothers of the
bride and groom. Galatian couples, when they
came together, did not eat bread but traditionally
drank from the same cup. Among the Spartans, the
bride's woman, in their chamber, offered the bride
to her spouse dressed as a man, with her hair cut;
and it was permitted that the thing be accomplished
without any torches. But on the island of Cos, the

---

[50]Plutarch, *Roman Questions* 86; Ovid, *Fasti* 5.487–490 ("wicked women marry in
the month of May" is the proverb, verse 490).

[51]Presumably to provide for the witnessing by the community that is such a prominent feature of Roman legal arrangements.

[52]These were the hinge-points of Roman months, the Calends being the first day,
the Ides a day around mid-month, and the Nones a day in between.

groom was dressed as a woman. Yet of these customs, the Spartan was by far the more licentious;
for young men were shut up in a very dark place
with as many virgins, and the one that each youth
got he used to bring home for himself in marriage,
even if she had no dowry. The result, whether it
occurred by prior arrangement or by happenstance,
no one was allowed to fault or alter; indeed, no opportunity for redress was offered. On this account
the Ephors decreed a fine against Lysander[53] because he divorced the wife who had fallen to him in
order to procure a prettier one. At Carthage the
custom held that no one be joined in marriage who
had not previously tasted sliced tunafish. At Athens, quinces had to be served and eaten at the banquet according to the law of Solon. Fragrances were
added by the Babylonians, and the Persians ate ap-
ples with camel's marrow. Athenæus writes in his
fourth book[54] that at Naucratis the people were
cautioned by law not to bring to the nuptial banquet
an egg or any μελίπηκτον,[55] that is, honey dessert. *melipēkton,* 'honey-compound'
At Athens when the groom entered, a fig, dates, and
legumes were scattered upon his head from above.
Even now in certain places they throw wheat. Spartan virgins used no veils; widows who were remar-
rying would come forth with their faces veiled but
their heads uncovered. The following custom will
give special encouragement to wedlock: for also
among the Spartans, at a certain festival bachelors
would be dragged around an altar by women and
beaten with whips, so that by this ignominy they
might be stimulated to give their attention to pro-

[53]The Ephors were five magistrates, the governing board of the Spartan state;
Lysander was the great Spartan commander who among many other distinctions su-
pervised the humiliation of Athens at the end of the Peloponnesian war in 404 B.C.
This story is from Athenæus (second–third century), *Deipnosophistæ* 13 (555c).

[54]Athenæus was from Naucratis on the Nile delta; see *Deipnosophistæ* 4 (150a).

[55]The ancients compounded honey with seeds and nuts. A similar food was conveyed by nocturnal swimmers to the Spartan warriors trapped on Pylos (Thucydides,
Peloponnesian War 4.26) and is still served in the Eastern Mediterranean under such
names as the Hebrew *halva* and the Turkish *helva*.

creation. It will be suitable also to recall Cecrops,[56] who first corrected the random and unstable sexual practices at Athens by restricting them to the union of one man with one woman. (For what they say of Socrates, that he had two wives, Xanthippe and Myrto, is false, as Panætius of Rhodes has handed down, among others.)[57]

There is a northern people, the Lapps, living by Sweden; they bring fire to their weddings as did the Romans of old, and also flint. About the fire there is no question, for nothing is more necessary in that region; and I take it that flint was brought for the same reason, in order to keep the fire burning. They say that in Bœotia brides were crowned with asparagus, in order to learn to put aside their wildness and be tamed to another's will. (A succulent and flavorful vegetable is in fact obtainable from wild asparagus.)[58]

Nothing indeed will prevent you from evoking in most tender poetry two springs of Attica, Callirrhoe and Enneacrunon,[59] from which the water was drawn in which a virgin bathed before she reclined upon the nuptial couch. Nor ought it be omitted that the more noble Greek brides were drawn to their grooms in a cart (if any went on foot, she was called χαμάπους). The axle of this cart was burned before his doors to demonstrate constancy and self-control, so that no thought of another union or new marriage might occupy her vacillating spirit, nor the impulse seize her to wander off here or there, a vice especially congenial to women. In the city of Lepta there was a custom that on the day following the wedding the bride would send to her mother-in-law to ask for a jar. The slaves

'pretty-flowing' and 'nine-spouted' in Greek

chamapous, 'foot to ground'

---

[56]Mythical first king of Athens.

[57]Scaliger could have known the tradition of Panætius from either Plutarch, *Life of Aristides* 27.3–4 (335cd), or Athenæus, *Deipnosophistæ* 13.2 (555d–556b).

[58]Scaliger could have learned of wild asparagus, *corruda*, from Cato the Elder, *On Agriculture* 6.3–4, or Pliny the Elder, *Natural History* 19.54 and 145.

[59]It is generally thought that both names refer to the same well.

would answer her that they neither had one nor, if they did, would they give it. In this way she would be trained to endure the ways of her mother-in-law (for they are generally troublesome). But enough of all this.

Now the singing [at weddings] is of various sorts. For at the dinner itself drinking songs used to be sung, which have been described above in the chapter on Pæans.[60] After the dinner came the Epithalamium, when the couple were being led to their chamber. A third type is found among the poets, in which the ceremony itself is described, for example Musæus's poem about Leander, Ovid's about the marriage of Orpheus, Statius's about Stella. Claudian wrote one such about Honorius and Maria, and there is also an elaborate one by Ausonius.[61]

A final type is one in which narration and song are mixed. There is a very beautiful example by Catullus which has been ineptly titled *Argonautica,* for in fact it is an epithalamium in the mixed style for Peleus.[62] There is also extant a most delightful epithalamium by Claudian of the sort that used to be sung [at weddings]. Wherefore, in order to set you upon the track, I will append several examples of Catullus. May you avail so to place your step in his footprints that you may the more easily reach the finish-line of his glory. Here are three different openings, the first immediately addressing Hymen:

> O thou who hauntest Mt. Helicon,
> of the race of Urania,
> who snatchest the tender maid
> for a husband, O Hymen . . .
>
> [61.1–4]

[60]Book 1, chapter 44.

[61]Musæus (grammarian, fifth–sixth century), *Hero and Leander;* Ovid, *Metamorphoses* 10.1–102; Statius, *Silvae* 1.2; Claudian, *Epithalamium de Nuptiis Honorii,* poems 9 and 10 (Birt's enumeration; he also wrote Fescennine verses, a set for Honorius, and three others—see poems 11–14. Flavius Honorius was Roman emperor 393–423); Ausonius, *Cento Nuptialis,* poem 17, justly called "elaborate" from its being an extremely learned production created solely from lines and fragments of classical verse.

[62]Catullus 64, never called *Argonautica* today.

Now the second begins with a reference to the time
of day and is addressed to the band of youths:

It is evening, lads; rise up! At last Hesperus
is just lofting his long-awaited rays over Olympus.
[62.1–2]

The third is addressed to Peleus himself:

O thou, augmenting exceeding loveliness with
great virtues, prop of Macedon, Peleus . . . [63]
[64.323–324]

Catullus mentioned the bridal veil in the words
"Seize the bridal veil" [61.8]. Claudian, because he
was not able to accommodate the singular form to
the heroic verse, used the plural[64]:

[Venus] herself fits the bridal veils to
the maiden's tresses.
[*Epithalamion* 285]

Claudian also mentioned the chariot that was discussed earlier:

. . . and brightly shines
the sacred chariot which will convey the bride—
[286–287]

true enough when one's lot is imperial.[65] Catullus
attributes one torch to Hymen, but that is because
he is a single individual:

[63]Scaliger reads *O decus eximium, et magnis virtutibus augens / Æmathiæ columen,
Peleu*. Today, following Housman's emendation *Emathiæ tutamen, Opis carissime nato*,
we translate verse 324 as "guardian of Emathia, most dear to the son of Ops."
[64]This situation, quite frequent in Latin hexameter verse, is sometimes called the
"poetic plural."
[65]Claudian refers to the epithet "sacred" applied to the chariot; such was the language in late antiquity when referring to the Imperial family and their trappings.

> . . . in your hand
> shake the piney torch!
> [61.14–15]

But in fact there are more torches than one, since he says

> Do you see how the torches
> shake their golden hair?
> [61.77–78]

An amœbœic[66] poem can be made not only with the name of Hymen as the refrain, but also another expression, as in

> Run, run, ye spindles, leading out the threads![67]
> [64.333, 337, 342, etc.]

This line appears several times in the same poem, not just once, as occurs elsewhere in Catullus:

> Who would dare to be
> compared with this god?
> [61.64–65, 69–70, 74–75]

and

> . . . the day wanes.
> Come forth, new bride!
> [61.90–91, 105–106]

and

> Boy-love, cast nuts!
> [61.128, 133]

The maidens would sing these verses at the prompting of a cantor. For Catullus says,

[66]The term refers properly to poetry written with voices in dialogue, but Scaliger seems to widen it to include poetry with a refrain; cf. Theocritus, *Idylls* 1 and 2.

[67]The threads are those of destiny, unwound, measured, and cut by the three Fates.

> You likewise, O pure
> maidens, for whom a similar
> day approaches, sing together
> in rhythm, "O Hymen, Hymen,
> O Hymen, Hymen!"
> [61.36–40]

Likewise in the other epithalamium,

> See how the unmarried maids reach for what they
> have rehearsed!
> [62.12]

> Now they are beginning to sing, now will be the time
> to respond,
> "Hymen, O Hymen! Draw near, Hymen, O Hymen!"
> [62.18–19]

As to the word ἀπαυλίζειν, which we noted
above and interpreted to mean *decubare* according to
the ancient pontifical texts, Catullus in fact writes
secubare:

apaulizein, 'to chamber apart'

'to lie apart'

'to lie apart'

> He will not wish to sleep
> apart from your tender breasts.
> [61.100–101]

He has also included an allusion to the bawdy Fes-
cennines (I quote that you may recognize it, but not
for imitation):

> Let not the insolent Fescennine
> sayings be long silent![68]
> [61.119–120]

and what follows. Indeed, for my part, I prefer that
you abstain from such material, or else preserve the
tradition with a cultivated modesty. For he who

---

[68]Here Scaliger reads *locutio*, "utterance," whereas the text commonly accepted today is *iocatio*, "jest."

speaks shamefully is involved in great danger, not only to reputation, but to life, since of whatever sort your composition is, so also your mind would seem to be. Concerning moreover the custom we noted, that the bride ought not touch the threshold,

> With good omen carry your
> golden feet across the threshold.
> [61.159–160]

From this passage it would seem that it was *not* in her father's house that this was done; however, if the usual opinion *is* correct, then perhaps the new bride was carried across the threshold in order to show her reluctance at leaving her father's house.

Hopes of offspring are also expressed:

> May a little Torquatus (so I wish),
> stretching out his tender hands
> from his mother's lap,
> smile sweetly at his father!
> [61.209–212]

In the *Argonauticus*,[69] moreover, almost the whole poem contains that idea. Claudian also gives an example:

> Born thus in the purple,
> let a little scion of Honorius sit on his grandfather's
> knees.
> [*Epithalamion* 340–341]

Aristophanes concluded his play *The Peace* with a chorus; there, after certain vows and prayers, he added a kind of parody of the marriage-rite, just as also in another play, *The Birds*.[70] A poem [61] of

[69]That is, Catullus 64; Scaliger is no doubt thinking of verses 23–30 and 328–375.
[70]Aristophanes, *Peace* 1332–1357 and *Birds* 1720–1765. It is of course normal for Greek plays to end with choral passages.

Catullus uses glyconic stanzas composed of four glyconic verses[71] plus a pherecratean,[72] thus producing stanzas of five verses. (When occasionally he uses a spondee in the first foot instead of a trochee,[73] he does it by example of the ancients, just as when he makes the same substitution for the dactyl in the second foot, as in the verse

nutriunt umore.[74]

[61.25]

'they nourish with moisture'

For indeed you have a similar metrical structure in Aristophanes' play *The Knights.* Here you may notice an even greater license. For in place of the dactyl he actually used an amphibrach,[75] in the line

τοῖς ἀφικνομένοισι[76]

[975]

tois aphiknomenoisi, 'to arrivals'

What is more, in another place he uses an amphimacron:[77]

ὡς εἰ μὴ 'γένοιθ' οὗτος ἐν,[78]

[981]

hōs ei mē 'genoith' houtos en, 'if only he were not [great] in [the city]'

[71]Glyconics are of the metrical form ×× – ᵕ – ᵕ –, where x indicates space for either a long or a short syllable (*syllaba anceps*).

[72]A pherecratean is of the form ×× – ᵕ ᵕ – –.

[73]The spondee has two long syllables, and the trochee a long followed by a short. What Scaliger notes is not a license according to modern metrical theory, for each of the first two syllables of these verses is *anceps,* that is, may be long or short.

[74]Scaliger is saying that in this pherecratean, *-unt u-* are two long syllables, making a spondee, instead of the expected – ᵕ ᵕ, a dactyl.

[75] ᵕ – ᵕ.

[76]The form ἀφικνομένοισι is impossible; nor do the mss. read as Scaliger says, but rather τοῖσιν ἀφικνουμένοισιν, *toisin aphiknoumenoisin.* But this scans – ᵕ ᵕ – – ᵕ – –, unacceptably for a glyconic; so the line is emended to τοῖσι δεῦρ' ἀφικνουμένοις, *toisi deur' aphiknoumenois,* "to arrivals hither," in order to scan correctly, – ᵕ – ᵕ ᵕ – ᵕ –. One may note that in Scaliger's day, ancient Greek texts were still rather crude compared to what the later Humanist editors were able to achieve.

[77] – ᵕ –, more often called a cretic.

[78]Again, modern editions receive an emendation to 'γένεθ', *'geneth',* which removes the anomaly and translates "if only he had not become great. . . ." The emendation is in fact attributed to Scaliger, evidently Julius Cæsar's son, Joseph Juste.

and also in that passage,

-στην σκεύη δύω χρησίμω.)[79]

[983]

*[e]stēn skeuē dyō
chrēsimō,* 'two useful
tools would [not] have
been'

[79]In this line, Scaliger read an erroneous form, δύω (*dyō*). When it is corrected to δύο (*dyo*, "two"), the anomalous long syllable is removed and another perfect glyconic results.

Index

297

Library of Congress Cataloging-in-Publication Data

Dubrow, Heather
  A happier Eden : the politics of marriage in the Stuart epithalamium /
Heather Dubrow.
    p. cm.
  ISBN 0–8014–2296–5 (alk. paper)
    1. English poetry—Early modern. 1500–1700—History and criticism.
2. Epithalamia—History and criticism. 3. Marriage in literature. 4. Weddings
in literature. 5. Politics in literature. 6. Stuart, House of. 7. Marriage—
Great Britain—History—17th century. I. Title
PR545.M29D83 1990
821'.309354—dc20   89–71200